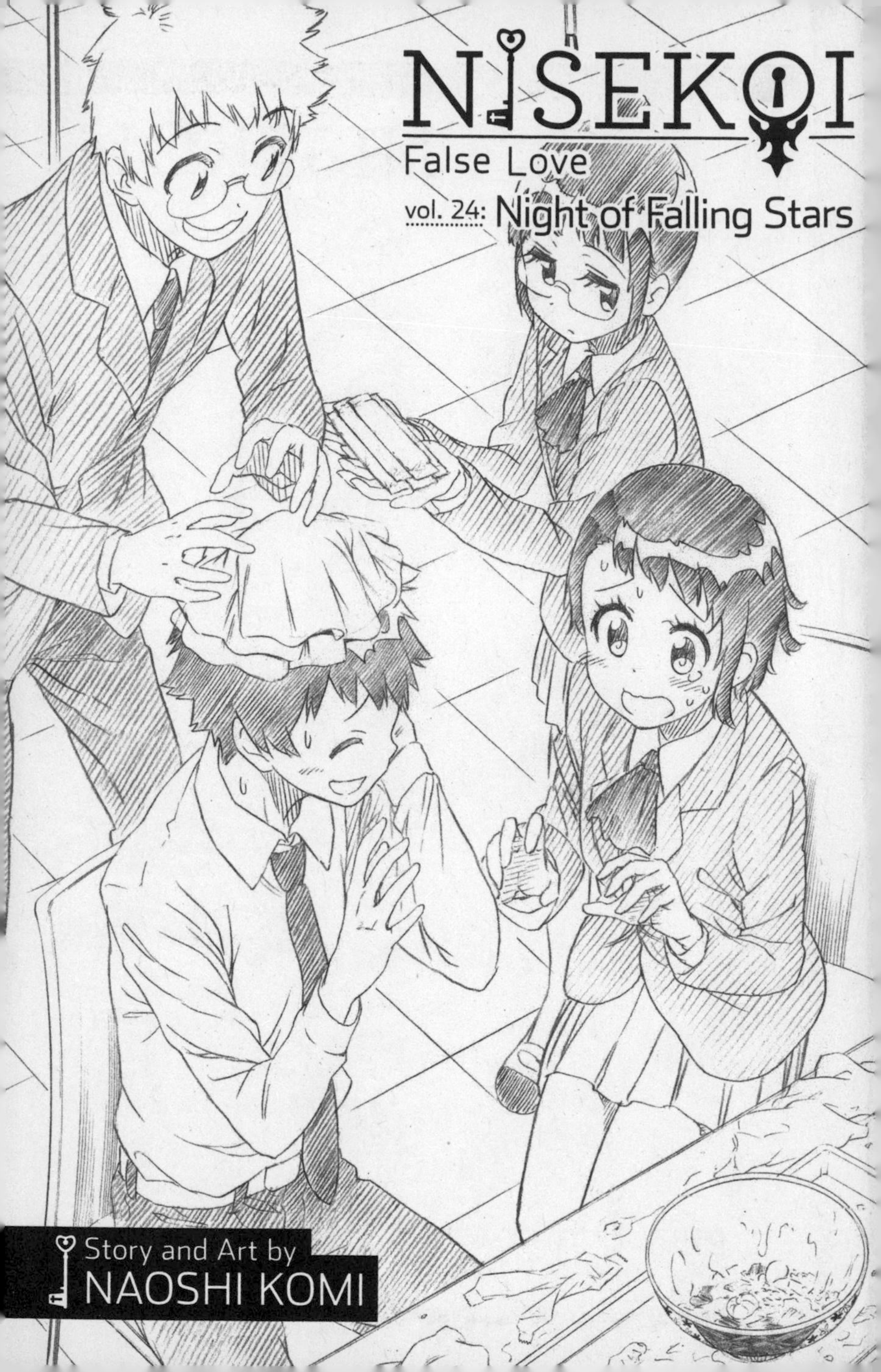

NISEKOI

False Love

vol. 24: Night of Falling Stars

Story and Art by
NAOSHI KOMI

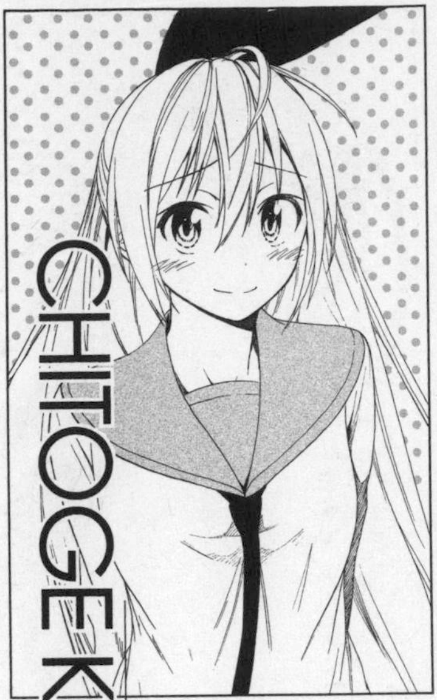

CHITOGE KIRISAKI

A half-Japanese bombshell with stellar athletic abilities. Short-tempered and violent. Comes from a family of gangsters.

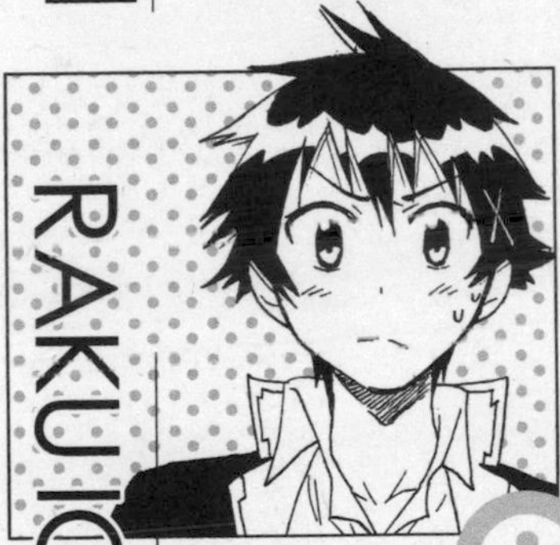

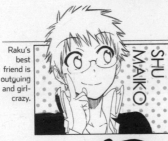

RAKU ICHIJO

A normal teen whose family happens to be yakuza. Cherishes a pendant given to him by a girl he met ten years ago.

KOSAKI ONODERA

A girl Raku has a crush on. Beautiful and sweet, Kosaki has no shortage of admirers. She's a terrible cook but makes food that *looks* amazing.

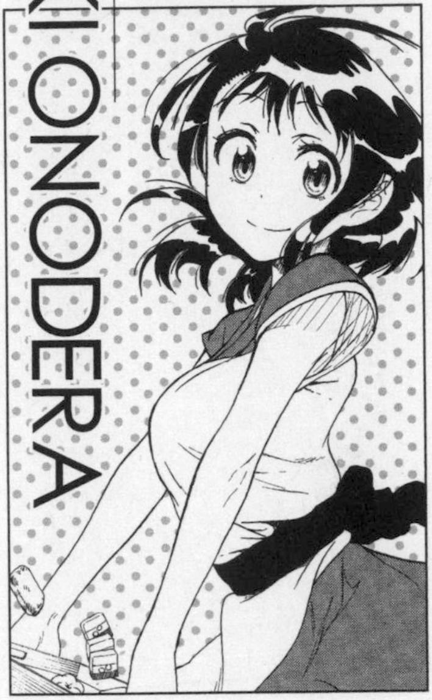

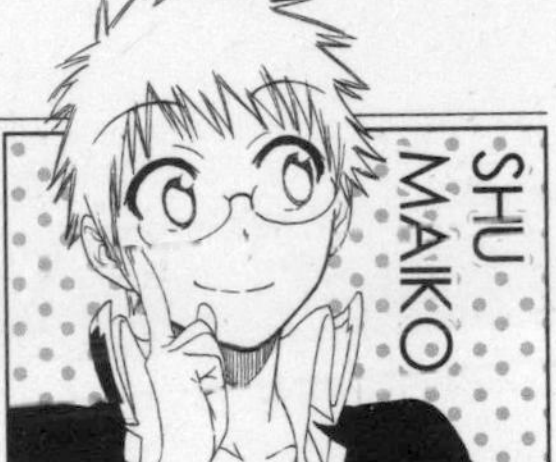

SHU MAIKO

Raku's best friend is outgoing and girl-crazy.

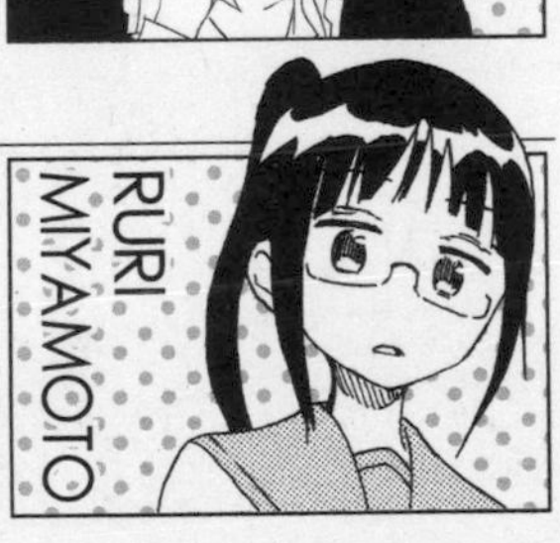

RURI MIYAMOTO

Kosaki's best gal pal. Comes off as aloof, but is actually a devoted and highly intuitive friend.

YUI KANAKURA

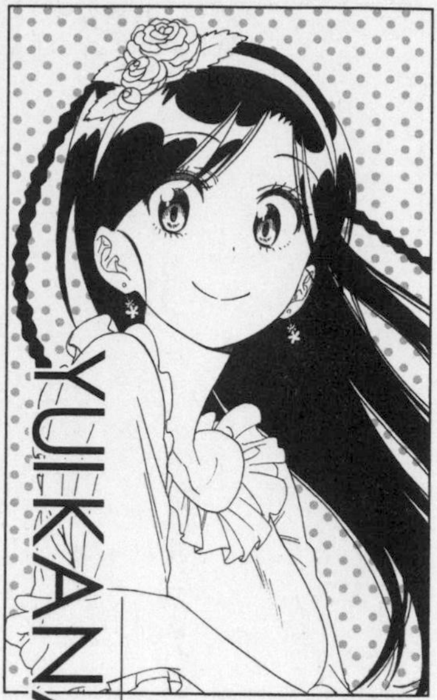

A childhood friend of Raku's, Yui is the head of a Chinese mafia gang and the homeroom teacher of Raku's class at his school. She was staying at Raku's house and professed her love to him. She also has a key that's linked to some kind of promise.

MARIKA TACHIBANA

Daughter of the chief of police, Marika is Raku's fiancée, according to an agreement made by their fathers—an agreement Marika takes very seriously! Also has a key and remembers making a promise with Raku ten years ago. Due to a physical condition, she has to leave Japan for treatment in an American hospital.

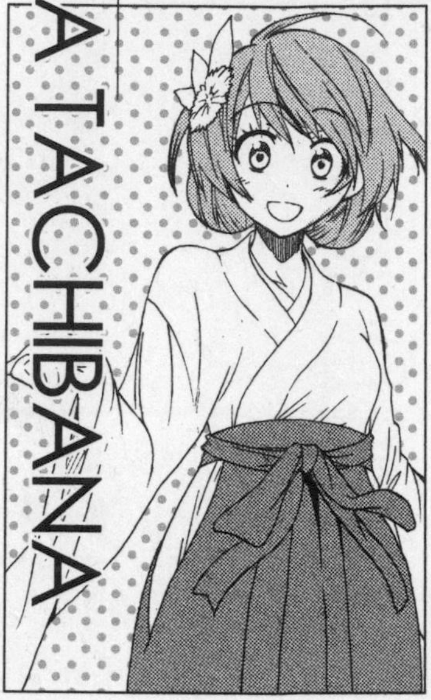

CHARACTERS & STORY

Ten years ago, Raku Ichijo made a promise with a girl he loved that they would get married when they met again...and he still treasures the pendant she gave him to seal their pledge.

Thanks to his family's circumstances, Raku has to pretend he's dating Chitoge Kirisaki, the daughter of a rival gangster. Despite their constant spats, Raku and Chitoge manage to fool everyone. Chitoge also has a token from her first love ten years ago—an old key. Meanwhile, Raku's crush, Kosaki, also has a key, as do Marika, the girl Raku's father has arranged for him to marry, and Yui, a childhood friend who's their homeroom teacher. Raku still doesn't know who his promise girl is when he realizes he has feelings for Chitoge. Torn between his love for Kosaki and Chitoge, Raku knows he has to make a choice. As the friends start their final year of high school, they begin to discuss their plans for the future. In the middle of one such conversation, Ruri and Maiko encounter a lost child looking for her parents...!

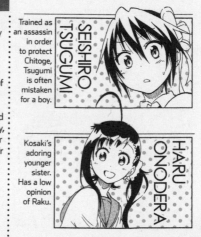

SEISHIRO TSUGUMI

Trained as an assassin in order to protect Chitoge, Tsugumi is often mistaken for a boy.

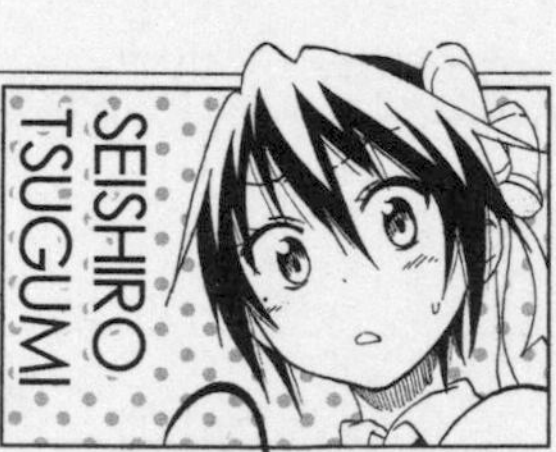

HARU ONODERA

Kosaki's adoring younger sister. Has a low opinion of Raku.

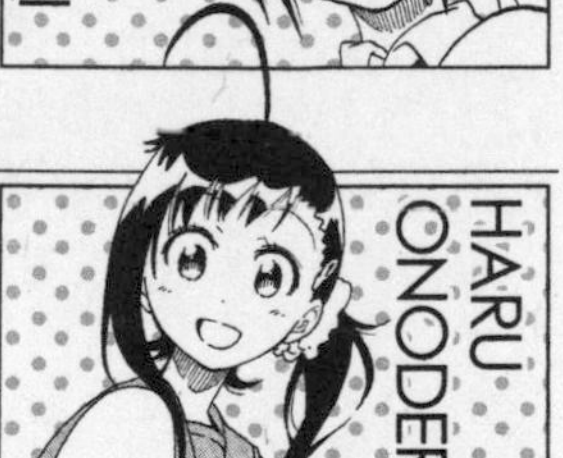

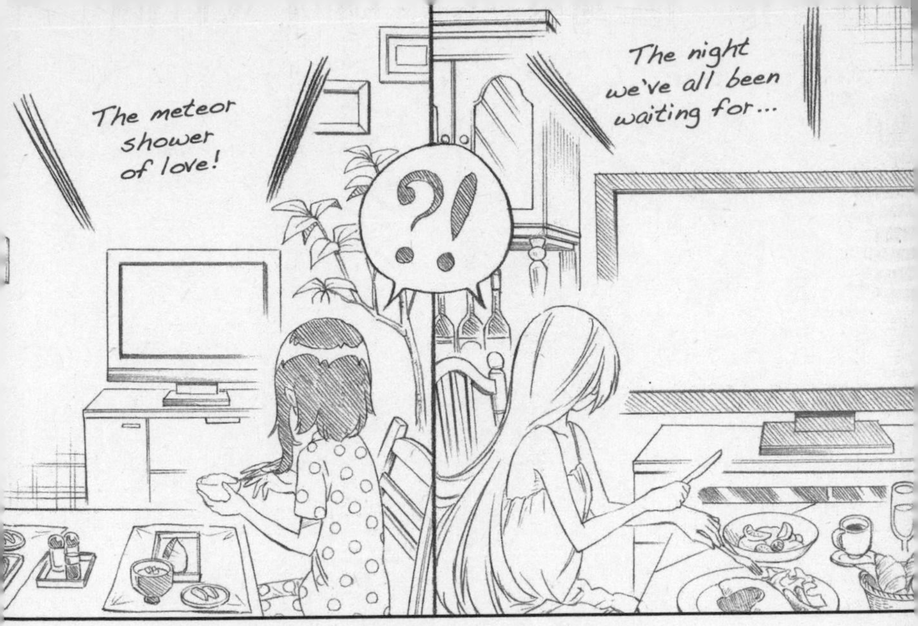
The night we've all been waiting for...
?!
The meteor shower of love!

NISEKOI
False Love
vol. 24: Night of Falling Stars

TABLE OF CONTENTS

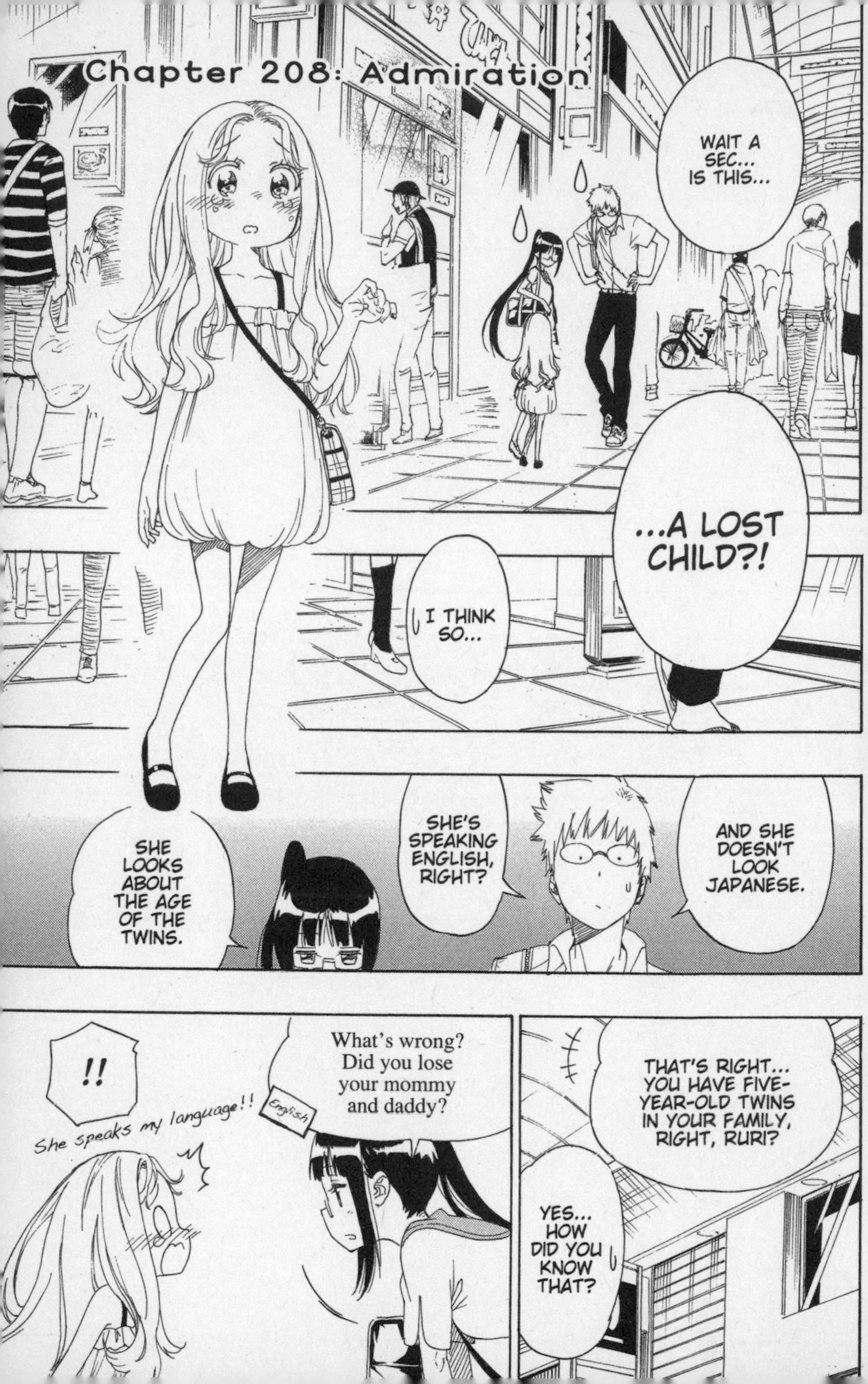
Chapter 208: Admiration
WAIT A SEC... IS THIS...
...A LOST CHILD?!
I THINK SO...
AND SHE DOESN'T LOOK JAPANESE.
SHE'S SPEAKING ENGLISH, RIGHT?
SHE LOOKS ABOUT THE AGE OF THE TWINS.
THAT'S RIGHT... YOU HAVE FIVE-YEAR-OLD TWINS IN YOUR FAMILY, RIGHT, RURI?
YES... HOW DID YOU KNOW THAT?
What's wrong? Did you lose your mommy and daddy?
English
!!
She speaks my language!!

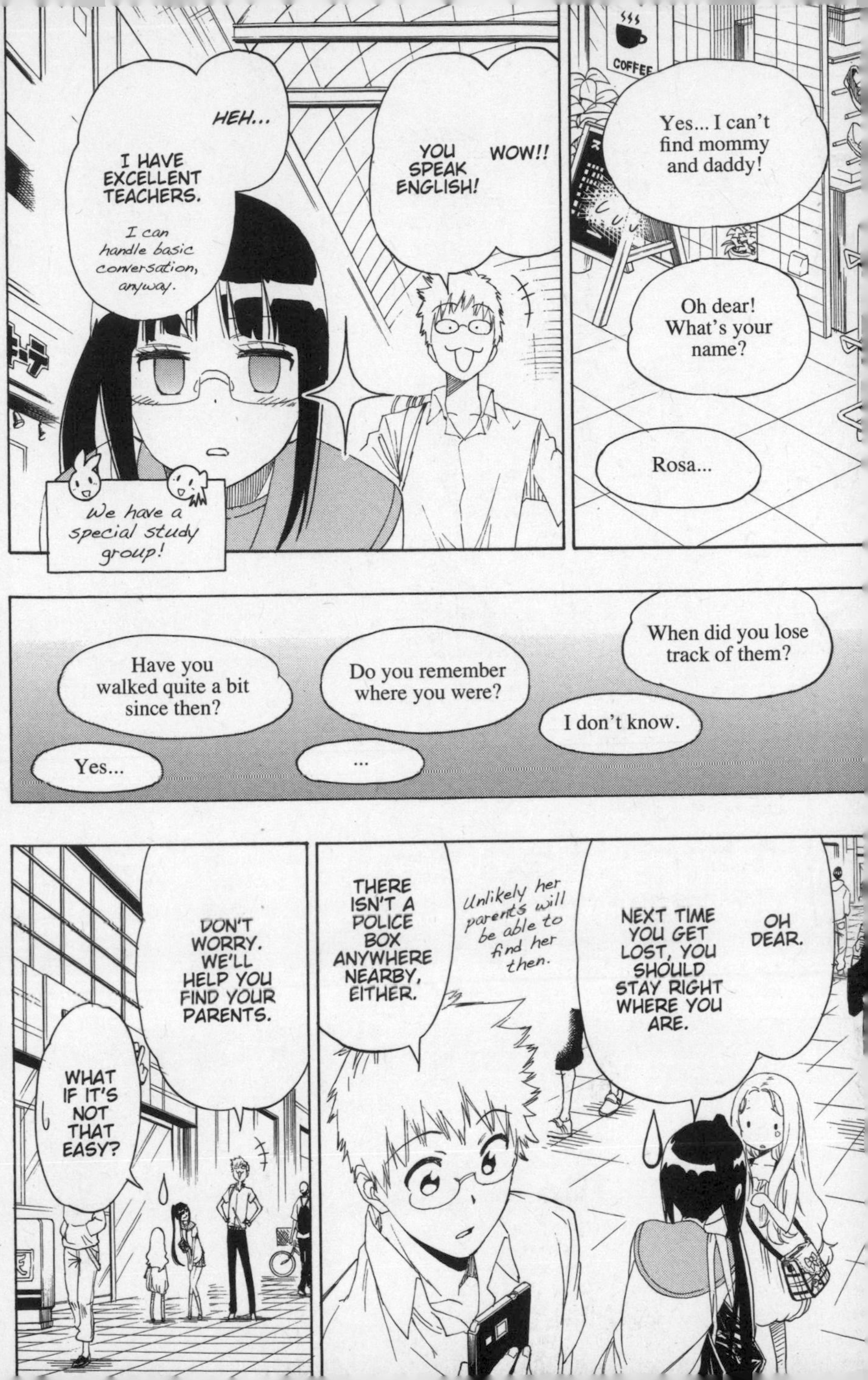
COFFEE
Yes... I can't find mommy and daddy!
Oh dear! What's your name?
Rosa...
WOW!!
YOU SPEAK ENGLISH!
HEH...
I HAVE EXCELLENT TEACHERS.
I can handle basic conversation, anyway.
We have a special study group!
When did you lose track of them?
I don't know.
Do you remember where you were?
...
Have you walked quite a bit since then?
Yes...
OH DEAR.
NEXT TIME YOU GET LOST, YOU SHOULD STAY RIGHT WHERE YOU ARE.
Unlikely her parents will be able to find her then.
THERE ISN'T A POLICE BOX ANYWHERE NEARBY, EITHER.
DON'T WORRY. WE'LL HELP YOU FIND YOUR PARENTS.
WHAT IF IT'S NOT THAT EASY?

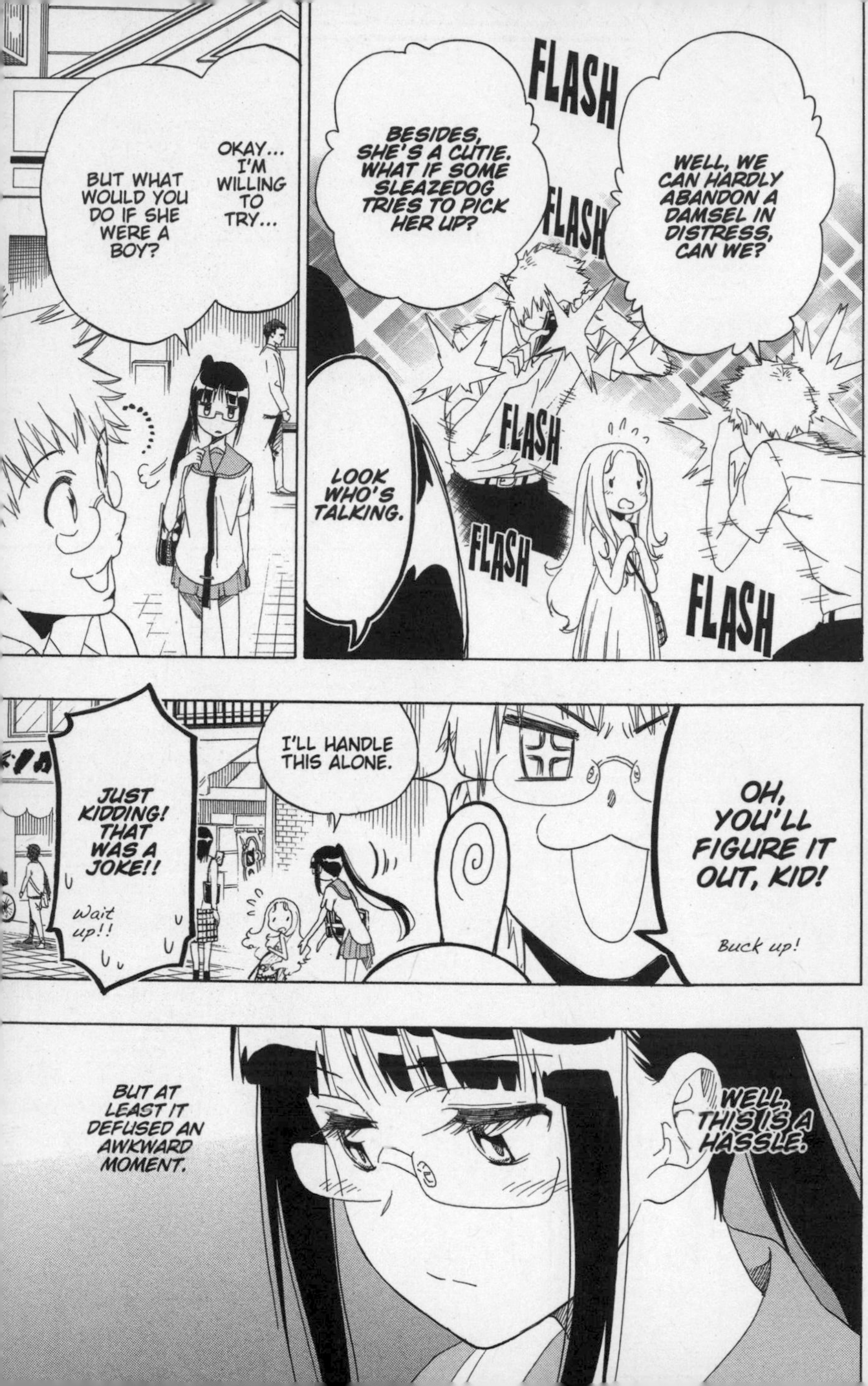
FLASH
WELL, WE CAN HARDLY ABANDON A DAMSEL IN DISTRESS, CAN WE?
BESIDES, SHE'S A CUTIE. WHAT IF SOME SLEAZEDOG TRIES TO PICK HER UP?
FLASH
FLASH
FLASH
FLASH
LOOK WHO'S TALKING.
OKAY... I'M WILLING TO TRY...
BUT WHAT WOULD YOU DO IF SHE WERE A BOY?
OH, YOU'LL FIGURE IT OUT, KID!
Buck up!
I'LL HANDLE THIS ALONE.
JUST KIDDING! THAT WAS A JOKE!!
Wait up!!
WELL, THIS IS A HASSLE.
BUT AT LEAST IT DEFUSED AN AWKWARD MOMENT.

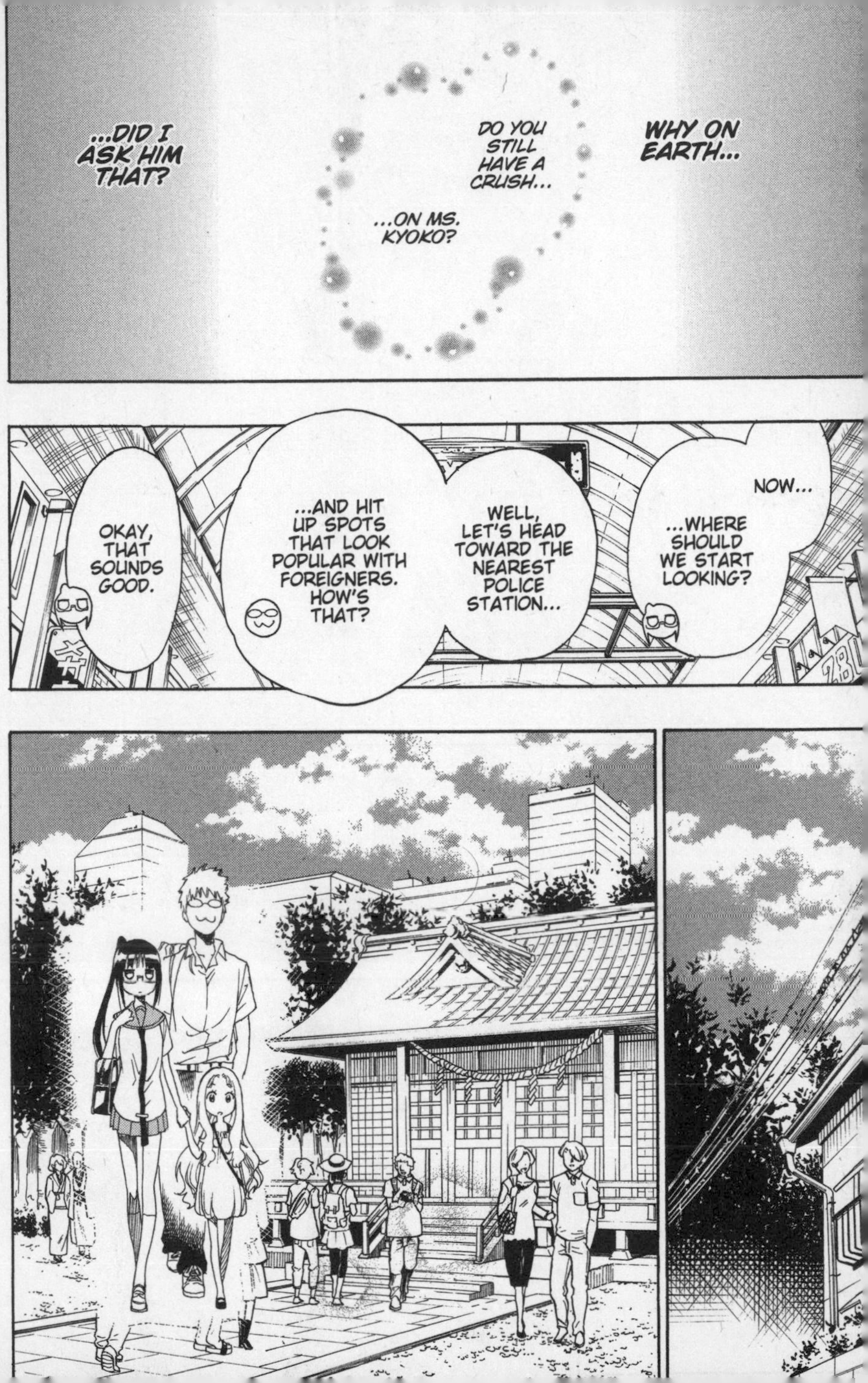
WHY ON EARTH...
DO YOU STILL HAVE A CRUSH...
...ON MS. KYOKO?
...DID I ASK HIM THAT?
NOW...
...WHERE SHOULD WE START LOOKING?
WELL, LET'S HEAD TOWARD THE NEAREST POLICE STATION...
...AND HIT UP SPOTS THAT LOOK POPULAR WITH FOREIGNERS. HOW'S THAT?
OKAY, THAT SOUNDS GOOD.

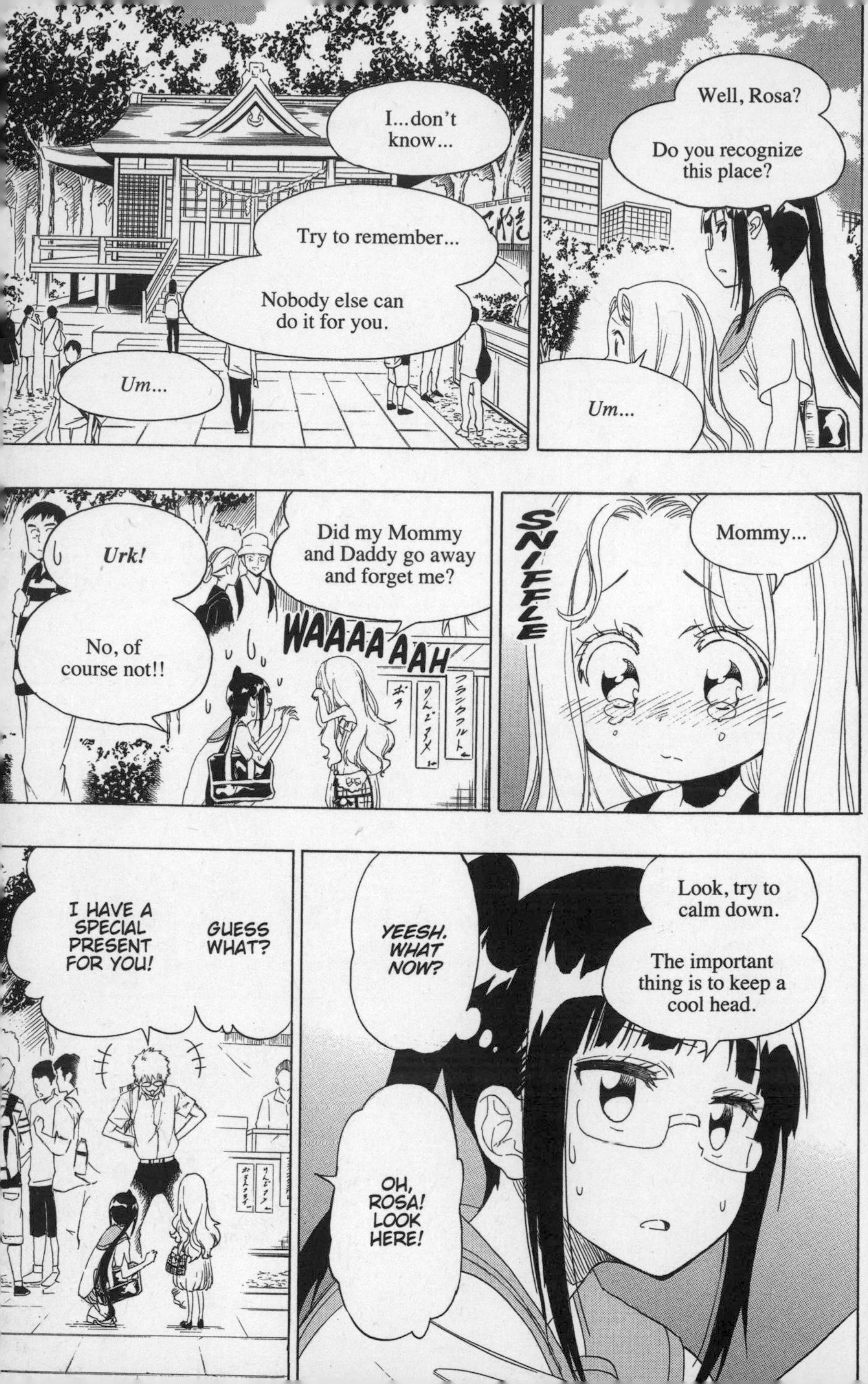
Well, Rosa?
Do you recognize this place?
Um...
I...don't know...
Try to remember...
Nobody else can do it for you.
Um...
SNIFFLE
Mommy...
Did my Mommy and Daddy go away and forget me?
WAAAAAAH
Urk!
No, of course not!!
Look, try to calm down.
The important thing is to keep a cool head.
YEESH. WHAT NOW?
OH, ROSA! LOOK HERE!
GUESS WHAT?
I HAVE A SPECIAL PRESENT FOR YOU!

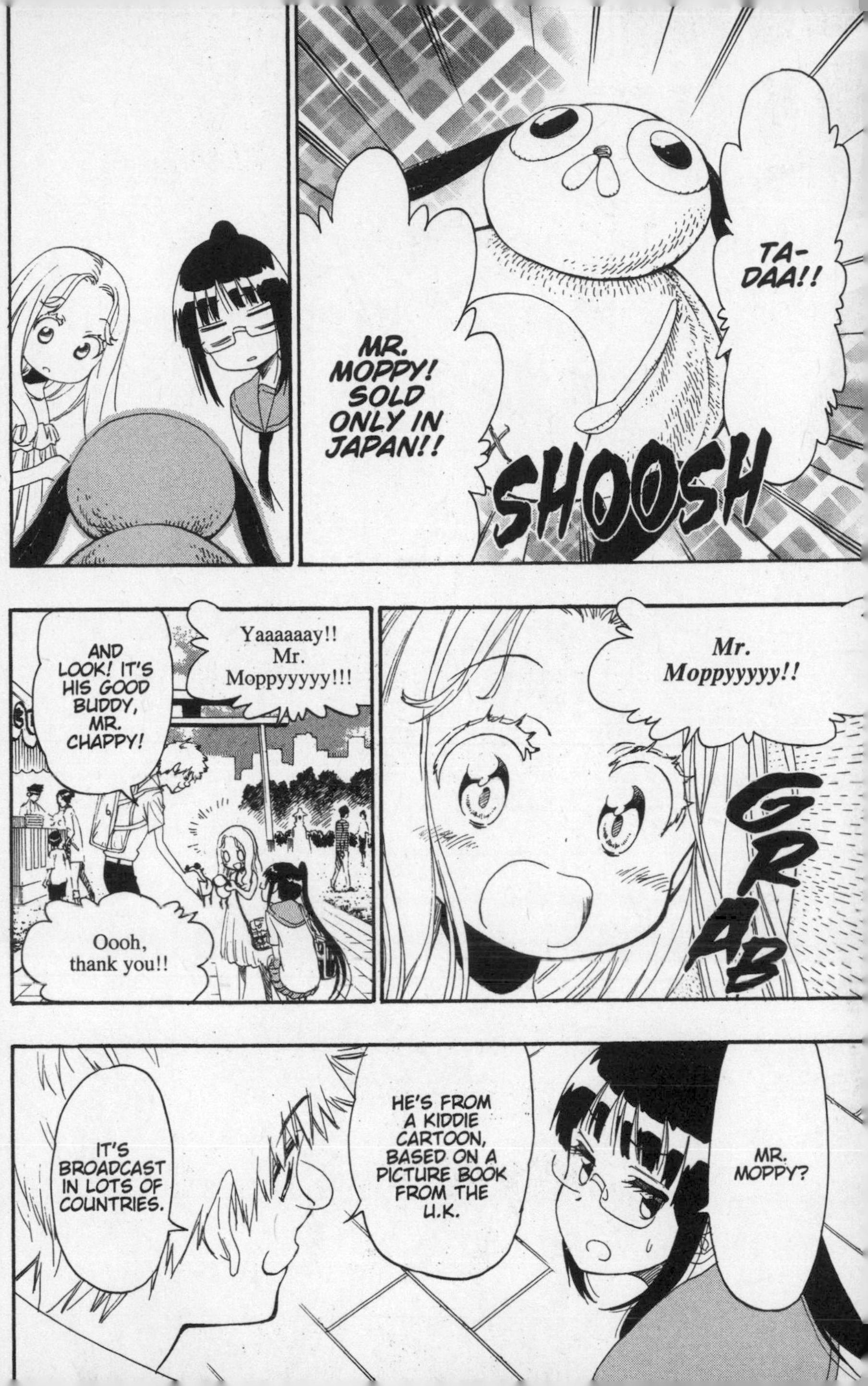
TA-DAA!!
MR. MOPPY! SOLD ONLY IN JAPAN!!
SHOOSH
Mr. Moppyyyyy!!
GRAB
Yaaaaaay!! Mr. Moppyyyyy!!!
AND LOOK! IT'S HIS GOOD BUDDY, MR. CHAPPY!
Oooh, thank you!!
MR. MOPPY?
HE'S FROM A KIDDIE CARTOON, BASED ON A PICTURE BOOK FROM THE U.K.
IT'S BROADCAST IN LOTS OF COUNTRIES.

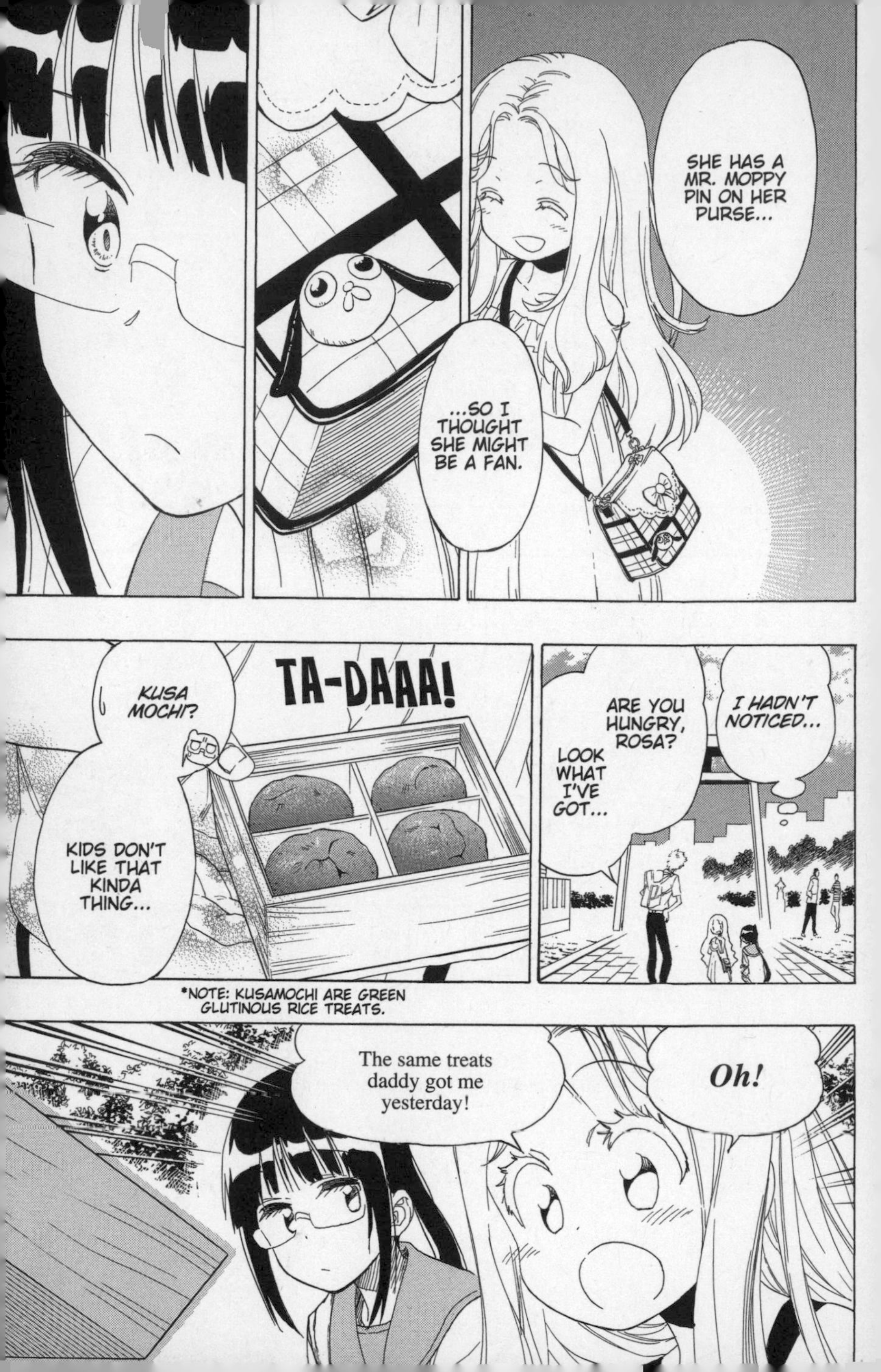
SHE HAS A MR. MOPPY PIN ON HER PURSE...
...SO I THOUGHT SHE MIGHT BE A FAN.
I HADN'T NOTICED...
ARE YOU HUNGRY, ROSA?
LOOK WHAT I'VE GOT...
TA-DAAA!
KUSA MOCHI?
KIDS DON'T LIKE THAT KINDA THING...
*NOTE: KUSAMOCHI ARE GREEN GLUTINOUS RICE TREATS.
Oh!
The same treats daddy got me yesterday!

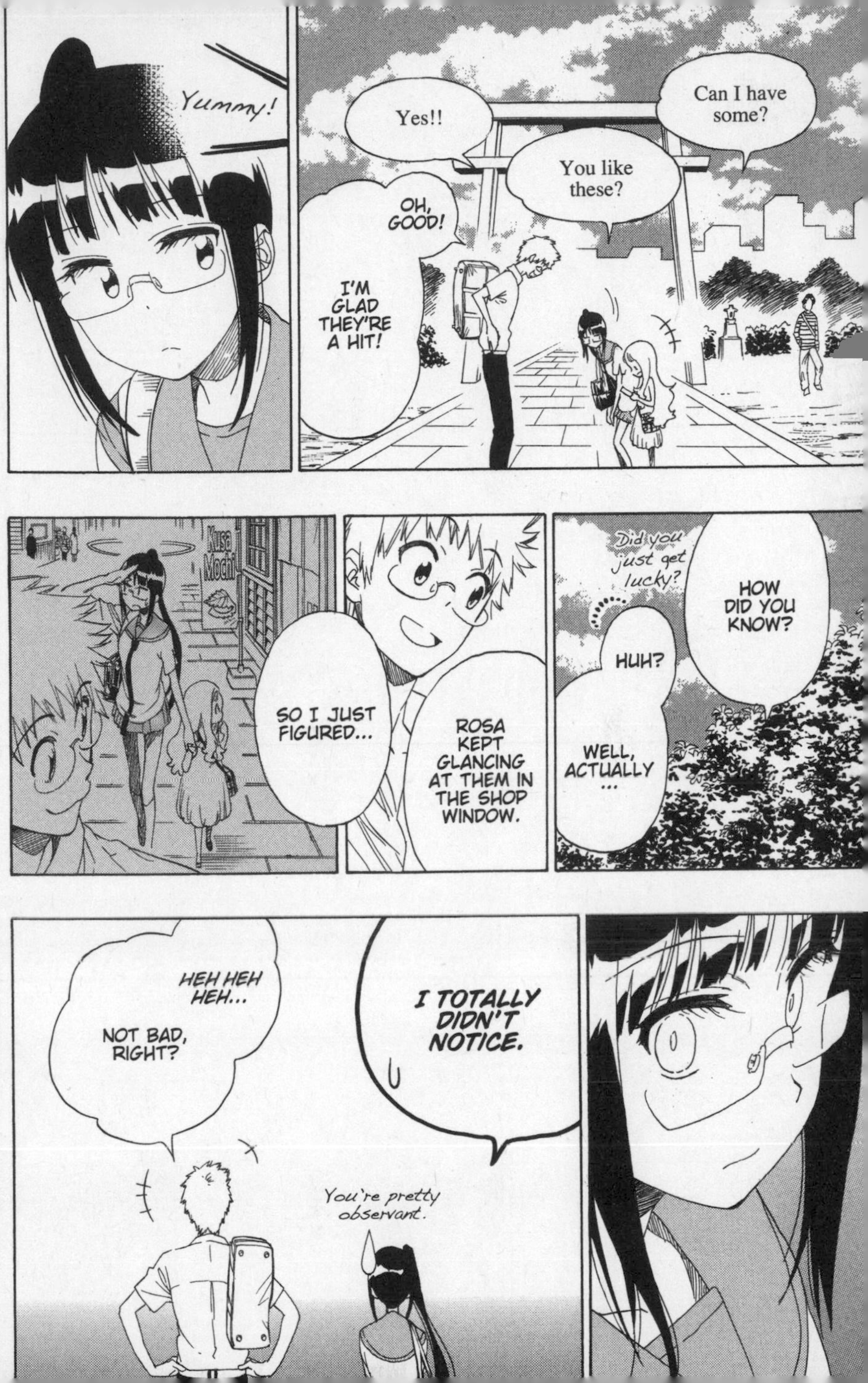
Can I have some?
You like these?
Yes!!
OH, GOOD!
I'M GLAD THEY'RE A HIT!
Yummy!
Did you just get lucky?
HOW DID YOU KNOW?
HUH?
WELL, ACTUALLY...
ROSA KEPT GLANCING AT THEM IN THE SHOP WINDOW.
SO I JUST FIGURED...
Kusa Mochi
I TOTALLY DIDN'T NOTICE.
HEH HEH HEH...
NOT BAD, RIGHT?
You're pretty observant.

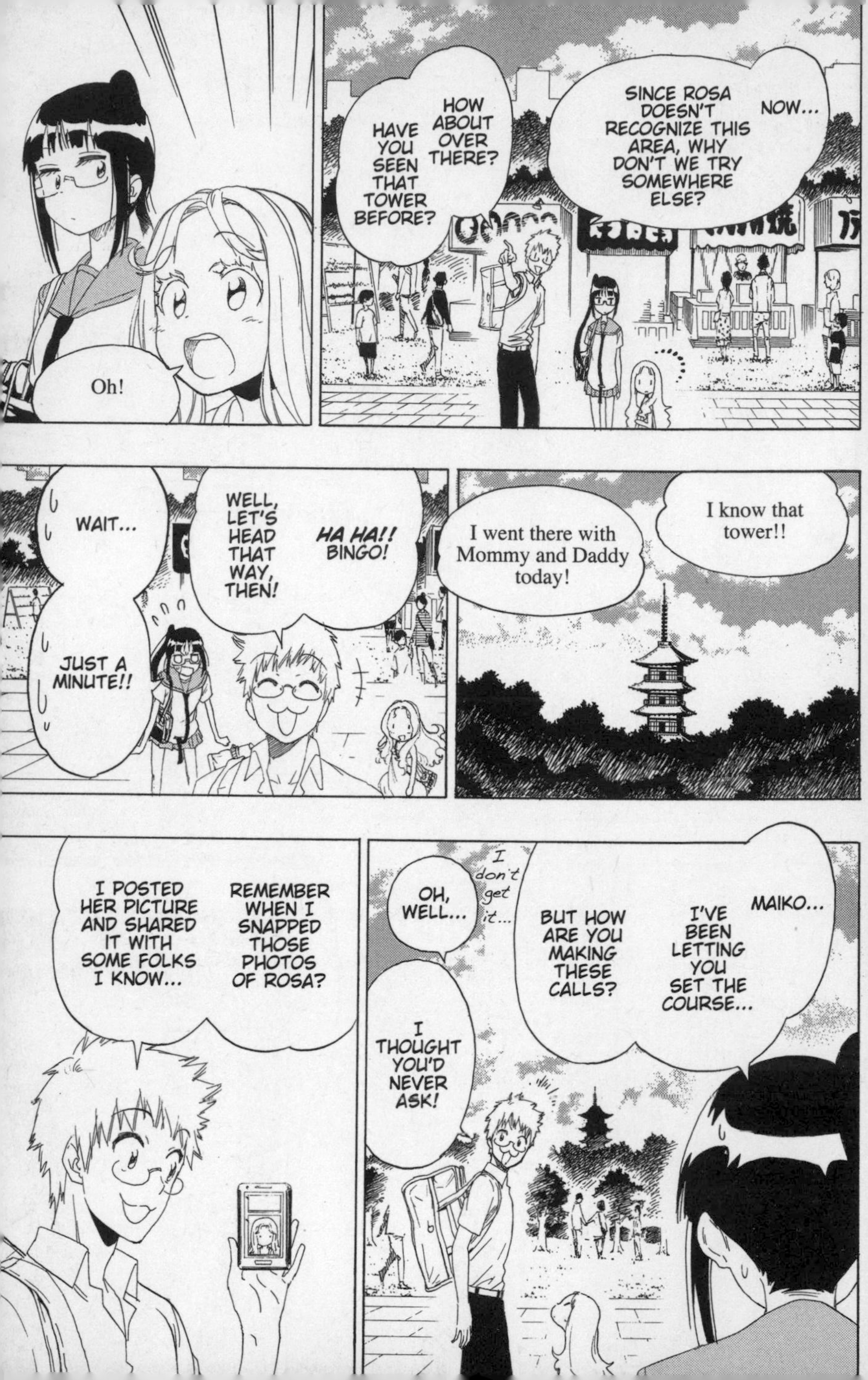
NOW...
SINCE ROSA DOESN'T RECOGNIZE THIS AREA, WHY DON'T WE TRY SOMEWHERE ELSE?
HOW ABOUT OVER THERE?
HAVE YOU SEEN THAT TOWER BEFORE?
Oh!
I know that tower!!
I went there with Mommy and Daddy today!
HA HA!! BINGO!
WELL, LET'S HEAD THAT WAY, THEN!
WAIT...
JUST A MINUTE!!
MAIKO...
I'VE BEEN LETTING YOU SET THE COURSE...
BUT HOW ARE YOU MAKING THESE CALLS?
I don't get it...
OH, WELL...
I THOUGHT YOU'D NEVER ASK!
REMEMBER WHEN I SNAPPED THOSE PHOTOS OF ROSA?
I POSTED HER PICTURE AND SHARED IT WITH SOME FOLKS I KNOW...

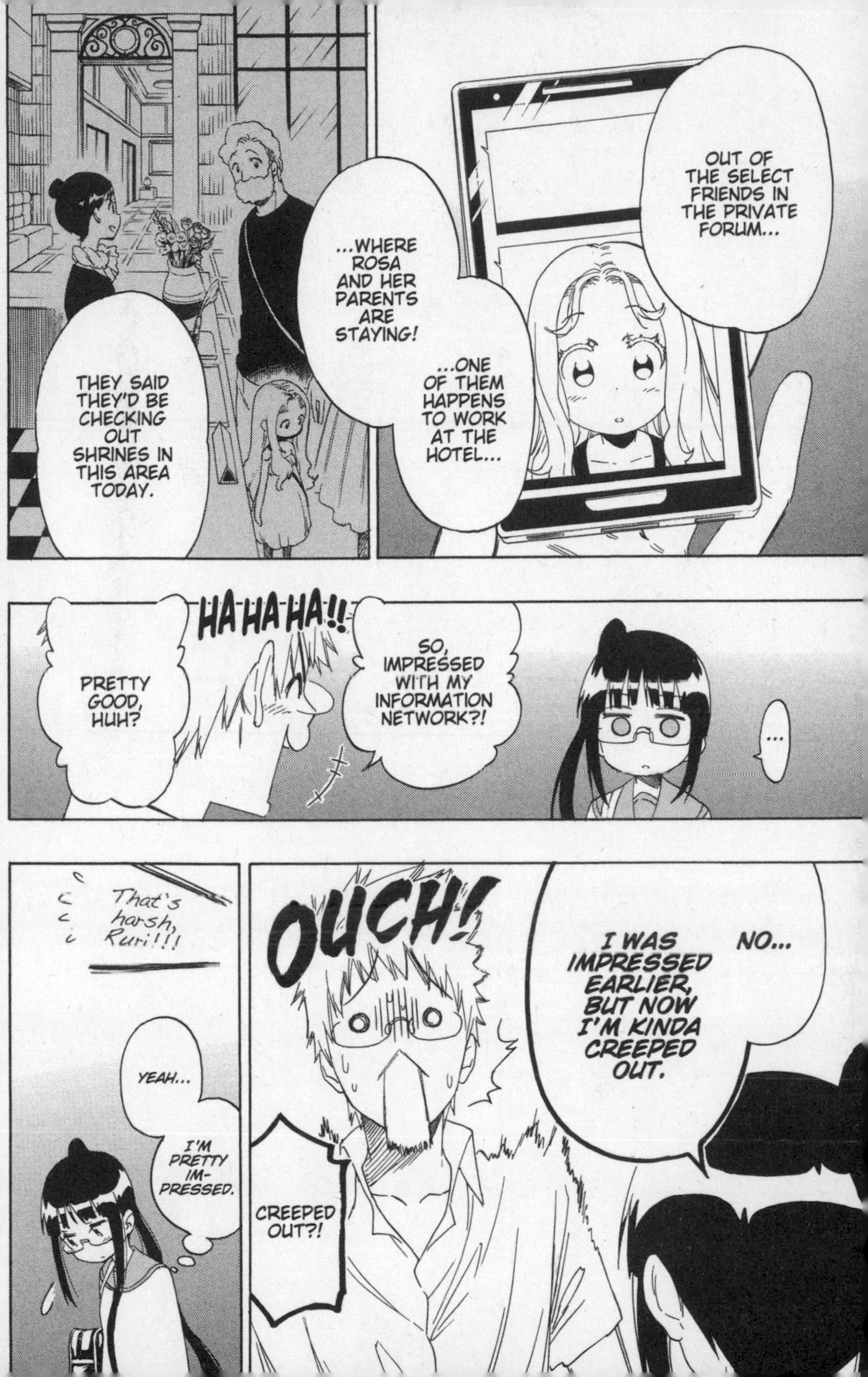
OUT OF THE SELECT FRIENDS IN THE PRIVATE FORUM...
...ONE OF THEM HAPPENS TO WORK AT THE HOTEL...
...WHERE ROSA AND HER PARENTS ARE STAYING!
THEY SAID THEY'D BE CHECKING OUT SHRINES IN THIS AREA TODAY.
HA HA HA!!
PRETTY GOOD, HUH?
SO, IMPRESSED WITH MY INFORMATION NETWORK?!
...
NO...
I WAS IMPRESSED EARLIER, BUT NOW I'M KINDA CREEPED OUT.
OUCH!
CREEPED OUT?!
That's harsh, Ruri!!!
YEAH...
I'M PRETTY IM-PRESSED.

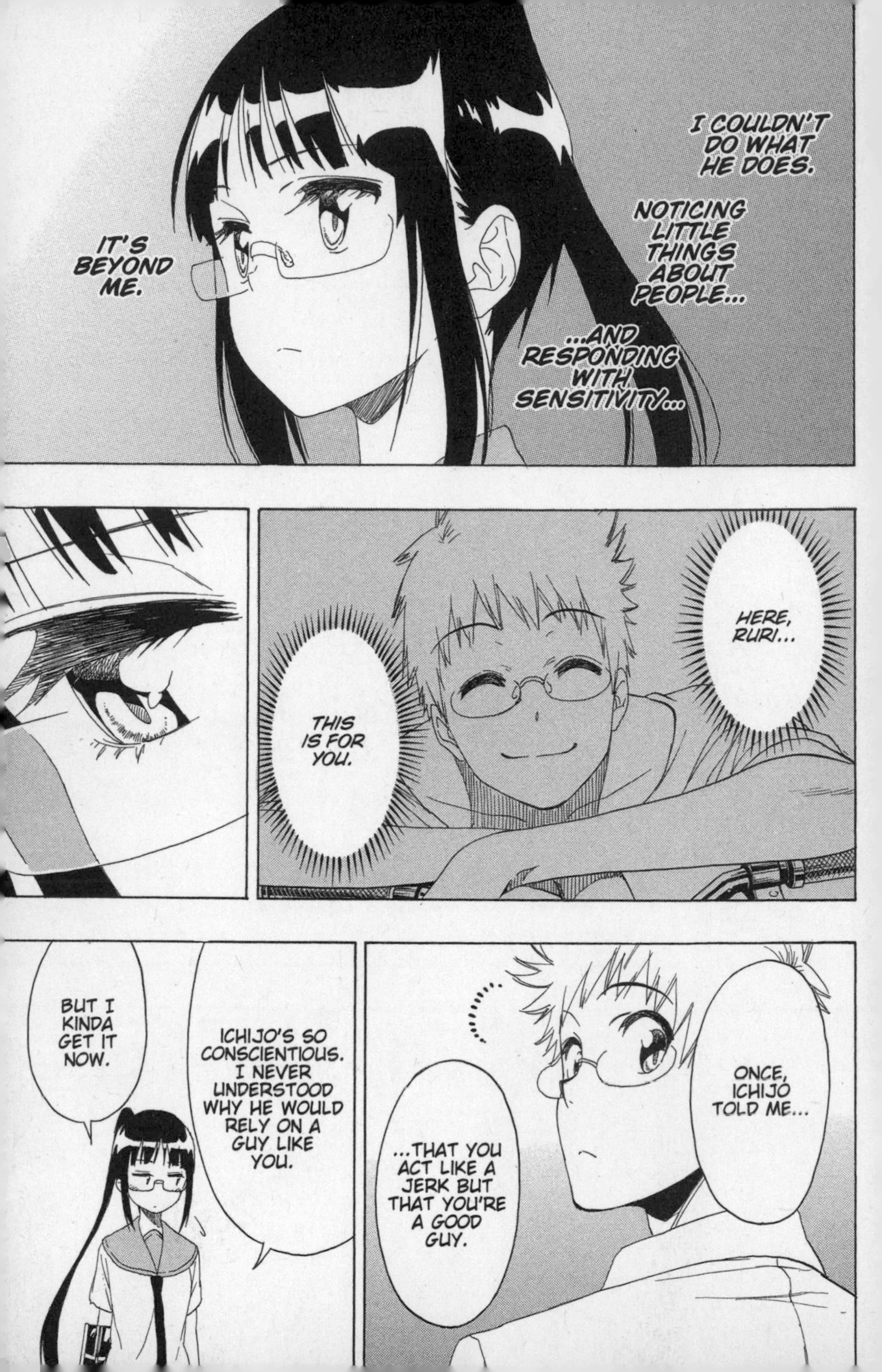
I COULDN'T DO WHAT HE DOES.
NOTICING LITTLE THINGS ABOUT PEOPLE...
...AND RESPONDING WITH SENSITIVITY...
IT'S BEYOND ME.
HERE, RURI...
THIS IS FOR YOU.
ONCE, ICHIJO TOLD ME...
...THAT YOU ACT LIKE A JERK BUT THAT YOU'RE A GOOD GUY.
ICHIJO'S SO CONSCIENTIOUS. I NEVER UNDERSTOOD WHY HE WOULD RELY ON A GUY LIKE YOU.
BUT I KINDA GET IT NOW.

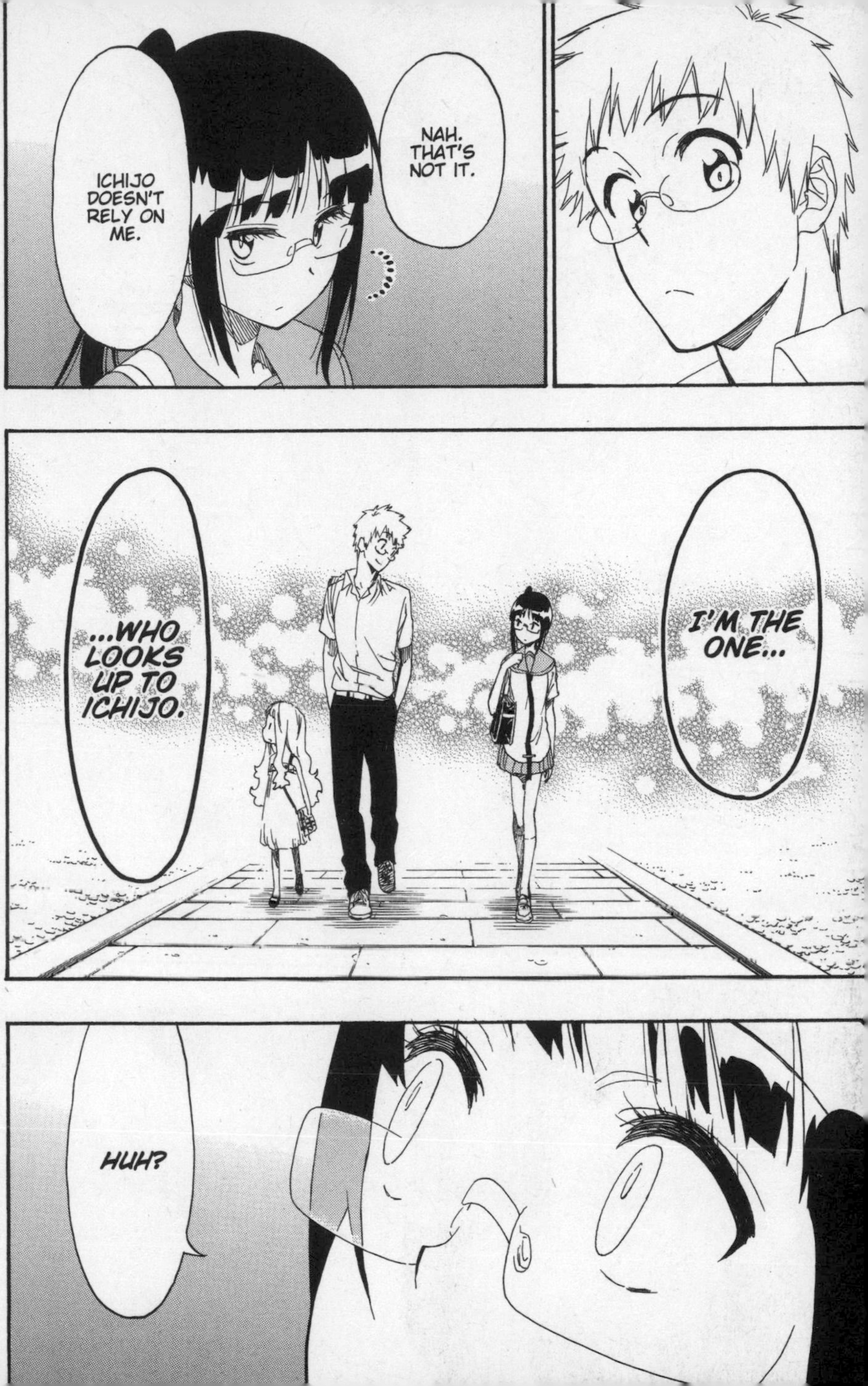
NAH. THAT'S NOT IT.
ICHIJO DOESN'T RELY ON ME.
I'M THE ONE...
...WHO LOOKS UP TO ICHIJO.
HUH?

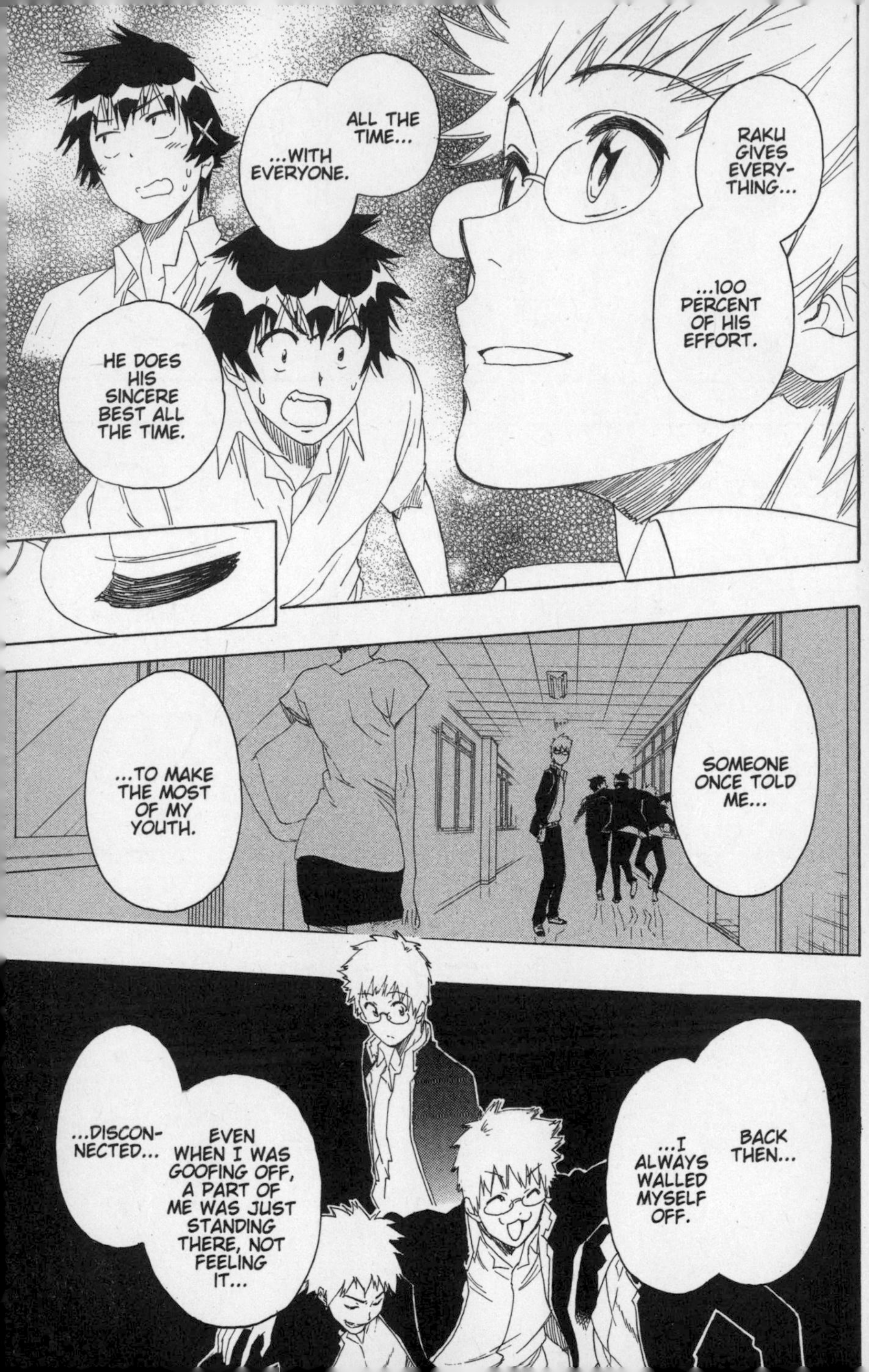
RAKU GIVES EVERY-THING...
...100 PERCENT OF HIS EFFORT.
ALL THE TIME...
...WITH EVERYONE.
HE DOES HIS SINCERE BEST ALL THE TIME.
SOMEONE ONCE TOLD ME...
...TO MAKE THE MOST OF MY YOUTH.
BACK THEN...
...I ALWAYS WALLED MYSELF OFF.
EVEN WHEN I WAS GOOFING OFF, A PART OF ME WAS JUST STANDING THERE, NOT FEELING IT...
...DISCON-NECTED...

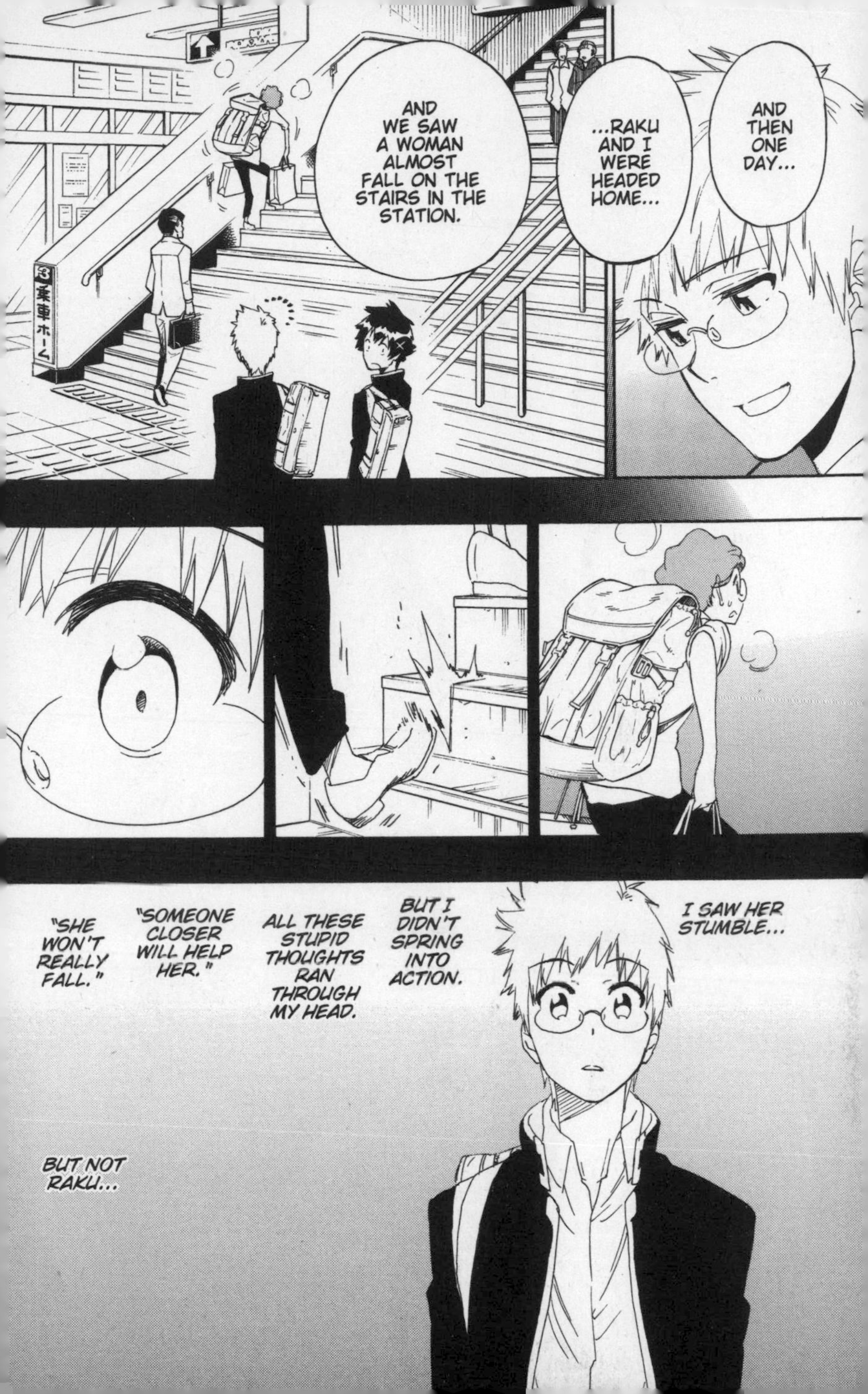
AND THEN ONE DAY...
...RAKU AND I WERE HEADED HOME...
AND WE SAW A WOMAN ALMOST FALL ON THE STAIRS IN THE STATION.
3 乗車ホーム
I SAW HER STUMBLE...
BUT I DIDN'T SPRING INTO ACTION.
ALL THESE STUPID THOUGHTS RAN THROUGH MY HEAD.
"SOMEONE CLOSER WILL HELP HER."
"SHE WON'T REALLY FALL."
BUT NOT RAKU...

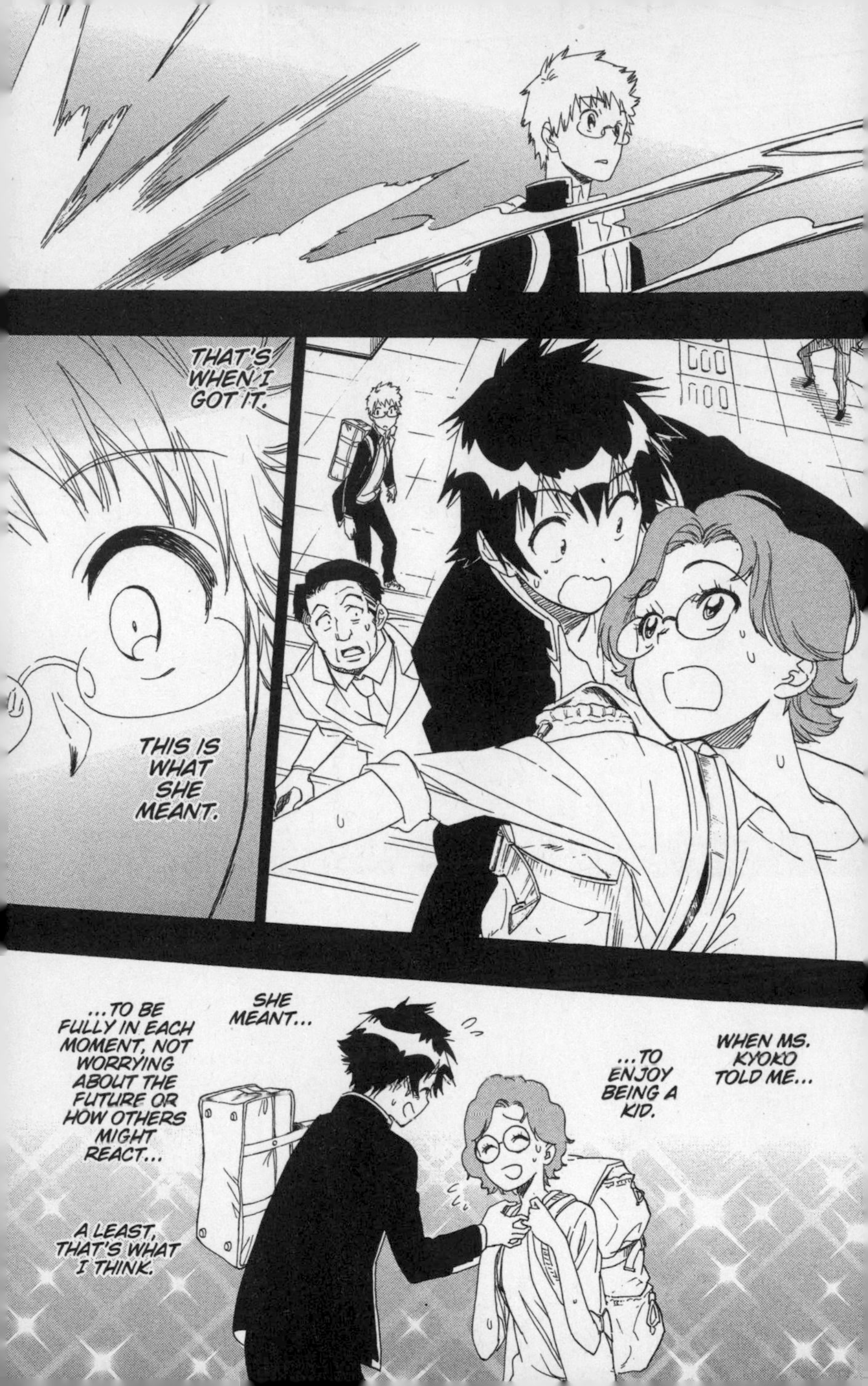
THAT'S WHEN I GOT IT.
THIS IS WHAT SHE MEANT.
WHEN MS. KYOKO TOLD ME...
...TO ENJOY BEING A KID.
SHE MEANT...
...TO BE FULLY IN EACH MOMENT, NOT WORRYING ABOUT THE FUTURE OR HOW OTHERS MIGHT REACT...
A LEAST, THAT'S WHAT I THINK.

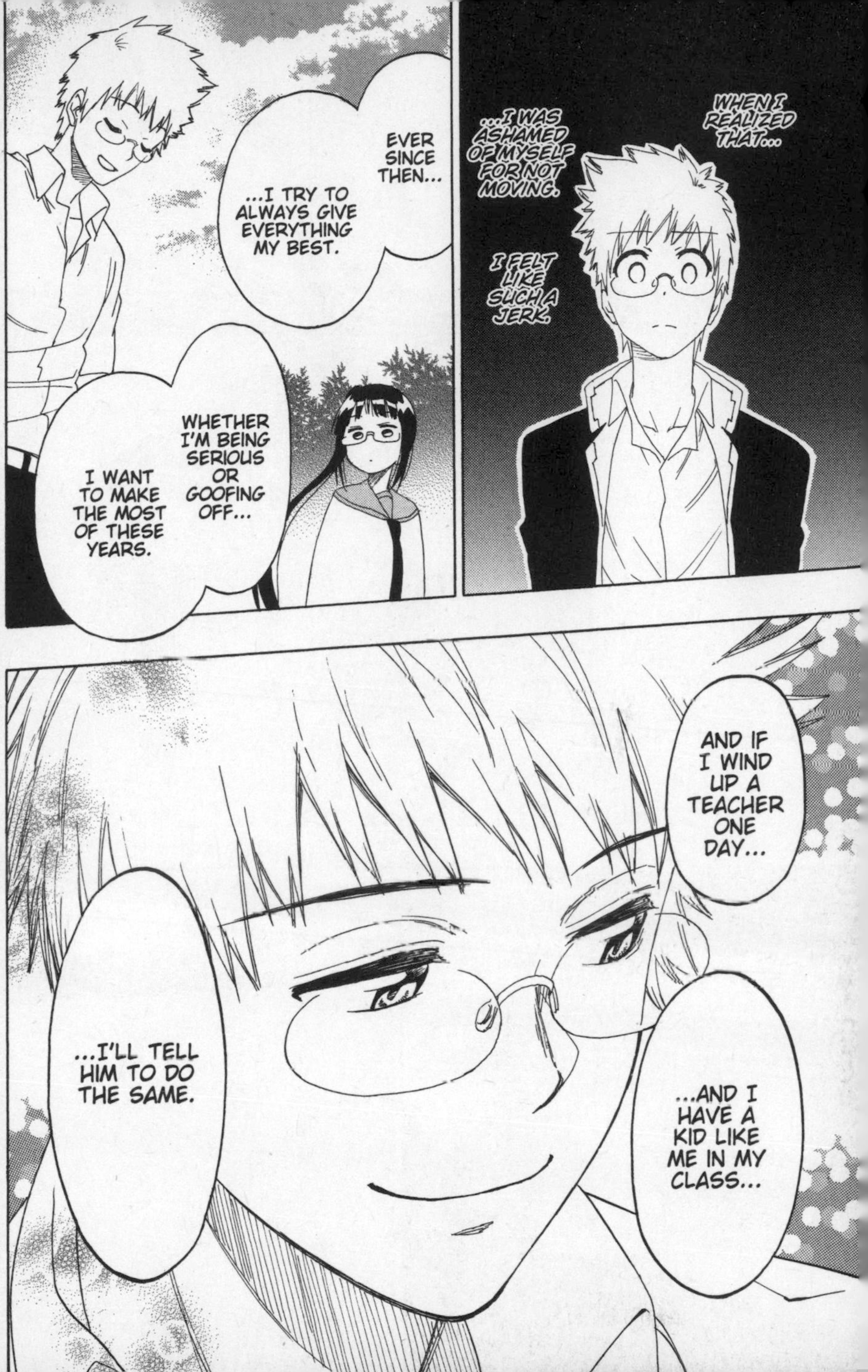
WHEN I REALIZED THAT...
...I WAS ASHAMED OF MYSELF FOR NOT MOVING.
I FELT LIKE SUCH A JERK.
EVER SINCE THEN...
...I TRY TO ALWAYS GIVE EVERYTHING MY BEST.
WHETHER I'M BEING SERIOUS OR GOOFING OFF...
I WANT TO MAKE THE MOST OF THESE YEARS.
AND IF I WIND UP A TEACHER ONE DAY...
...AND I HAVE A KID LIKE ME IN MY CLASS...
...I'LL TELL HIM TO DO THE SAME.

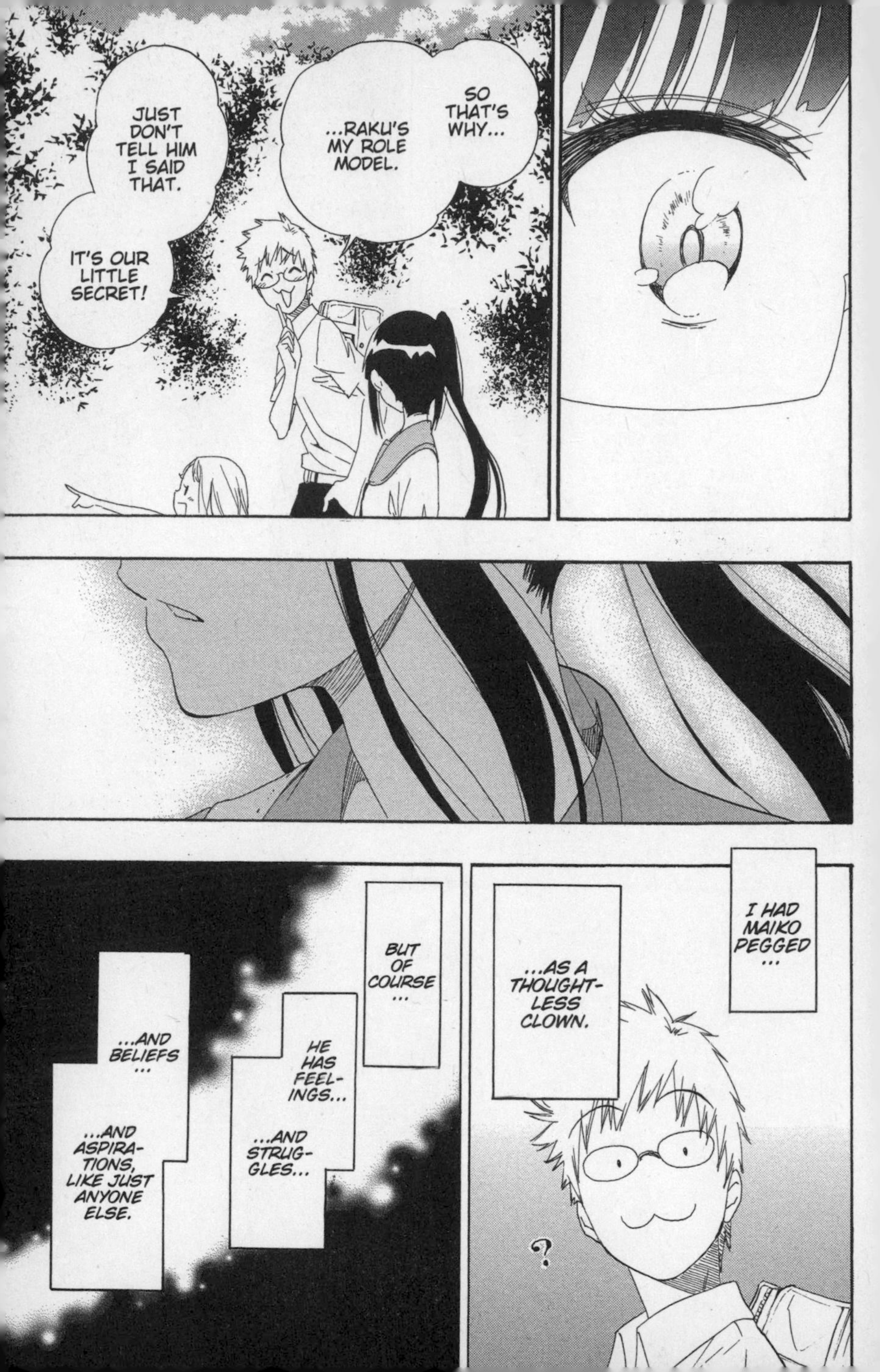
SO THAT'S WHY...
...RAKU'S MY ROLE MODEL.
JUST DON'T TELL HIM I SAID THAT.
IT'S OUR LITTLE SECRET!
I HAD MAIKO PEGGED...
...AS A THOUGHTLESS CLOWN.
?
BUT OF COURSE...
HE HAS FEELINGS...
...AND STRUGGLES...
...AND BELIEFS...
...AND ASPIRATIONS, LIKE JUST ANYONE ELSE.

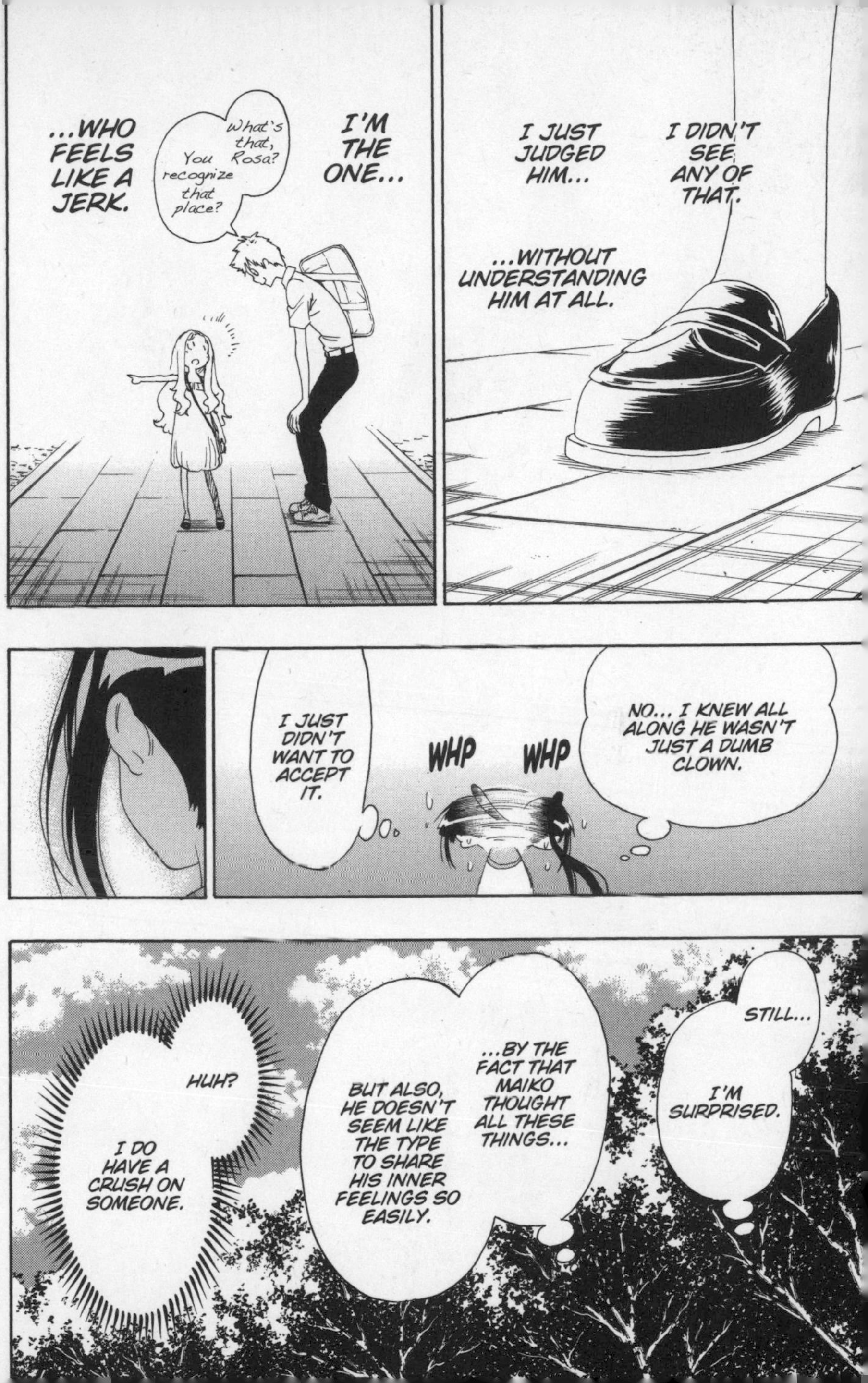
I DIDN'T SEE ANY OF THAT.
I JUST JUDGED HIM...
...WITHOUT UNDERSTANDING HIM AT ALL.
I'M THE ONE...
What's that, Rosa? You recognize that place?
...WHO FEELS LIKE A JERK.
NO... I KNEW ALL ALONG HE WASN'T JUST A DUMB CLOWN.
WHP
WHP
I JUST DIDN'T WANT TO ACCEPT IT.
STILL...
I'M SURPRISED.
...BY THE FACT THAT MAIKO THOUGHT ALL THESE THINGS...
BUT ALSO, HE DOESN'T SEEM LIKE THE TYPE TO SHARE HIS INNER FEELINGS SO EASILY.
HUH?
I DO HAVE A CRUSH ON SOMEONE.

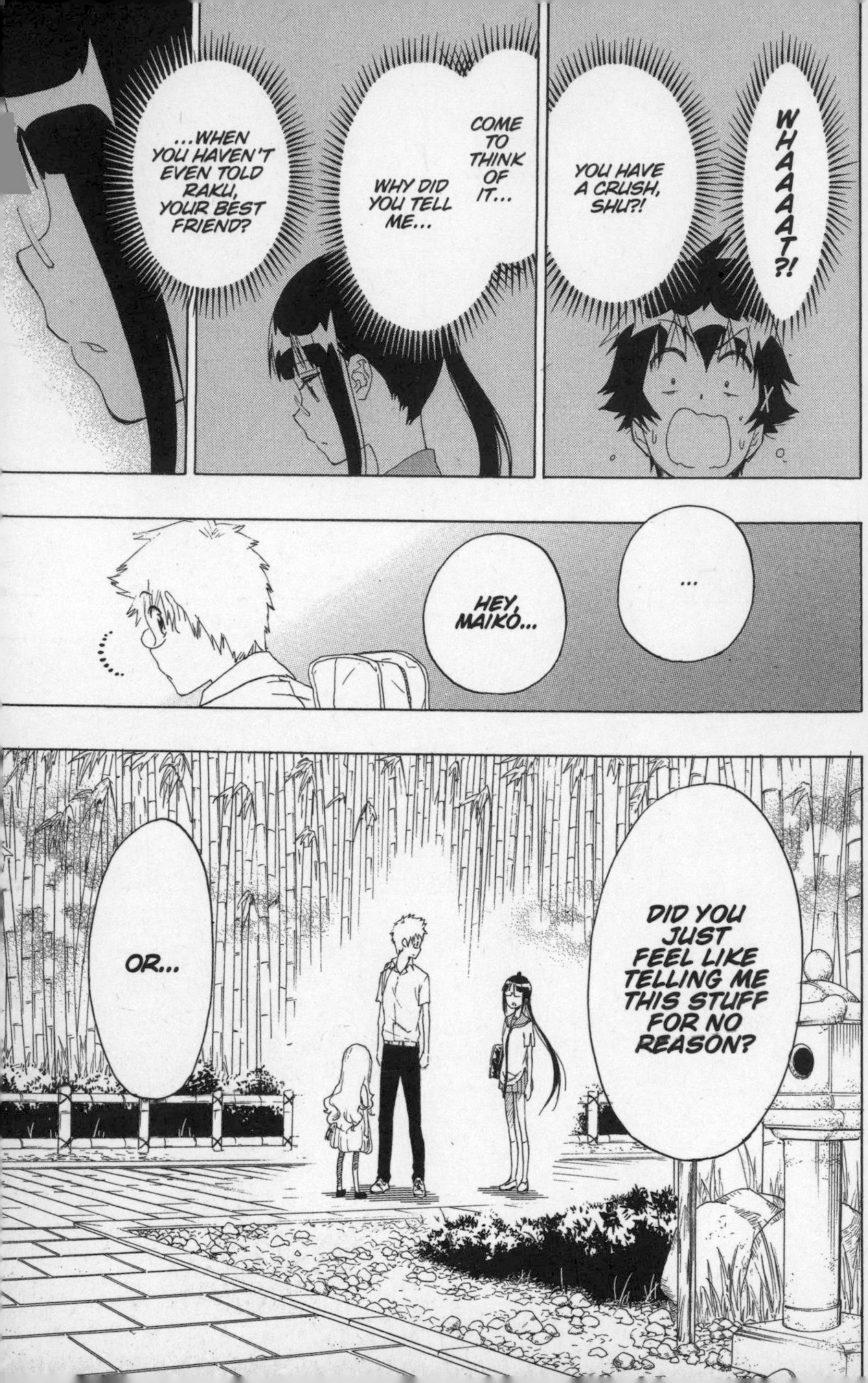
WHAAAAAT?!
YOU HAVE A CRUSH, SHU?!
COME TO THINK OF IT...
WHY DID YOU TELL ME...
...WHEN YOU HAVEN'T EVEN TOLD RAKU, YOUR BEST FRIEND?
...
HEY, MAIKO...
DID YOU JUST FEEL LIKE TELLING ME THIS STUFF FOR NO REASON?
OR...

Profile of Mr. Moppy

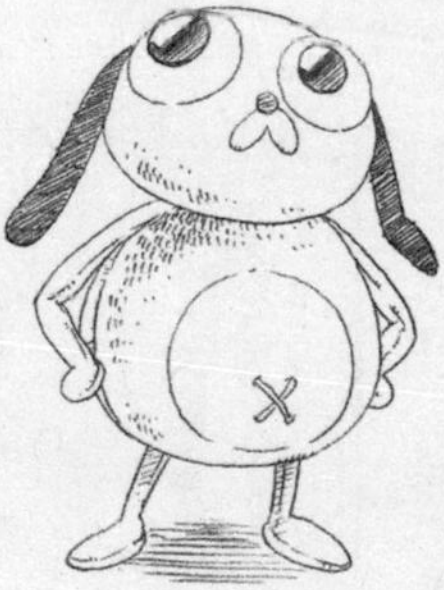

Mr. Moppy is a cute and dependable stuffed animal.

But that persona is actually a disguise.

Mr. Moppy is actually possessed of the ancient spirit of General Marazoroff!! Mr. Moppy traverses the land from East to West having great adventures and making clever quips with his beloved horse Chappy from his past life. One day they will overthrow Ussona, the evil underground organization...!

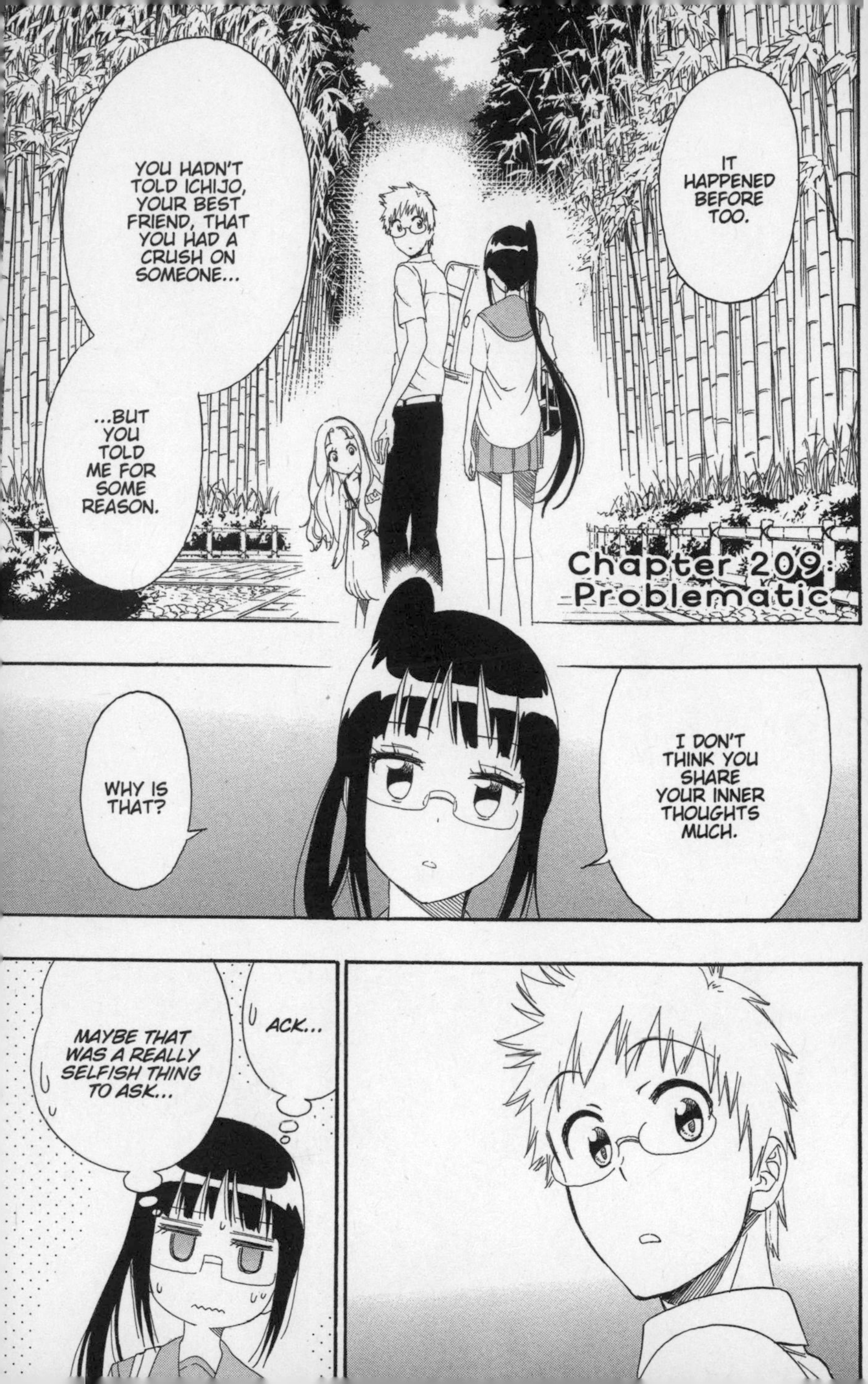
IT HAPPENED BEFORE TOO.
YOU HADN'T TOLD ICHIJO, YOUR BEST FRIEND, THAT YOU HAD A CRUSH ON SOMEONE...
...BUT YOU TOLD ME FOR SOME REASON.
Chapter 209: Problematic
I DON'T THINK YOU SHARE YOUR INNER THOUGHTS MUCH.
WHY IS THAT?
ACK...
MAYBE THAT WAS A REALLY SELFISH THING TO ASK...

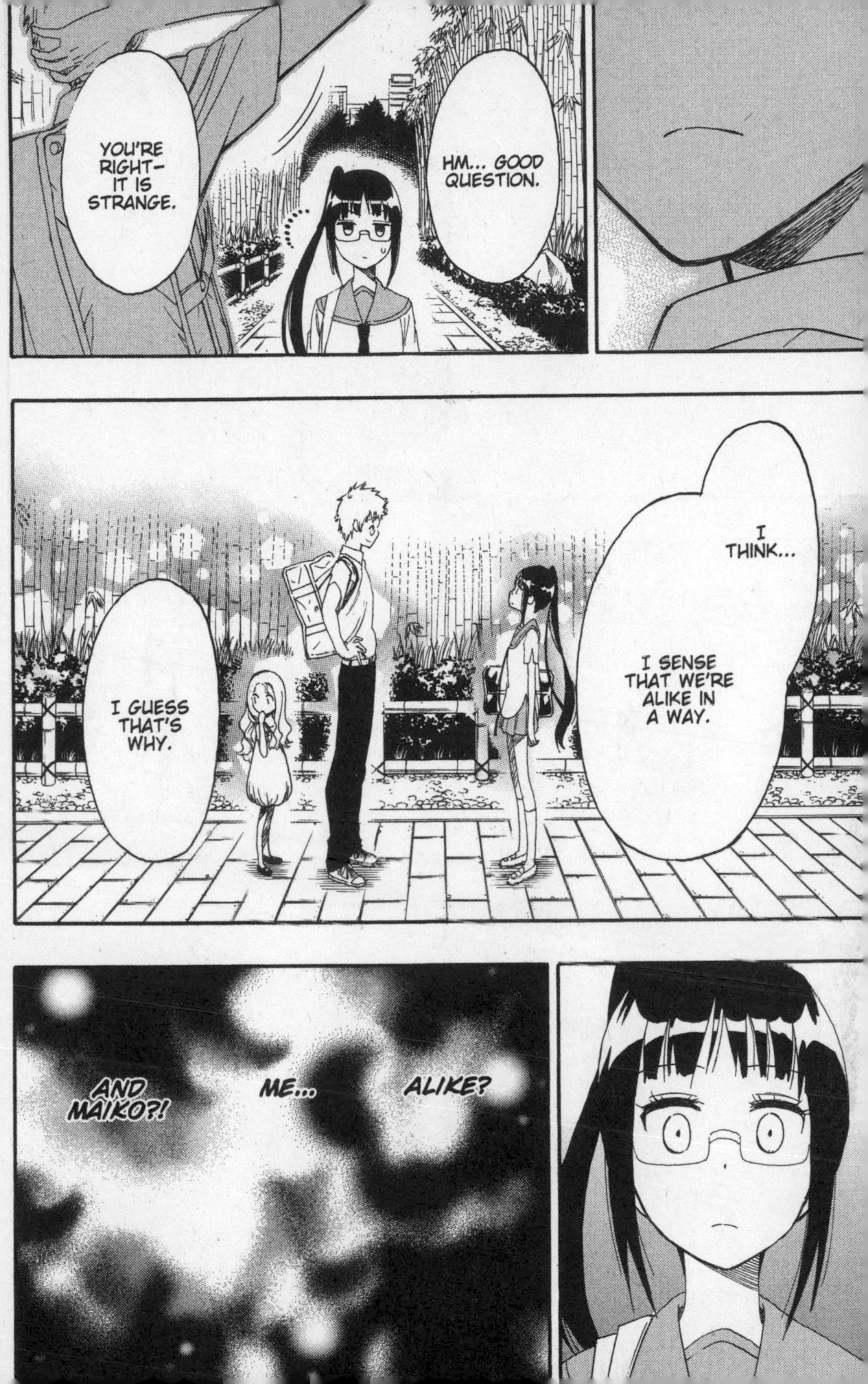
HM... GOOD QUESTION.
YOU'RE RIGHT- IT IS STRANGE.
I THINK...
I SENSE THAT WE'RE ALIKE IN A WAY.
I GUESS THAT'S WHY.
ALIKE?
ME...
AND MAIKO?!

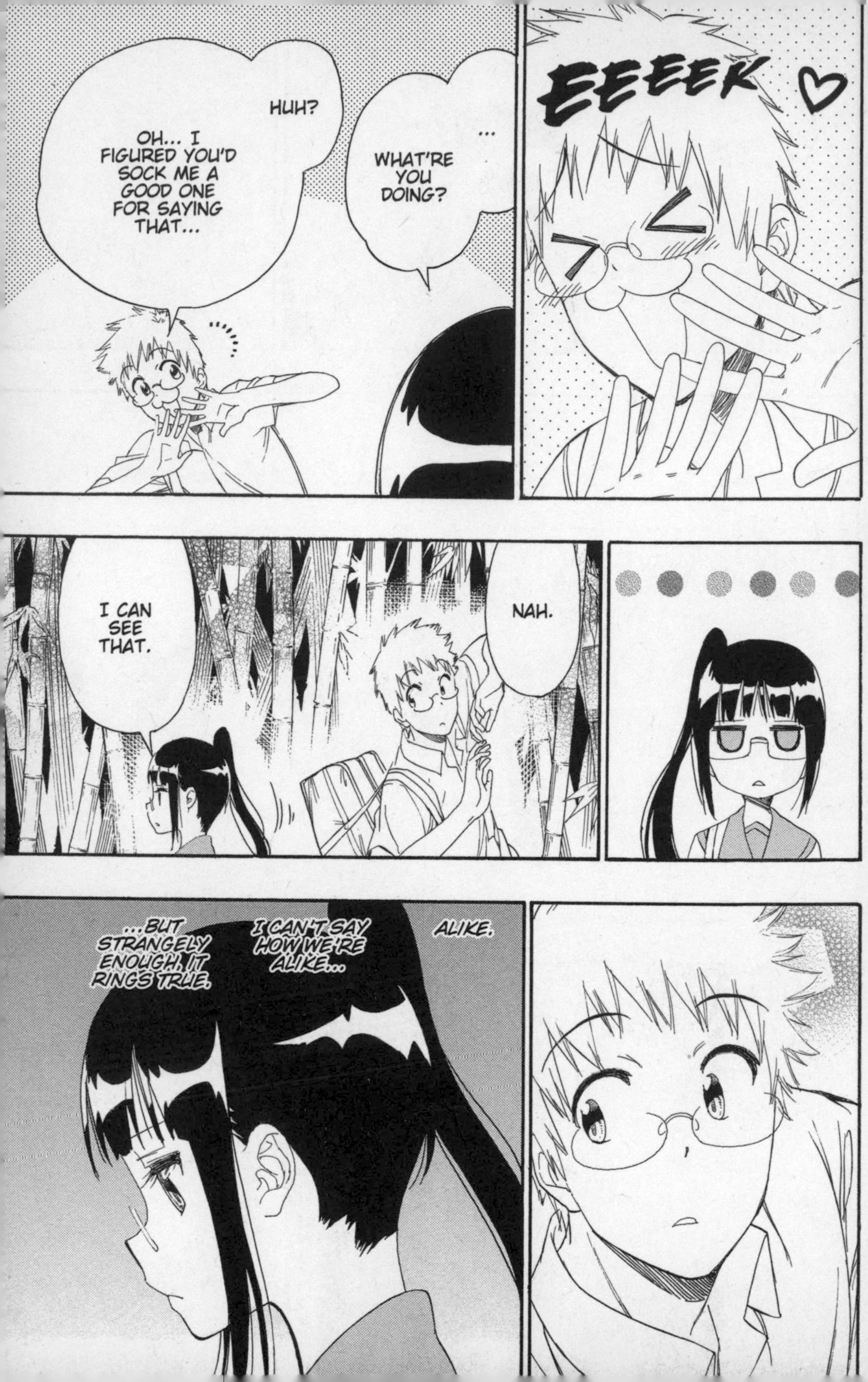
EEEEEK ♥
...
WHAT'RE YOU DOING?
HUH?
OH... I FIGURED YOU'D SOCK ME A GOOD ONE FOR SAYING THAT...
NAH.
I CAN SEE THAT.
ALIKE.
I CAN'T SAY HOW WE'RE ALIKE...
...BUT STRANGELY ENOUGH, IT RINGS TRUE.

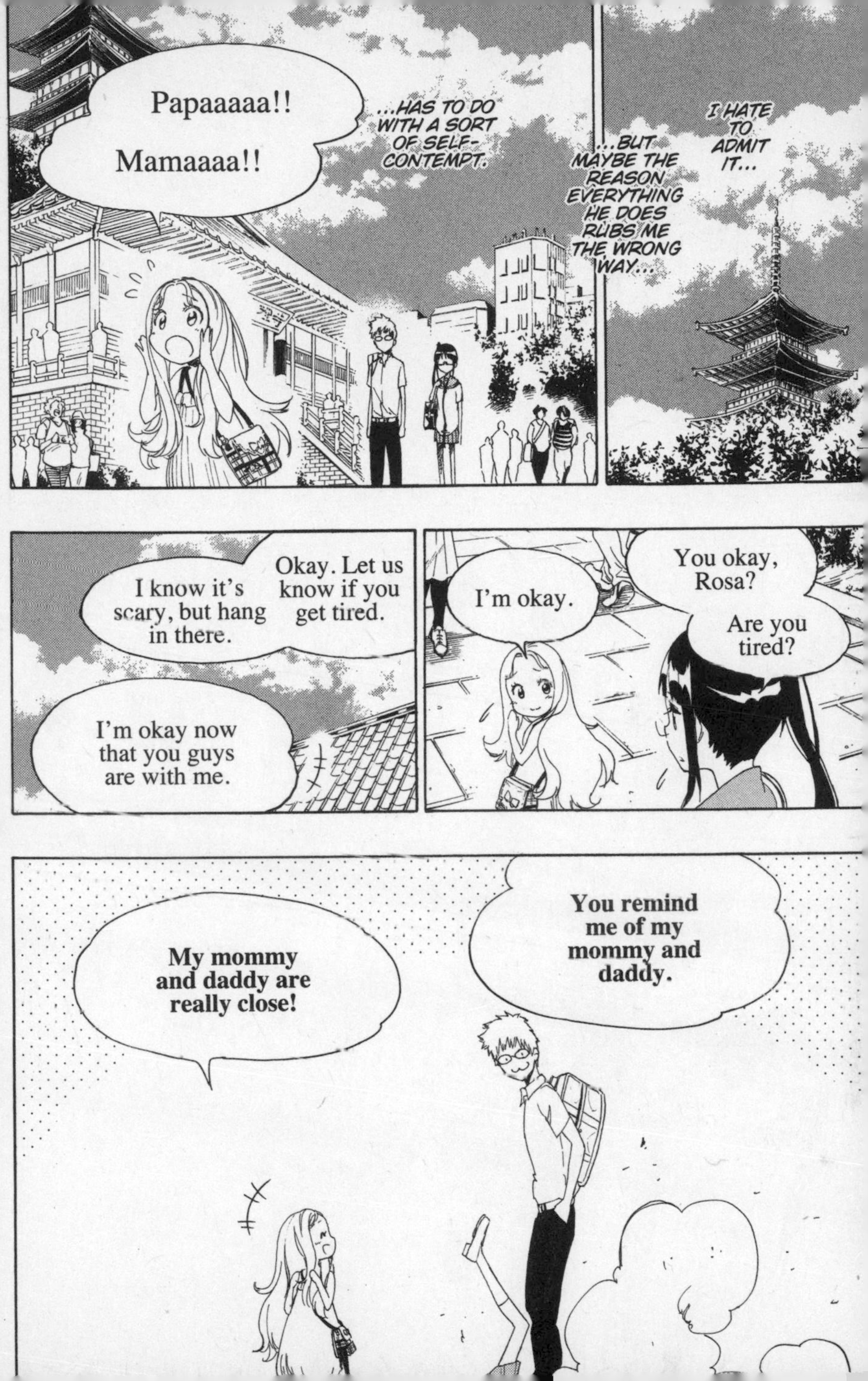
I HATE TO ADMIT IT...
...BUT MAYBE THE REASON EVERYTHING HE DOES RUBS ME THE WRONG WAY...
...HAS TO DO WITH A SORT OF SELF-CONTEMPT.
Papaaaaa!! Mamaaaa!!
You okay, Rosa?
Are you tired?
I'm okay.
Okay. Let us know if you get tired.
I know it's scary, but hang in there.
I'm okay now that you guys are with me.
You remind me of my mommy and daddy.
My mommy and daddy are really close!

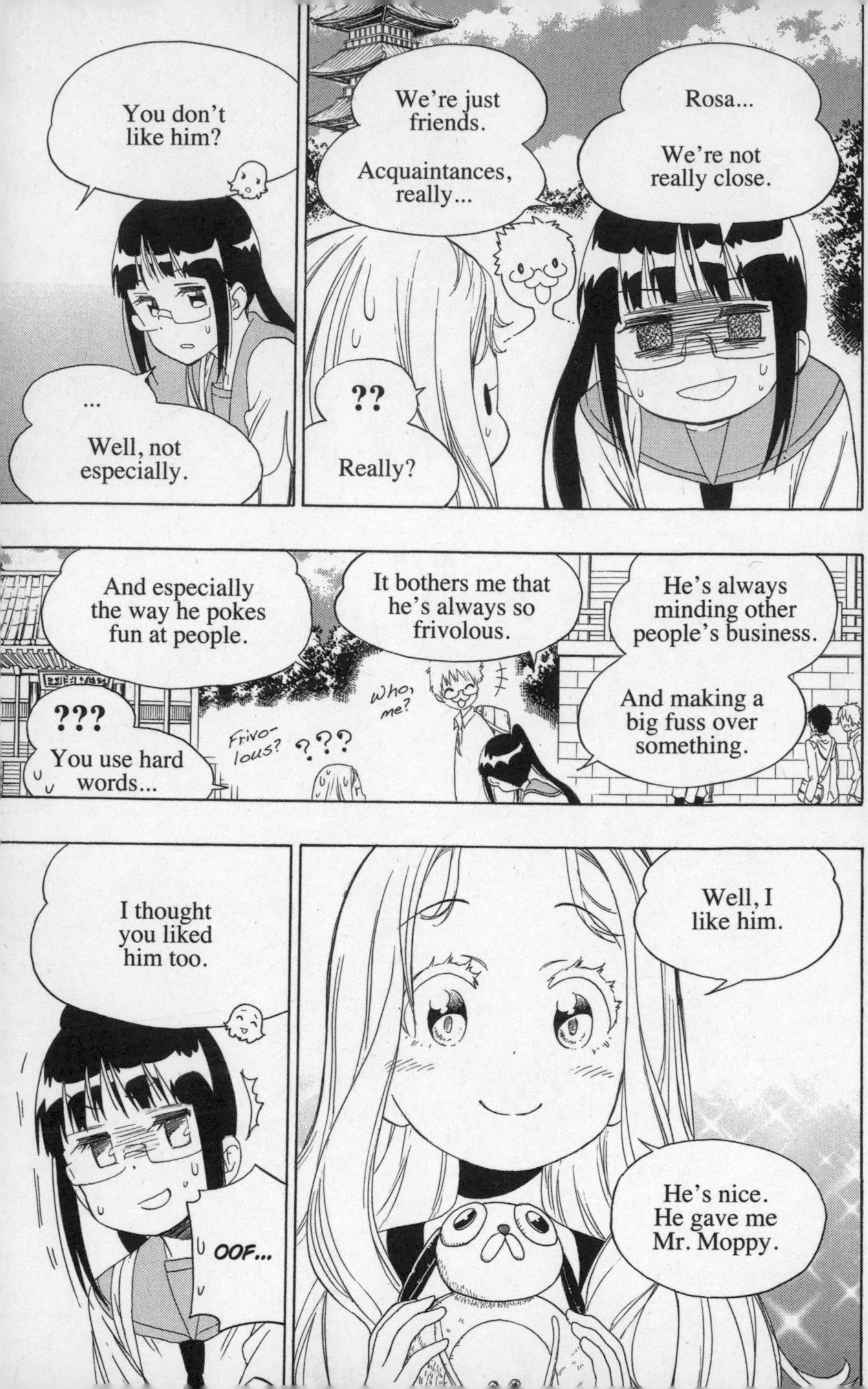
Rosa... We're not really close.
We're just friends. Acquaintances, really...
?? Really?
You don't like him?
... Well, not especially.
He's always minding other people's business.
And making a big fuss over something.
It bothers me that he's always so frivolous.
Who, me?
And especially the way he pokes fun at people.
Frivo-lous? ???
??? You use hard words...
Well, I like him.
He's nice. He gave me Mr. Moppy.
I thought you liked him too.
OOF...

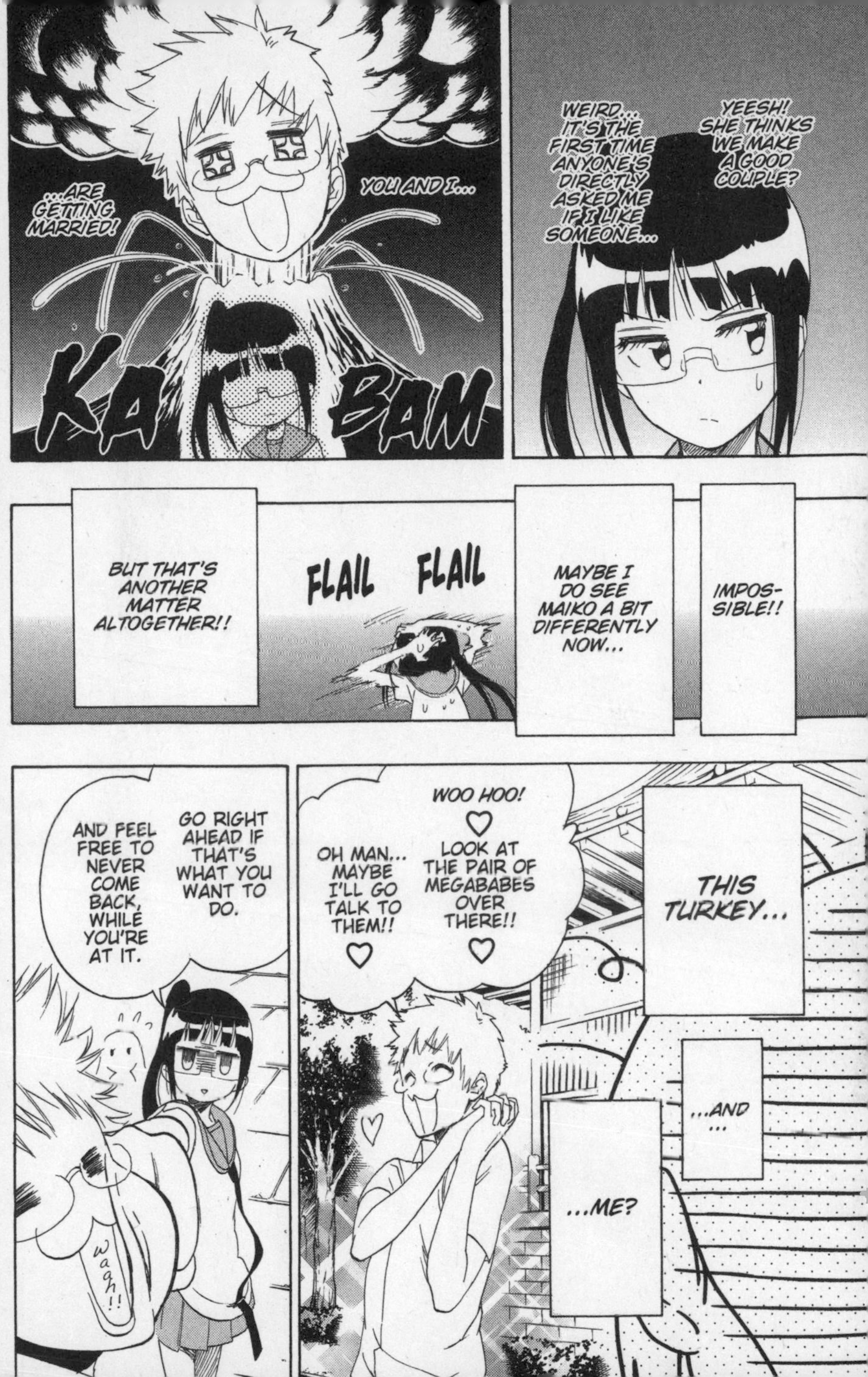
YEESH! SHE THINKS WE MAKE A GOOD COUPLE?
WEIRD... IT'S THE FIRST TIME ANYONE'S DIRECTLY ASKED ME IF I LIKE SOMEONE...
YOU AND I...
...ARE GETTING MARRIED!
KA BAM
IMPOS-SIBLE!!
MAYBE I DO SEE MAIKO A BIT DIFFERENTLY NOW...
FLAIL FLAIL
BUT THAT'S ANOTHER MATTER ALTOGETHER!!
THIS TURKEY...
WOO HOO! ♡ LOOK AT THE PAIR OF MEGABABES OVER THERE!! ♡
OH MAN... MAYBE I'LL GO TALK TO THEM!! ♡
...AND ...
...ME?
GO RIGHT AHEAD IF THAT'S WHAT YOU WANT TO DO.
AND FEEL FREE TO NEVER COME BACK, WHILE YOU'RE AT IT.
Waah!!

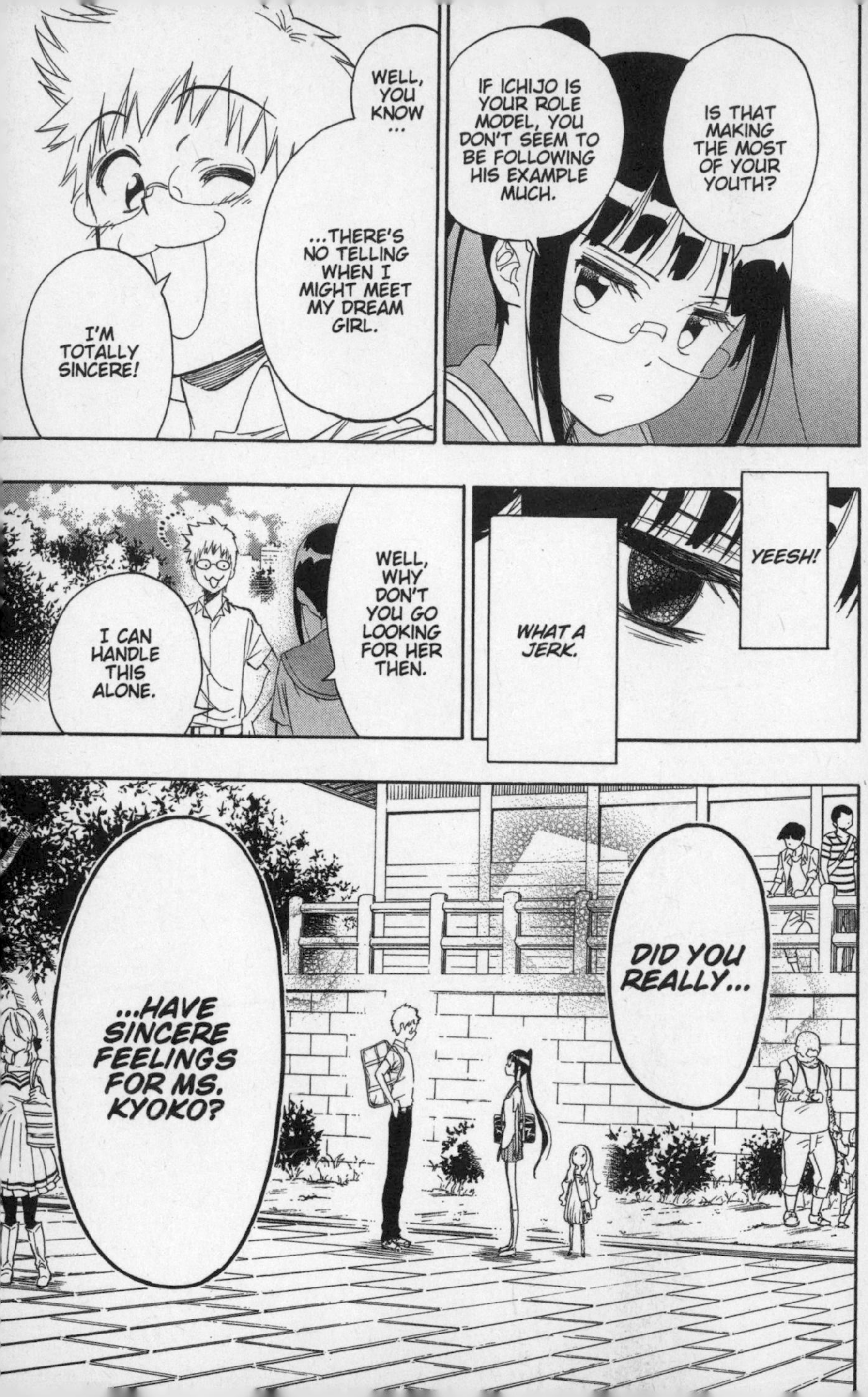
IS THAT MAKING THE MOST OF YOUR YOUTH?
IF ICHIJO IS YOUR ROLE MODEL, YOU DON'T SEEM TO BE FOLLOWING HIS EXAMPLE MUCH.
WELL, YOU KNOW ...
...THERE'S NO TELLING WHEN I MIGHT MEET MY DREAM GIRL.
I'M TOTALLY SINCERE!
YEESH!
WHAT A JERK.
WELL, WHY DON'T YOU GO LOOKING FOR HER THEN.
I CAN HANDLE THIS ALONE.
DID YOU REALLY...
...HAVE SINCERE FEELINGS FOR MS. KYOKO?

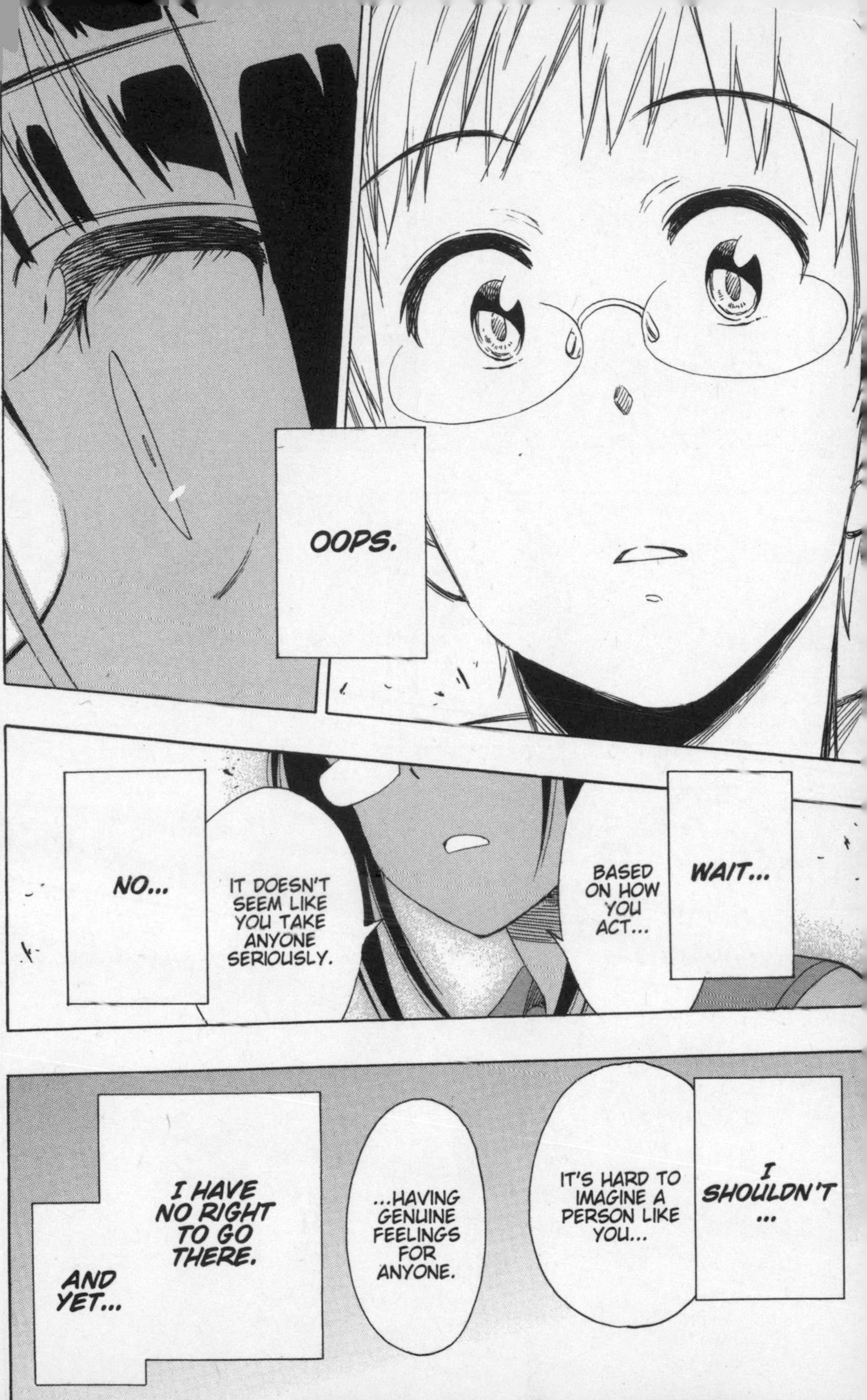
OOPS.
WAIT...
BASED ON HOW YOU ACT...
IT DOESN'T SEEM LIKE YOU TAKE ANYONE SERIOUSLY.
NO...
I SHOULDN'T ...
IT'S HARD TO IMAGINE A PERSON LIKE YOU...
...HAVING GENUINE FEELINGS FOR ANYONE.
I HAVE NO RIGHT TO GO THERE.
AND YET...

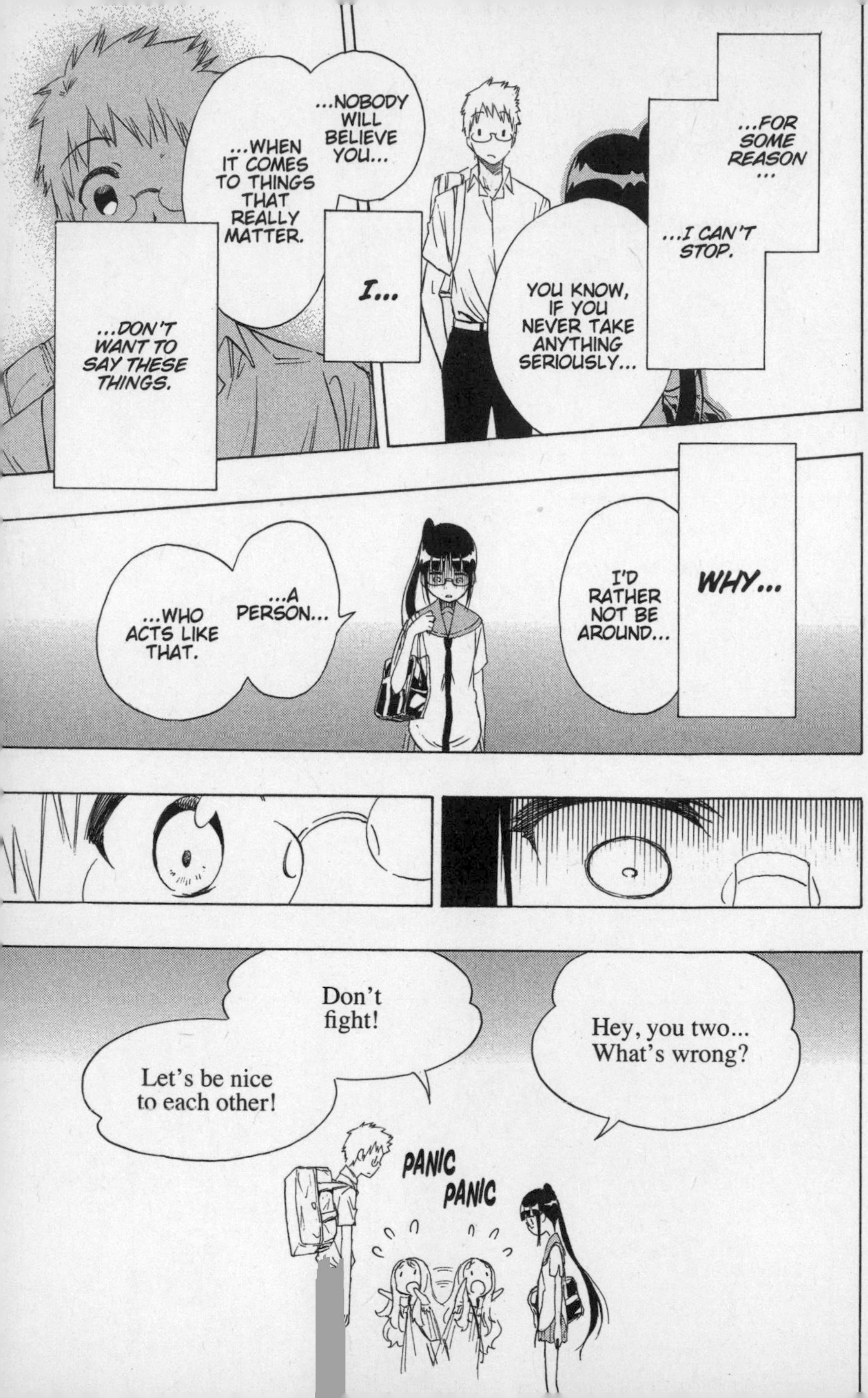
...FOR SOME REASON ...
...I CAN'T STOP.
YOU KNOW, IF YOU NEVER TAKE ANYTHING SERIOUSLY...
...NOBODY WILL BELIEVE YOU...
...WHEN IT COMES TO THINGS THAT REALLY MATTER.
I...
...DON'T WANT TO SAY THESE THINGS.
WHY...
I'D RATHER NOT BE AROUND...
...A PERSON...
...WHO ACTS LIKE THAT.
Hey, you two... What's wrong?
Don't fight!
Let's be nice to each other!
PANIC
PANIC

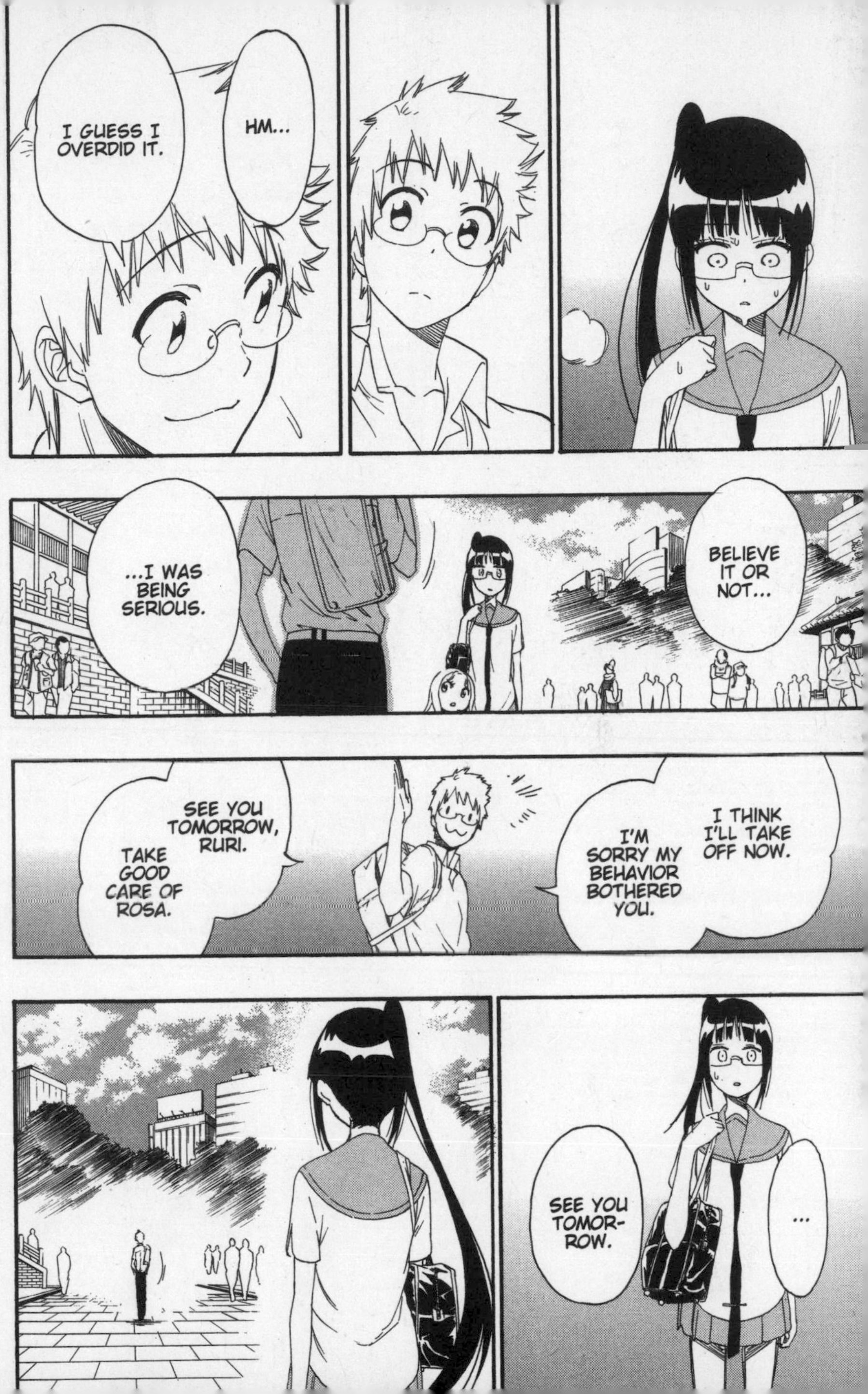
HM...
I GUESS I OVERDID IT.
BELIEVE IT OR NOT...
...I WAS BEING SERIOUS.
I THINK I'LL TAKE OFF NOW.
I'M SORRY MY BEHAVIOR BOTHERED YOU.
SEE YOU TOMORROW, RURI.
TAKE GOOD CARE OF ROSA.
...
SEE YOU TOMOR-ROW.

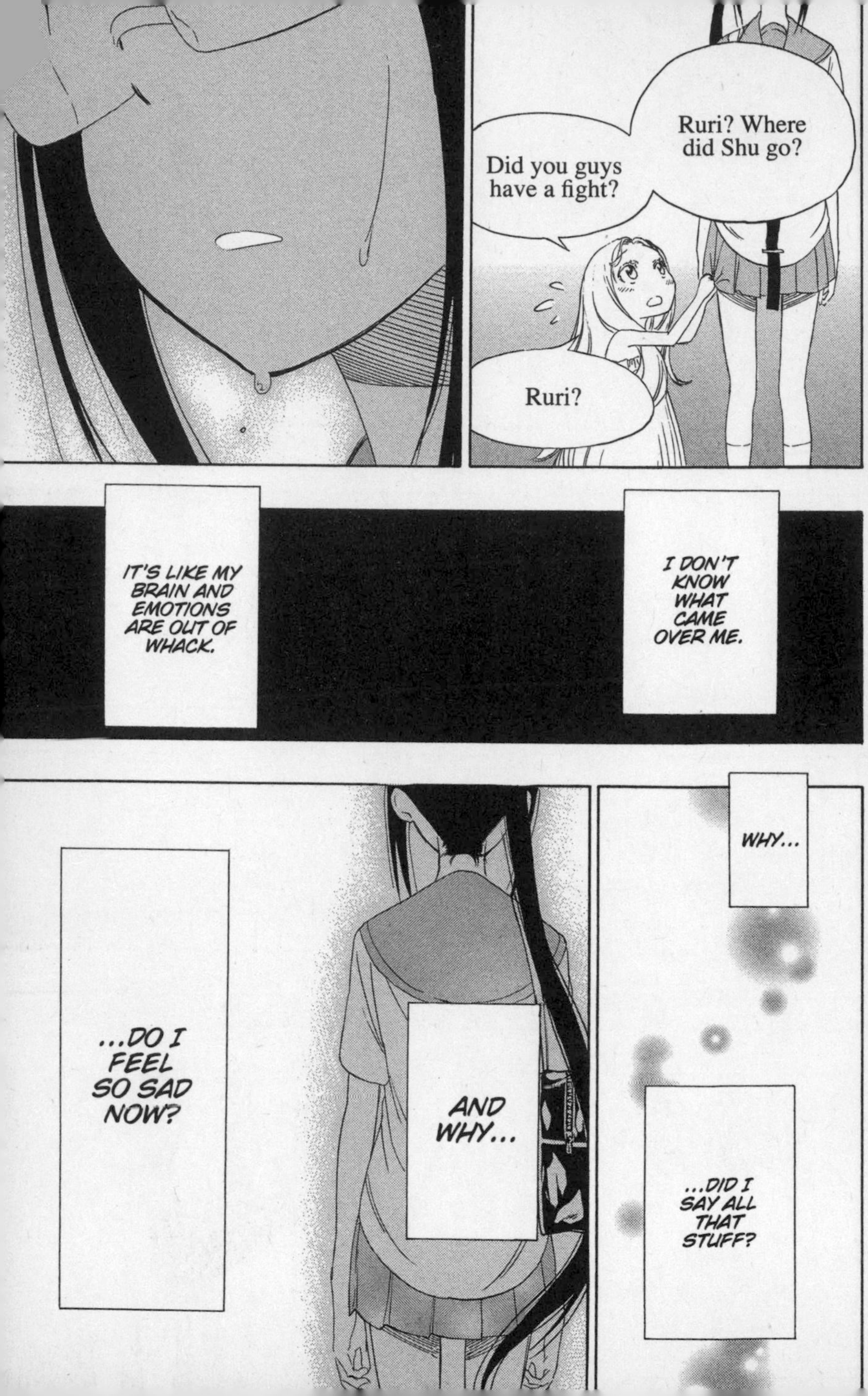
Ruri? Where did Shu go?
Did you guys have a fight?
Ruri?
I DON'T KNOW WHAT CAME OVER ME.
IT'S LIKE MY BRAIN AND EMOTIONS ARE OUT OF WHACK.
WHY...
...DID I SAY ALL THAT STUFF?
AND WHY...
...DO I FEEL SO SAD NOW?

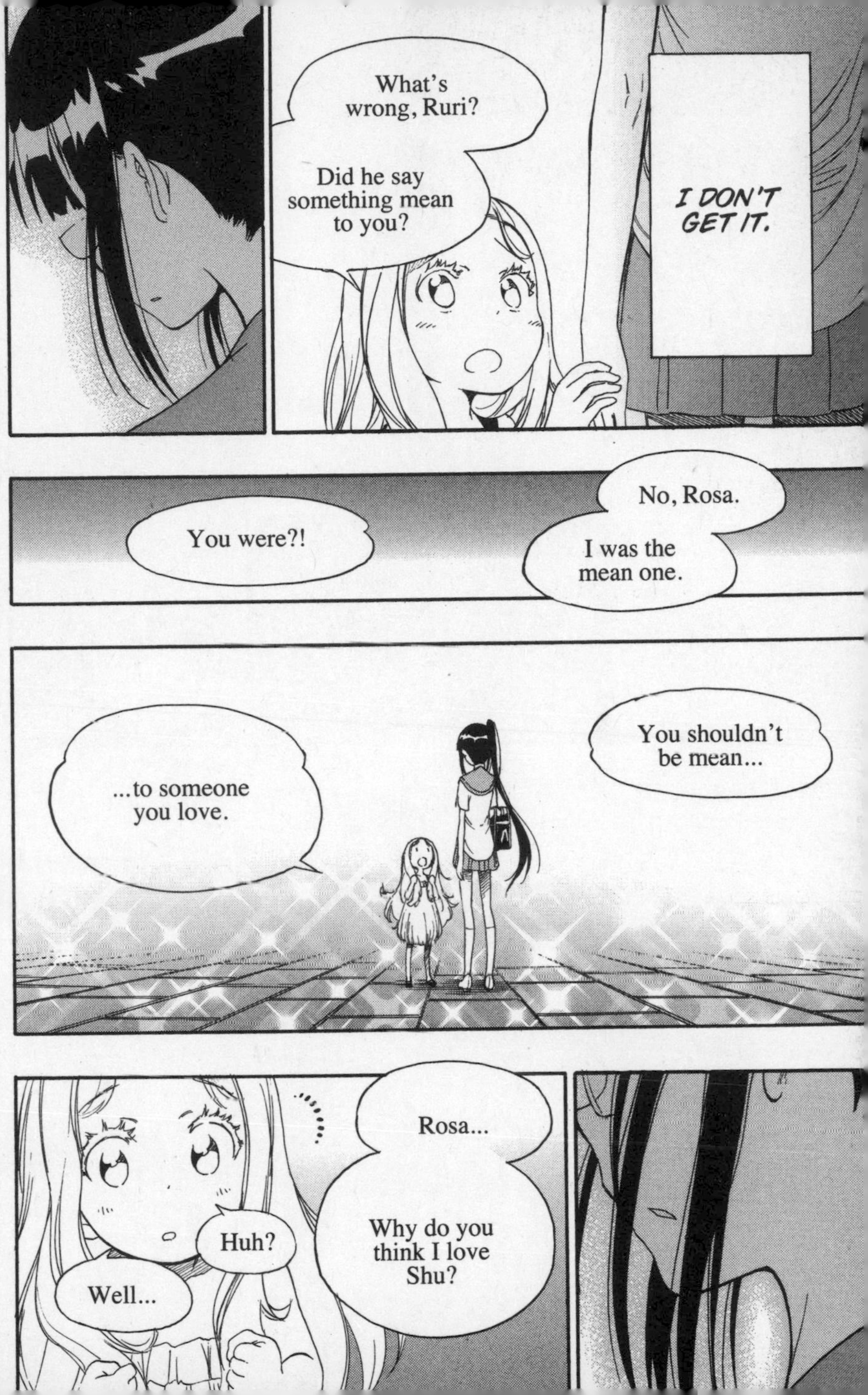
I DON'T GET IT.
What's wrong, Ruri?
Did he say something mean to you?
No, Rosa.
I was the mean one.
You were?!
You shouldn't be mean...
...to someone you love.
Rosa...
Why do you think I love Shu?
Huh?
Well...

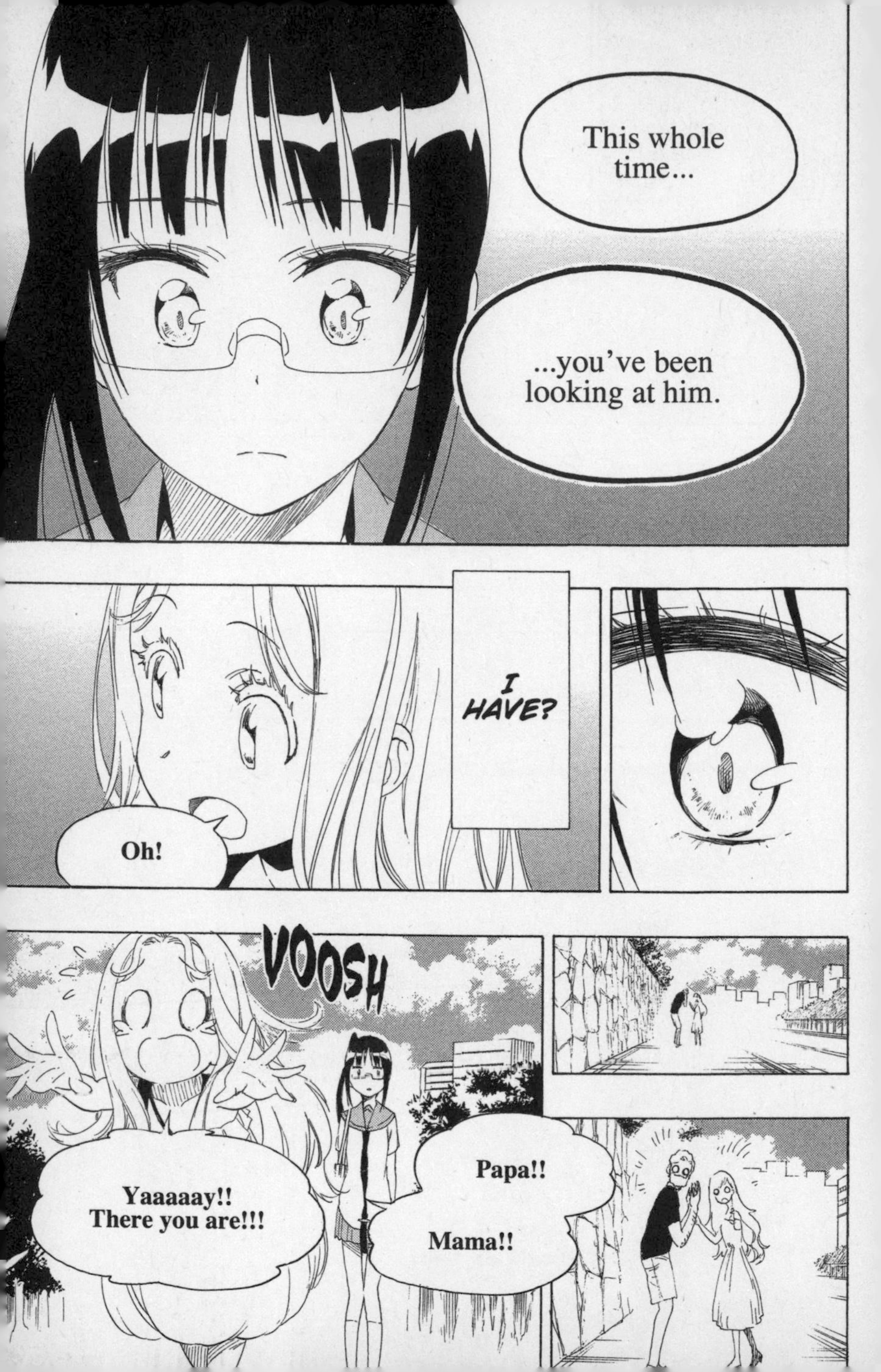
This whole time...
...you've been looking at him.
I HAVE?
Oh!
Papa!!
Mama!!
VOOSH
Yaaaaay!! There you are!!!

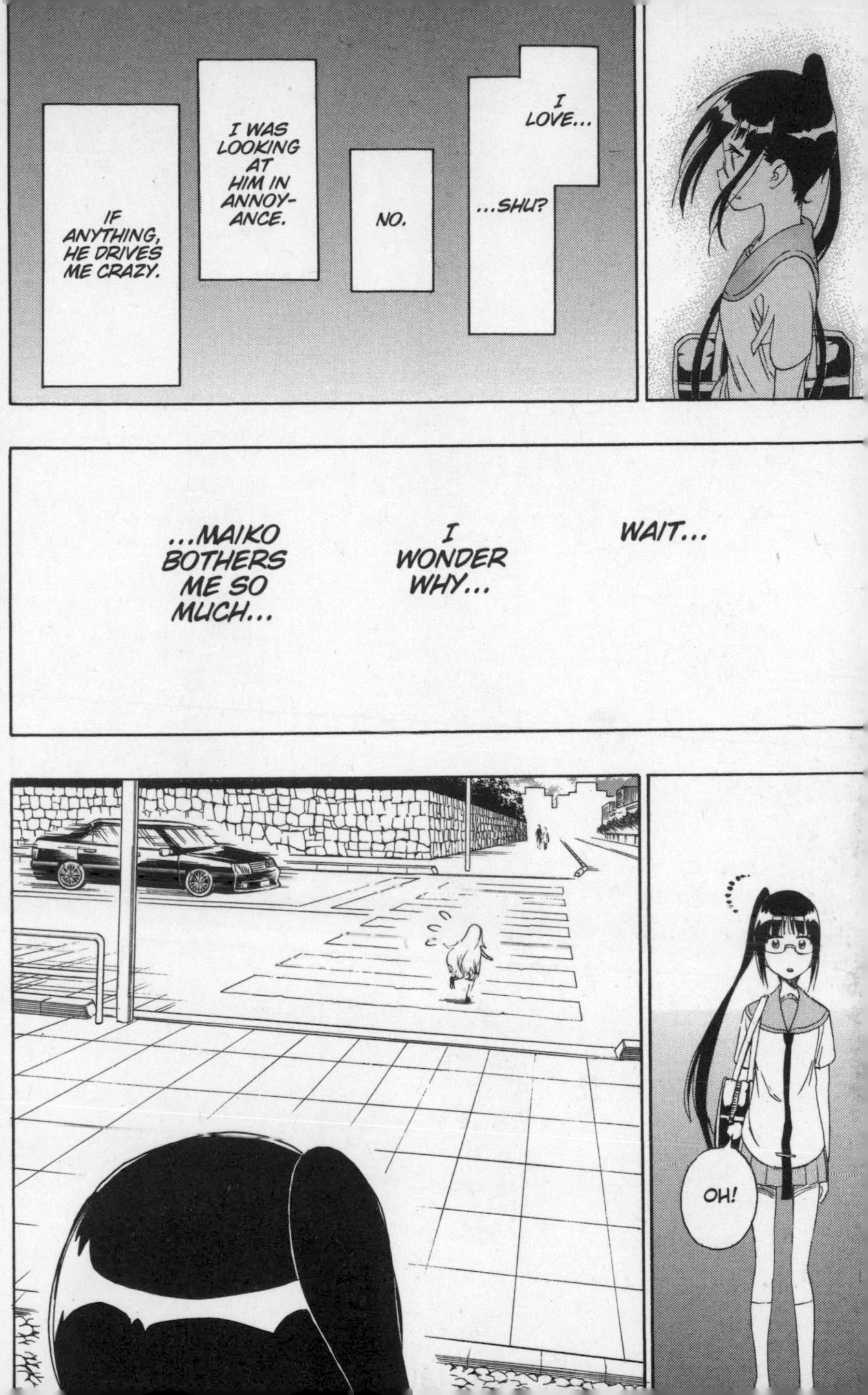
I LOVE...
...SHU?
NO.
I WAS LOOKING AT HIM IN ANNOY-ANCE.
IF ANYTHING, HE DRIVES ME CRAZY.
WAIT...
I WONDER WHY...
...MAIKO BOTHERS ME SO MUCH...
OH!

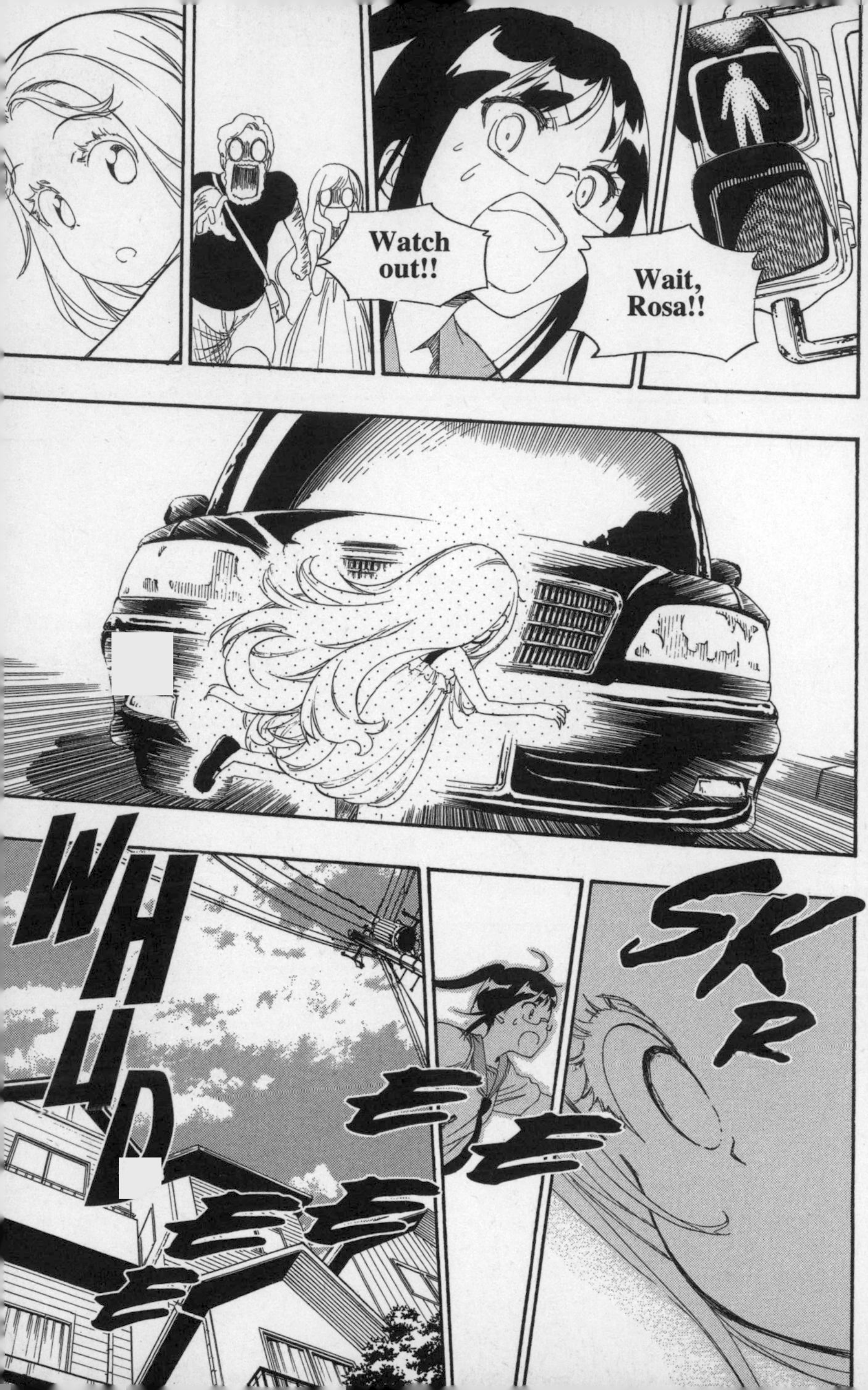
Wait, Rosa!!
Watch out!!
SKREEEEE
WHUD

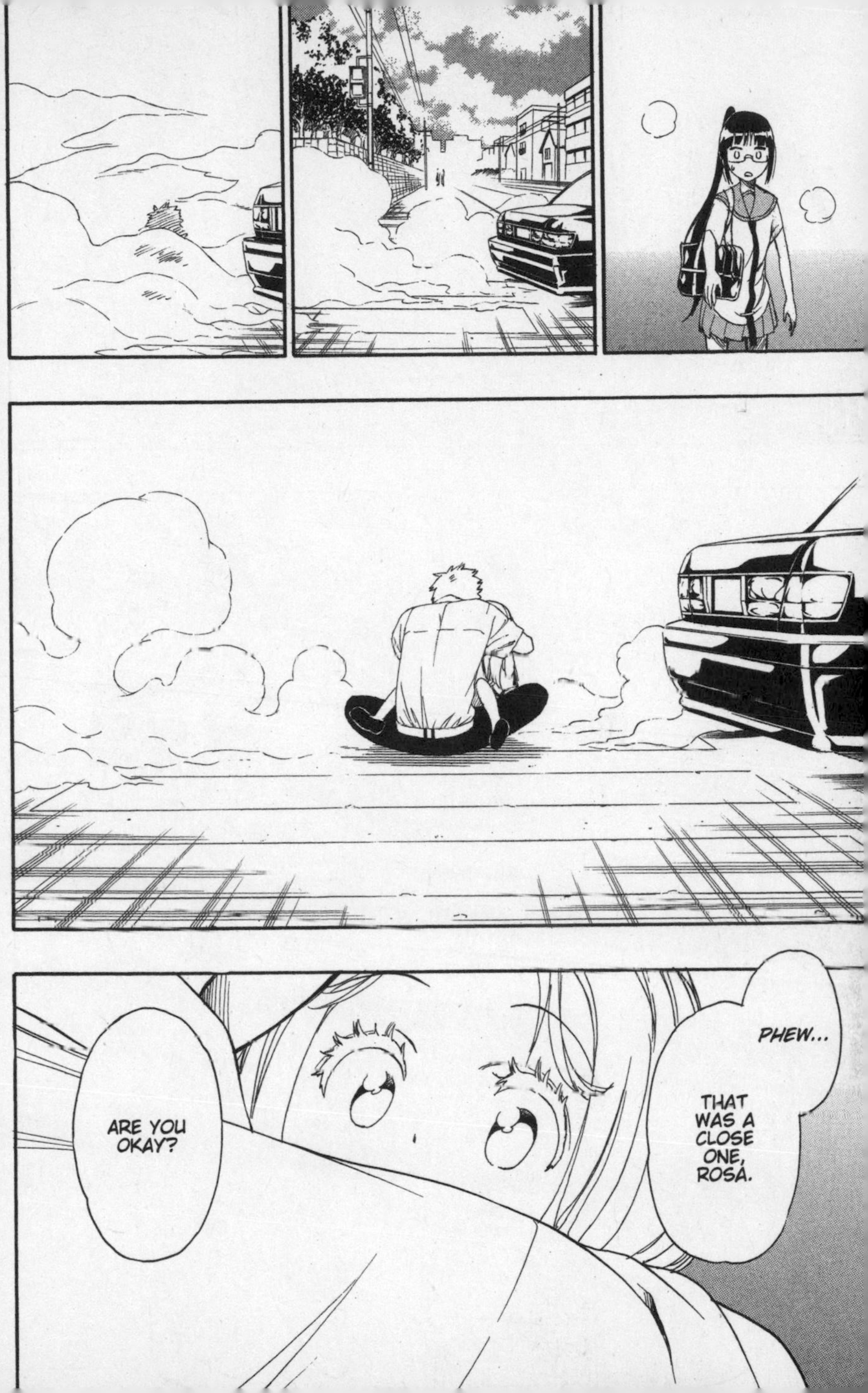
PHEW...
THAT WAS A CLOSE ONE, ROSA.
ARE YOU OKAY?

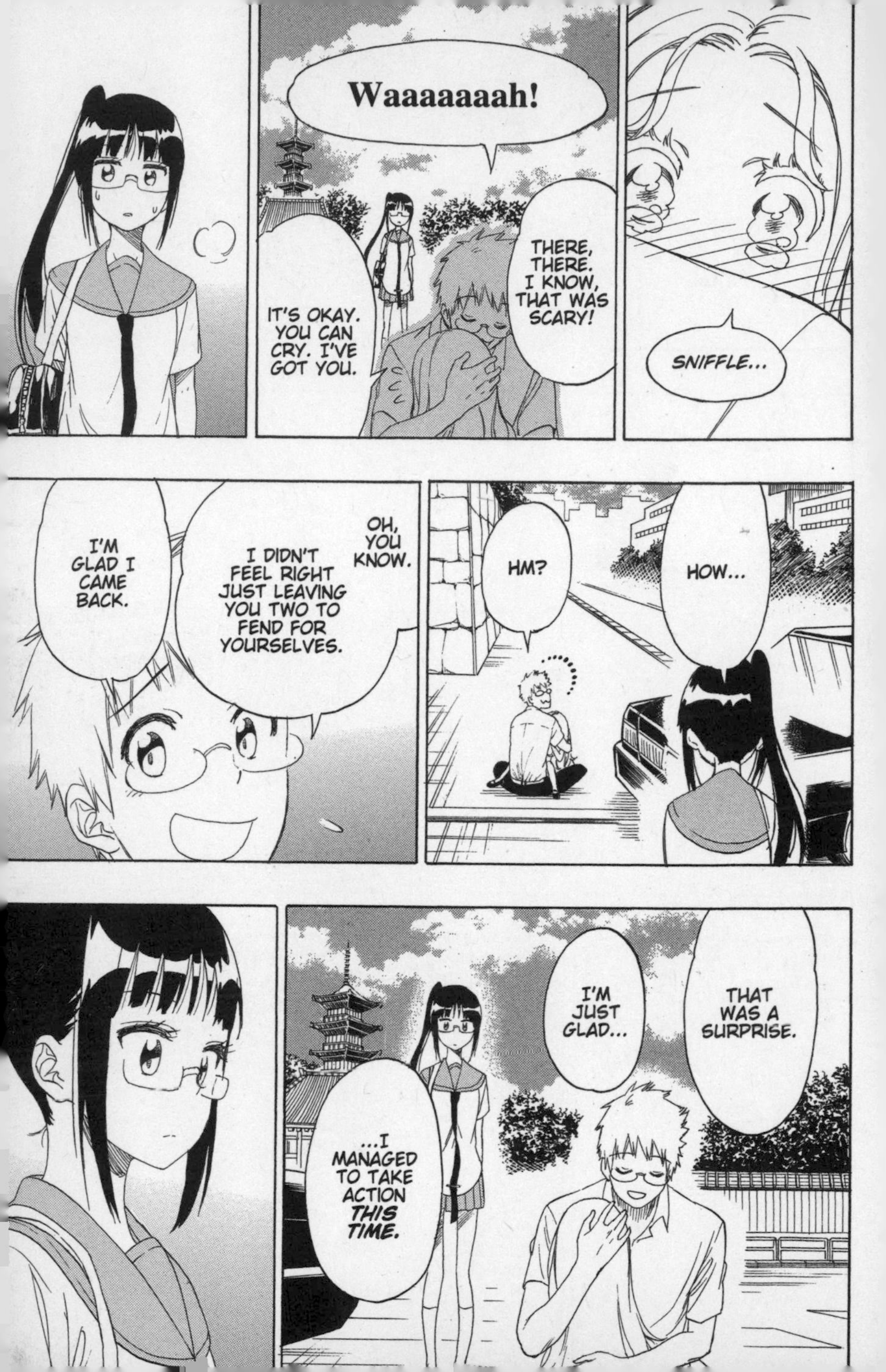
SNIFFLE...
Waaaaaaah!
THERE, THERE. I KNOW, THAT WAS SCARY!
IT'S OKAY. YOU CAN CRY. I'VE GOT YOU.
HOW...
HM?
OH, YOU KNOW.
I DIDN'T FEEL RIGHT JUST LEAVING YOU TWO TO FEND FOR YOURSELVES.
I'M GLAD I CAME BACK.
THAT WAS A SURPRISE.
I'M JUST GLAD...
...I MANAGED TO TAKE ACTION *THIS TIME.*

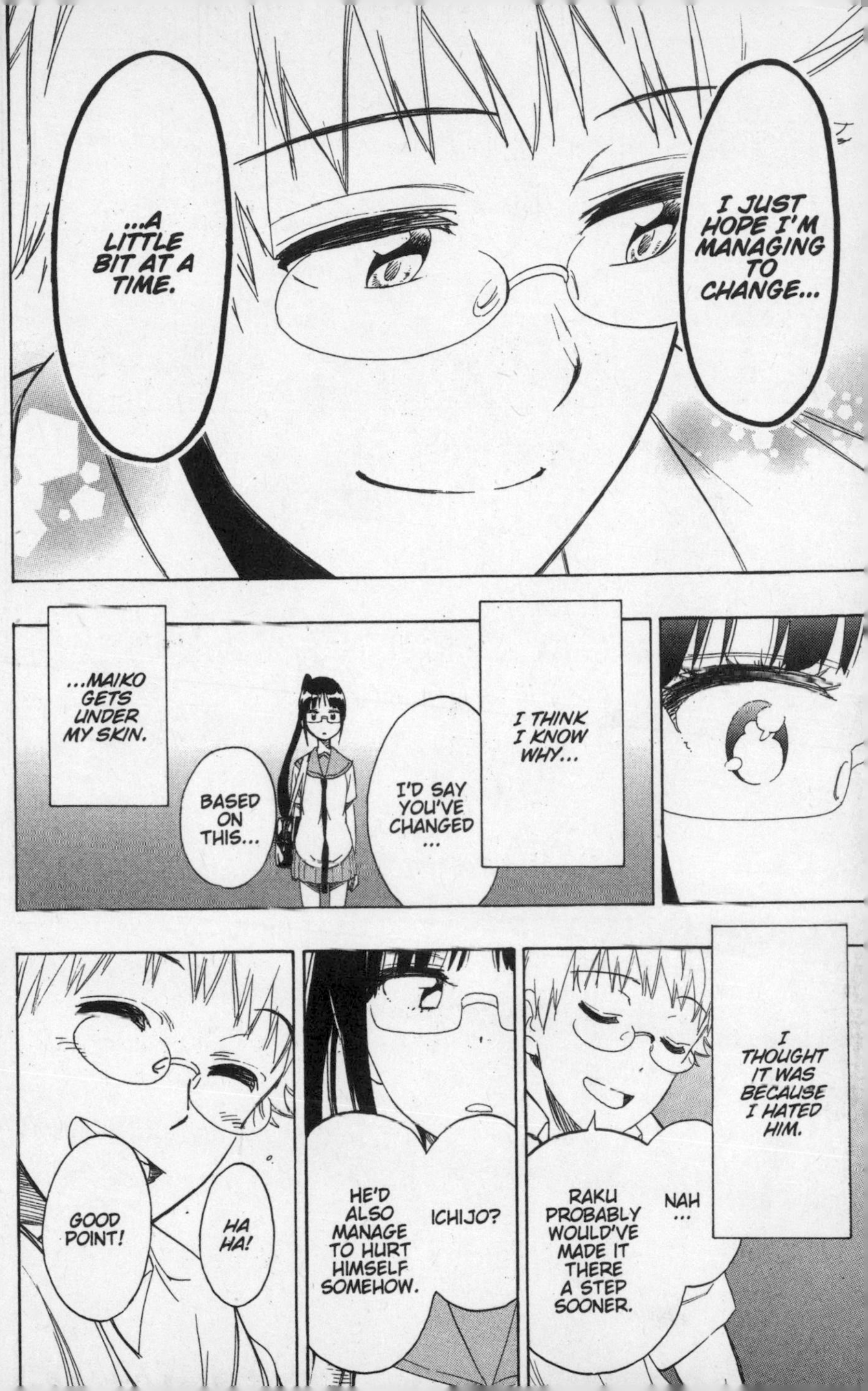
I JUST HOPE I'M MANAGING TO CHANGE...
...A LITTLE BIT AT A TIME.
I THINK I KNOW WHY...
I'D SAY YOU'VE CHANGED ...
BASED ON THIS...
...MAIKO GETS UNDER MY SKIN.
I THOUGHT IT WAS BECAUSE I HATED HIM.
NAH ...
RAKU PROBABLY WOULD'VE MADE IT THERE A STEP SOONER.
ICHIJO?
HE'D ALSO MANAGE TO HURT HIMSELF SOMEHOW.
HA HA!
GOOD POINT!

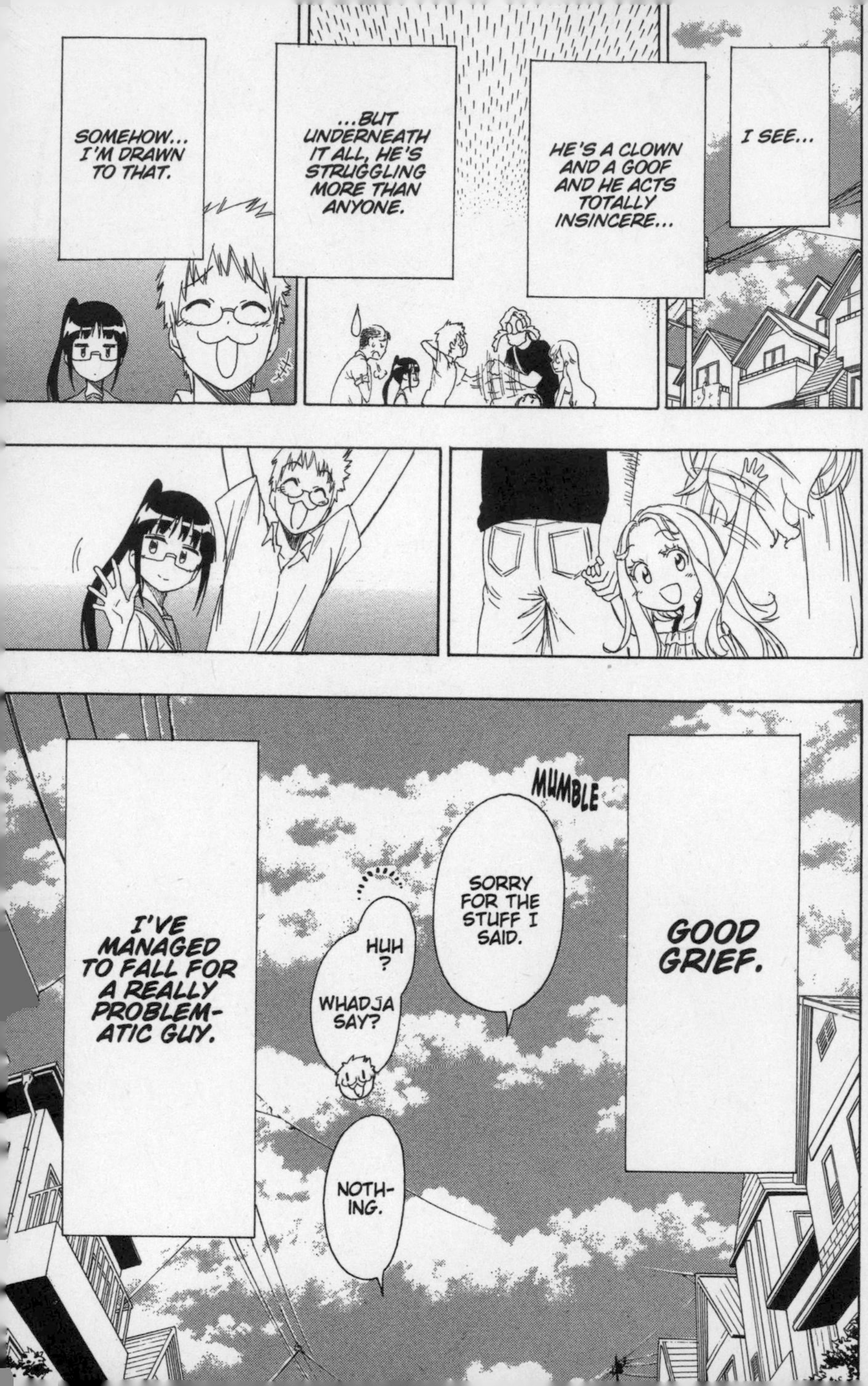

I SEE...
HE'S A CLOWN AND A GOOF AND HE ACTS TOTALLY INSINCERE...
...BUT UNDERNEATH IT ALL, HE'S STRUGGLING MORE THAN ANYONE.
SOMEHOW... I'M DRAWN TO THAT.
GOOD GRIEF.
MUMBLE
SORRY FOR THE STUFF I SAID.
I'VE MANAGED TO FALL FOR A REALLY PROBLEM-ATIC GUY.
HUH?
WHADJA SAY?
NOTH-ING.

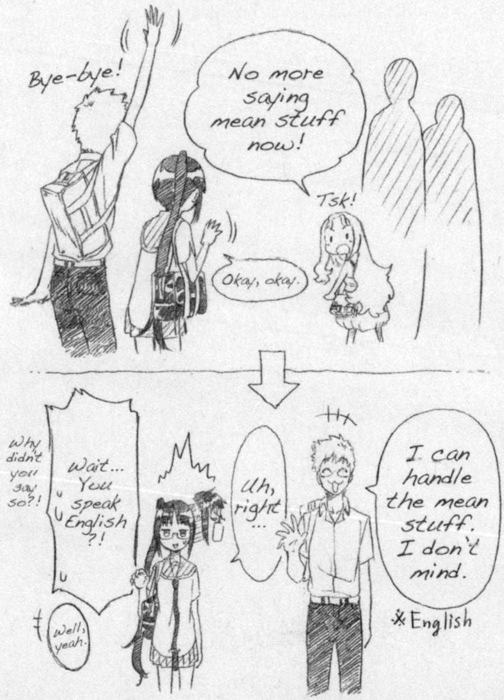
No more saying mean stuff now!
Tsk!
Okay, okay.
Bye-bye!
I can handle the mean stuff. I don't mind.
※English
Uh, right...
Wait... You speak English?!
Why didn't you say so?!
Well, yeah.

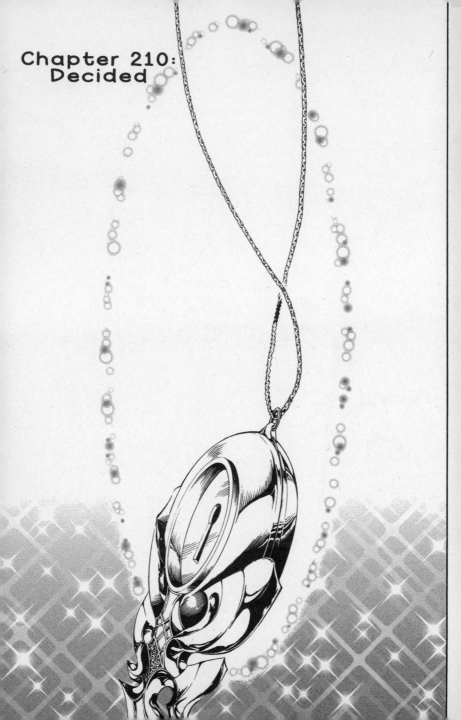

Chapter 210:
Decided

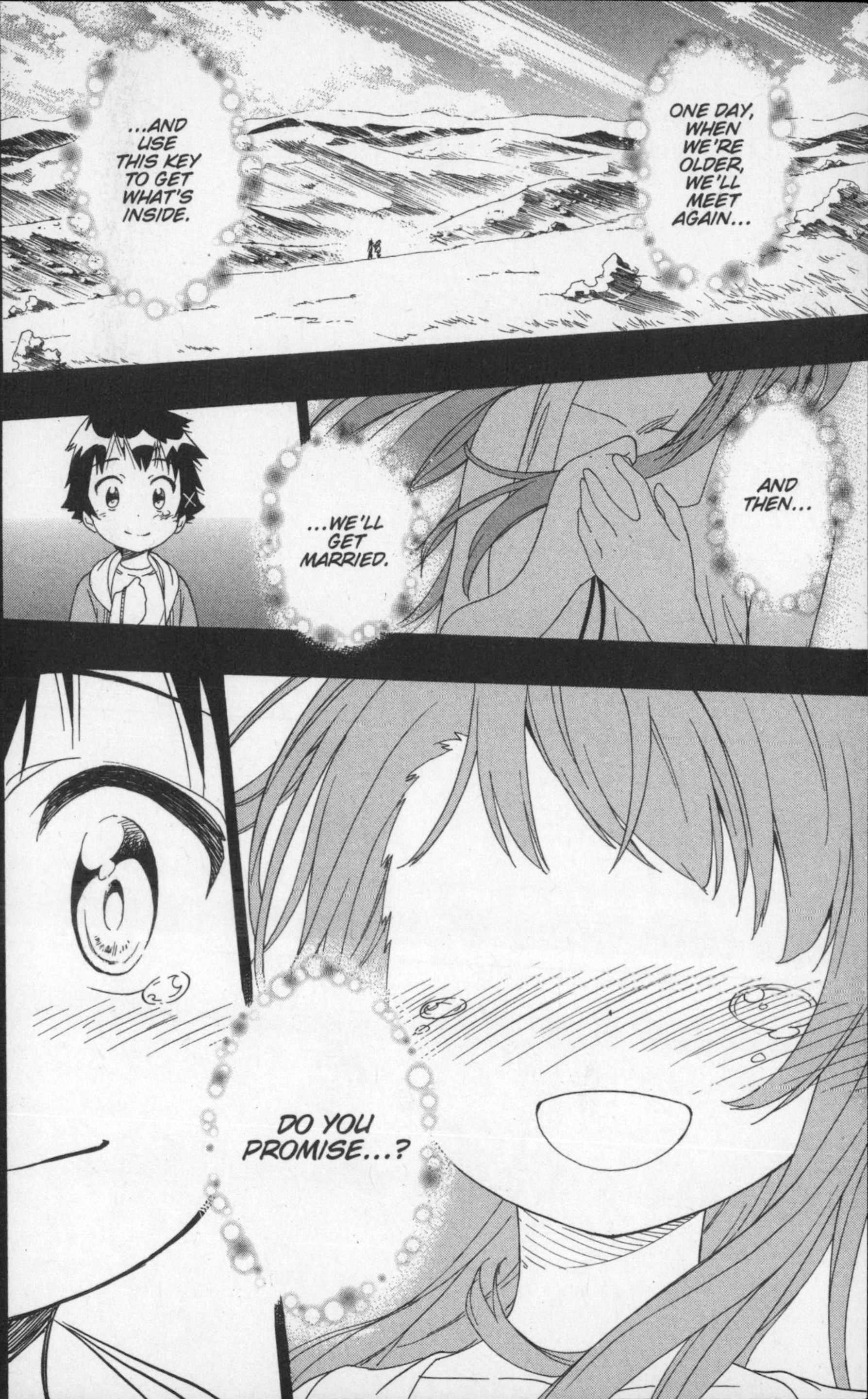
ONE DAY, WHEN WE'RE OLDER, WE'LL MEET AGAIN...
...AND USE THIS KEY TO GET WHAT'S INSIDE.
AND THEN...
...WE'LL GET MARRIED.
DO YOU PROMISE...?

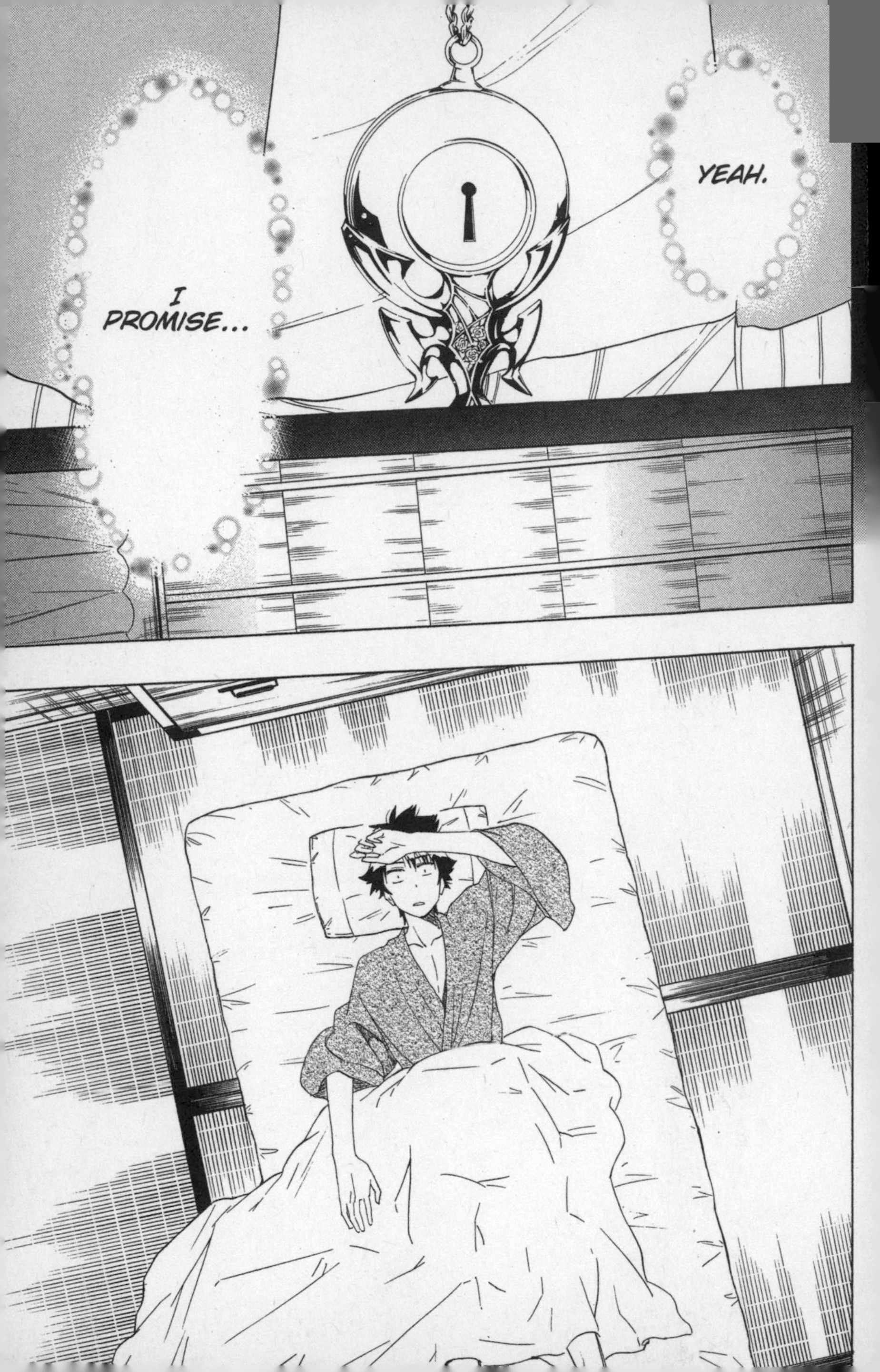
YEAH.
I PROMISE...

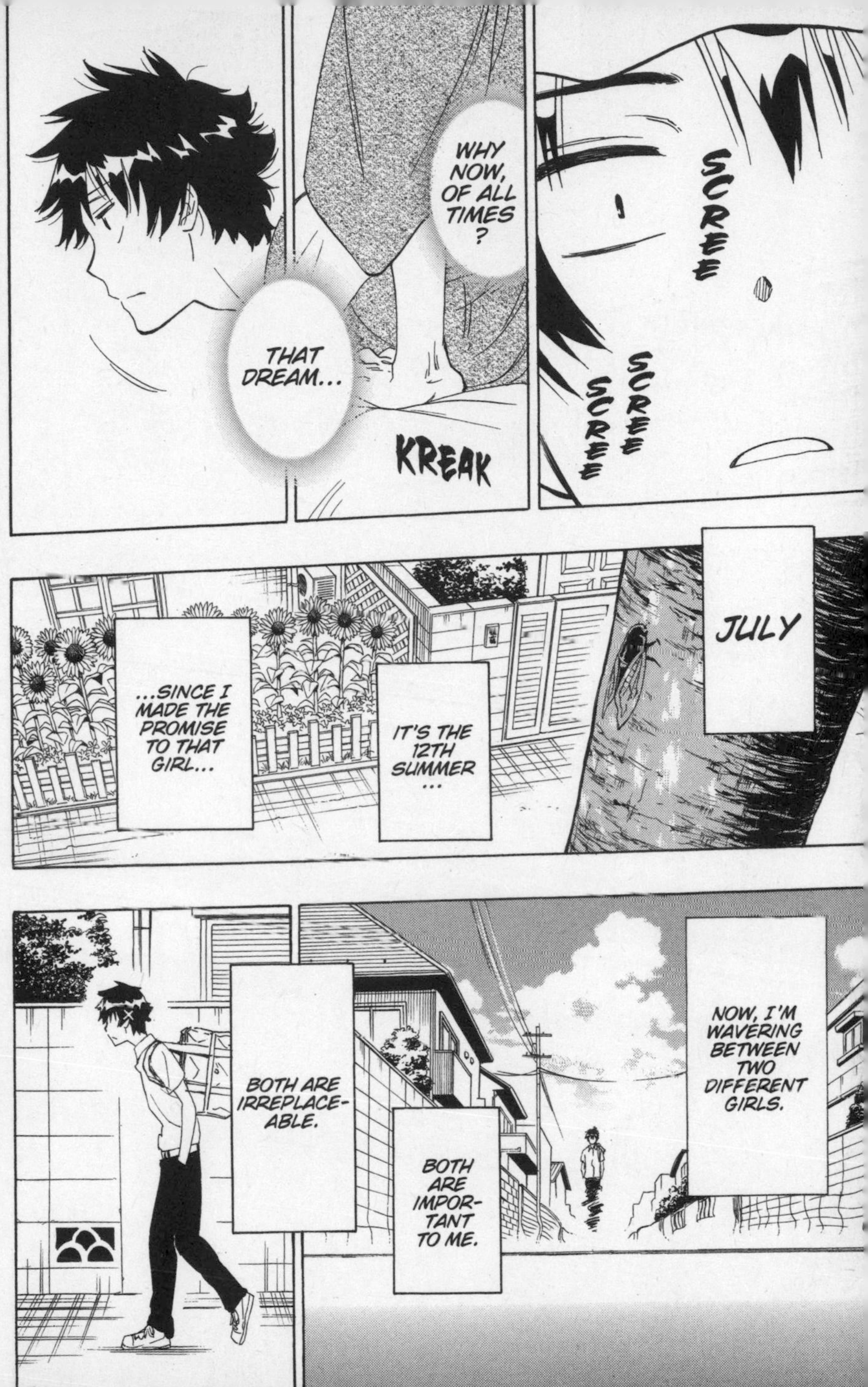
SCREE
SCREE
SCREE
WHY NOW, OF ALL TIMES?
THAT DREAM...
KREAK
JULY
IT'S THE 12TH SUMMER...
...SINCE I MADE THE PROMISE TO THAT GIRL...
NOW, I'M WAVERING BETWEEN TWO DIFFERENT GIRLS.
BOTH ARE IRREPLACE-ABLE.
BOTH ARE IMPOR-TANT TO ME.

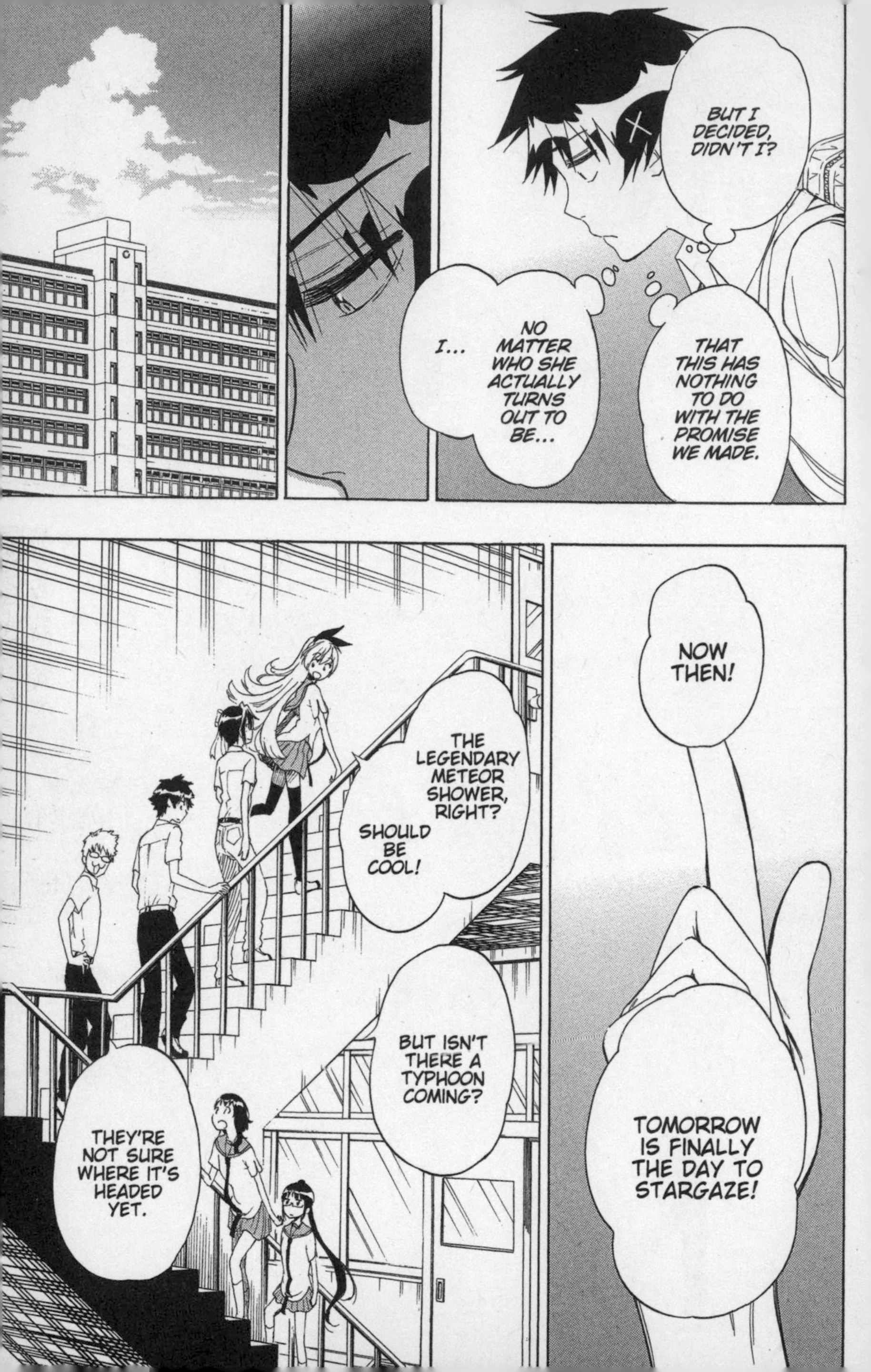
BUT I DECIDED, DIDN'T I?
THAT THIS HAS NOTHING TO DO WITH THE PROMISE WE MADE.
NO MATTER WHO SHE ACTUALLY TURNS OUT TO BE...
I...
NOW THEN!
TOMORROW IS FINALLY THE DAY TO STARGAZE!
THE LEGENDARY METEOR SHOWER, RIGHT?
SHOULD BE COOL!
BUT ISN'T THERE A TYPHOON COMING?
THEY'RE NOT SURE WHERE IT'S HEADED YET.

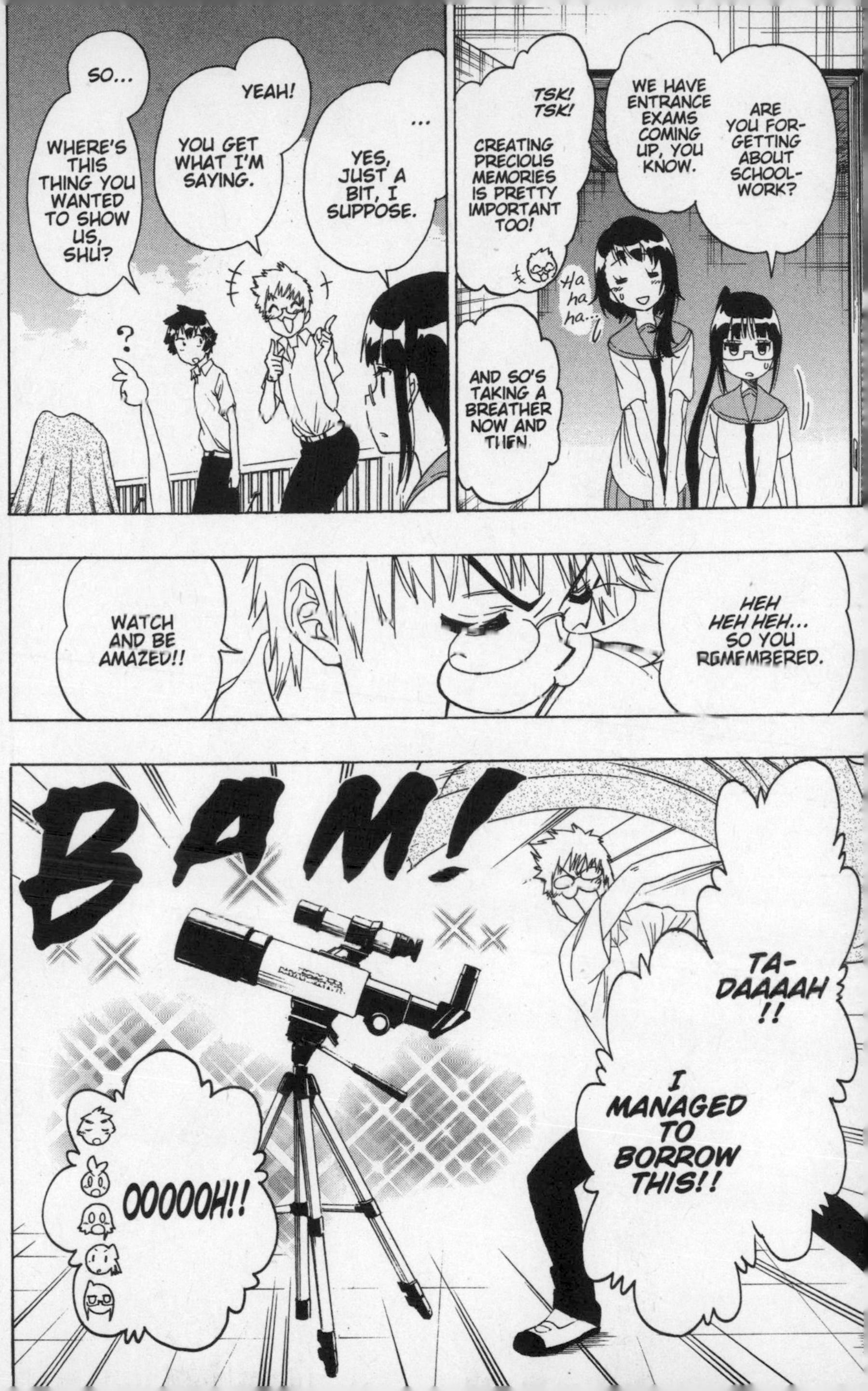
ARE YOU FORGETTING ABOUT SCHOOLWORK?
WE HAVE ENTRANCE EXAMS COMING UP, YOU KNOW.
TSK! TSK!
CREATING PRECIOUS MEMORIES IS PRETTY IMPORTANT TOO!
Ha ha ha...
AND SO'S TAKING A BREATHER NOW AND THEN.
...
YES, JUST A BIT, I SUPPOSE.
YEAH!
YOU GET WHAT I'M SAYING.
SO...
WHERE'S THIS THING YOU WANTED TO SHOW US, SHU?
?
HEH HEH HEH... SO YOU REMEMBERED.
WATCH AND BE AMAZED!!
TA-DAAAAH!!
BAM!
I MANAGED TO BORROW THIS!!
OOOOOH!!

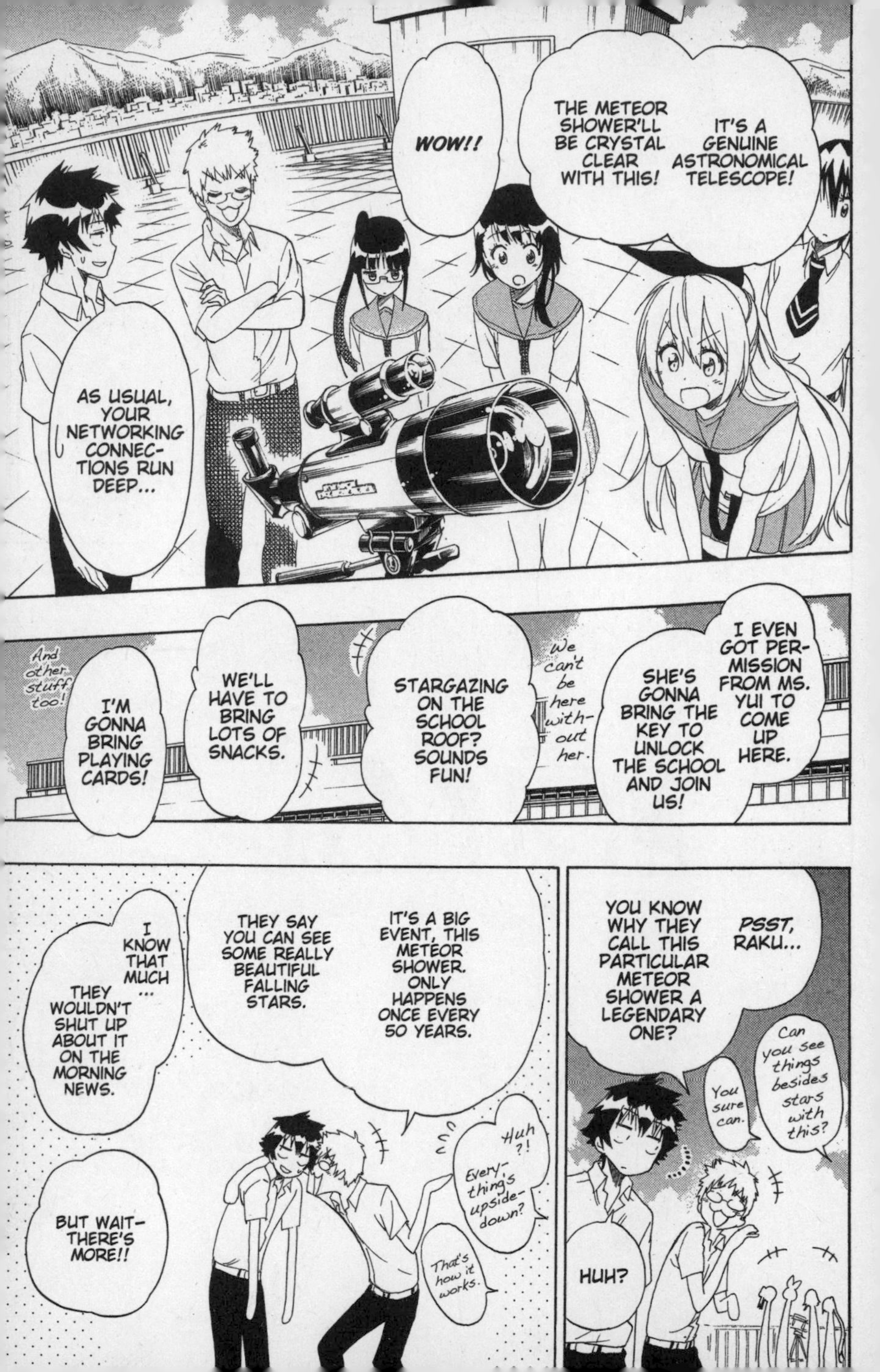
IT'S A GENUINE ASTRONOMICAL TELESCOPE!
THE METEOR SHOWER'LL BE CRYSTAL CLEAR WITH THIS!
WOW!!
AS USUAL, YOUR NETWORKING CONNECTIONS RUN DEEP...
I EVEN GOT PERMISSION FROM MS. YUI TO COME UP HERE.
SHE'S GONNA BRING THE KEY TO UNLOCK THE SCHOOL AND JOIN US!
We can't be here without her.
STARGAZING ON THE SCHOOL ROOF? SOUNDS FUN!
WE'LL HAVE TO BRING LOTS OF SNACKS.
I'M GONNA BRING PLAYING CARDS!
And other stuff too!
PSST, RAKU...
YOU KNOW WHY THEY CALL THIS PARTICULAR METEOR SHOWER A LEGENDARY ONE?
Can you see things besides stars with this?
You sure can.
HUH?
IT'S A BIG EVENT, THIS METEOR SHOWER. ONLY HAPPENS ONCE EVERY 50 YEARS.
THEY SAY YOU CAN SEE SOME REALLY BEAUTIFUL FALLING STARS.
I KNOW THAT MUCH...
THEY WOULDN'T SHUT UP ABOUT IT ON THE MORNING NEWS.
Huh?!
Everything's upside-down?
That's how it works.
BUT WAIT—THERE'S MORE!!

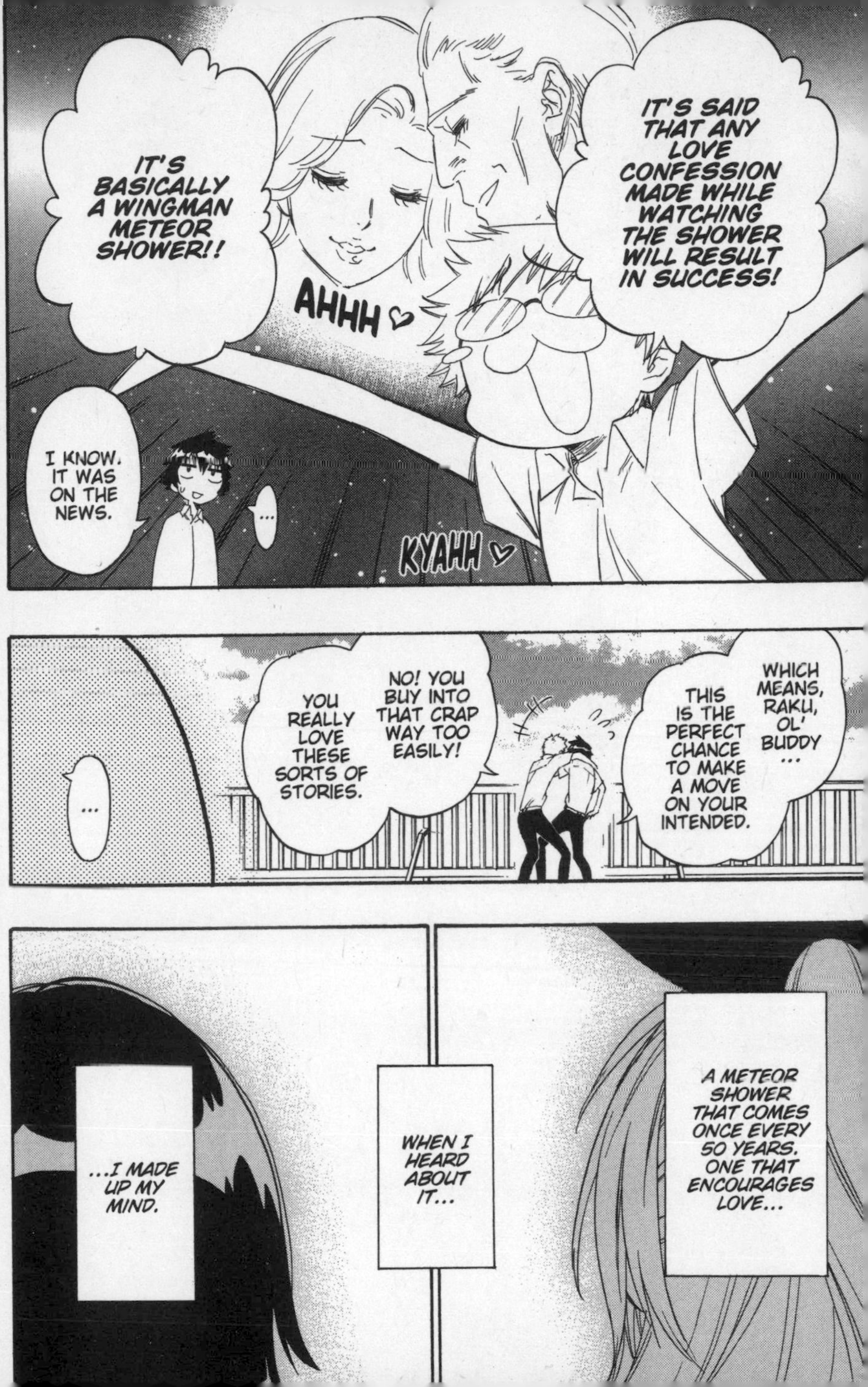

IT'S SAID THAT ANY LOVE CONFESSION MADE WHILE WATCHING THE SHOWER WILL RESULT IN SUCCESS!
AHHH ♡
IT'S BASICALLY A WINGMAN METEOR SHOWER!!
KYAHH ♡
...
I KNOW. IT WAS ON THE NEWS.
WHICH MEANS, RAKU, OL' BUDDY...
THIS IS THE PERFECT CHANCE TO MAKE A MOVE ON YOUR INTENDED.
NO! YOU BUY INTO THAT CRAP WAY TOO EASILY!
YOU REALLY LOVE THESE SORTS OF STORIES.
...
A METEOR SHOWER THAT COMES ONCE EVERY 50 YEARS. ONE THAT ENCOURAGES LOVE...
WHEN I HEARD ABOUT IT...
...I MADE UP MY MIND.

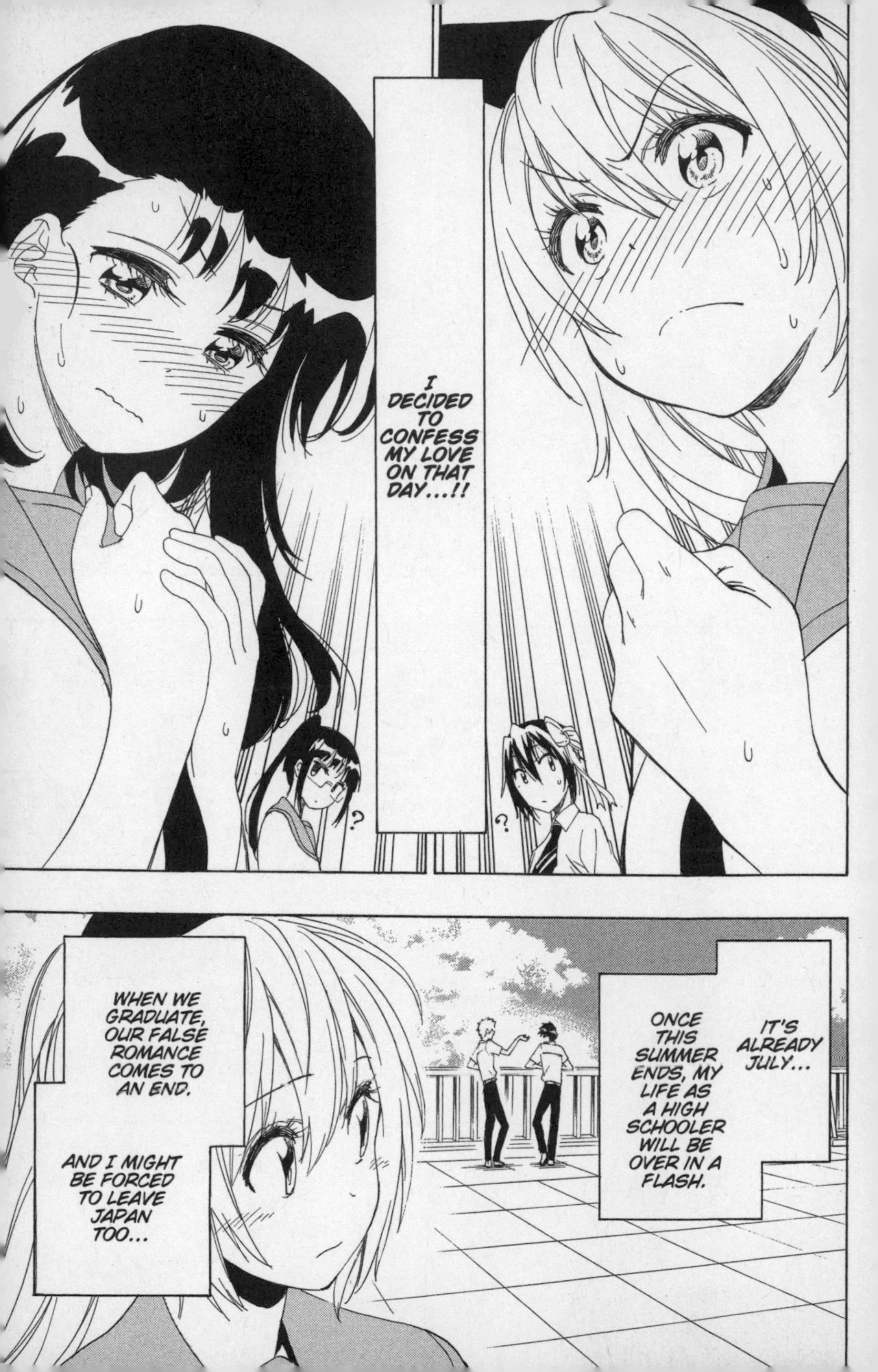
I DECIDED TO CONFESS MY LOVE ON THAT DAY...!!
?
?
IT'S ALREADY JULY...
ONCE THIS SUMMER ENDS, MY LIFE AS A HIGH SCHOOLER WILL BE OVER IN A FLASH.
WHEN WE GRADUATE, OUR FALSE ROMANCE COMES TO AN END.
AND I MIGHT BE FORCED TO LEAVE JAPAN TOO...

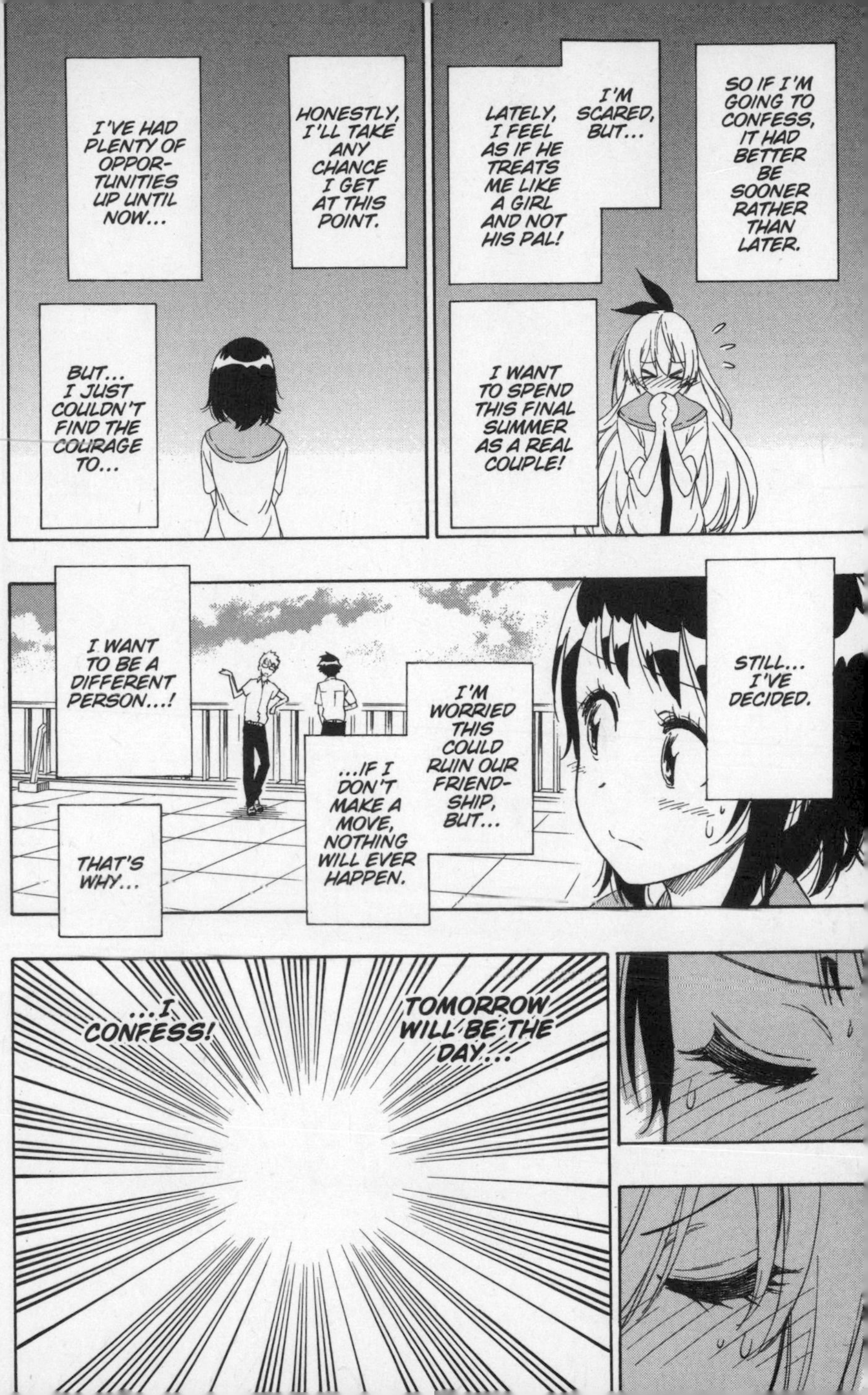
SO IF I'M GOING TO CONFESS, IT HAD BETTER BE SOONER RATHER THAN LATER.
I'M SCARED, BUT...
LATELY, I FEEL AS IF HE TREATS ME LIKE A GIRL AND NOT HIS PAL!
I WANT TO SPEND THIS FINAL SUMMER AS A REAL COUPLE!
HONESTLY, I'LL TAKE ANY CHANCE I GET AT THIS POINT.
I'VE HAD PLENTY OF OPPOR-TUNITIES UP UNTIL NOW...
BUT... I JUST COULDN'T FIND THE COURAGE TO...
STILL... I'VE DECIDED.
I'M WORRIED THIS COULD RUIN OUR FRIEND-SHIP, BUT...
...IF I DON'T MAKE A MOVE, NOTHING WILL EVER HAPPEN.
I WANT TO BE A DIFFERENT PERSON...!
THAT'S WHY...
TOMORROW WILL BE THE DAY...
...I CONFESS!

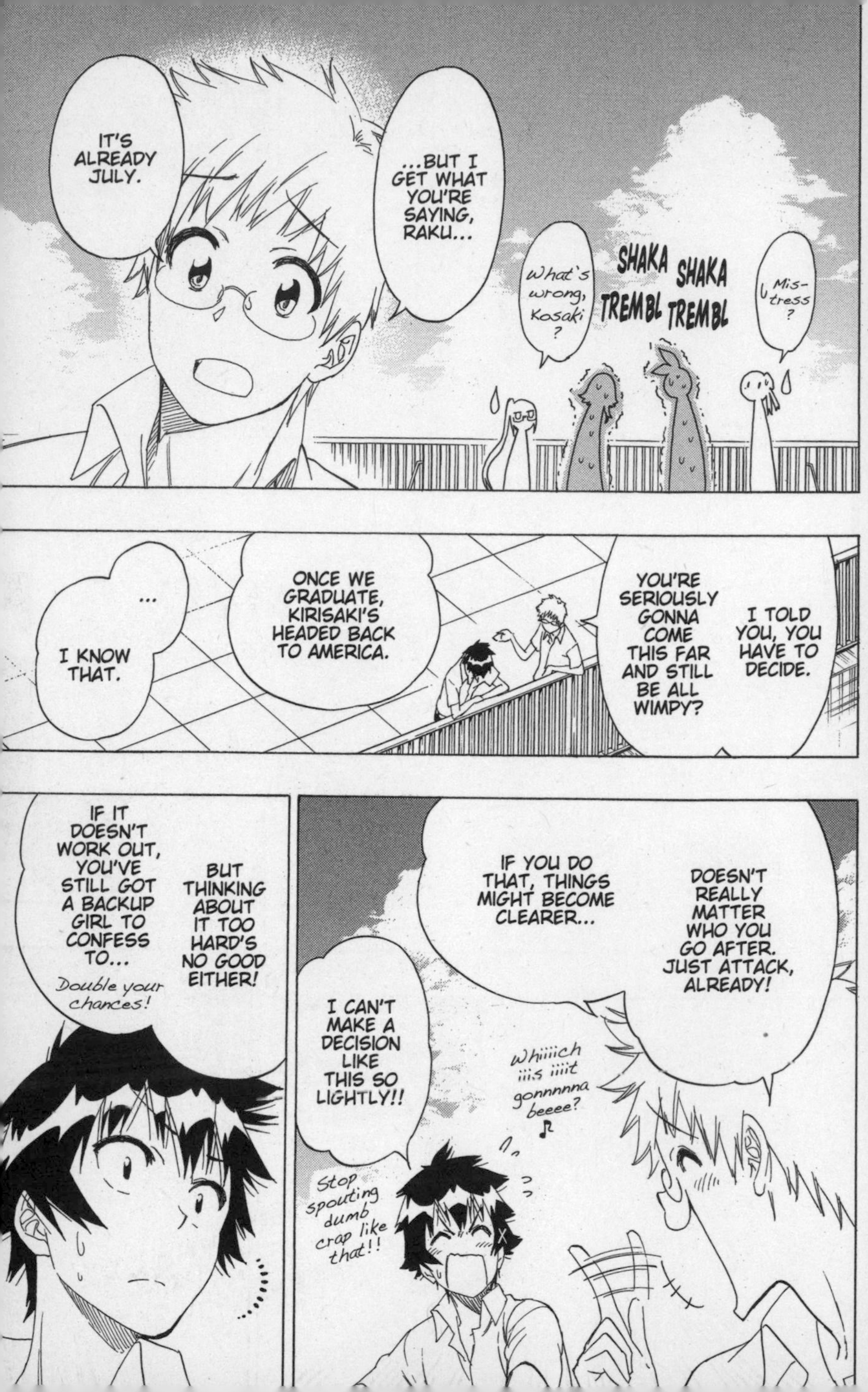
Mis-tress?
SHAKA TREMBL
SHAKA TREMBL
What's wrong, Kosaki?
...BUT I GET WHAT YOU'RE SAYING, RAKU...
IT'S ALREADY JULY.
I TOLD YOU, YOU HAVE TO DECIDE.
YOU'RE SERIOUSLY GONNA COME THIS FAR AND STILL BE ALL WIMPY?
ONCE WE GRADUATE, KIRISAKI'S HEADED BACK TO AMERICA.
... I KNOW THAT.
DOESN'T REALLY MATTER WHO YOU GO AFTER. JUST ATTACK, ALREADY!
IF YOU DO THAT, THINGS MIGHT BECOME CLEARER...
Whiiiich iiiis iiiit gonnnnna beeee? ♪
I CAN'T MAKE A DECISION LIKE THIS SO LIGHTLY!!
Stop spouting dumb crap like that!!
BUT THINKING ABOUT IT TOO HARD'S NO GOOD EITHER!
IF IT DOESN'T WORK OUT, YOU'VE STILL GOT A BACKUP GIRL TO CONFESS TO...
Double your chances!

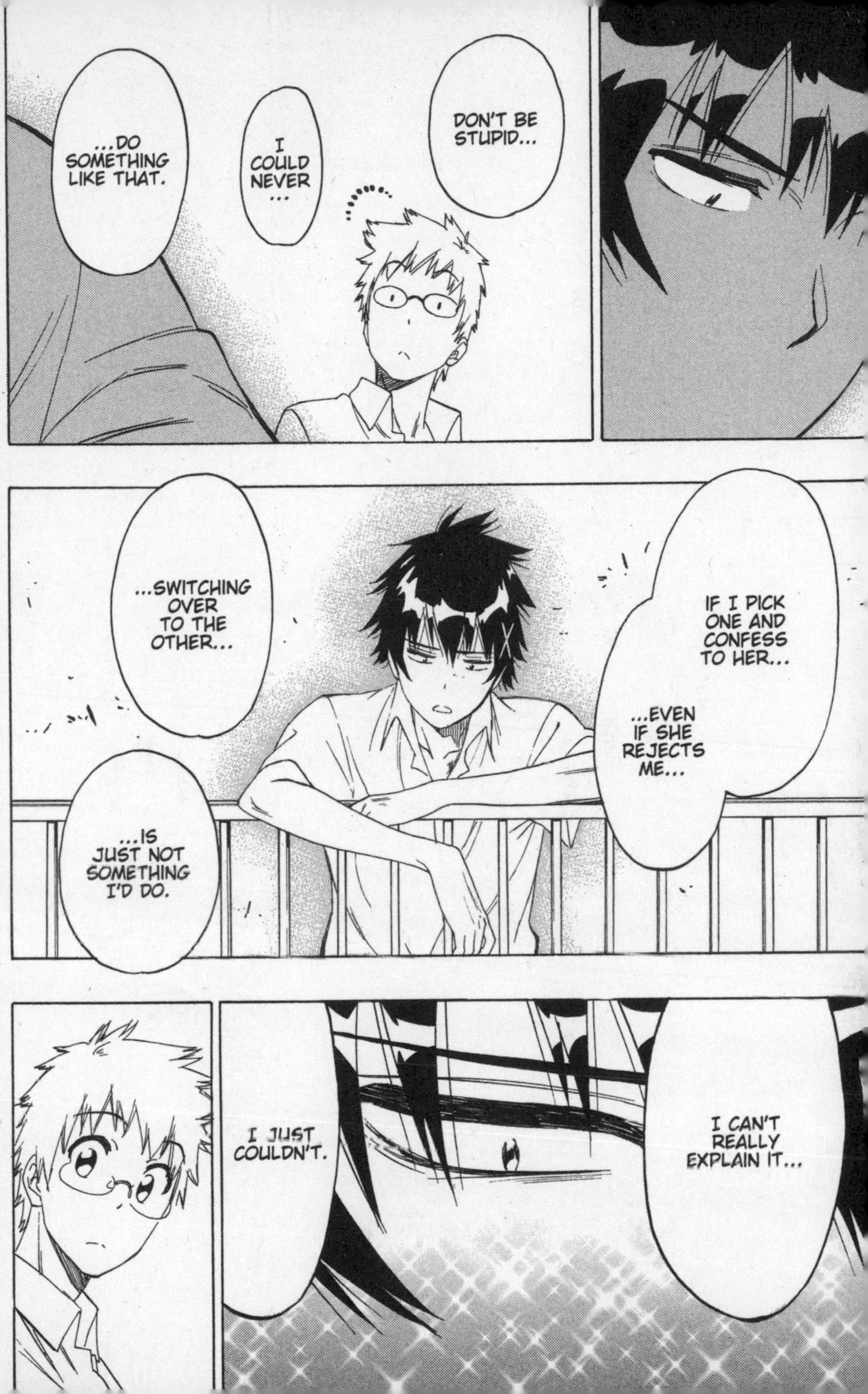
DON'T BE STUPID...
I COULD NEVER ...
...DO SOMETHING LIKE THAT.
IF I PICK ONE AND CONFESS TO HER...
...EVEN IF SHE REJECTS ME...
...SWITCHING OVER TO THE OTHER...
...IS JUST NOT SOMETHING I'D DO.
I CAN'T REALLY EXPLAIN IT...
I JUST COULDN'T.

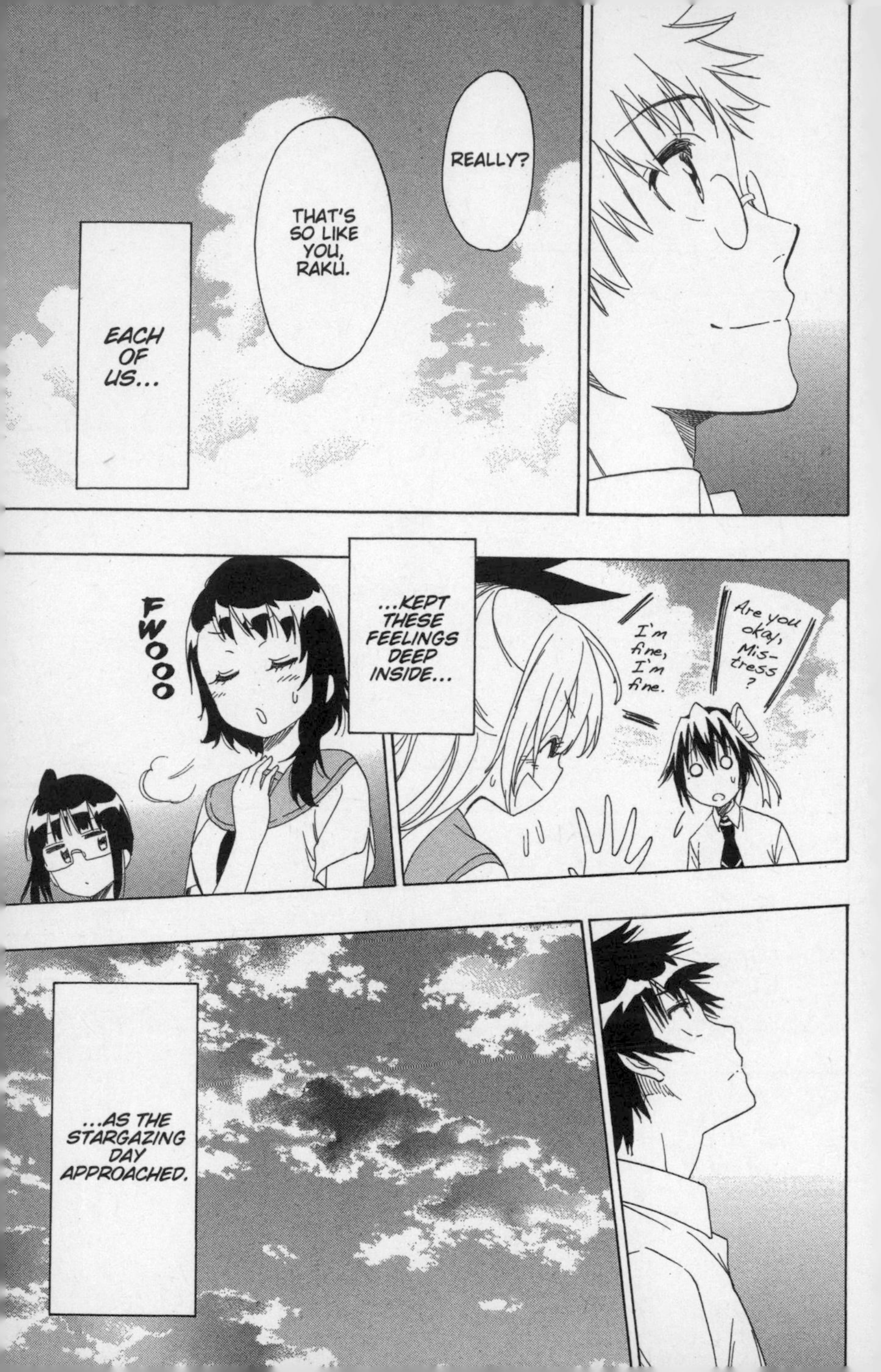
REALLY?
THAT'S SO LIKE YOU, RAKU.
EACH OF US...
Are you okay, Mistress?
I'm fine, I'm fine.
...KEPT THESE FEELINGS DEEP INSIDE...
FWOOO
...AS THE STARGAZING DAY APPROACHED.

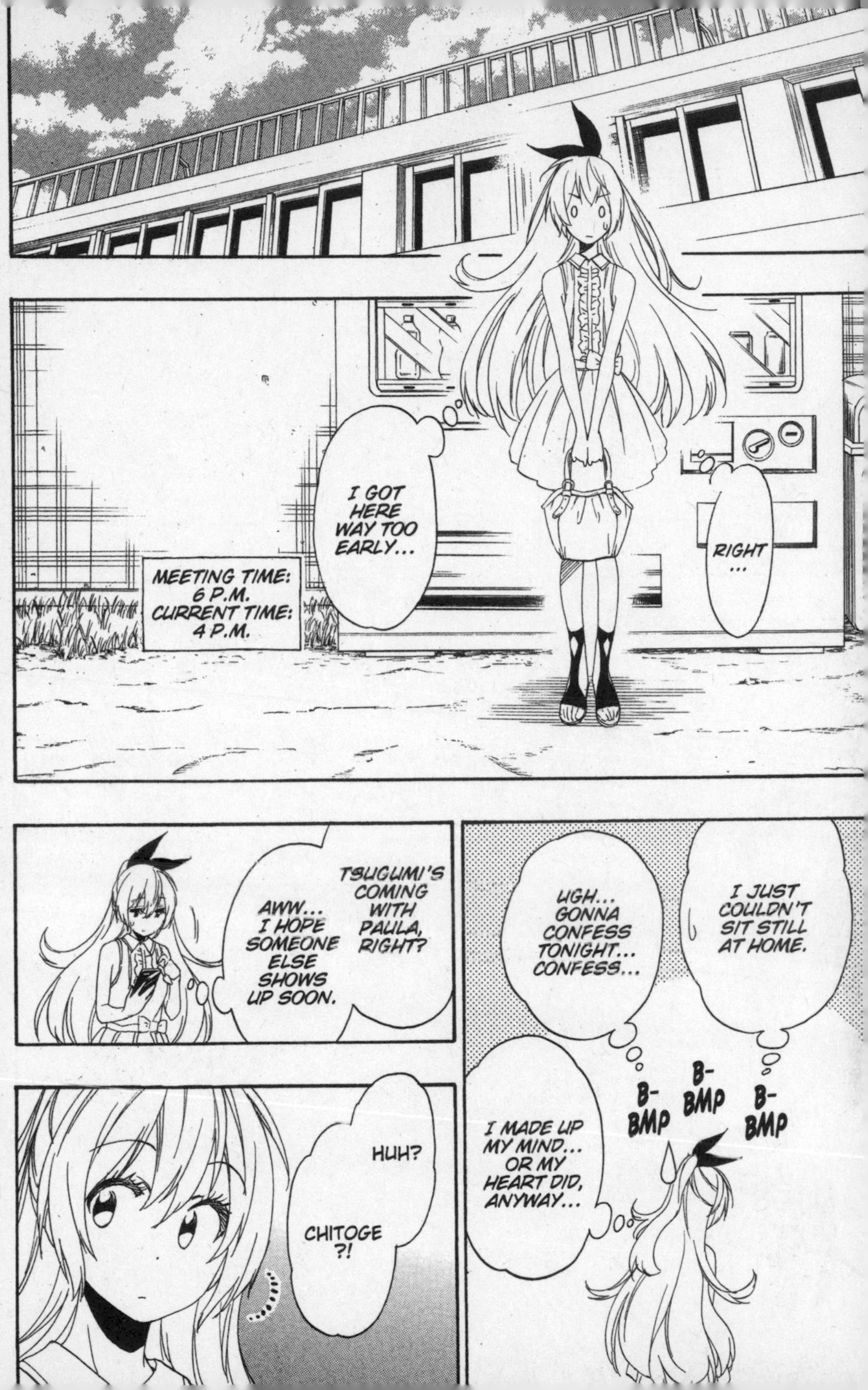
RIGHT...
I GOT HERE WAY TOO EARLY...
MEETING TIME: 6 P.M. CURRENT TIME: 4 P.M.
I JUST COULDN'T SIT STILL AT HOME.
UGH... GONNA CONFESS TONIGHT... CONFESS...
B-BMP
B-BMP
B-BMP
I MADE UP MY MIND... OR MY HEART DID, ANYWAY...
TSUGUMI'S COMING WITH PAULA, RIGHT?
AWW... I HOPE SOMEONE ELSE SHOWS UP SOON.
HUH?
CHITOGE?!

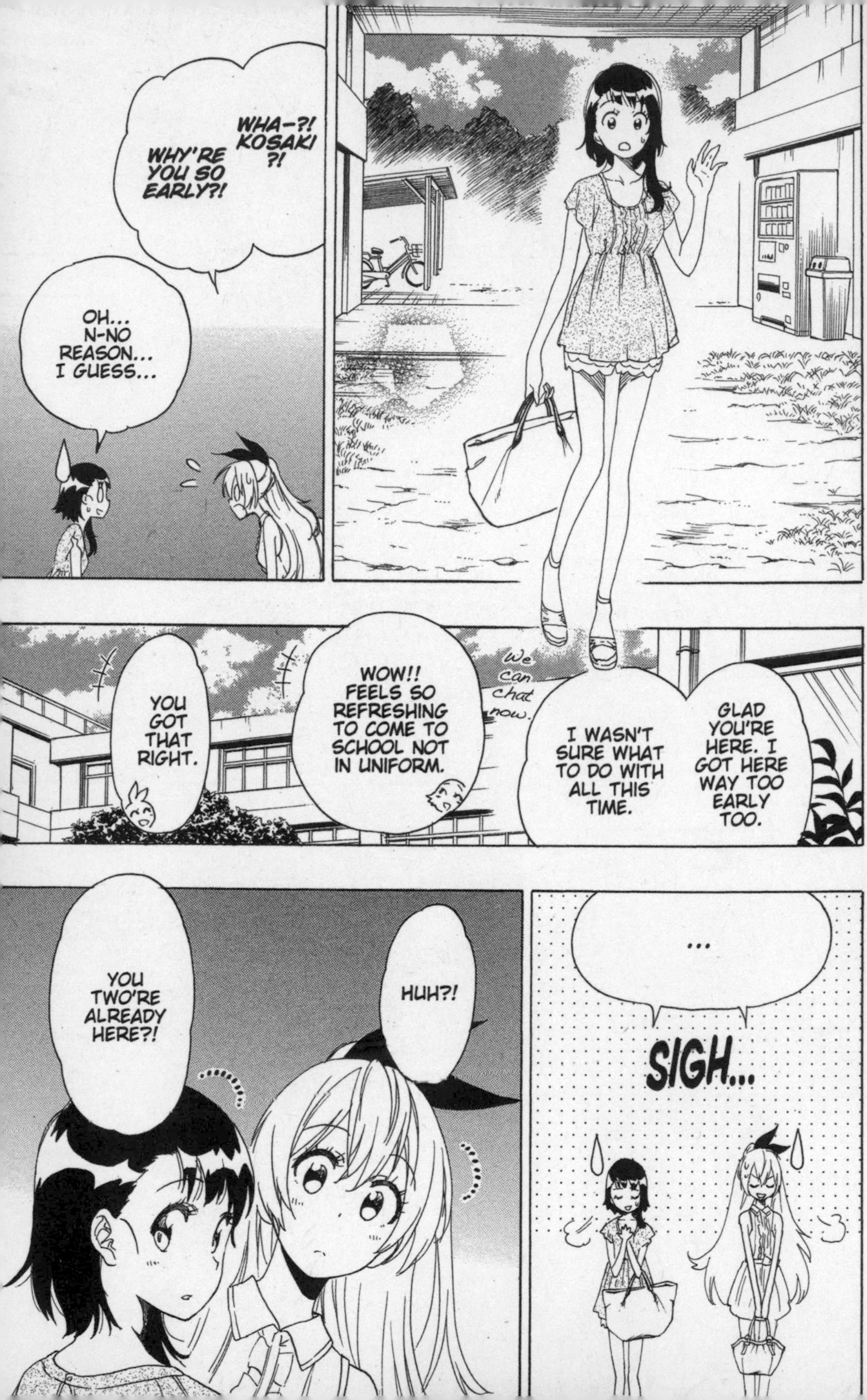
WHA-?! KOSAKI ?!
WHY'RE YOU SO EARLY?!
OH... N-NO REASON... I GUESS...
GLAD YOU'RE HERE. I GOT HERE WAY TOO EARLY TOO.
I WASN'T SURE WHAT TO DO WITH ALL THIS TIME.
We can chat now.
WOW!! FEELS SO REFRESHING TO COME TO SCHOOL NOT IN UNIFORM.
YOU GOT THAT RIGHT.
...
SIGH...
HUH?!
YOU TWO'RE ALREADY HERE?!

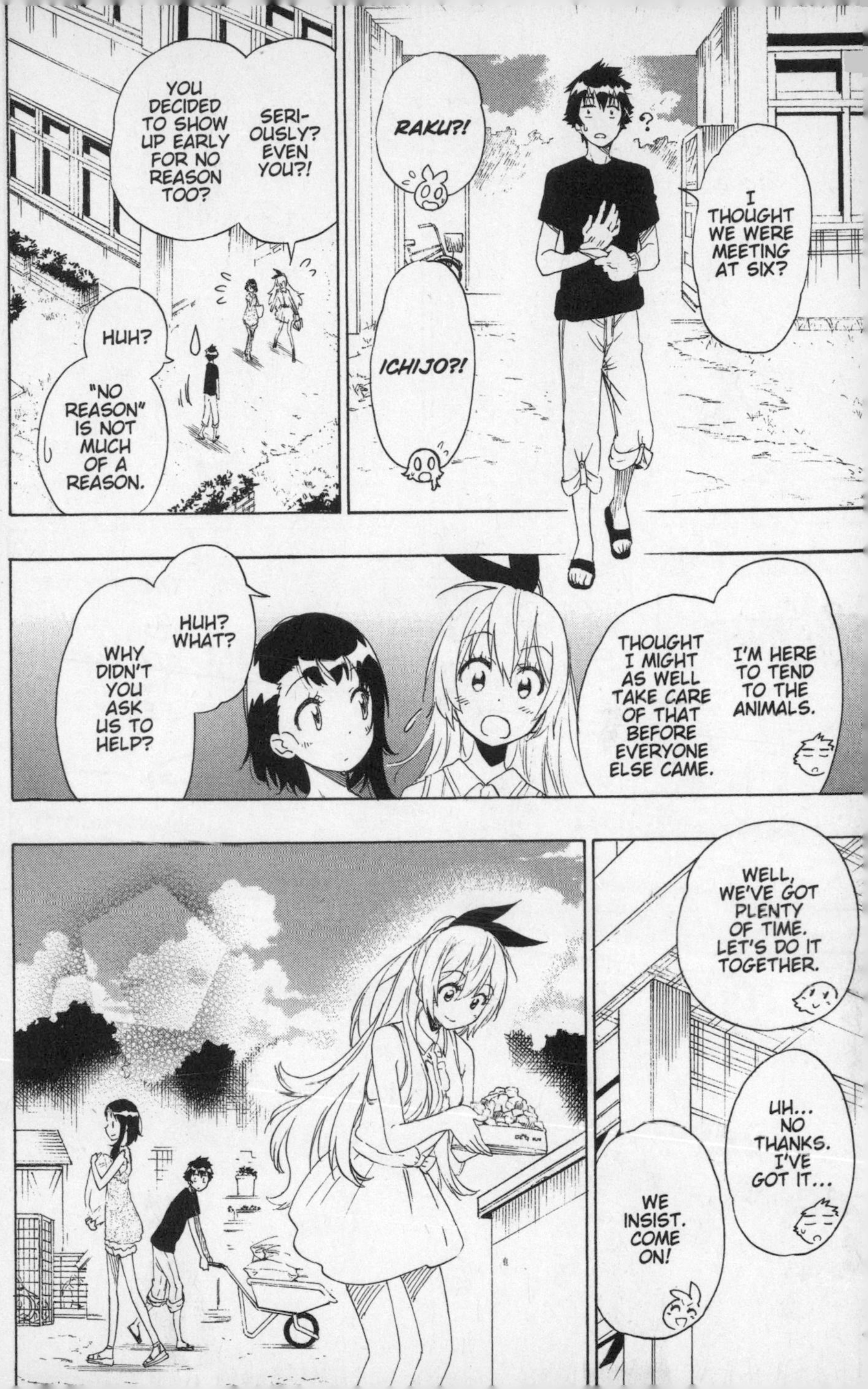
RAKU?!
ICHIJO?!
I THOUGHT WE WERE MEETING AT SIX?
YOU DECIDED TO SHOW UP EARLY FOR NO REASON TOO?
SERI-OUSLY? EVEN YOU?!
HUH?
"NO REASON" IS NOT MUCH OF A REASON.
I'M HERE TO TEND TO THE ANIMALS.
THOUGHT I MIGHT AS WELL TAKE CARE OF THAT BEFORE EVERYONE ELSE CAME.
HUH? WHAT?
WHY DIDN'T YOU ASK US TO HELP?
WELL, WE'VE GOT PLENTY OF TIME. LET'S DO IT TOGETHER.
UH... NO THANKS. I'VE GOT IT...
WE INSIST. COME ON!

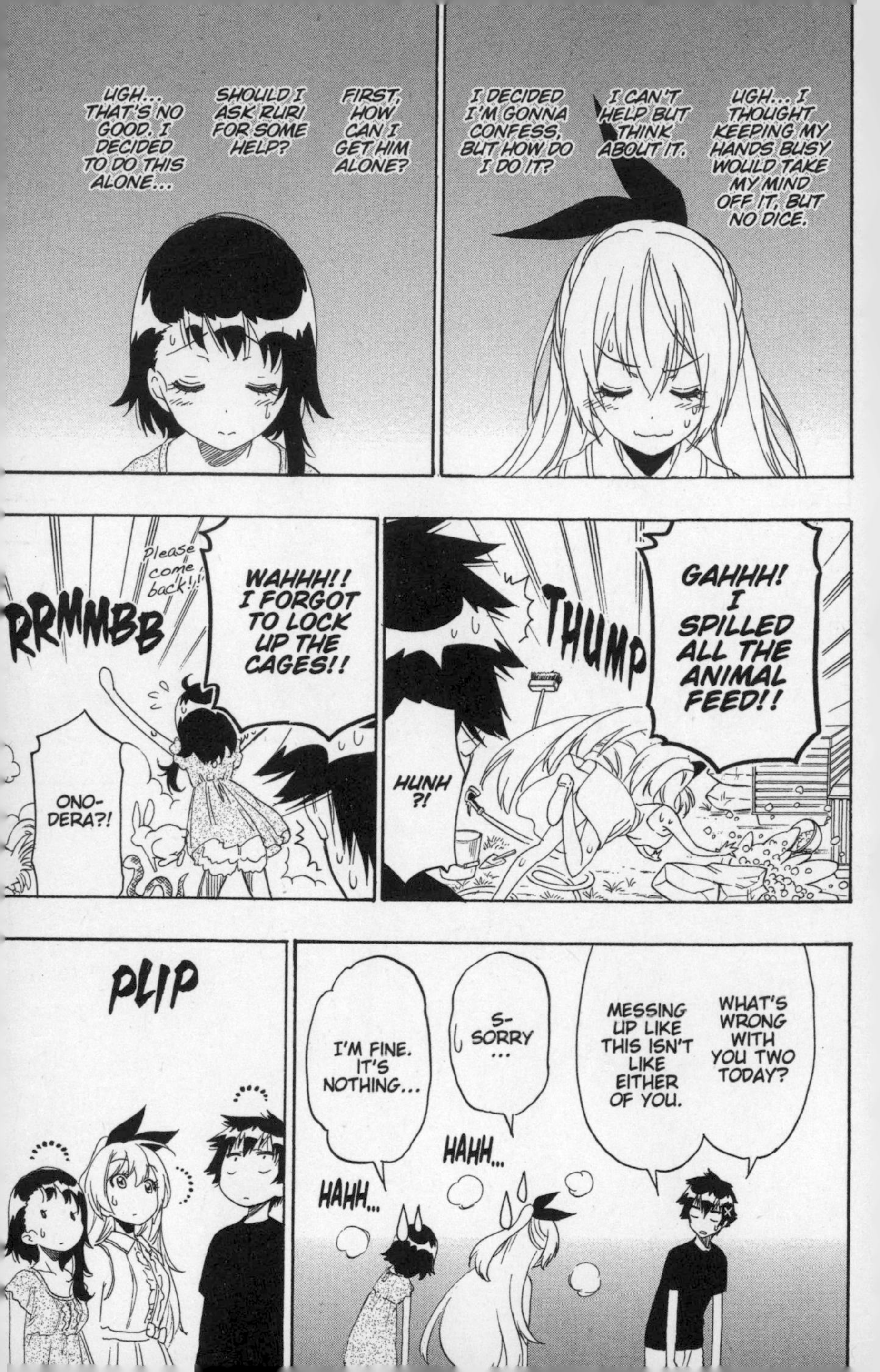
UGH... I THOUGHT KEEPING MY HANDS BUSY WOULD TAKE MY MIND OFF IT, BUT NO DICE.
I CAN'T HELP BUT THINK ABOUT IT.
I DECIDED I'M GONNA CONFESS, BUT HOW DO I DO IT?
FIRST, HOW CAN I GET HIM ALONE?
SHOULD I ASK RURI FOR SOME HELP?
UGH... THAT'S NO GOOD. I DECIDED TO DO THIS ALONE...
GAHHH! I SPILLED ALL THE ANIMAL FEED!!
THUMP
HUNH ?!
WAHHH!! I FORGOT TO LOCK UP THE CAGES!!
Please come back!!!
RRMMBB
ONO-DERA?!
WHAT'S WRONG WITH YOU TWO TODAY?
MESSING UP LIKE THIS ISN'T LIKE EITHER OF YOU.
S-SORRY...
HAHH...
I'M FINE. IT'S NOTHING...
HAHH...
PLIP

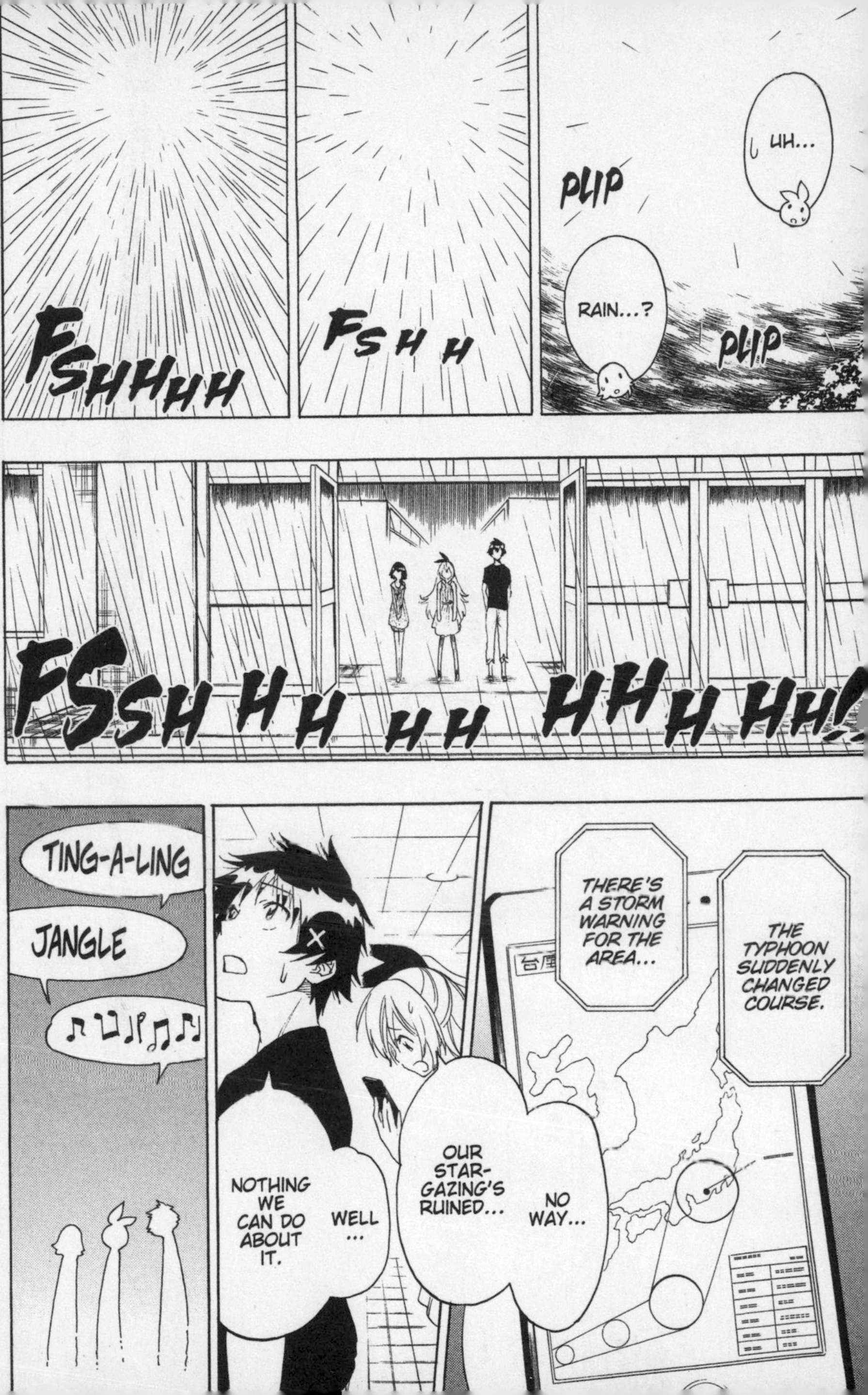
UH...
PLIP
RAIN...?
PLIP
FSHH
FSHHHHH
FSSHHHHHHHHHH!!
THE TYPHOON SUDDENLY CHANGED COURSE.
THERE'S A STORM WARNING FOR THE AREA...
NO WAY...
OUR STAR-GAZING'S RUINED...
WELL...
NOTHING WE CAN DO ABOUT IT.
TING-A-LING
JANGLE

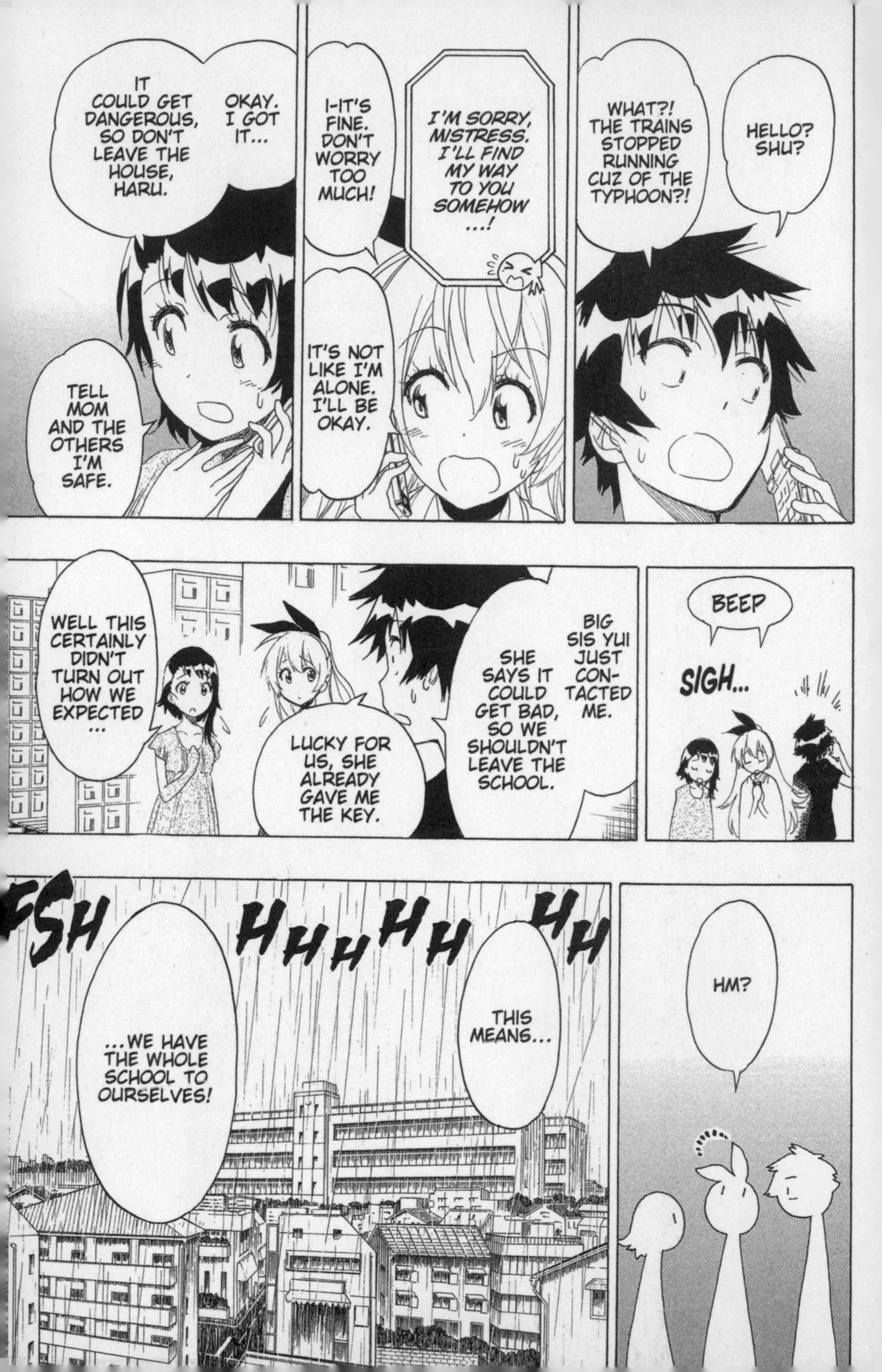
HELLO? SHU?
WHAT?! THE TRAINS STOPPED RUNNING CUZ OF THE TYPHOON?!
I'M SORRY, MISTRESS. I'LL FIND MY WAY TO YOU SOMEHOW ...!
I-IT'S FINE. DON'T WORRY TOO MUCH!
IT'S NOT LIKE I'M ALONE. I'LL BE OKAY.
OKAY. I GOT IT...
IT COULD GET DANGEROUS, SO DON'T LEAVE THE HOUSE, HARU.
TELL MOM AND THE OTHERS I'M SAFE.
BEEP
SIGH...
BIG SIS YUI JUST CONTACTED ME.
SHE SAYS IT COULD GET BAD, SO WE SHOULDN'T LEAVE THE SCHOOL.
LUCKY FOR US, SHE ALREADY GAVE ME THE KEY.
WELL THIS CERTAINLY DIDN'T TURN OUT HOW WE EXPECTED ...
HM?
THIS MEANS...
FSH HHHHHH HH
...WE HAVE THE WHOLE SCHOOL TO OURSELVES!

A sudden change in direc-tion...
I can relate!!!
KABAM

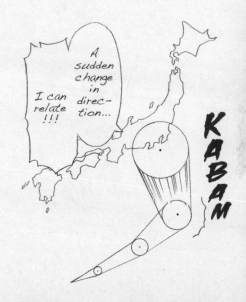

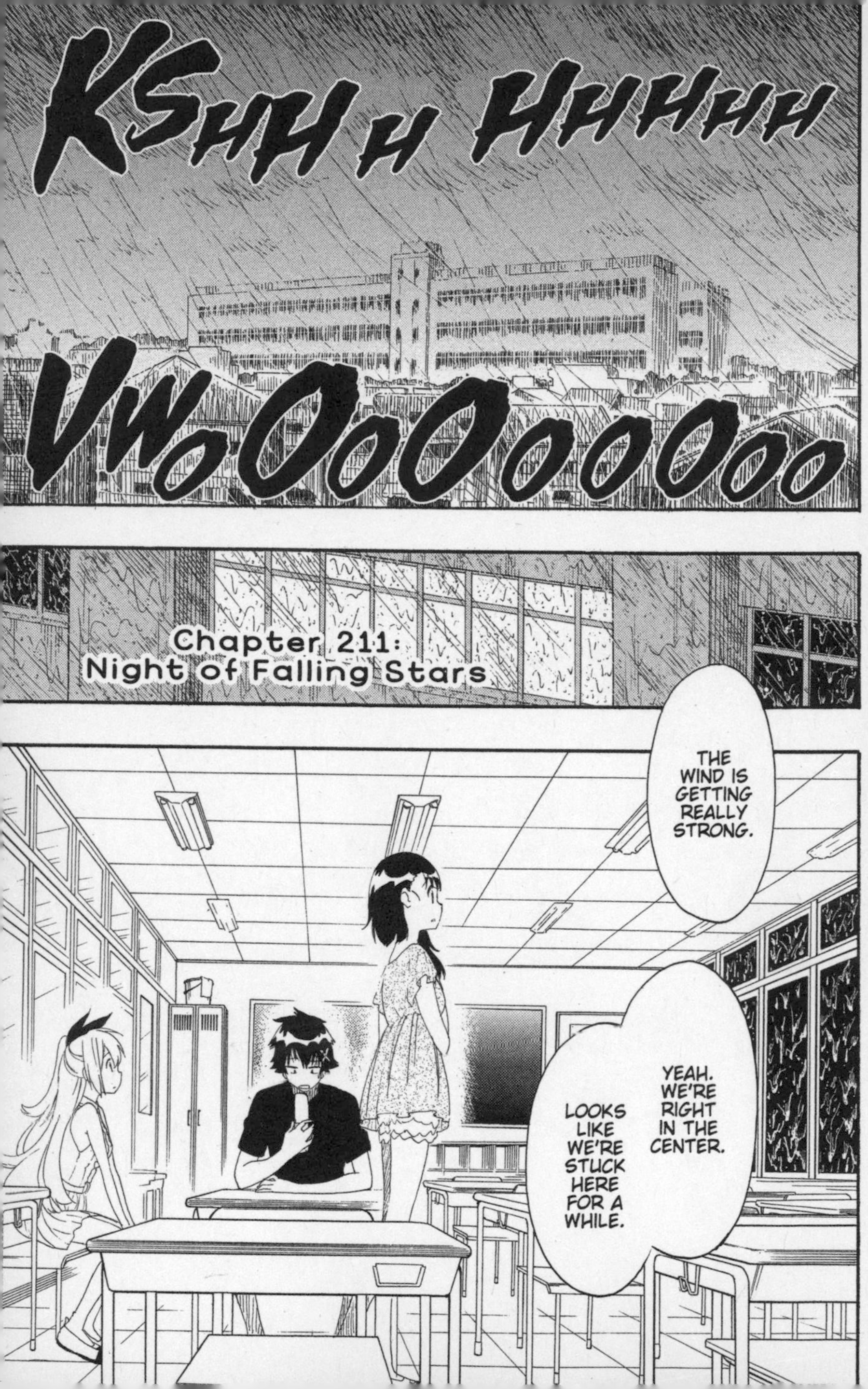
KSHHH HHHHH
VWOOOOOOOOOOO
Chapter 211:
Night of Falling Stars
THE WIND IS GETTING REALLY STRONG.
YEAH. WE'RE RIGHT IN THE CENTER.
LOOKS LIKE WE'RE STUCK HERE FOR A WHILE.

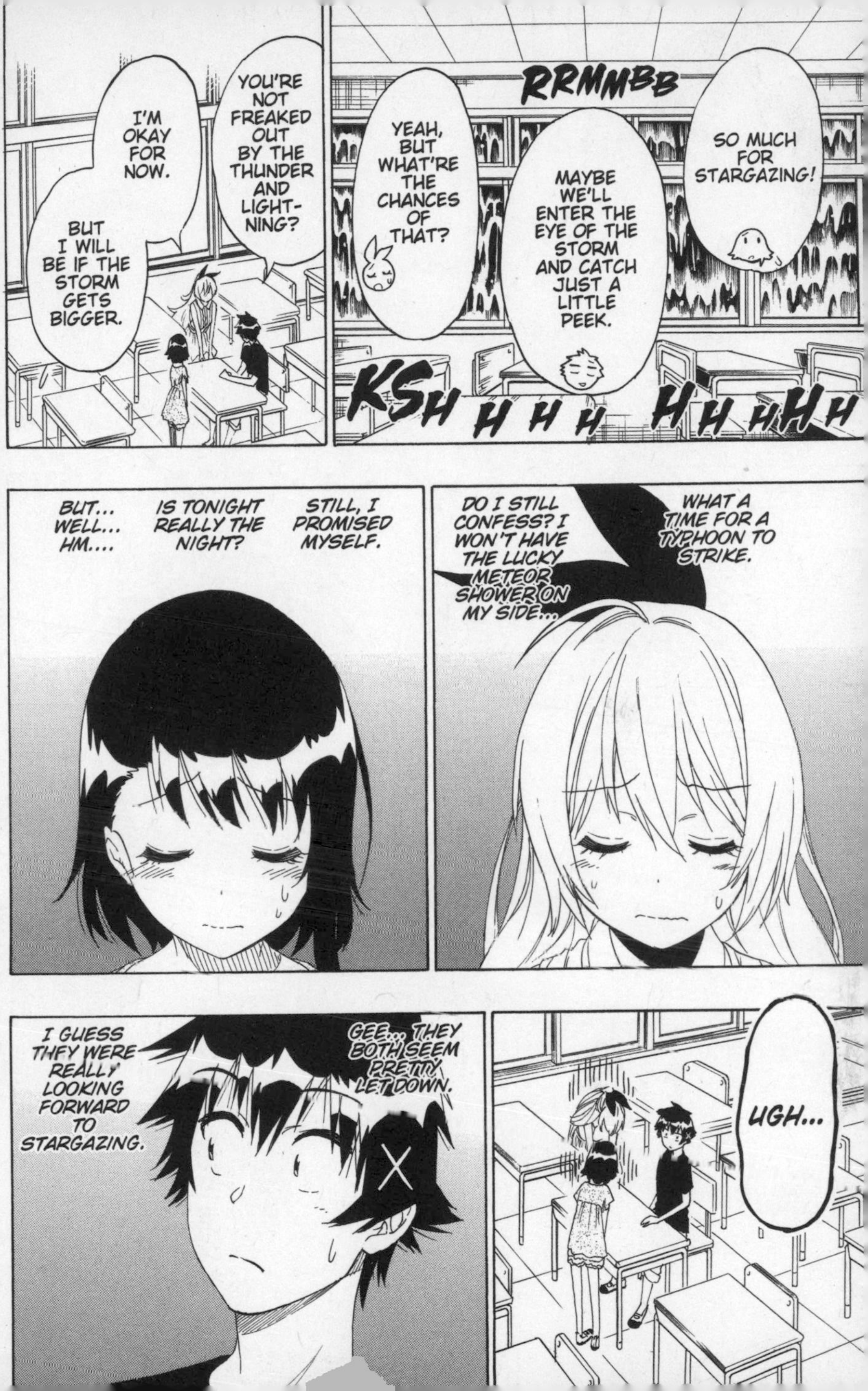
RRMMBB
SO MUCH FOR STARGAZING!
MAYBE WE'LL ENTER THE EYE OF THE STORM AND CATCH JUST A LITTLE PEEK.
YEAH, BUT WHAT'RE THE CHANCES OF THAT?
KSHHHH HHHHH
YOU'RE NOT FREAKED OUT BY THE THUNDER AND LIGHT-NING?
I'M OKAY FOR NOW.
BUT I WILL BE IF THE STORM GETS BIGGER.
WHAT A TIME FOR A TYPHOON TO STRIKE.
DO I STILL CONFESS? I WON'T HAVE THE LUCKY METEOR SHOWER ON MY SIDE...
STILL, I PROMISED MYSELF.
IS TONIGHT REALLY THE NIGHT?
BUT... WELL... HM....
UGH...
GEE... THEY BOTH SEEM PRETTY LET DOWN.
I GUESS THEY WERE REALLY LOOKING FORWARD TO STARGAZING.

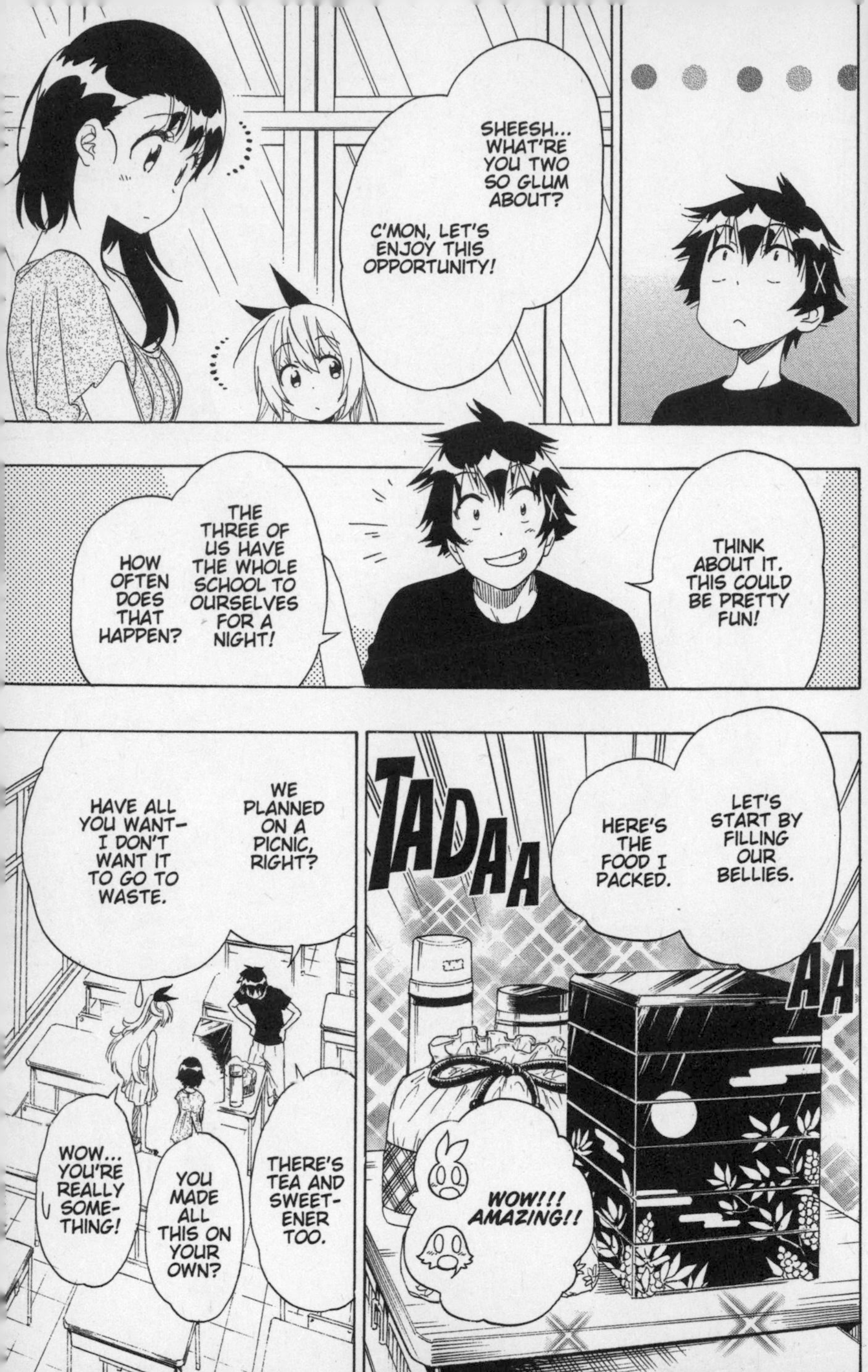
SHEESH... WHAT'RE YOU TWO SO GLUM ABOUT?
C'MON, LET'S ENJOY THIS OPPORTUNITY!
THINK ABOUT IT. THIS COULD BE PRETTY FUN!
THE THREE OF US HAVE THE WHOLE SCHOOL TO OURSELVES FOR A NIGHT!
HOW OFTEN DOES THAT HAPPEN?
LET'S START BY FILLING OUR BELLIES.
HERE'S THE FOOD I PACKED.
TADAAAA
WOW!!! AMAZING!!
WE PLANNED ON A PICNIC, RIGHT?
HAVE ALL YOU WANT— I DON'T WANT IT TO GO TO WASTE.
THERE'S TEA AND SWEET-ENER TOO.
YOU MADE ALL THIS ON YOUR OWN?
WOW... YOU'RE REALLY SOME-THING!

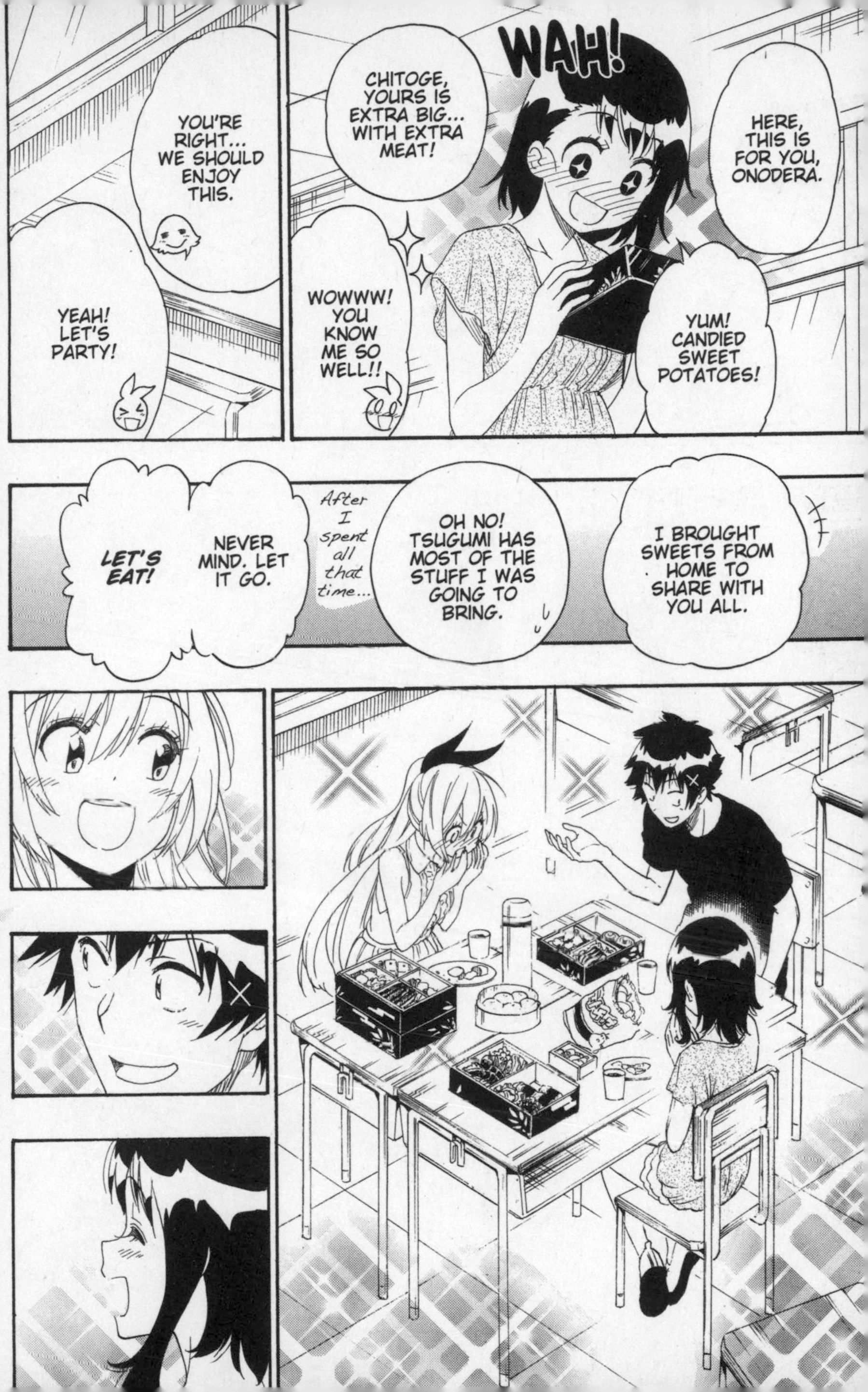
HERE, THIS IS FOR YOU, ONODERA.
WAH!
CHITOGE, YOURS IS EXTRA BIG... WITH EXTRA MEAT!
YUM! CANDIED SWEET POTATOES!
WOWWW! YOU KNOW ME SO WELL!!
YOU'RE RIGHT... WE SHOULD ENJOY THIS.
YEAH! LET'S PARTY!
I BROUGHT SWEETS FROM HOME TO SHARE WITH YOU ALL.
OH NO! TSUGUMI HAS MOST OF THE STUFF I WAS GOING TO BRING.
After I spent all that time...
NEVER MIND. LET IT GO.
LET'S EAT!

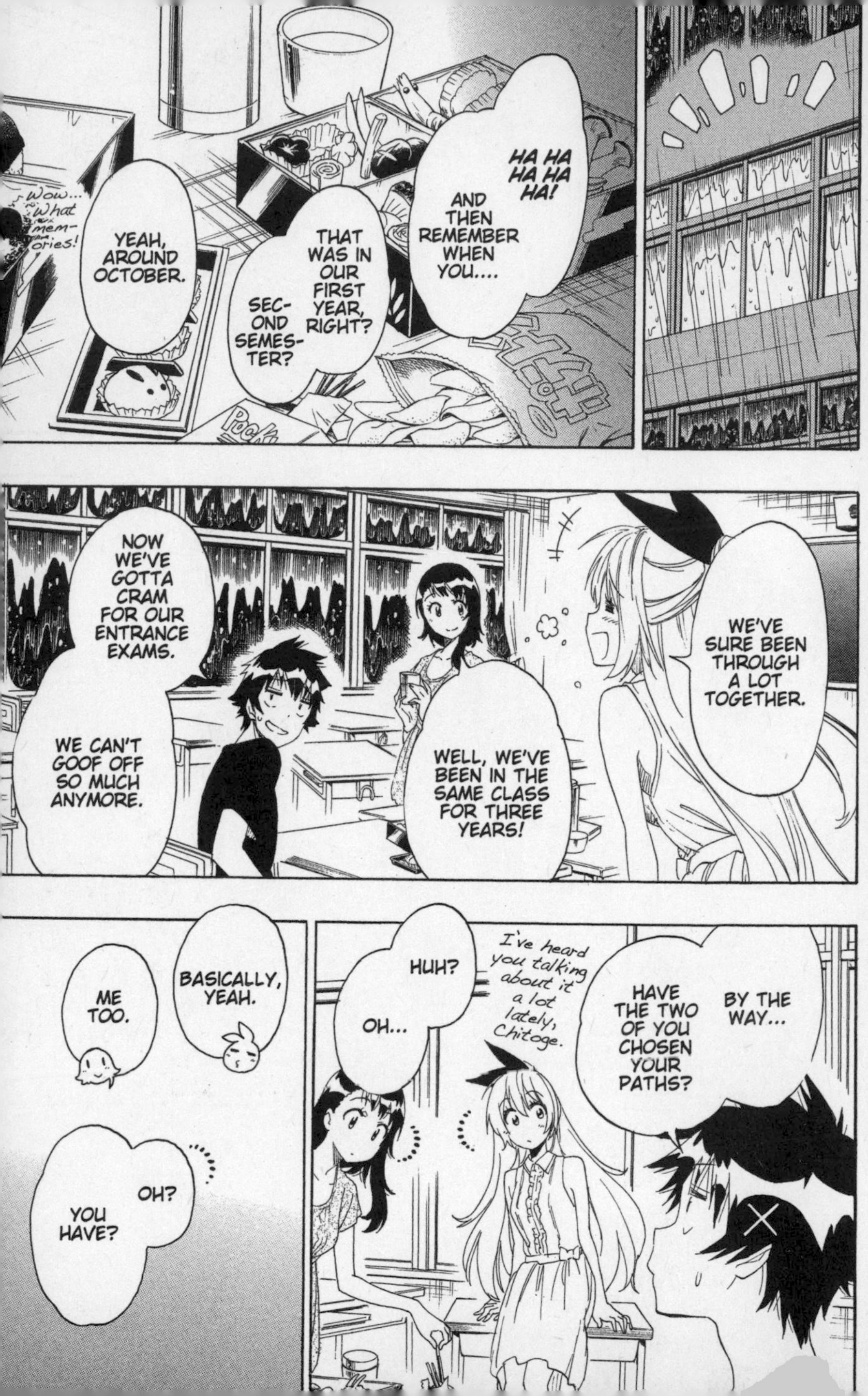
HA HA HA HA HA!
AND THEN REMEMBER WHEN YOU....
THAT WAS IN OUR FIRST YEAR, RIGHT?
SEC-OND SEMES-TER?
YEAH, AROUND OCTOBER.
Wow... What mem-ories!
WE'VE SURE BEEN THROUGH A LOT TOGETHER.
WELL, WE'VE BEEN IN THE SAME CLASS FOR THREE YEARS!
NOW WE'VE GOTTA CRAM FOR OUR ENTRANCE EXAMS.
WE CAN'T GOOF OFF SO MUCH ANYMORE.
BY THE WAY...
HAVE THE TWO OF YOU CHOSEN YOUR PATHS?
I've heard you talking about it a lot lately, Chitoge.
HUH?
OH...
BASICALLY, YEAH.
ME TOO.
OH?
YOU HAVE?

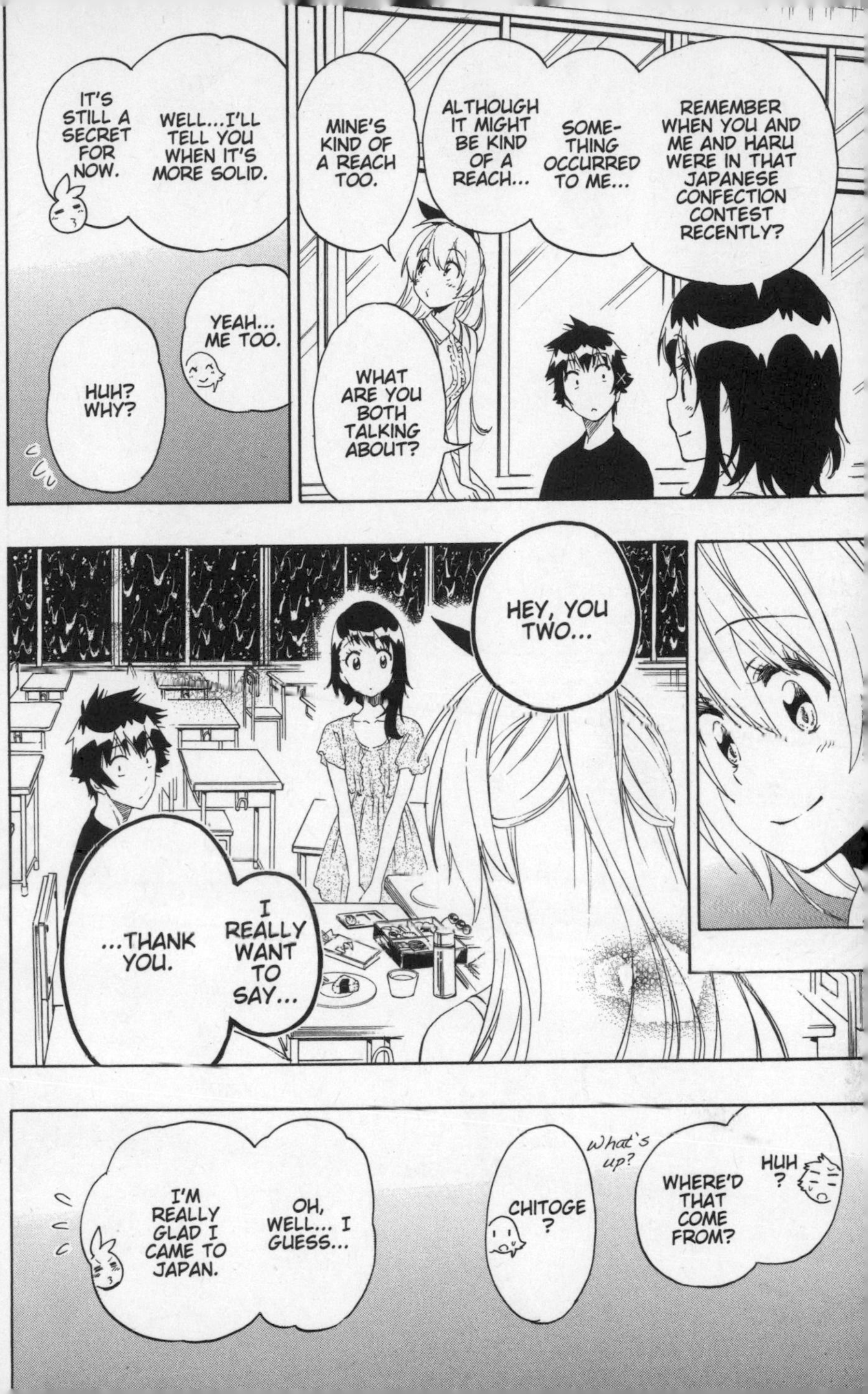
REMEMBER WHEN YOU AND ME AND HARU WERE IN THAT JAPANESE CONFECTION CONTEST RECENTLY?
SOME-THING OCCURRED TO ME...
ALTHOUGH IT MIGHT BE KIND OF A REACH...
MINE'S KIND OF A REACH TOO.
WHAT ARE YOU BOTH TALKING ABOUT?
WELL...I'LL TELL YOU WHEN IT'S MORE SOLID.
IT'S STILL A SECRET FOR NOW.
YEAH... ME TOO.
HUH? WHY?
HEY, YOU TWO...
I REALLY WANT TO SAY...
...THANK YOU.
HUH?
WHERE'D THAT COME FROM?
What's up?
CHITOGE?
OH, WELL... I GUESS...
I'M REALLY GLAD I CAME TO JAPAN.

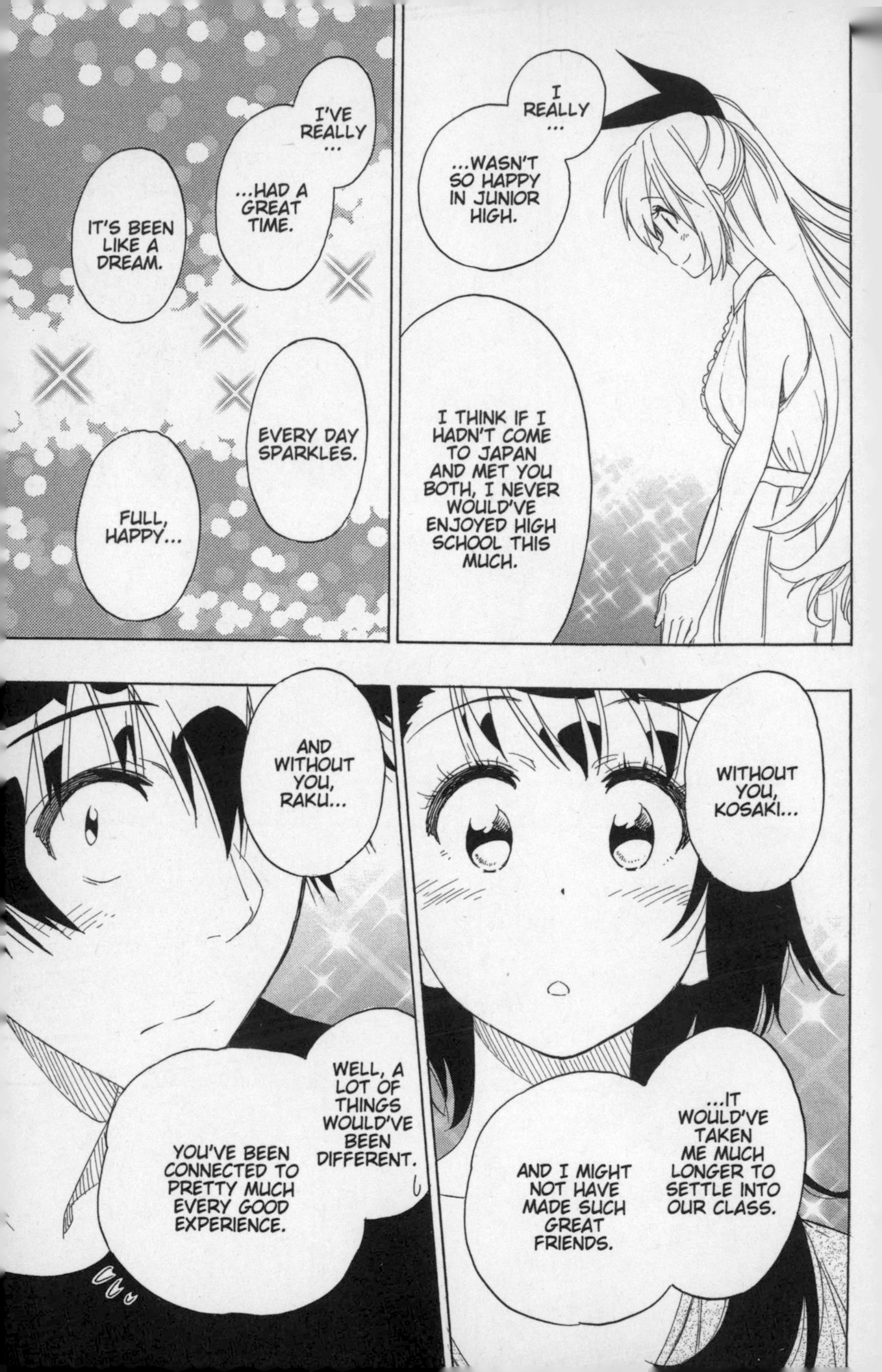
I REALLY...
...WASN'T SO HAPPY IN JUNIOR HIGH.
I THINK IF I HADN'T COME TO JAPAN AND MET YOU BOTH, I NEVER WOULD'VE ENJOYED HIGH SCHOOL THIS MUCH.
I'VE REALLY...
...HAD A GREAT TIME.
IT'S BEEN LIKE A DREAM.
EVERY DAY SPARKLES.
FULL, HAPPY...
WITHOUT YOU, KOSAKI...
...IT WOULD'VE TAKEN ME MUCH LONGER TO SETTLE INTO OUR CLASS.
AND I MIGHT NOT HAVE MADE SUCH GREAT FRIENDS.
AND WITHOUT YOU, RAKU...
WELL, A LOT OF THINGS WOULD'VE BEEN DIFFERENT.
YOU'VE BEEN CONNECTED TO PRETTY MUCH EVERY GOOD EXPERIENCE.

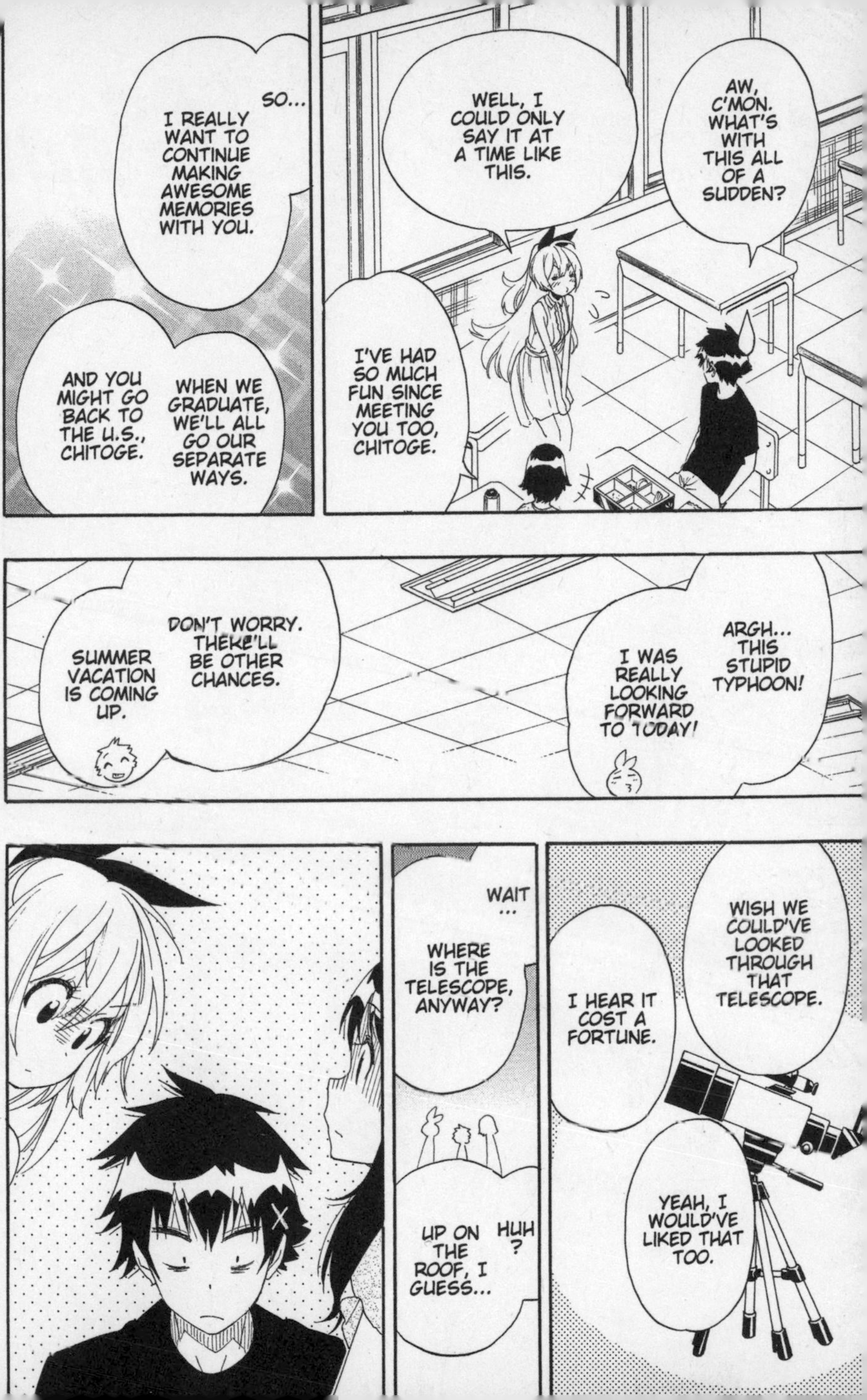
AW, C'MON. WHAT'S WITH THIS ALL OF A SUDDEN?
WELL, I COULD ONLY SAY IT AT A TIME LIKE THIS.
I'VE HAD SO MUCH FUN SINCE MEETING YOU TOO, CHITOGE.
SO... I REALLY WANT TO CONTINUE MAKING AWESOME MEMORIES WITH YOU.
WHEN WE GRADUATE, WE'LL ALL GO OUR SEPARATE WAYS.
AND YOU MIGHT GO BACK TO THE U.S., CHITOGE.
ARGH... THIS STUPID TYPHOON!
I WAS REALLY LOOKING FORWARD TO TODAY!
DON'T WORRY. THERE'LL BE OTHER CHANCES.
SUMMER VACATION IS COMING UP.
WISH WE COULD'VE LOOKED THROUGH THAT TELESCOPE.
I HEAR IT COST A FORTUNE.
YEAH, I WOULD'VE LIKED THAT TOO.
WAIT...
WHERE IS THE TELESCOPE, ANYWAY?
HUH?
UP ON THE ROOF, I GUESS...

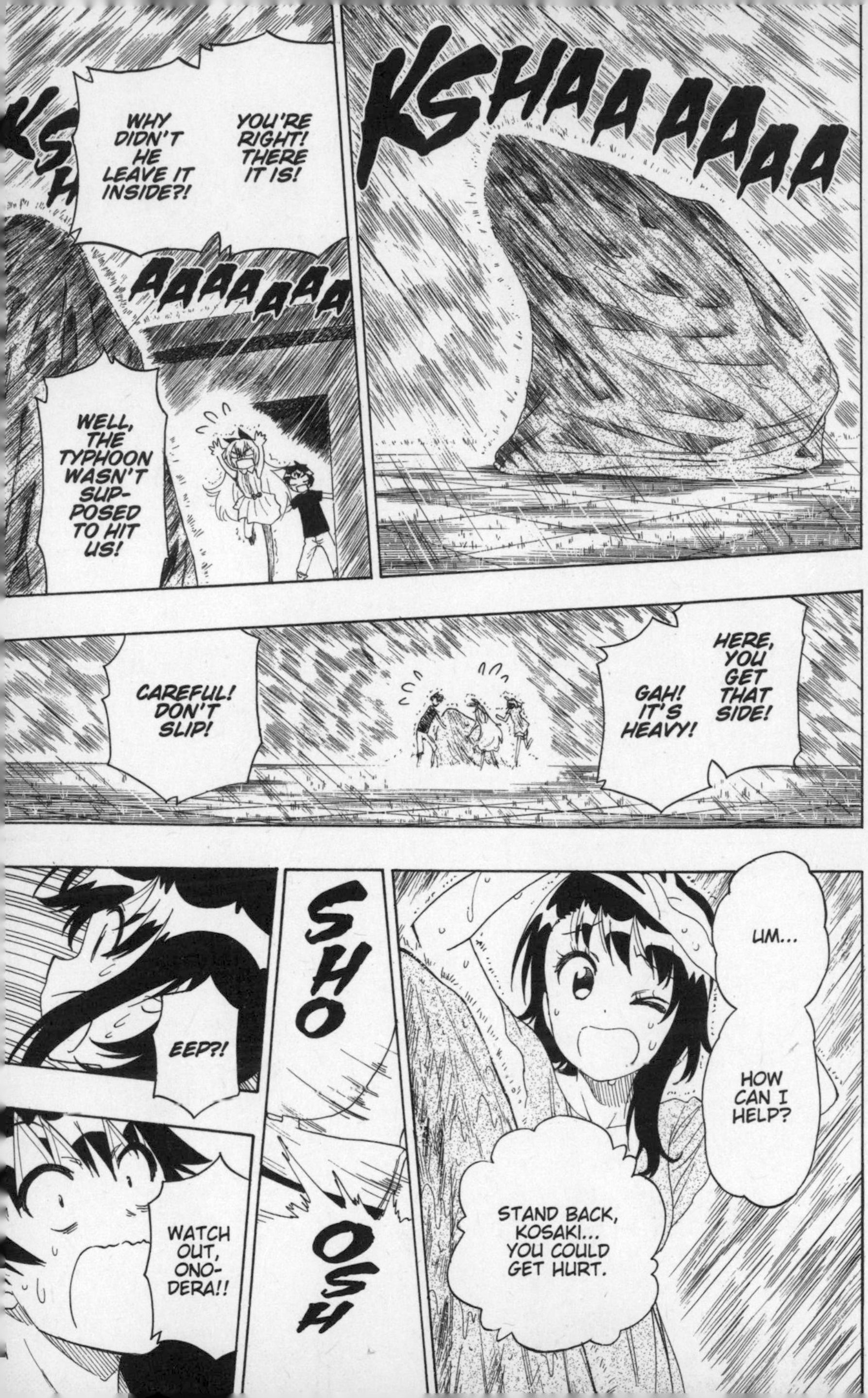
KSHAAAAAAA
YOU'RE RIGHT! THERE IT IS!
WHY DIDN'T HE LEAVE IT INSIDE?!
AAAAAAA
WELL, THE TYPHOON WASN'T SUP-POSED TO HIT US!
HERE, YOU GET THAT SIDE!
GAH! IT'S HEAVY!
CAREFUL! DON'T SLIP!
UM...
HOW CAN I HELP?
STAND BACK, KOSAKI... YOU COULD GET HURT.
SHO
OSH
EEP?!
WATCH OUT, ONO-DERA!!

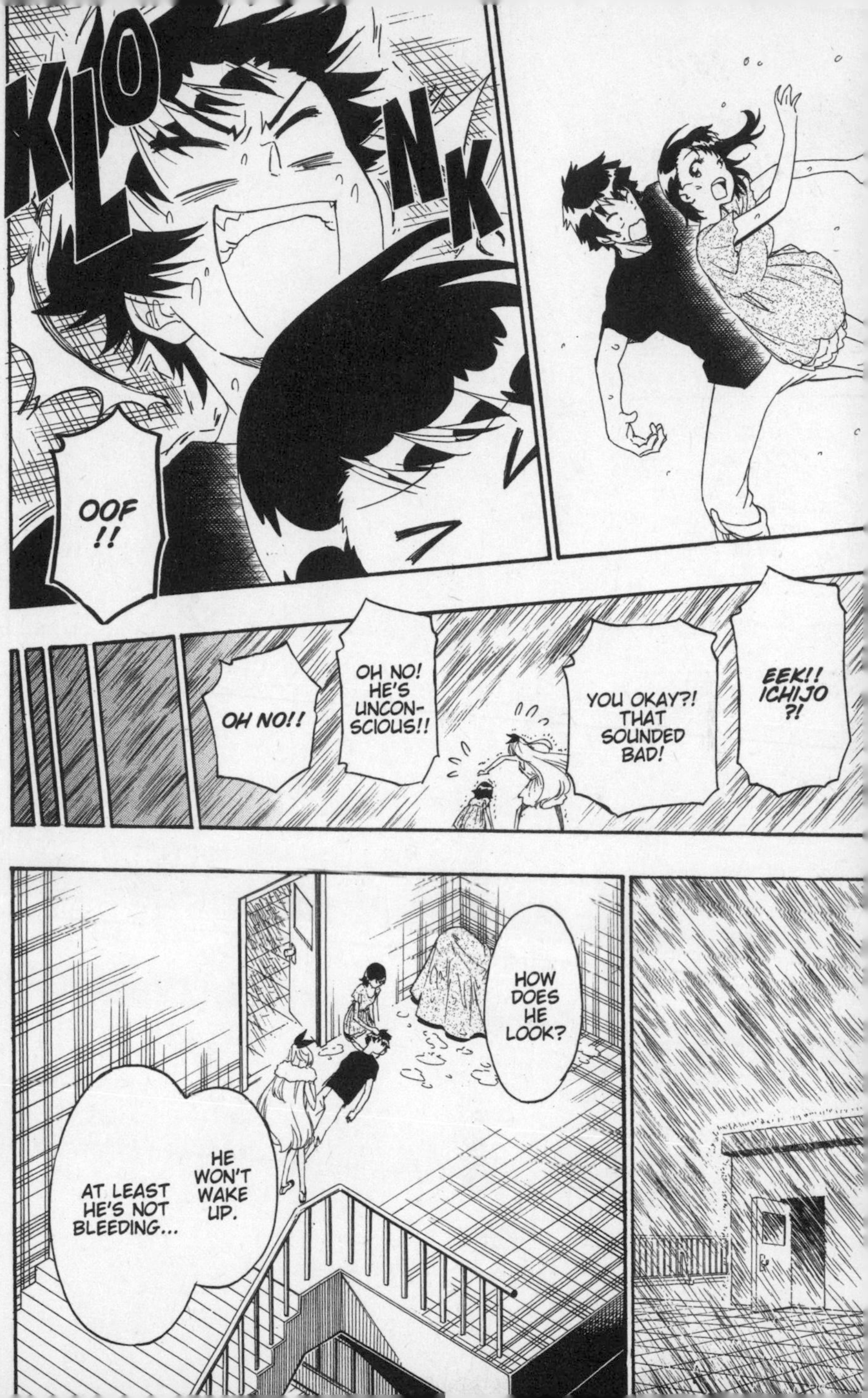
KLONK
OOF!!
EEK!! ICHIJO?!
YOU OKAY?! THAT SOUNDED BAD!
OH NO! HE'S UNCON-SCIOUS!!
OH NO!!
HOW DOES HE LOOK?
HE WON'T WAKE UP.
AT LEAST HE'S NOT BLEEDING...

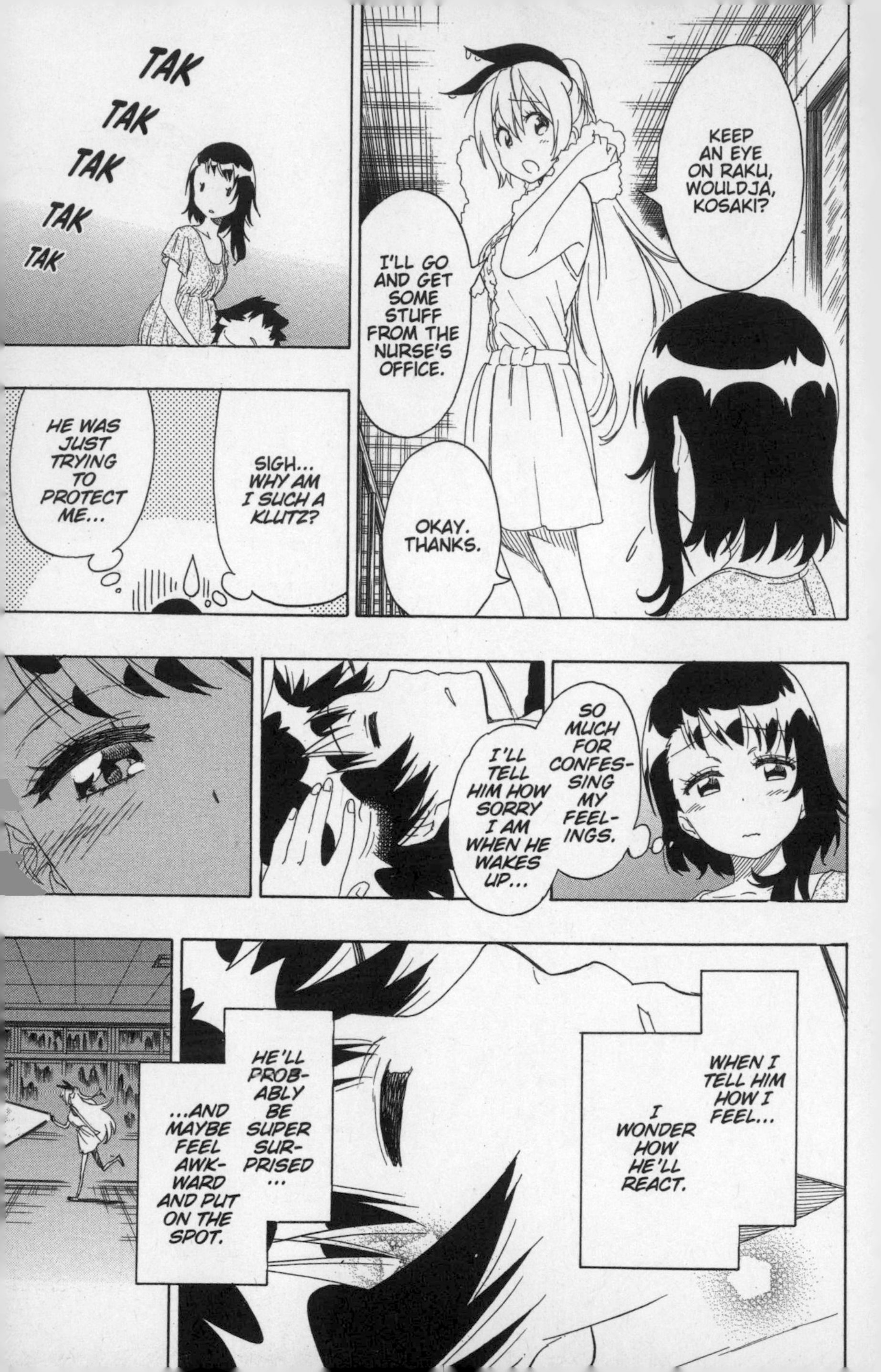
KEEP AN EYE ON RAKU, WOULDJA, KOSAKI?
I'LL GO AND GET SOME STUFF FROM THE NURSE'S OFFICE.
OKAY. THANKS.
TAK TAK TAK TAK TAK
SIGH... WHY AM I SUCH A KLUTZ?
HE WAS JUST TRYING TO PROTECT ME...
SO MUCH FOR CONFESSING MY FEELINGS.
I'LL TELL HIM HOW SORRY I AM WHEN HE WAKES UP...
WHEN I TELL HIM HOW I FEEL...
I WONDER HOW HE'LL REACT.
HE'LL PROBABLY BE SUPER SURPRISED...
...AND MAYBE FEEL AWKWARD AND PUT ON THE SPOT.

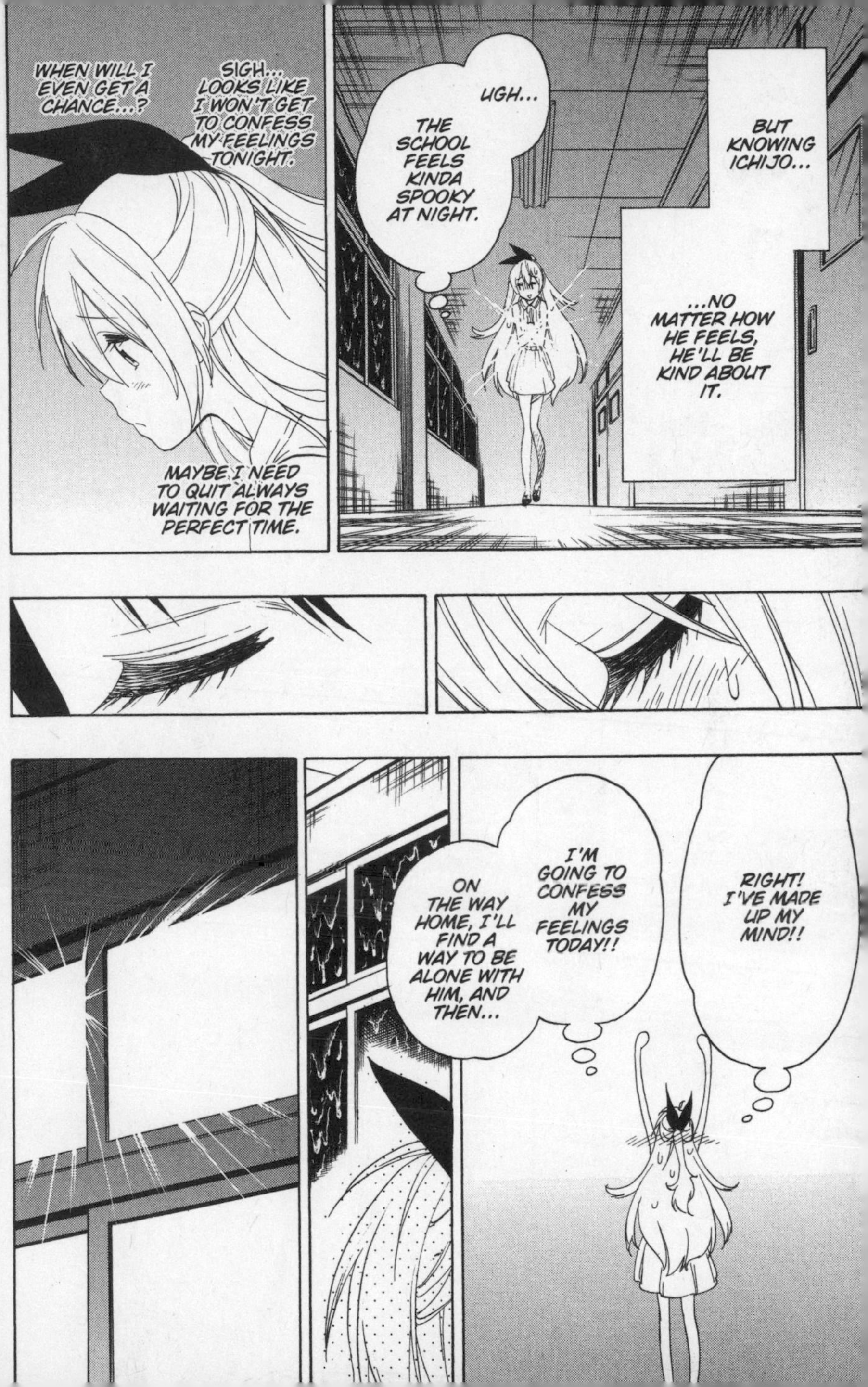
BUT KNOWING ICHIJO...
...NO MATTER HOW HE FEELS, HE'LL BE KIND ABOUT IT.
UGH... THE SCHOOL FEELS KINDA SPOOKY AT NIGHT.
SIGH... LOOKS LIKE I WON'T GET TO CONFESS MY FEELINGS TONIGHT.
WHEN WILL I EVEN GET A CHANCE...?
MAYBE I NEED TO QUIT ALWAYS WAITING FOR THE PERFECT TIME.
RIGHT! I'VE MADE UP MY MIND!!
I'M GOING TO CONFESS MY FEELINGS TODAY!!
ON THE WAY HOME, I'LL FIND A WAY TO BE ALONE WITH HIM, AND THEN...

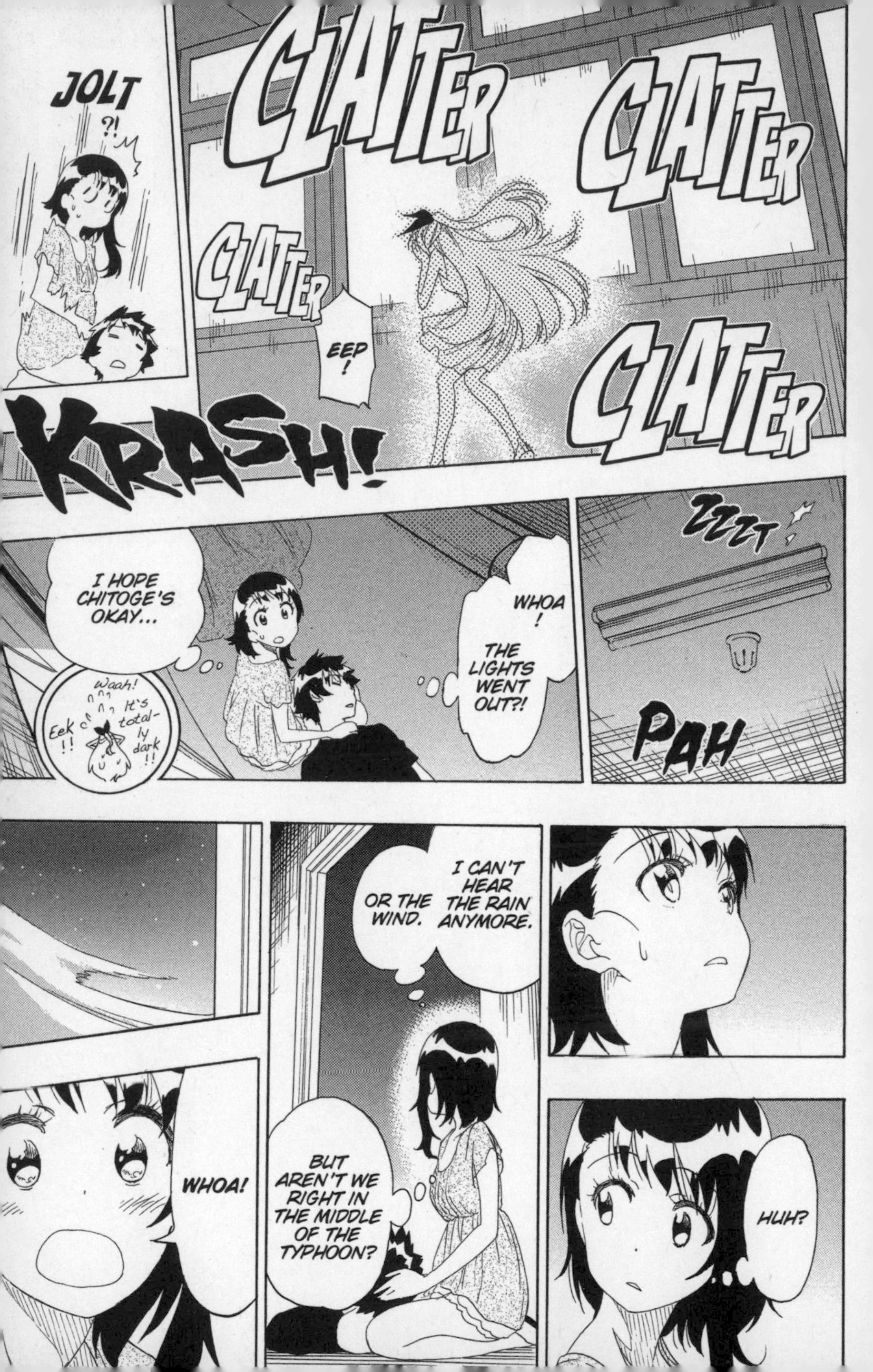
CLATTER
CLATTER
CLATTER
CLATTER
EEP!
JOLT
?!
KRASH!
ZZZT
PAH
WHOA! THE LIGHTS WENT OUT?!
I HOPE CHITOGE'S OKAY...
Waah! It's totally dark!!
Eek!!
HUH?
I CAN'T HEAR THE RAIN ANYMORE.
OR THE WIND.
BUT AREN'T WE RIGHT IN THE MIDDLE OF THE TYPHOON?
WHOA!

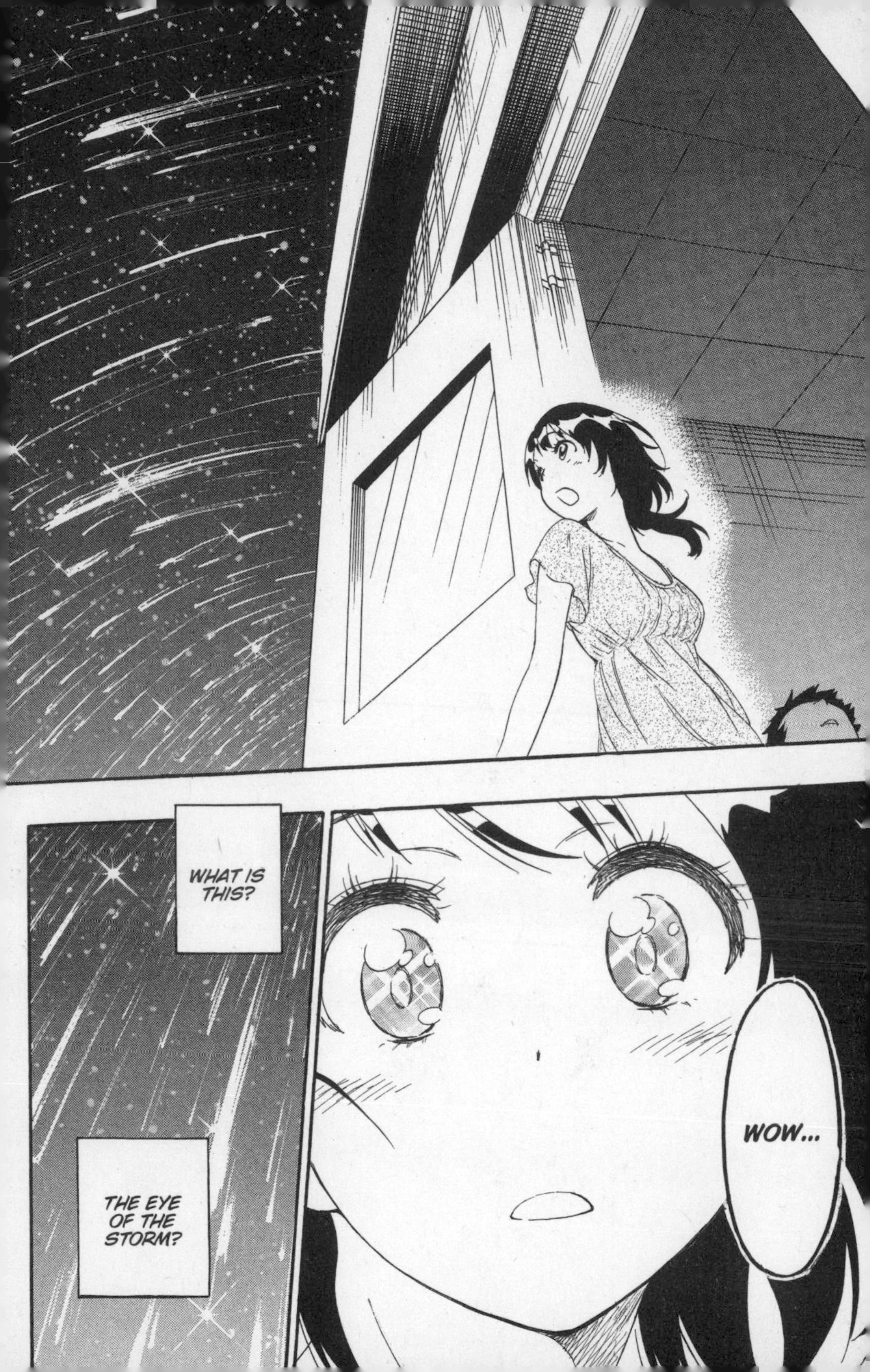
WOW...
WHAT IS THIS?
THE EYE OF THE STORM?

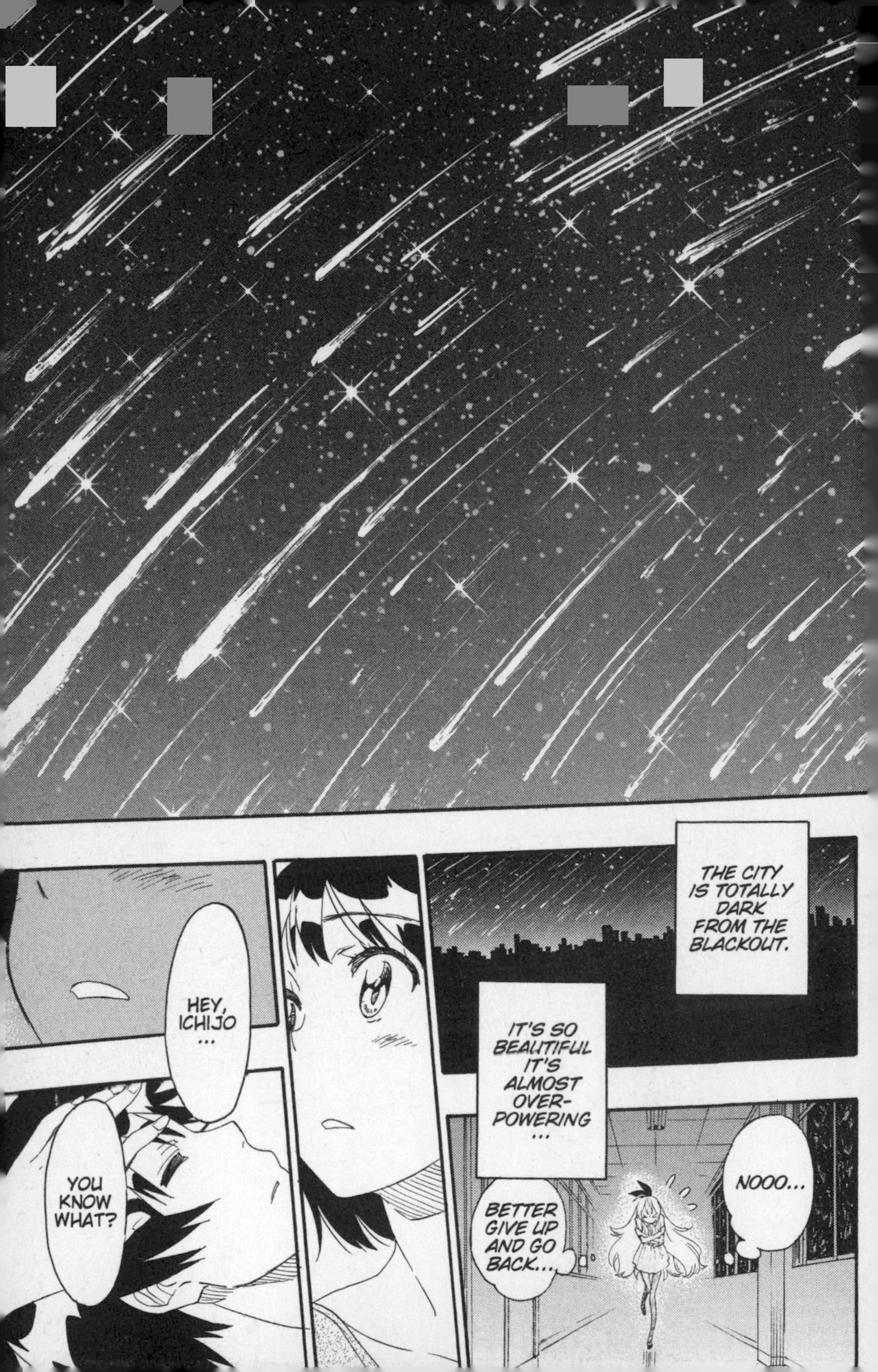
THE CITY IS TOTALLY DARK FROM THE BLACKOUT.
IT'S SO BEAUTIFUL IT'S ALMOST OVER-POWERING...
NOOO...
BETTER GIVE UP AND GO BACK...
HEY, ICHIJO...
YOU KNOW WHAT?

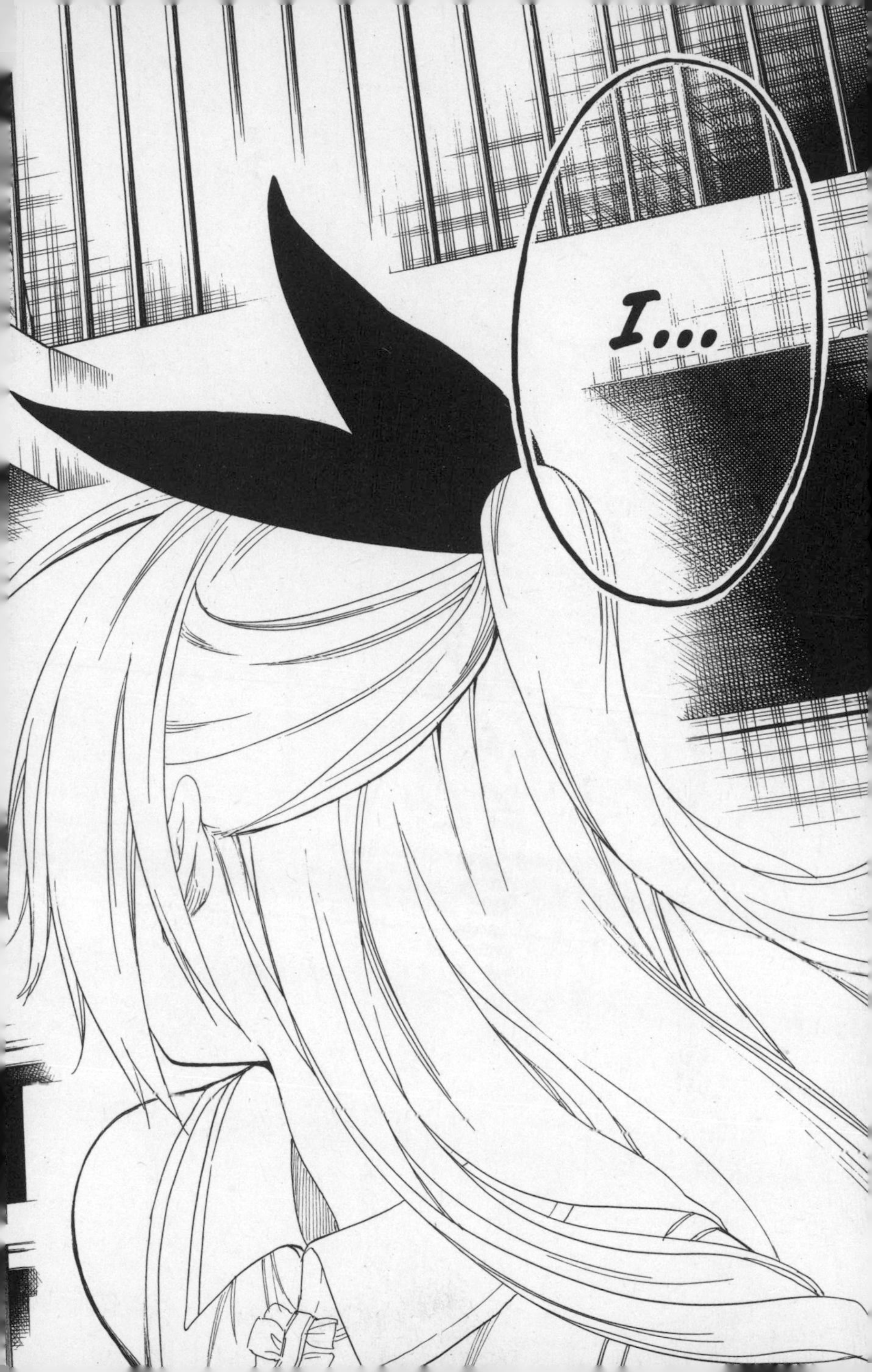
I...

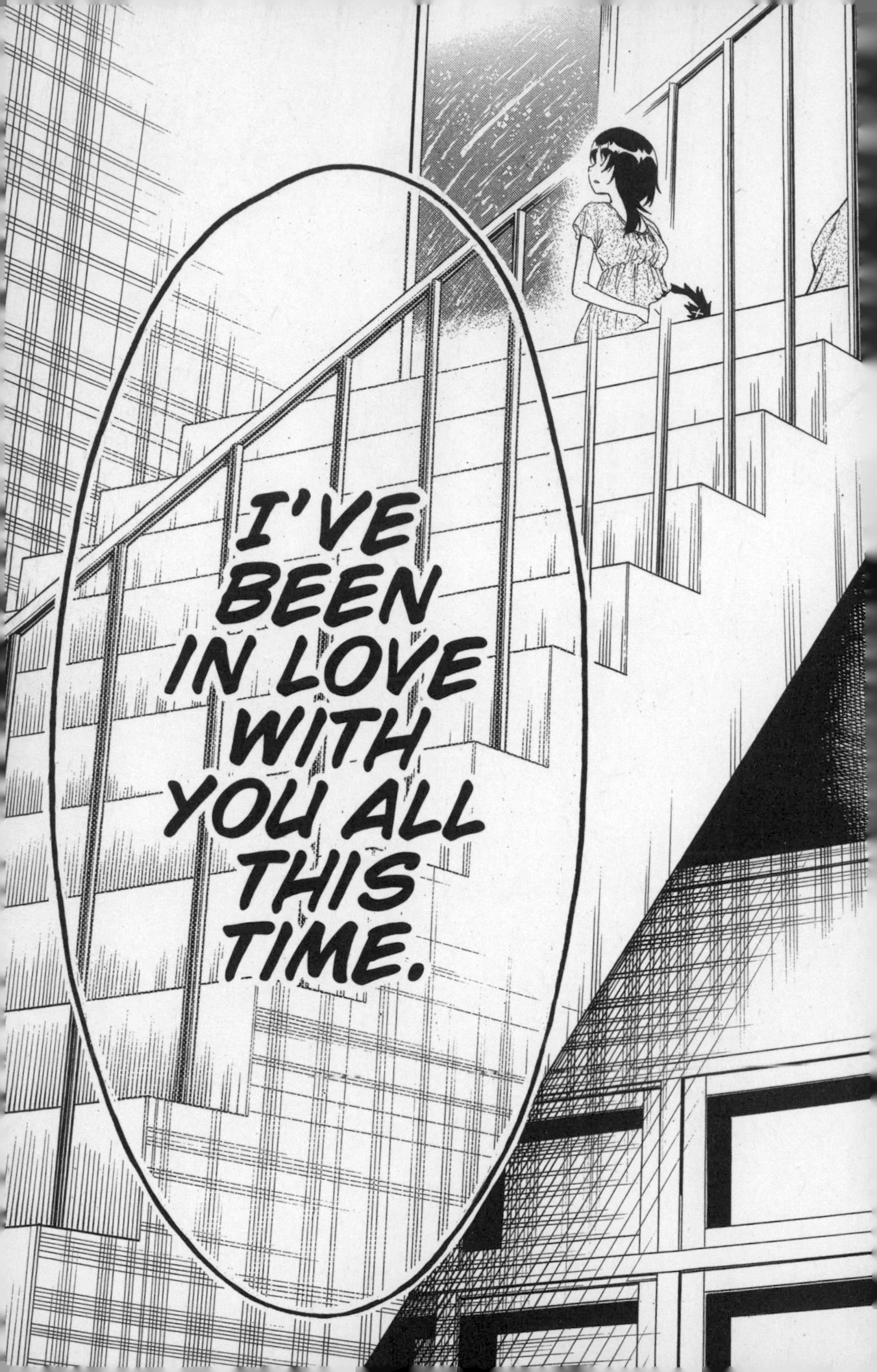
I'VE BEEN IN LOVE WITH YOU ALL THIS TIME.

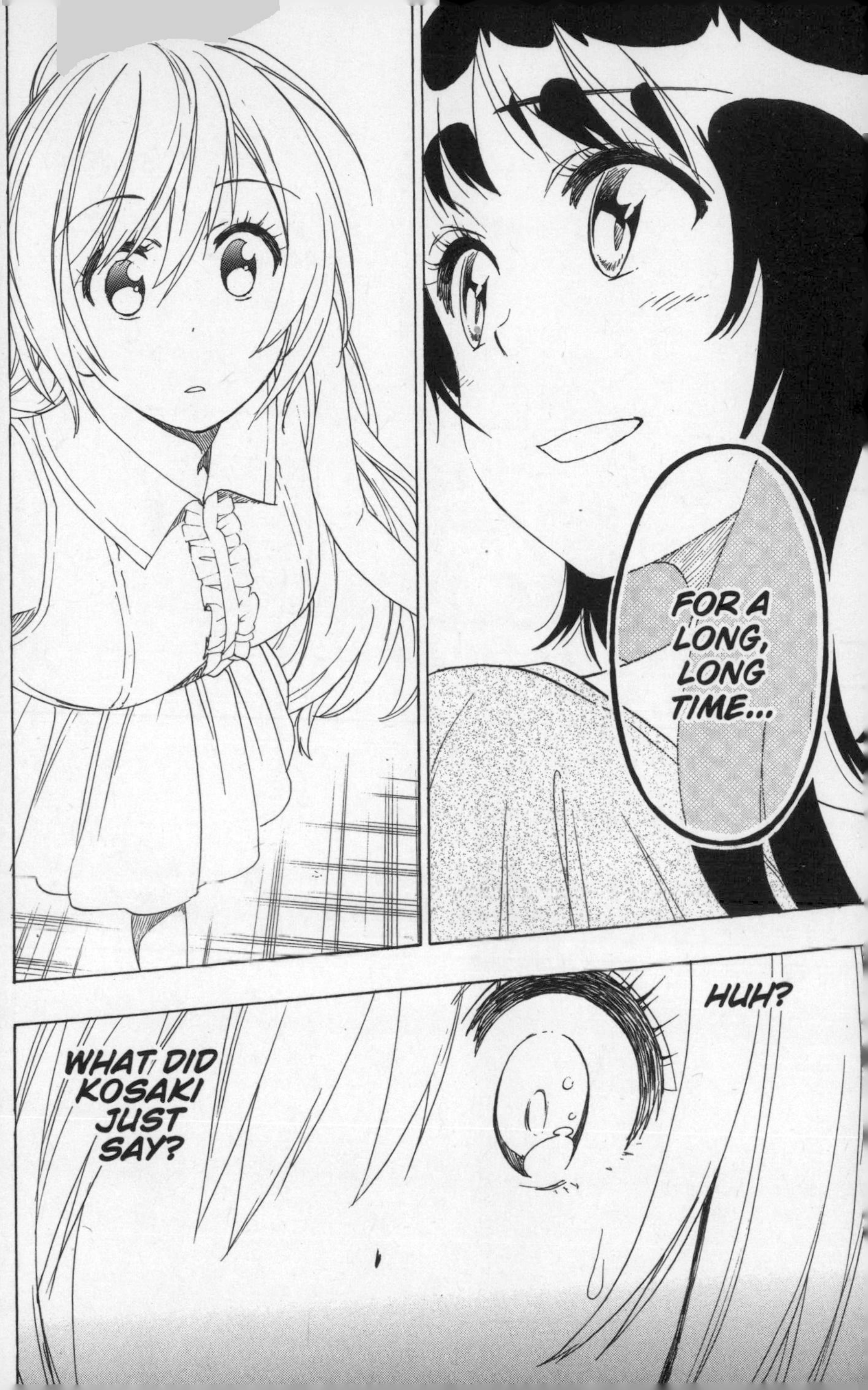
FOR A LONG, LONG TIME...
HUH?
WHAT DID KOSAKI JUST SAY?

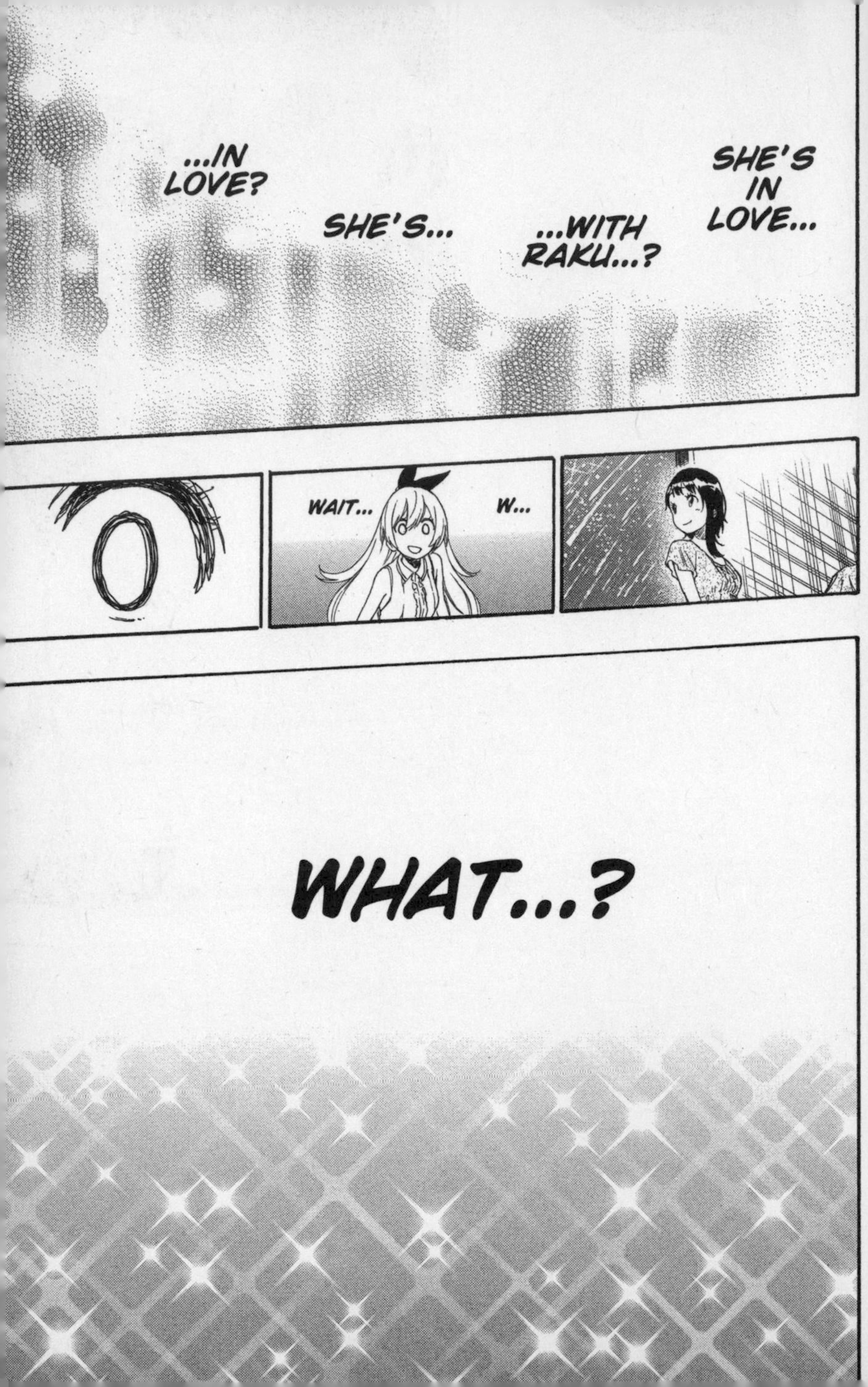
SHE'S IN LOVE...
...WITH RAKU...?
SHE'S...
...IN LOVE?
W...
WAIT...
WHAT...?

Chapter 212: Bye-Bye

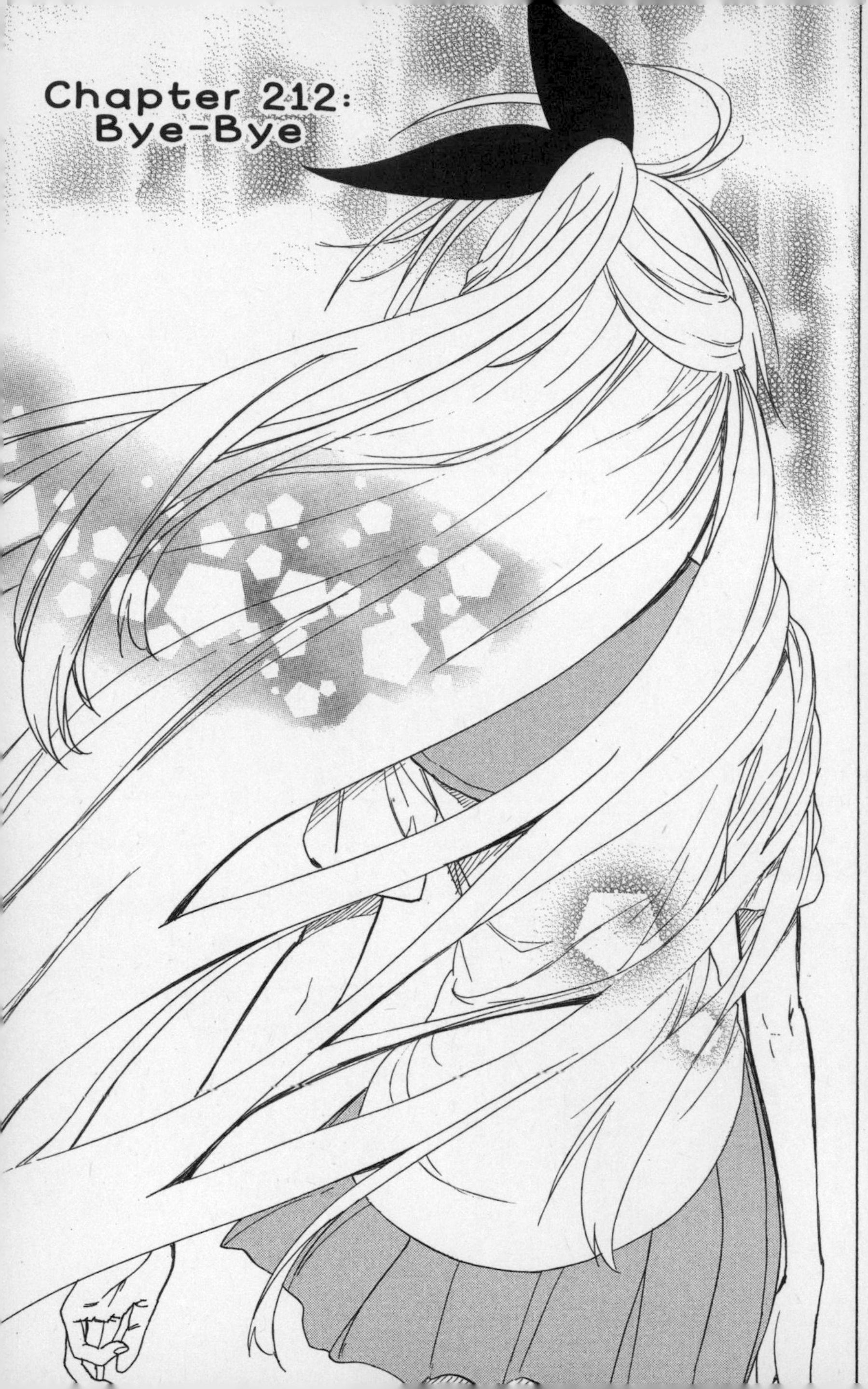

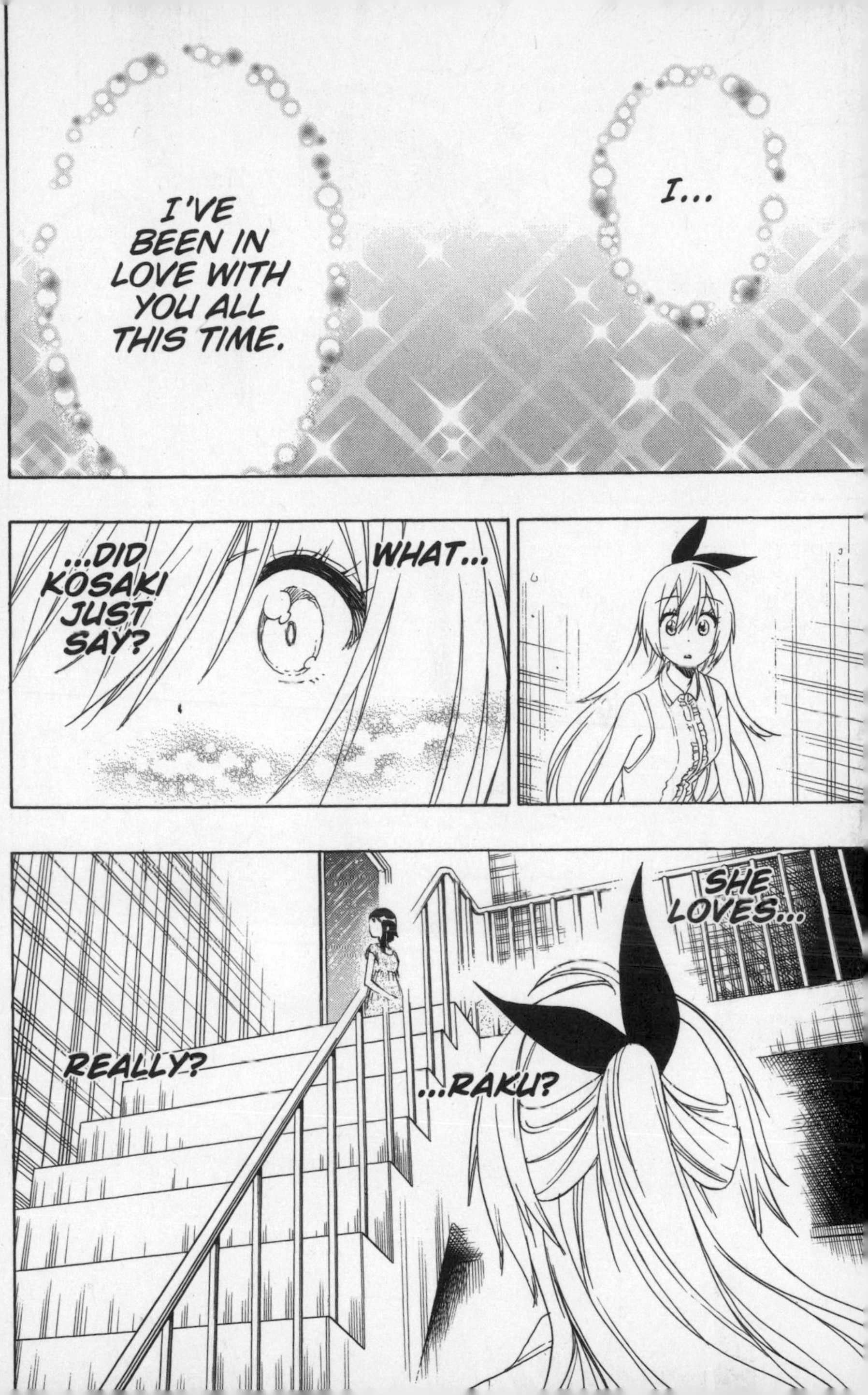
I...
I'VE BEEN IN LOVE WITH YOU ALL THIS TIME.
WHAT...
...DID KOSAKI JUST SAY?
SHE LOVES...
...RAKU?
REALLY?

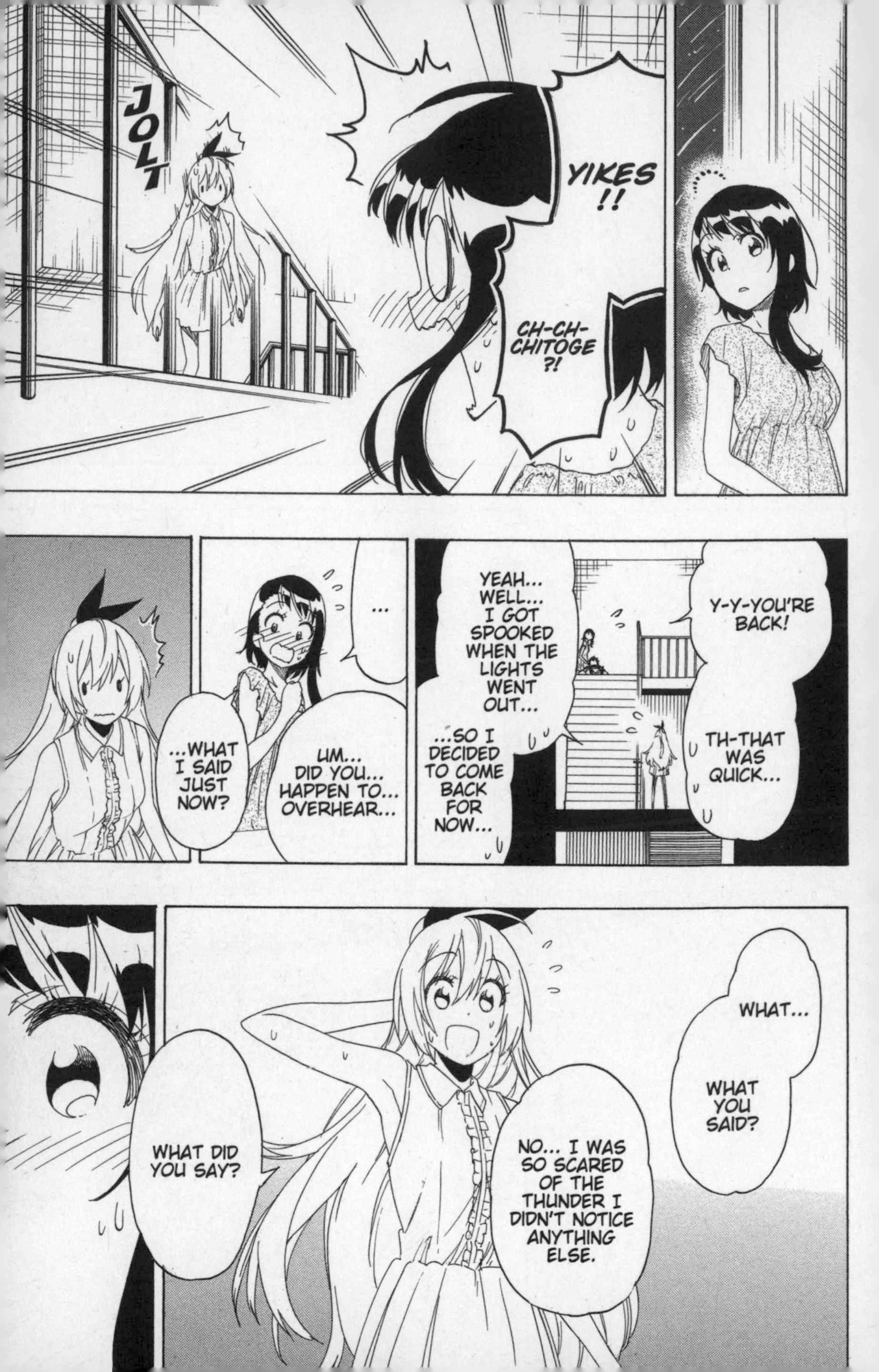
YIKES!!
CH-CH-CHITOGE?!
JOLT
Y-Y-YOU'RE BACK!
TH-THAT WAS QUICK...
YEAH... WELL... I GOT SPOOKED WHEN THE LIGHTS WENT OUT...
...SO I DECIDED TO COME BACK FOR NOW...
...
UM... DID YOU... HAPPEN TO... OVERHEAR...
...WHAT I SAID JUST NOW?
WHAT...
WHAT YOU SAID?
WHAT DID YOU SAY?
NO... I WAS SO SCARED OF THE THUNDER I DIDN'T NOTICE ANYTHING ELSE.

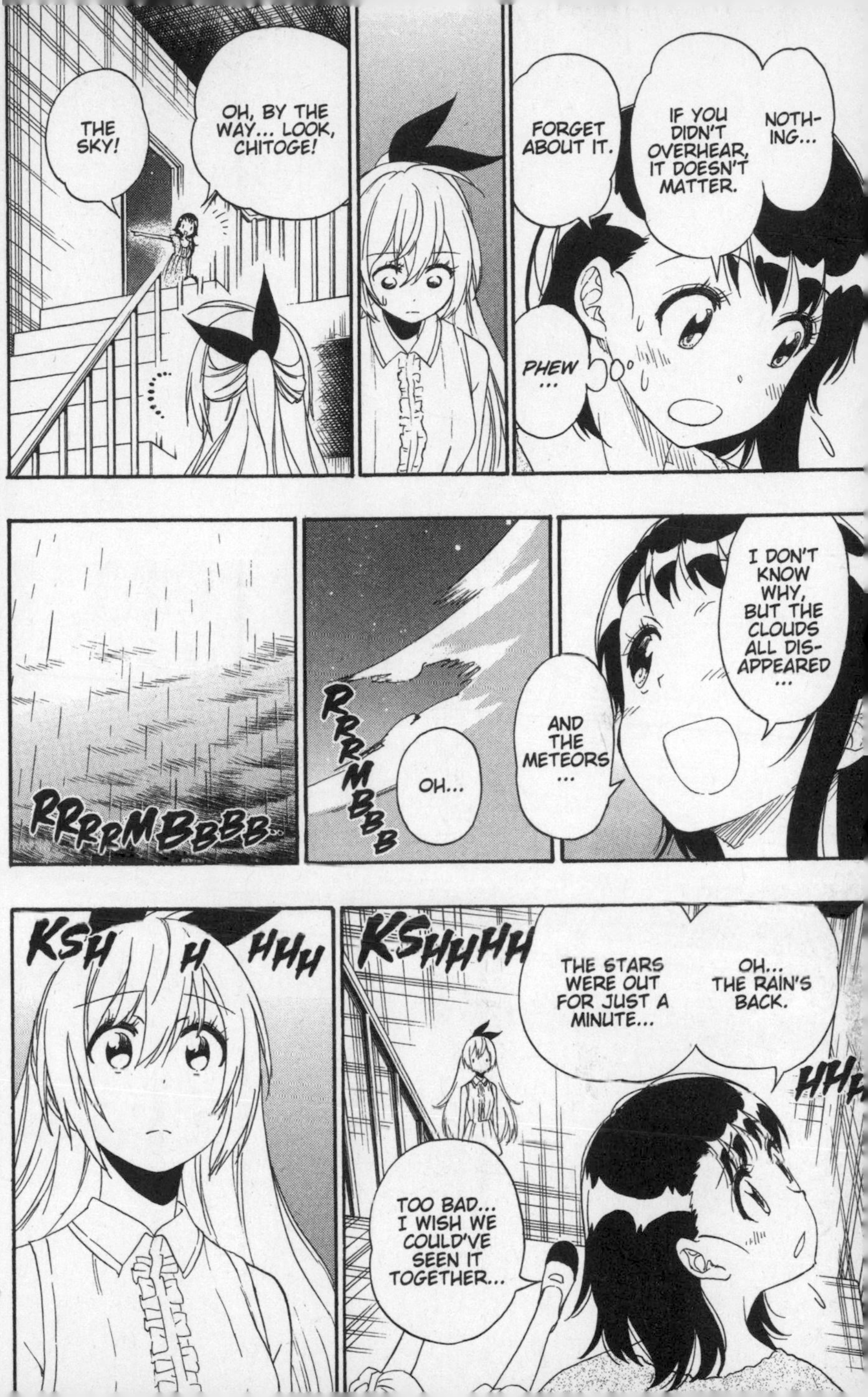
NOTH-ING...
IF YOU DIDN'T OVERHEAR, IT DOESN'T MATTER.
FORGET ABOUT IT.
PHEW...
OH, BY THE WAY... LOOK, CHITOGE!
THE SKY!
I DON'T KNOW WHY, BUT THE CLOUDS ALL DIS-APPEARED...
AND THE METEORS...
RRRRMBBB
OH...
RRRRMBBBB..
OH... THE RAIN'S BACK.
THE STARS WERE OUT FOR JUST A MINUTE...
KSHHHHH
HHH
TOO BAD... I WISH WE COULD'VE SEEN IT TOGETHER...
KSH H HHH

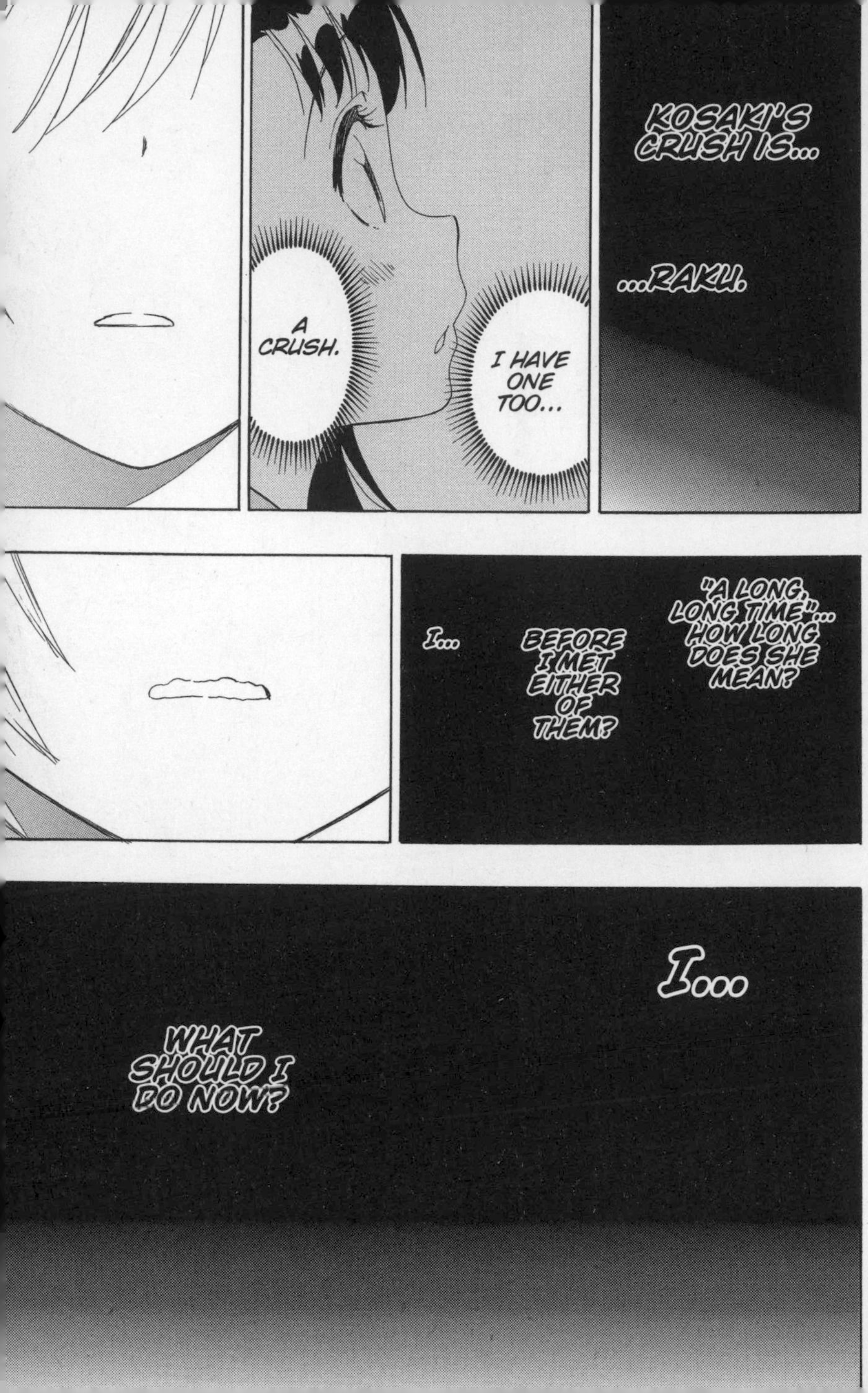
KOSAKI'S CRUSH IS...
...RAKU.
I HAVE ONE TOO...
A CRUSH.
"A LONG, LONG TIME"... HOW LONG DOES SHE MEAN?
BEFORE I MET EITHER OF THEM?
I...
I...
WHAT SHOULD I DO NOW?

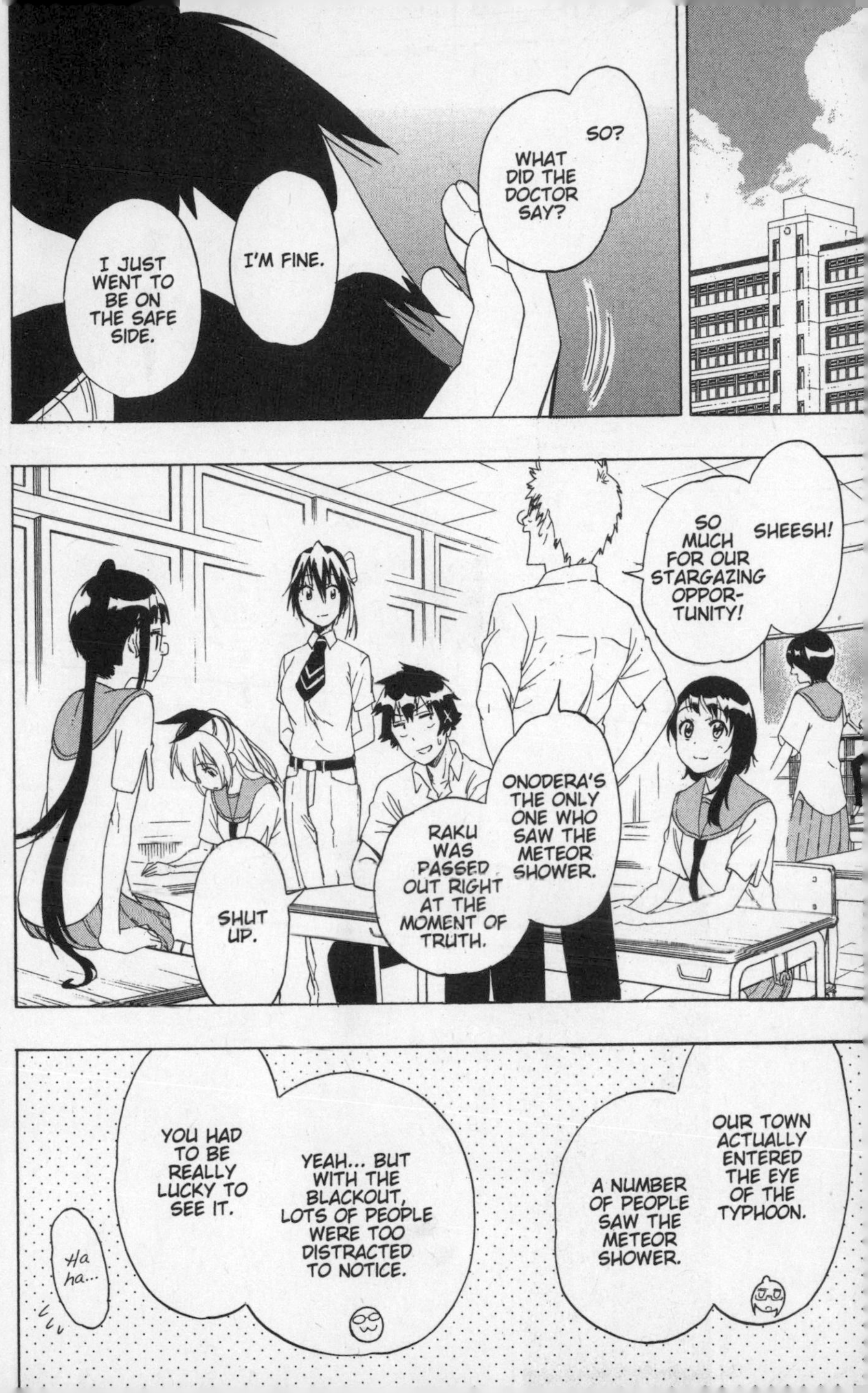
SO?
WHAT DID THE DOCTOR SAY?
I'M FINE.
I JUST WENT TO BE ON THE SAFE SIDE.
SHEESH!
SO MUCH FOR OUR STARGAZING OPPORTUNITY!
ONODERA'S THE ONLY ONE WHO SAW THE METEOR SHOWER.
RAKU WAS PASSED OUT RIGHT AT THE MOMENT OF TRUTH.
SHUT UP.
OUR TOWN ACTUALLY ENTERED THE EYE OF THE TYPHOON.
A NUMBER OF PEOPLE SAW THE METEOR SHOWER.
YEAH... BUT WITH THE BLACKOUT, LOTS OF PEOPLE WERE TOO DISTRACTED TO NOTICE.
YOU HAD TO BE REALLY LUCKY TO SEE IT.
Ha ha...

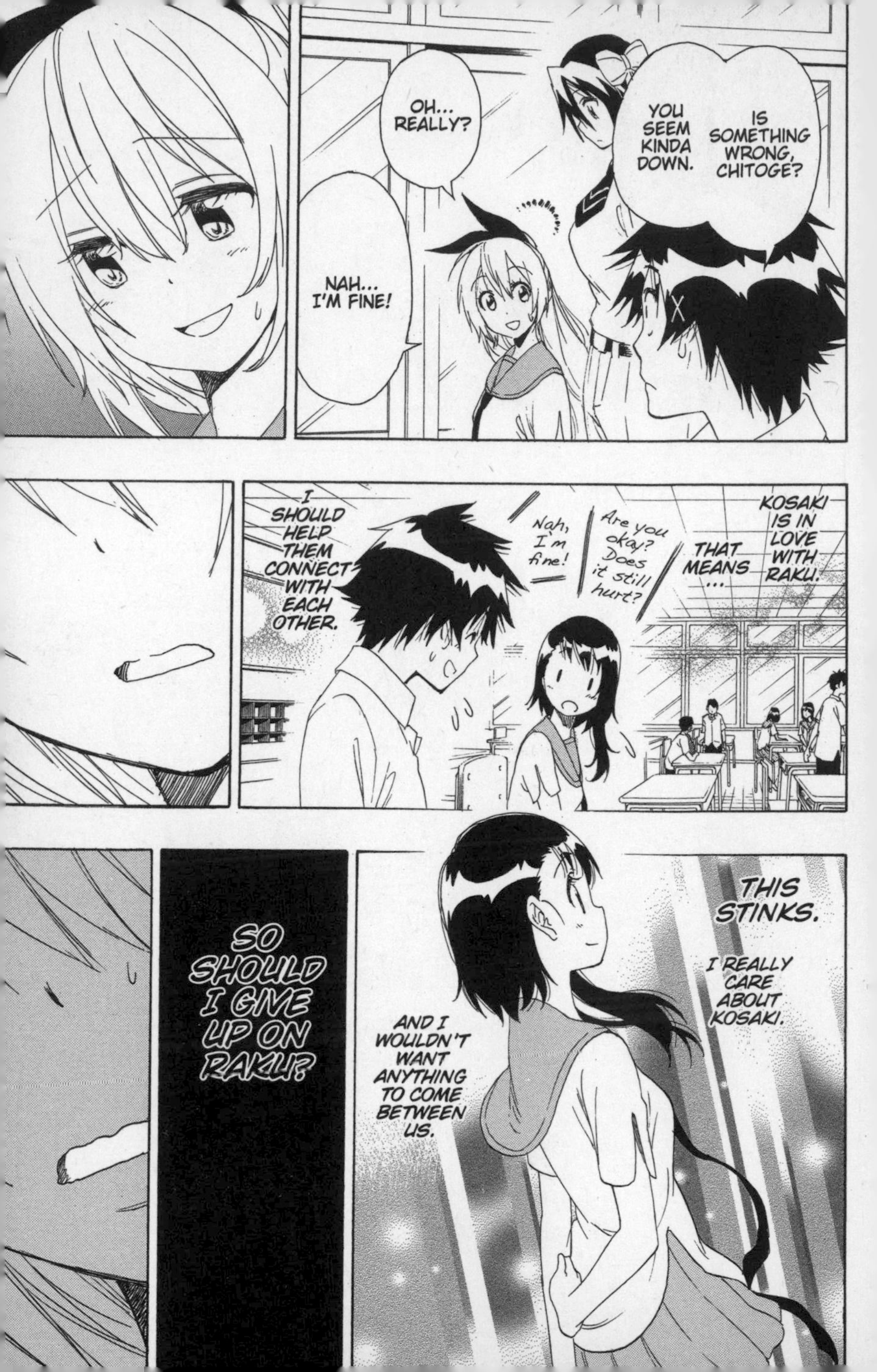
IS SOMETHING WRONG, CHITOGE?
YOU SEEM KINDA DOWN.
OH... REALLY?
NAH... I'M FINE!
KOSAKI IS IN LOVE WITH RAKU.
THAT MEANS...
Are you okay? Does it still hurt?
Nah, I'm fine!
I SHOULD HELP THEM CONNECT WITH EACH OTHER.
THIS STINKS.
I REALLY CARE ABOUT KOSAKI.
AND I WOULDN'T WANT ANYTHING TO COME BETWEEN US.
SO SHOULD I GIVE UP ON RAKU?

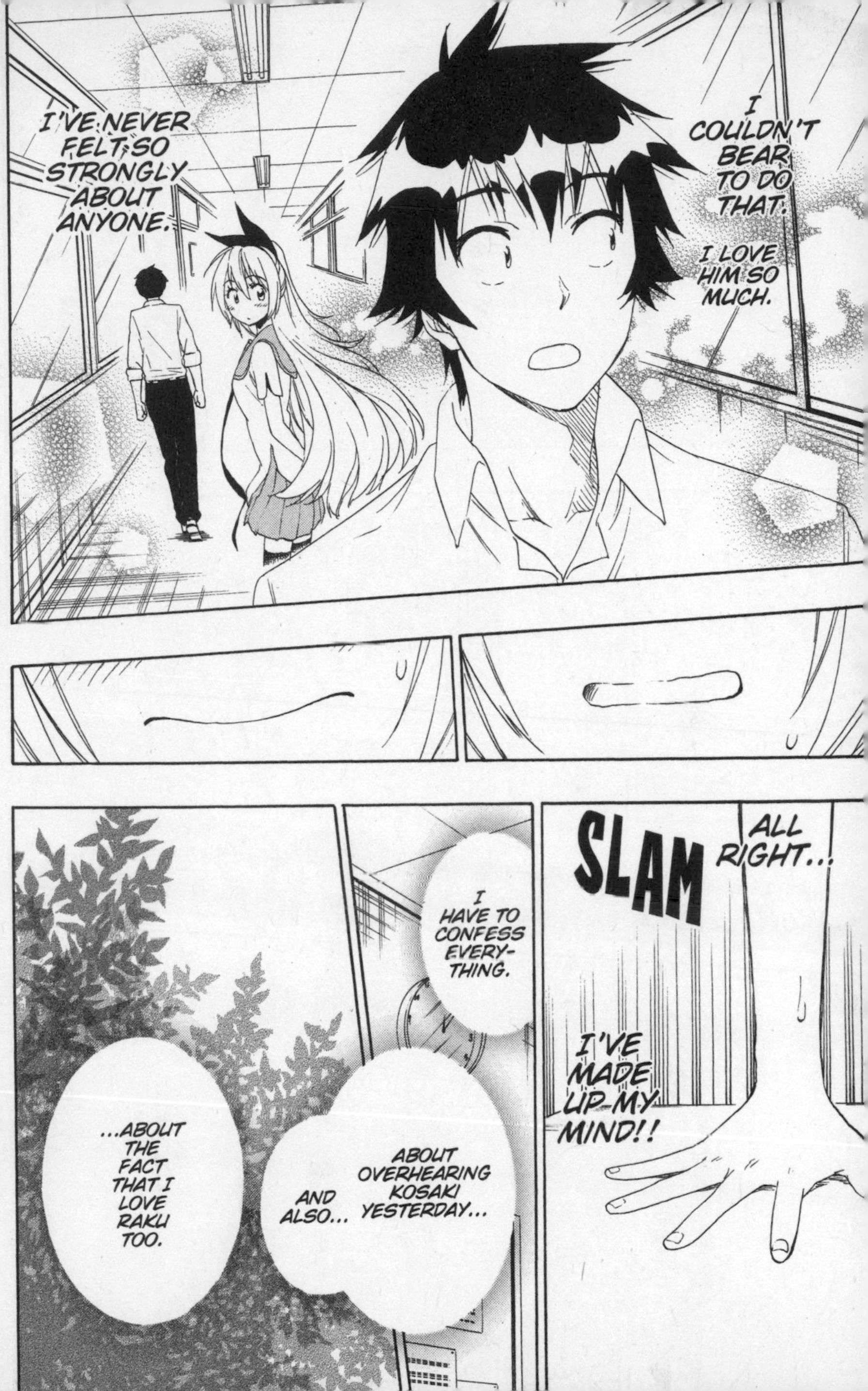
I COULDN'T BEAR TO DO THAT.
I LOVE HIM SO MUCH.
I'VE NEVER FELT SO STRONGLY ABOUT ANYONE.
ALL RIGHT...
SLAM
I'VE MADE UP MY MIND!!
I HAVE TO CONFESS EVERYTHING.
ABOUT OVERHEARING KOSAKI YESTERDAY...
AND ALSO...
...ABOUT THE FACT THAT I LOVE RAKU TOO.

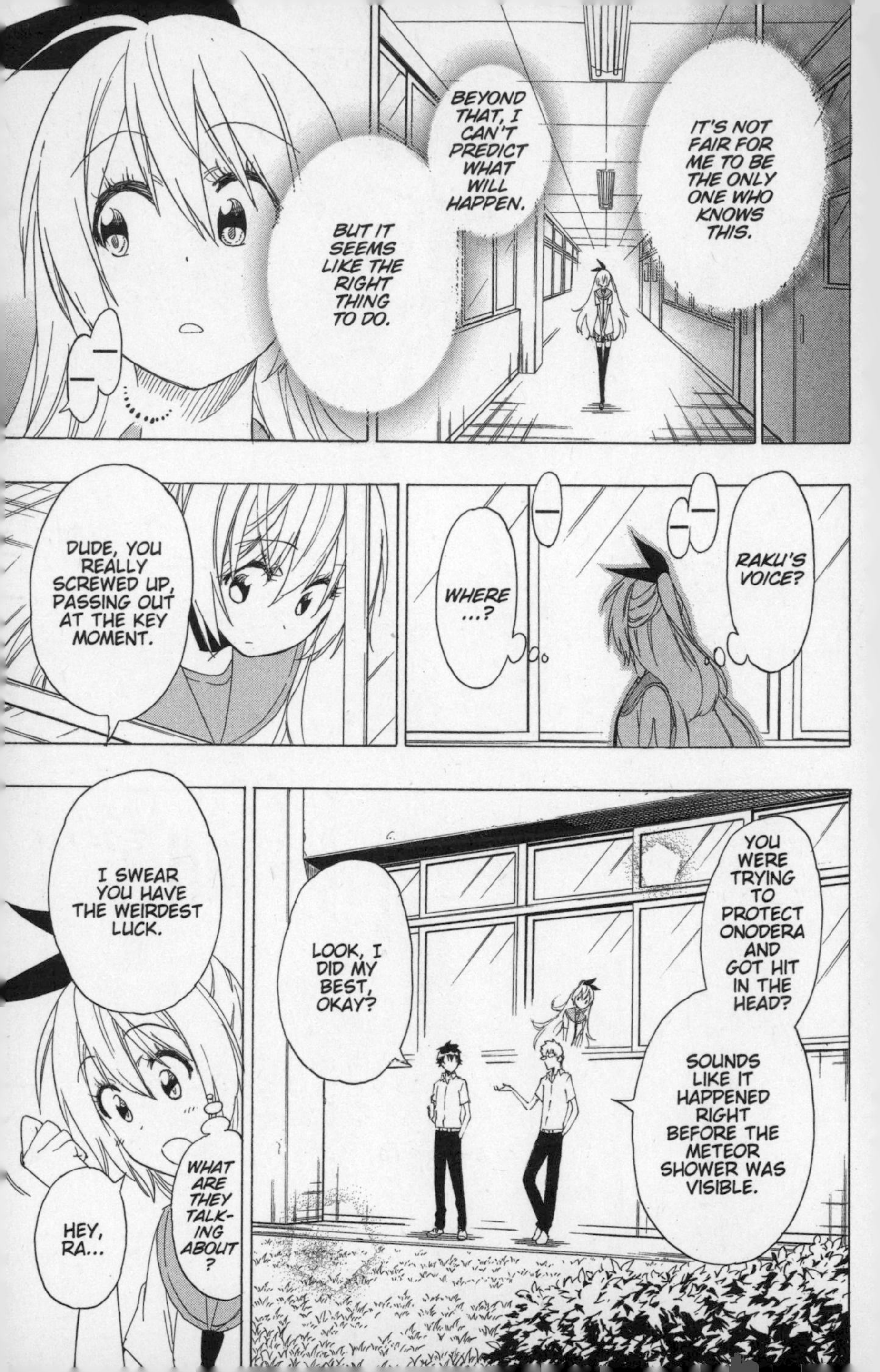
IT'S NOT FAIR FOR ME TO BE THE ONLY ONE WHO KNOWS THIS.
BEYOND THAT, I CAN'T PREDICT WHAT WILL HAPPEN.
BUT IT SEEMS LIKE THE RIGHT THING TO DO.
—
—
RAKU'S VOICE?
—
WHERE ...?
DUDE, YOU REALLY SCREWED UP, PASSING OUT AT THE KEY MOMENT.
YOU WERE TRYING TO PROTECT ONODERA AND GOT HIT IN THE HEAD?
SOUNDS LIKE IT HAPPENED RIGHT BEFORE THE METEOR SHOWER WAS VISIBLE.
LOOK, I DID MY BEST, OKAY?
I SWEAR YOU HAVE THE WEIRDEST LUCK.
WHAT ARE THEY TALKING ABOUT?
HEY, RA...

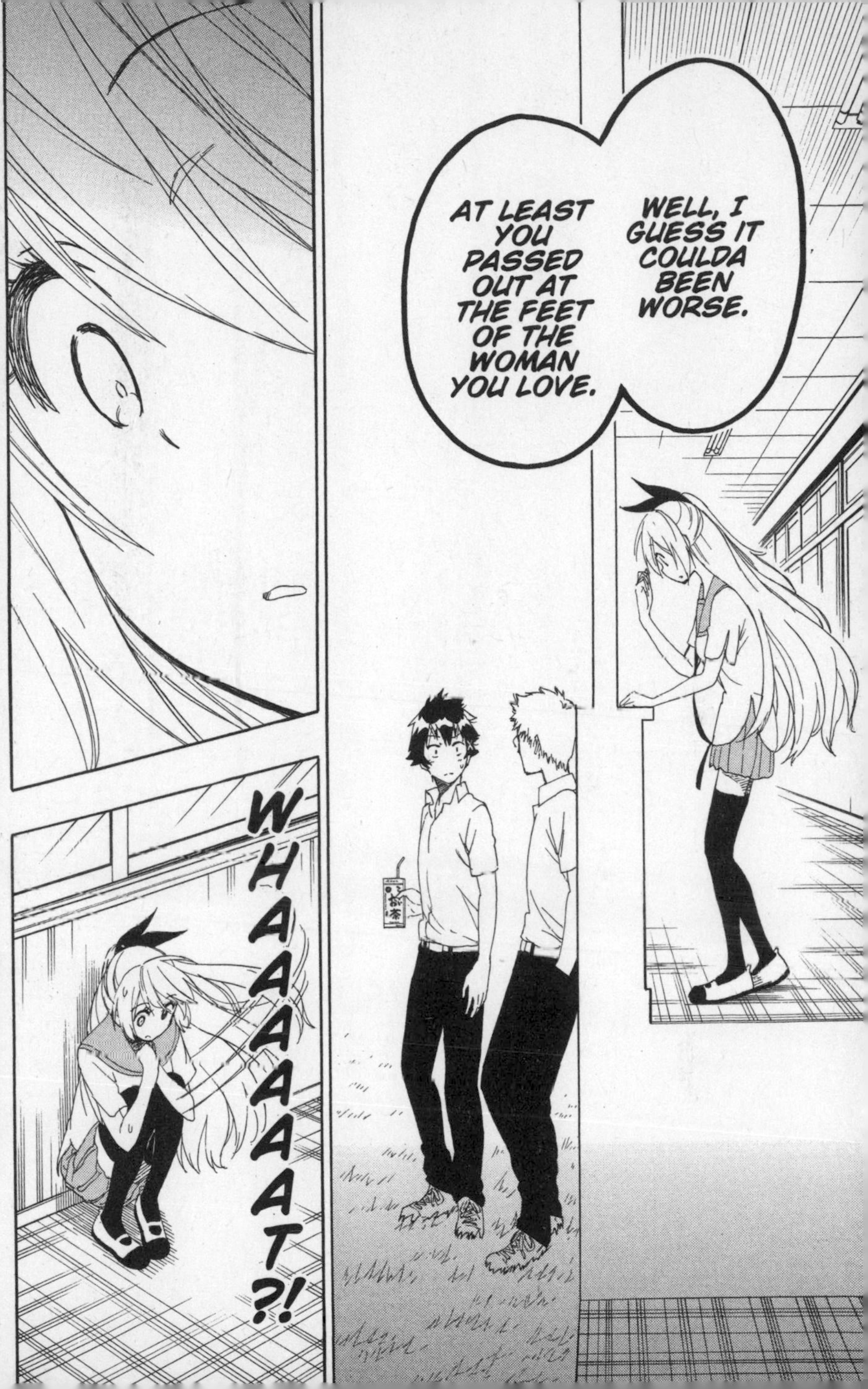
WELL, I GUESS IT COULDA BEEN WORSE.
AT LEAST YOU PASSED OUT AT THE FEET OF THE WOMAN YOU LOVE.
WHAAAAAAT?!

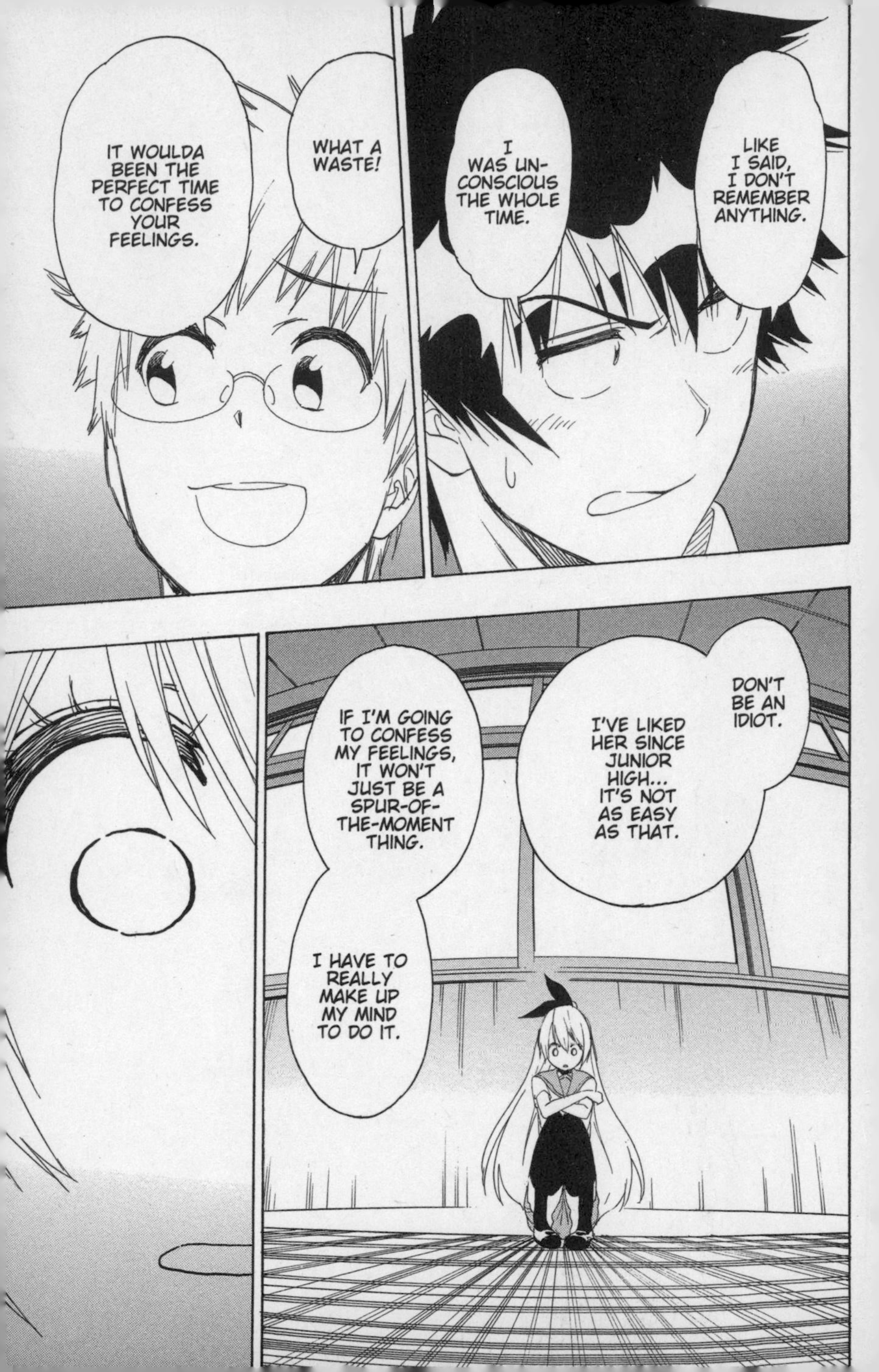
LIKE I SAID, I DON'T REMEMBER ANYTHING.
I WAS UN-CONSCIOUS THE WHOLE TIME.
WHAT A WASTE!
IT WOULDA BEEN THE PERFECT TIME TO CONFESS YOUR FEELINGS.
DON'T BE AN IDIOT.
I'VE LIKED HER SINCE JUNIOR HIGH... IT'S NOT AS EASY AS THAT.
IF I'M GOING TO CONFESS MY FEELINGS, IT WON'T JUST BE A SPUR-OF-THE-MOMENT THING.
I HAVE TO REALLY MAKE UP MY MIND TO DO IT.

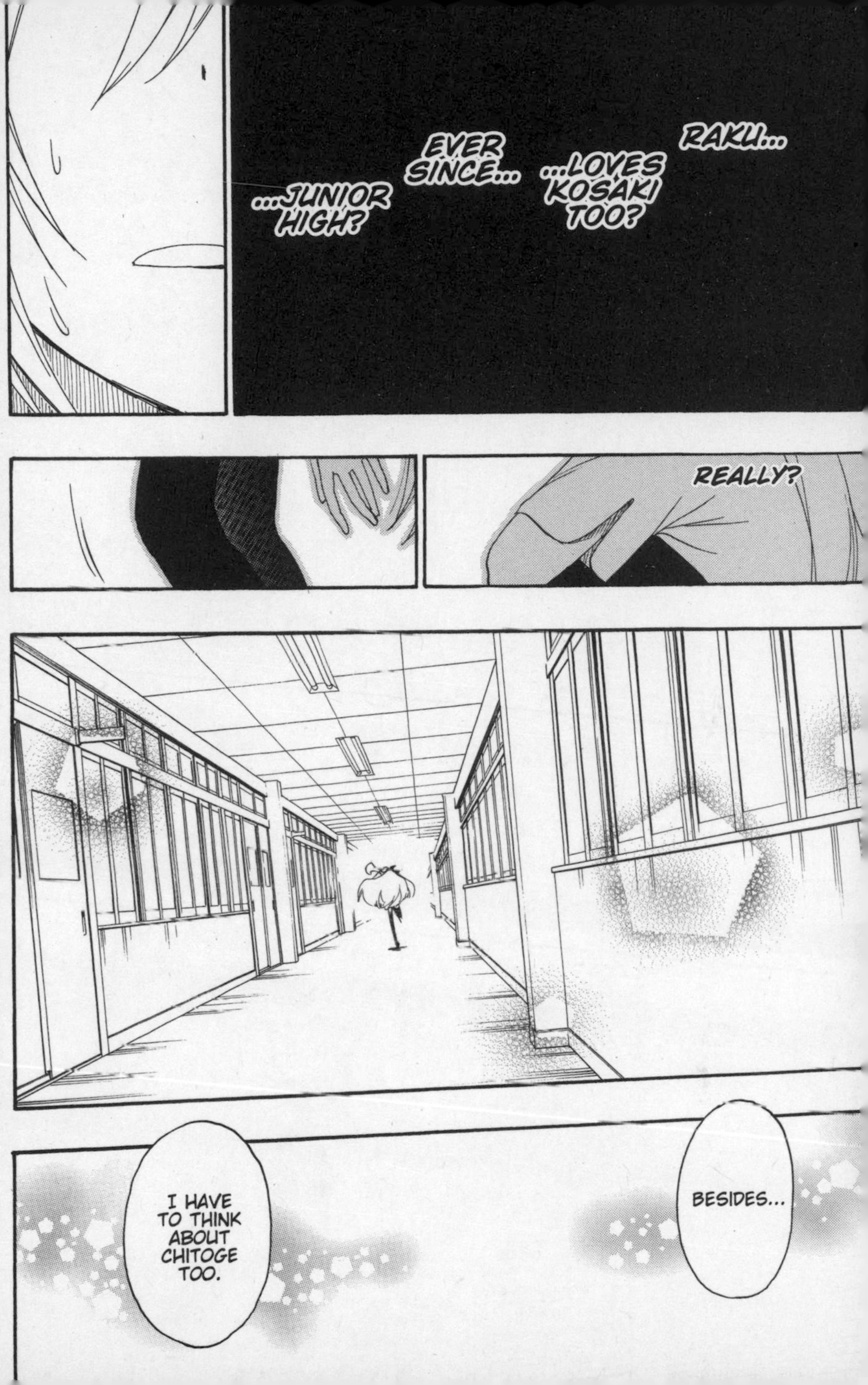
RAKU...
...LOVES KOSAKI TOO?
EVER SINCE...
...JUNIOR HIGH?
REALLY?
BESIDES...
I HAVE TO THINK ABOUT CHITOGE TOO.

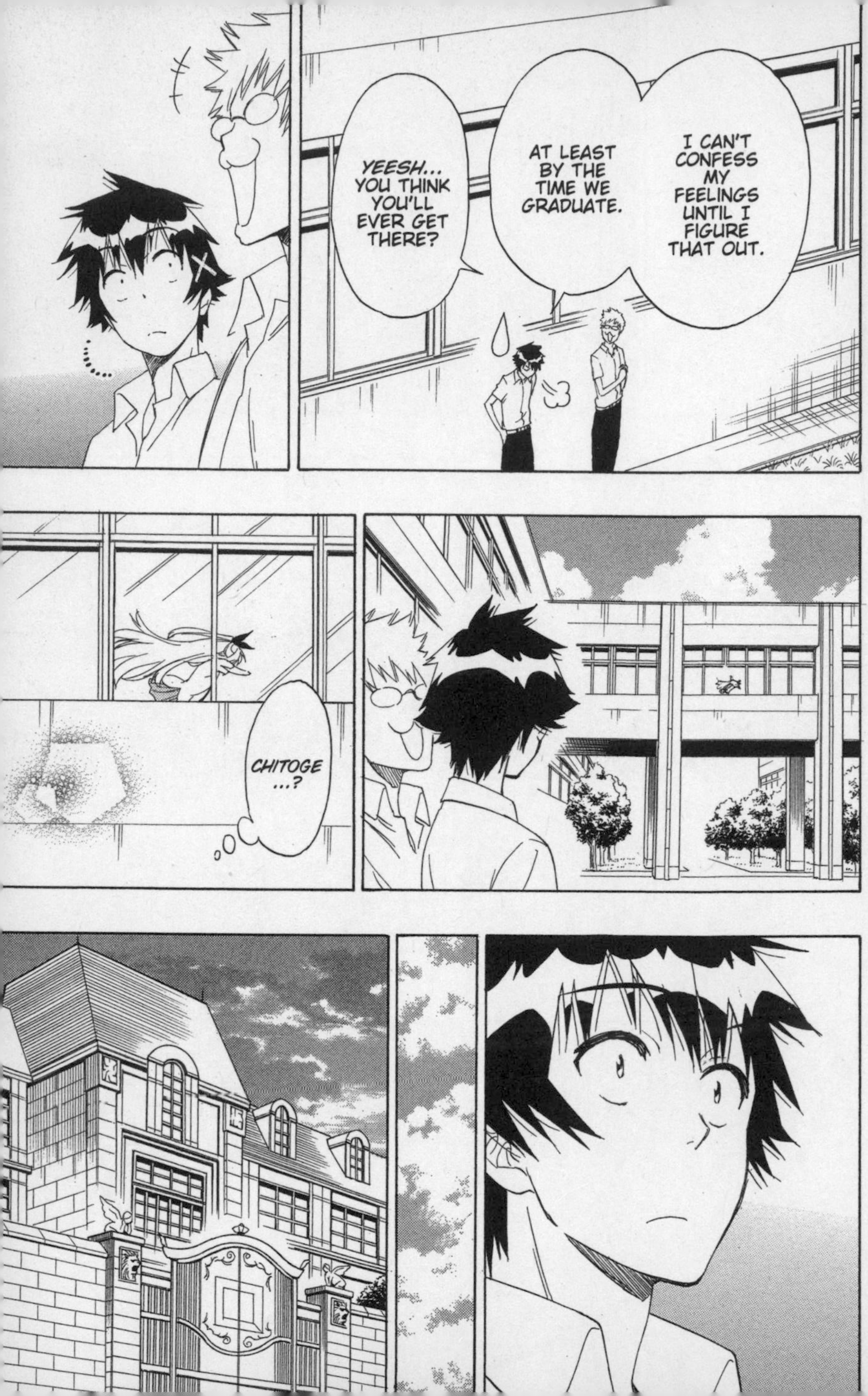
I CAN'T CONFESS MY FEELINGS UNTIL I FIGURE THAT OUT.
AT LEAST BY THE TIME WE GRADUATE.
YEESH... YOU THINK YOU'LL EVER GET THERE?
CHITOGE ...?

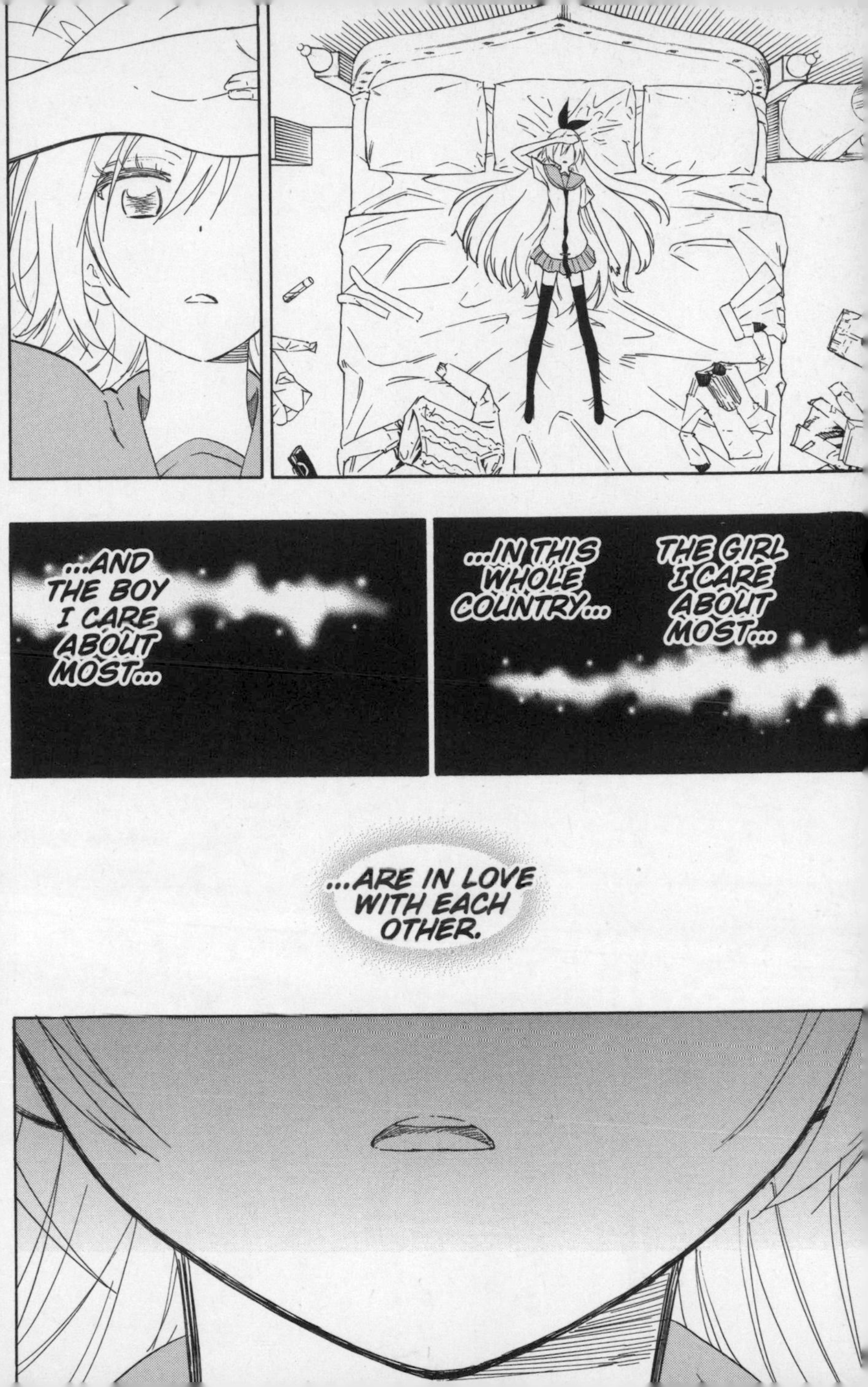
THE GIRL I CARE ABOUT MOST...
...IN THIS WHOLE COUNTRY...
...AND THE BOY I CARE ABOUT MOST...
...ARE IN LOVE WITH EACH OTHER.

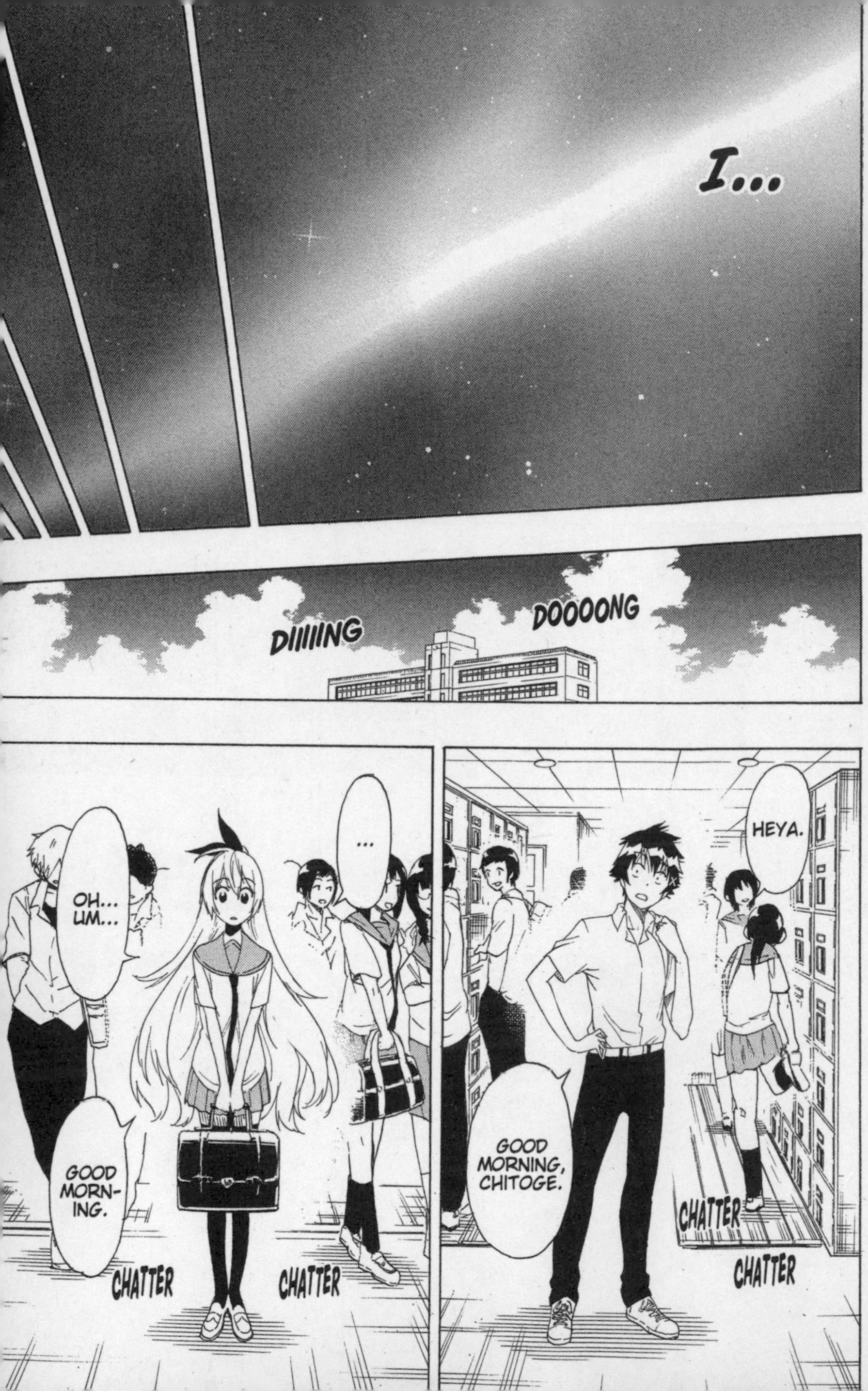
I...
DOOOONG
DIIIIING
HEYA.
GOOD MORNING, CHITOGE.
CHATTER
CHATTER
...
OH... UM...
GOOD MORN-ING.
CHATTER
CHATTER

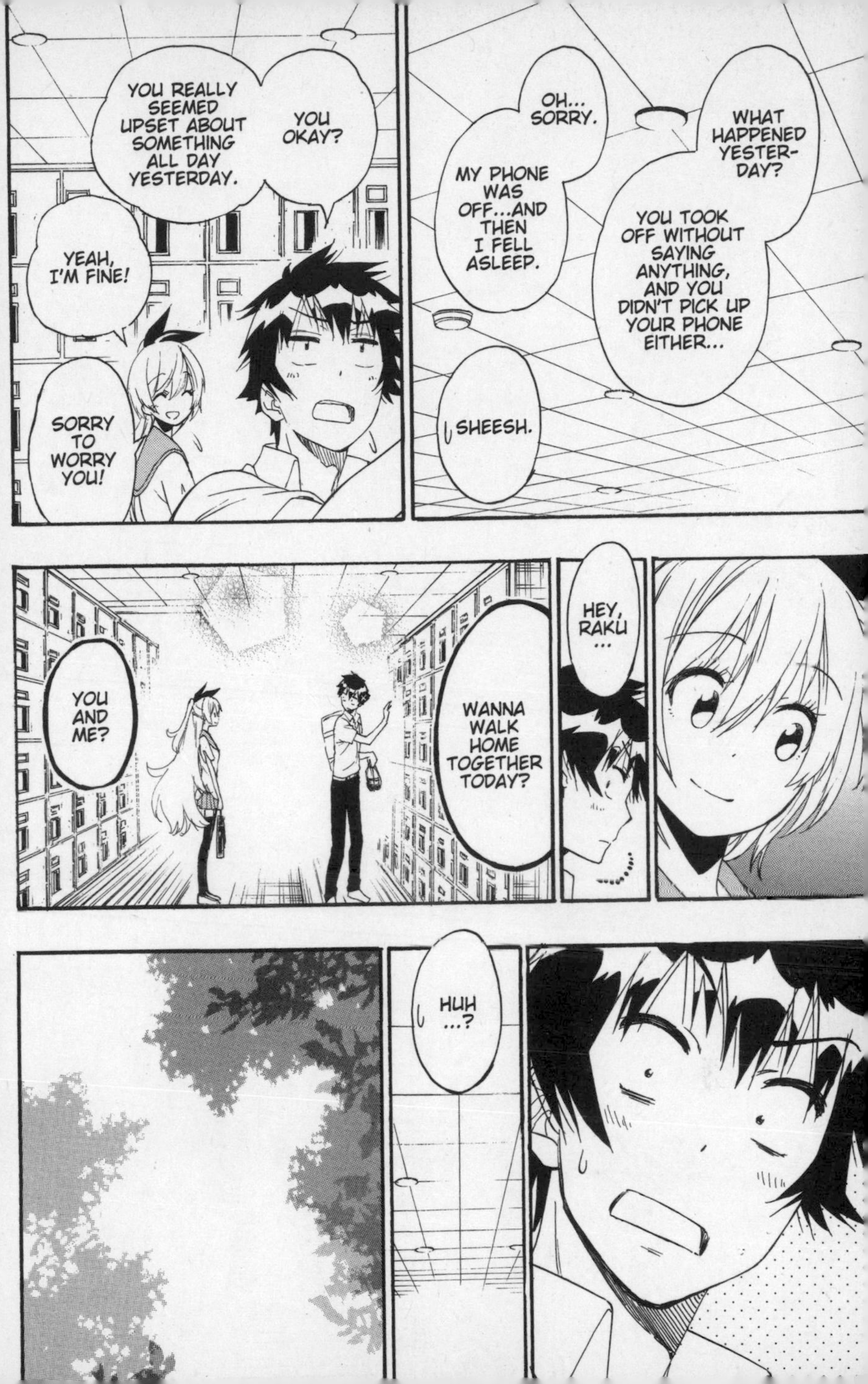
WHAT HAPPENED YESTERDAY?
YOU TOOK OFF WITHOUT SAYING ANYTHING, AND YOU DIDN'T PICK UP YOUR PHONE EITHER...
OH... SORRY.
MY PHONE WAS OFF...AND THEN I FELL ASLEEP.
SHEESH.
YOU OKAY?
YOU REALLY SEEMED UPSET ABOUT SOMETHING ALL DAY YESTERDAY.
YEAH, I'M FINE!
SORRY TO WORRY YOU!
HEY, RAKU...
WANNA WALK HOME TOGETHER TODAY?
YOU AND ME?
HUH...?

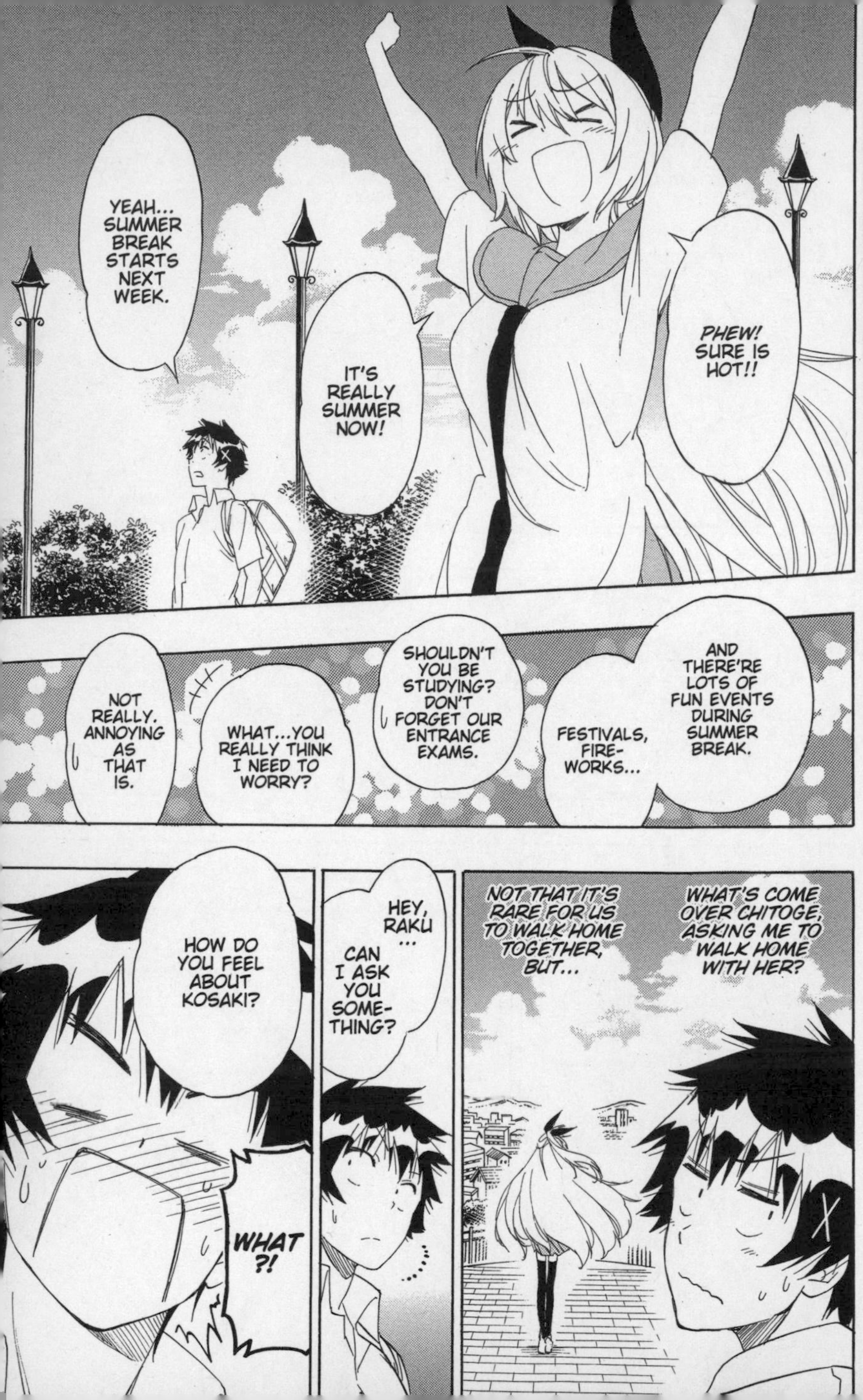
PHEW! SURE IS HOT!!
IT'S REALLY SUMMER NOW!
YEAH... SUMMER BREAK STARTS NEXT WEEK.
AND THERE'RE LOTS OF FUN EVENTS DURING SUMMER BREAK.
FESTIVALS, FIRE-WORKS...
SHOULDN'T YOU BE STUDYING? DON'T FORGET OUR ENTRANCE EXAMS.
WHAT...YOU REALLY THINK I NEED TO WORRY?
NOT REALLY. ANNOYING AS THAT IS.
WHAT'S COME OVER CHITOGE, ASKING ME TO WALK HOME WITH HER?
NOT THAT IT'S RARE FOR US TO WALK HOME TOGETHER, BUT...
HEY, RAKU...
CAN I ASK YOU SOME-THING?
HOW DO YOU FEEL ABOUT KOSAKI?
WHAT?!

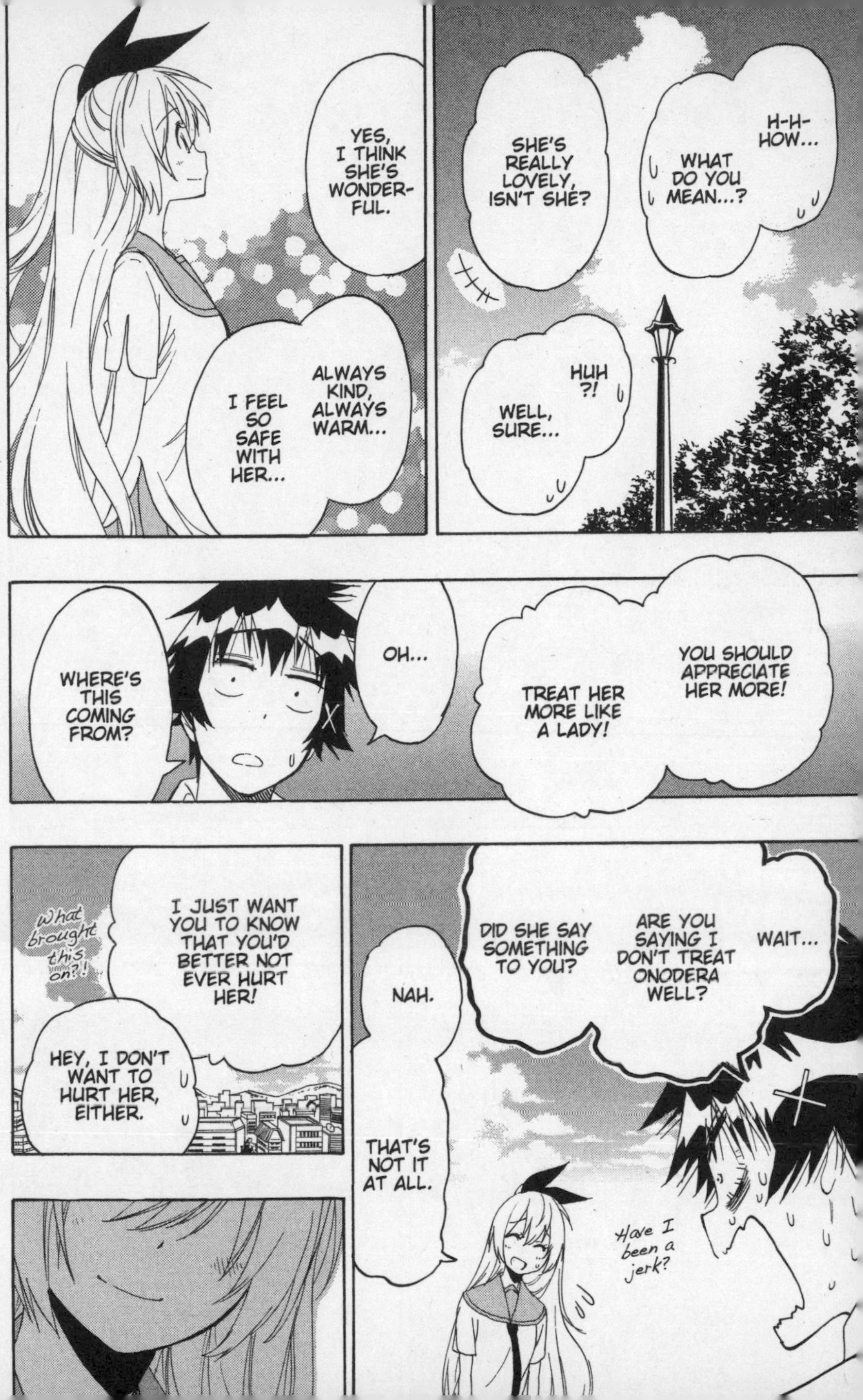
H-H-HOW...
WHAT DO YOU MEAN...?
SHE'S REALLY LOVELY, ISN'T SHE?
HUH?!
WELL, SURE...
YES, I THINK SHE'S WONDERFUL.
ALWAYS KIND, ALWAYS WARM...
I FEEL SO SAFE WITH HER...
YOU SHOULD APPRECIATE HER MORE!
TREAT HER MORE LIKE A LADY!
OH...
WHERE'S THIS COMING FROM?
WAIT...
ARE YOU SAYING I DON'T TREAT ONODERA WELL?
DID SHE SAY SOMETHING TO YOU?
Have I been a jerk?
NAH.
THAT'S NOT IT AT ALL.
I JUST WANT YOU TO KNOW THAT YOU'D BETTER NOT EVER HURT HER!
What brought this on?!
HEY, I DON'T WANT TO HURT HER, EITHER.

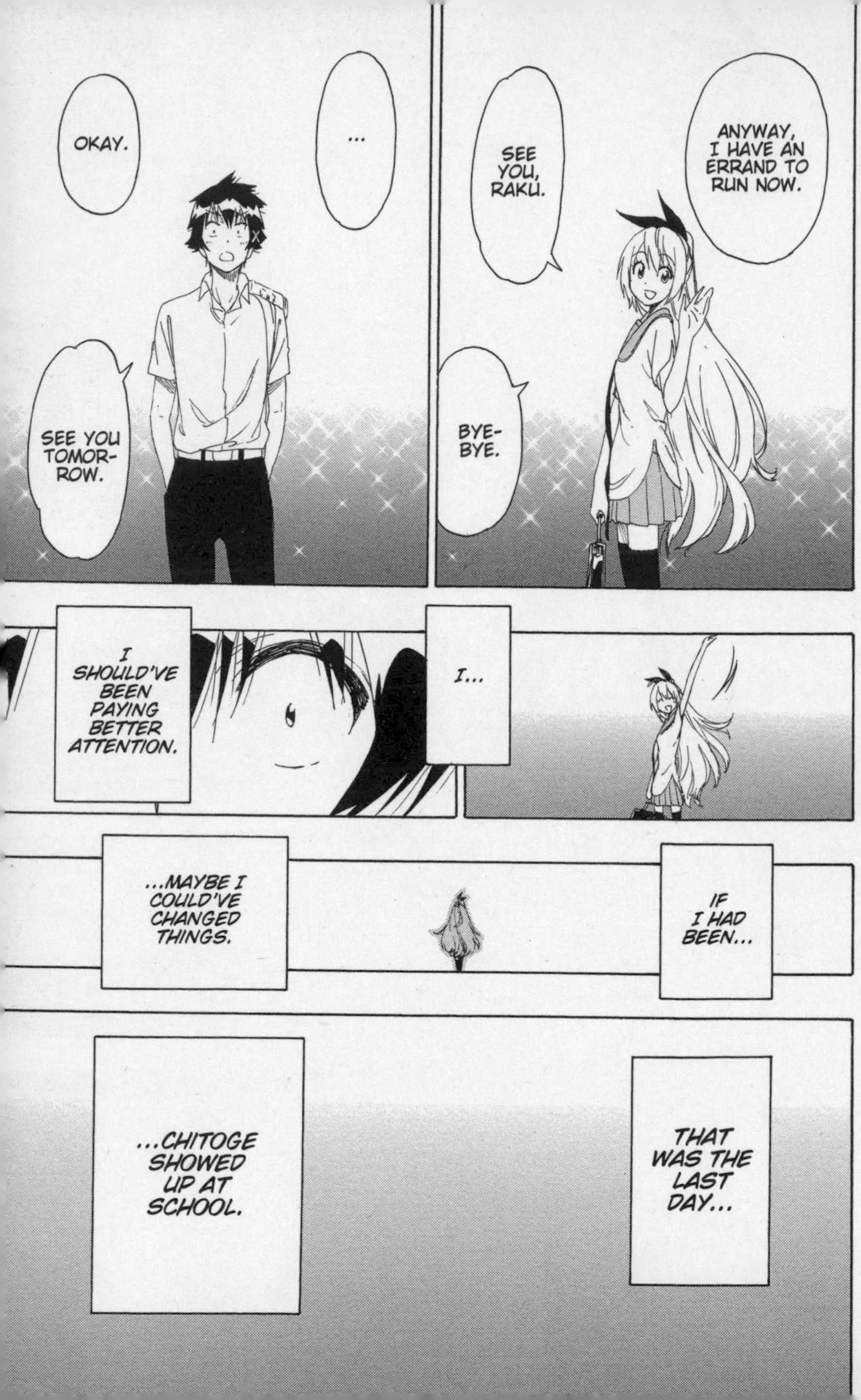
ANYWAY, I HAVE AN ERRAND TO RUN NOW.
SEE YOU, RAKU.
BYE-BYE.
...
OKAY.
SEE YOU TOMOR-ROW.
I...
I SHOULD'VE BEEN PAYING BETTER ATTENTION.
IF I HAD BEEN...
...MAYBE I COULD'VE CHANGED THINGS.
THAT WAS THE LAST DAY...
...CHITOGE SHOWED UP AT SCHOOL.

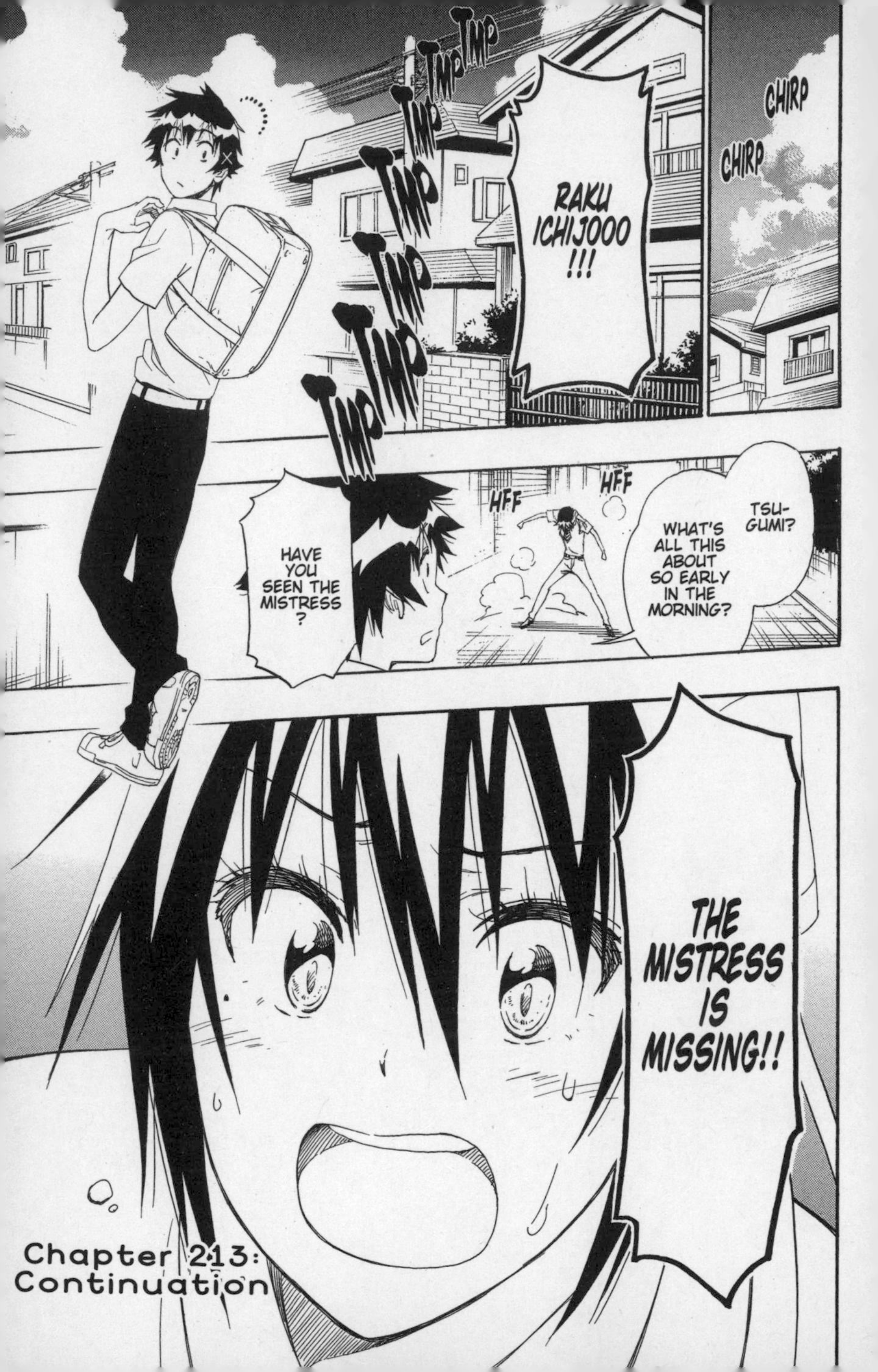
CHIRP
CHIRP
RAKU ICHIJOOO !!!
TMP TMP TMP TMP TMP TMP TMP TMP
TSU-GUMI?
WHAT'S ALL THIS ABOUT SO EARLY IN THE MORNING?
HFF
HFF
HAVE YOU SEEN THE MISTRESS ?
THE MISTRESS IS MISSING!!
Chapter 213:
Continuation

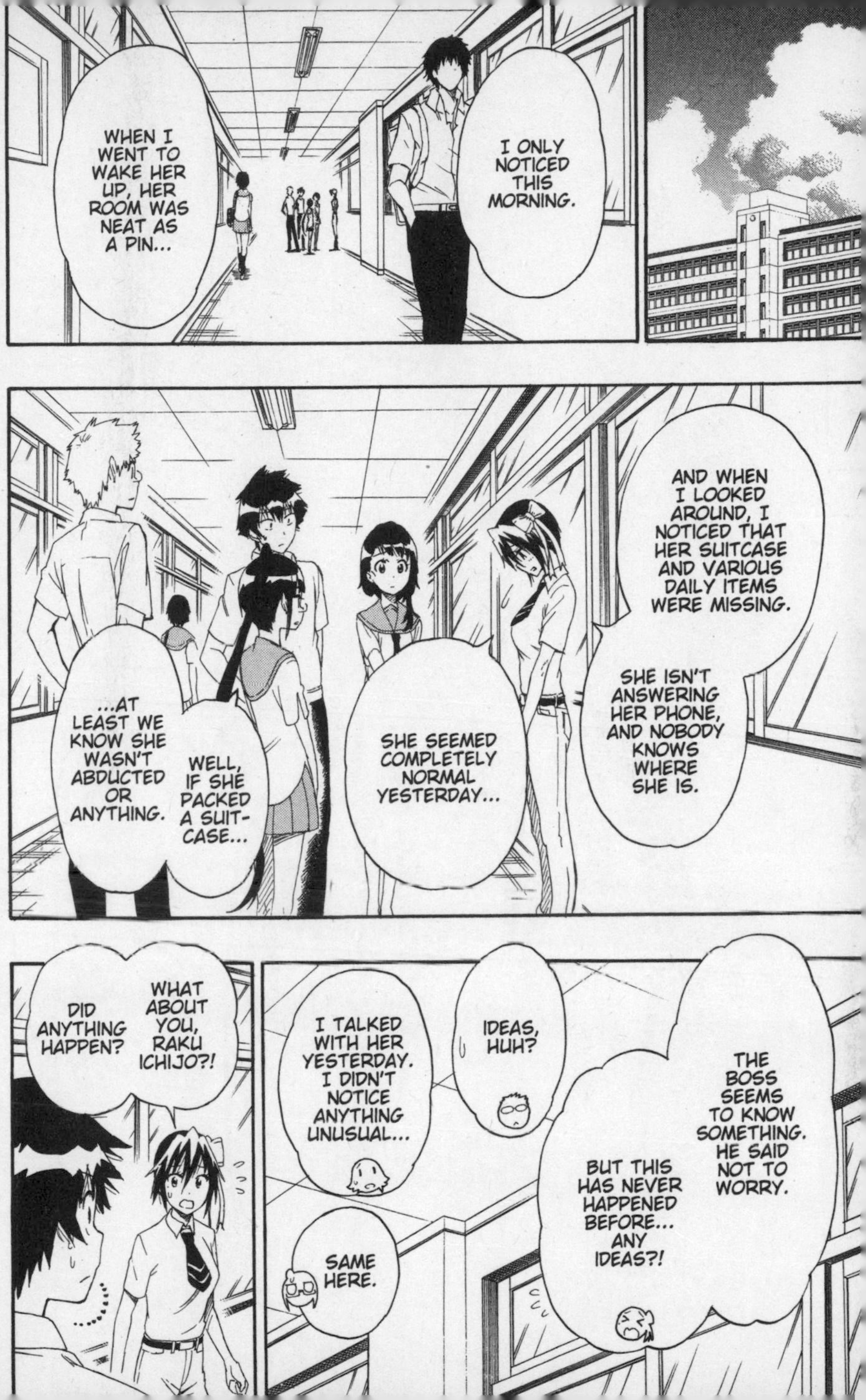
I ONLY NOTICED THIS MORNING.
WHEN I WENT TO WAKE HER UP, HER ROOM WAS NEAT AS A PIN...
AND WHEN I LOOKED AROUND, I NOTICED THAT HER SUITCASE AND VARIOUS DAILY ITEMS WERE MISSING.
SHE ISN'T ANSWERING HER PHONE, AND NOBODY KNOWS WHERE SHE IS.
SHE SEEMED COMPLETELY NORMAL YESTERDAY...
WELL, IF SHE PACKED A SUIT-CASE...
...AT LEAST WE KNOW SHE WASN'T ABDUCTED OR ANYTHING.
THE BOSS SEEMS TO KNOW SOMETHING. HE SAID NOT TO WORRY.
BUT THIS HAS NEVER HAPPENED BEFORE... ANY IDEAS?!
IDEAS, HUH?
I TALKED WITH HER YESTERDAY. I DIDN'T NOTICE ANYTHING UNUSUAL...
SAME HERE.
WHAT ABOUT YOU, RAKU ICHIJO?!
DID ANYTHING HAPPEN?
...

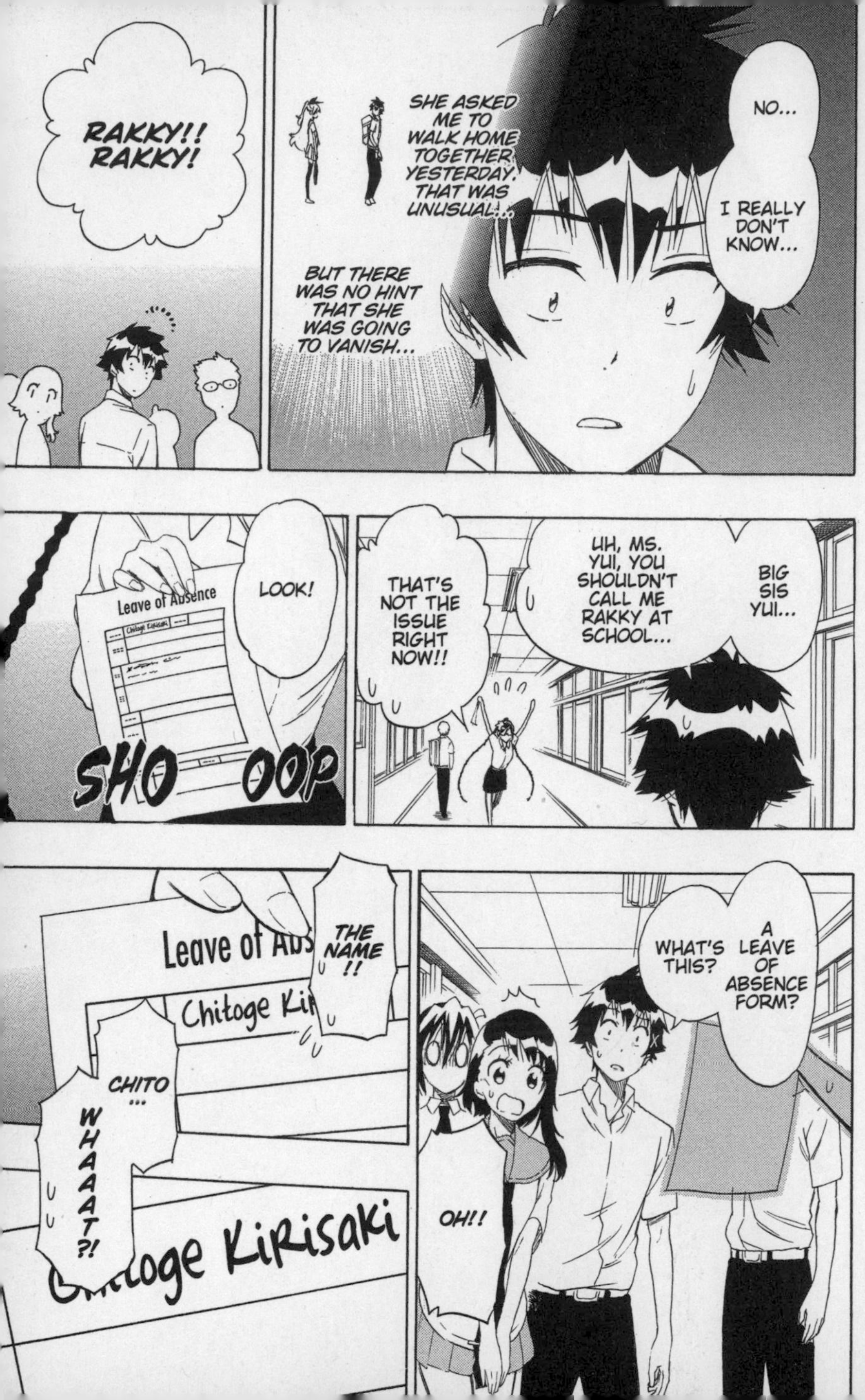
NO...
I REALLY DON'T KNOW...
SHE ASKED ME TO WALK HOME TOGETHER YESTERDAY. THAT WAS UNUSUAL...
BUT THERE WAS NO HINT THAT SHE WAS GOING TO VANISH...
RAKKY!! RAKKY!
BIG SIS YUI...
UH, MS. YUI, YOU SHOULDN'T CALL ME RAKKY AT SCHOOL...
THAT'S NOT THE ISSUE RIGHT NOW!!
LOOK!
Leave of Absence
Chitoge Kirisaki
SHO OOP
A LEAVE OF ABSENCE FORM?
WHAT'S THIS?
OH!!
THE NAME!!
Leave of Abs
Chitoge Ki
CHITO...
WHAAAAT?!
Chitoge Kirisaki

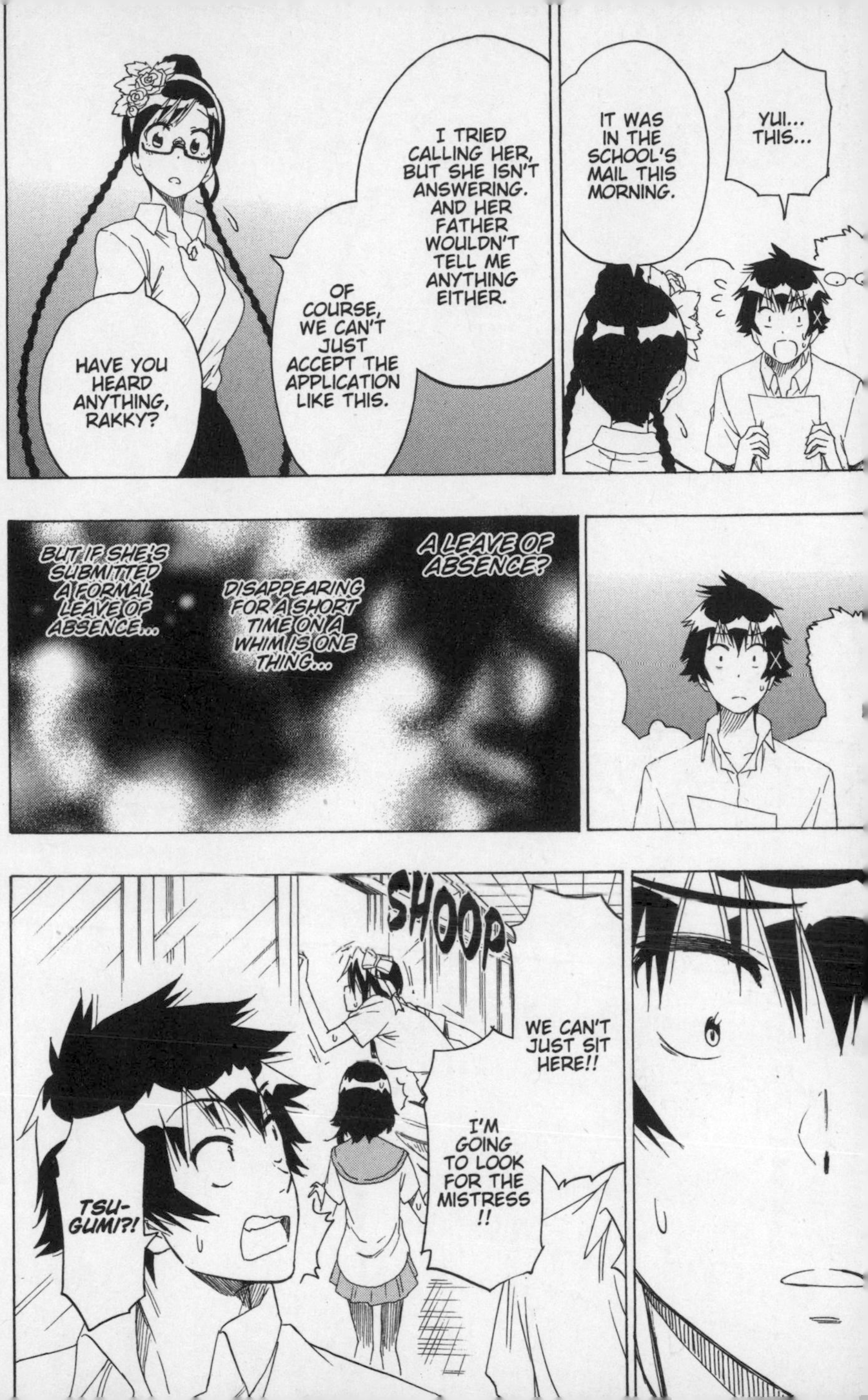
YUI... THIS...
IT WAS IN THE SCHOOL'S MAIL THIS MORNING.
I TRIED CALLING HER, BUT SHE ISN'T ANSWERING. AND HER FATHER WOULDN'T TELL ME ANYTHING EITHER.
OF COURSE, WE CAN'T JUST ACCEPT THE APPLICATION LIKE THIS.
HAVE YOU HEARD ANYTHING, RAKKY?
A LEAVE OF ABSENCE?
DISAPPEARING FOR A SHORT TIME ON A WHIM IS ONE THING...
BUT IF SHE'S SUBMITTED A FORMAL LEAVE OF ABSENCE...
SHOOP
WE CAN'T JUST SIT HERE!!
I'M GOING TO LOOK FOR THE MISTRESS!!
TSU-GUMI?!

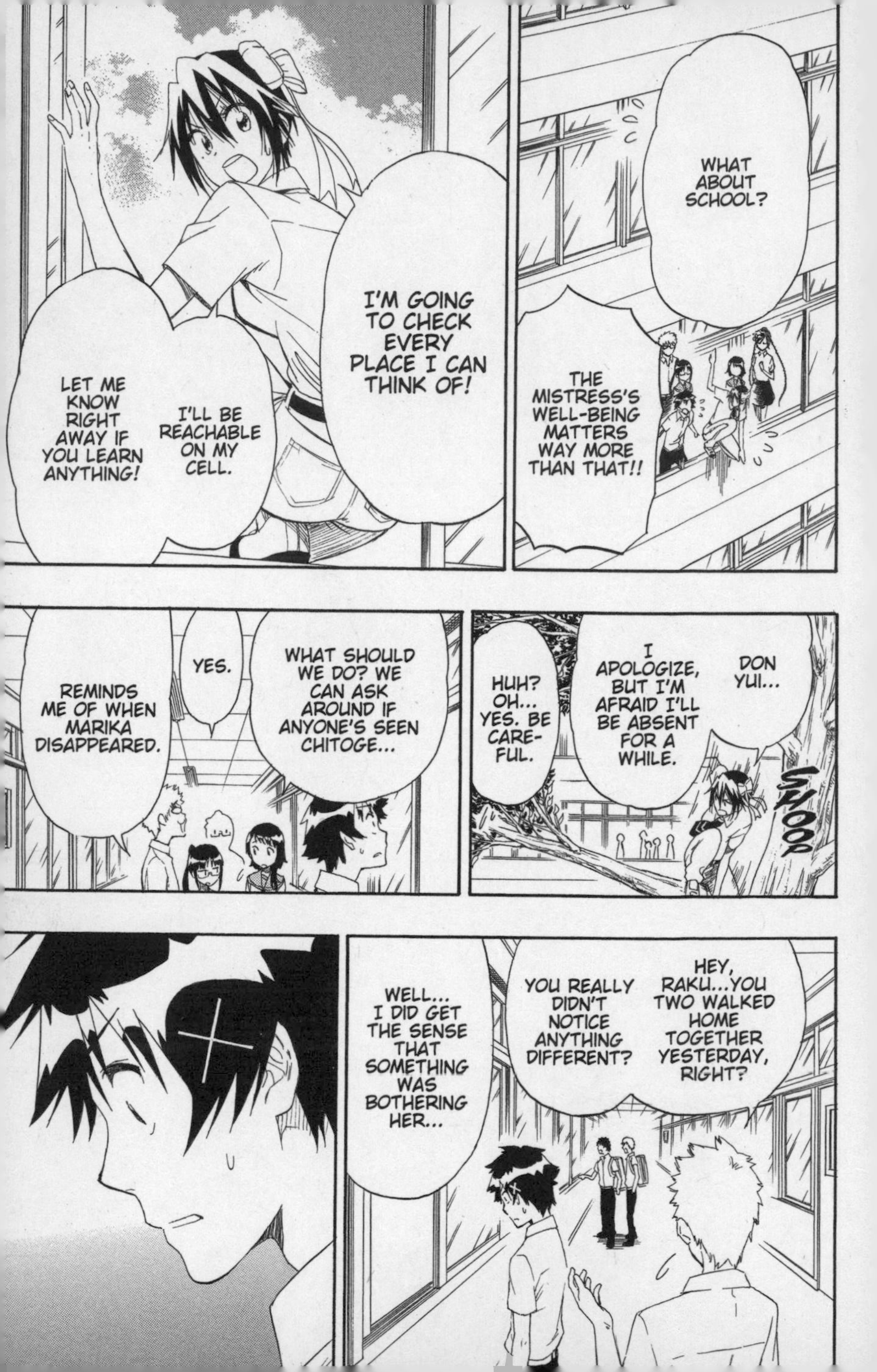
WHAT ABOUT SCHOOL?
THE MISTRESS'S WELL-BEING MATTERS WAY MORE THAN THAT!!
I'M GOING TO CHECK EVERY PLACE I CAN THINK OF!
I'LL BE REACHABLE ON MY CELL.
LET ME KNOW RIGHT AWAY IF YOU LEARN ANYTHING!
DON YUI...
I APOLOGIZE, BUT I'M AFRAID I'LL BE ABSENT FOR A WHILE.
SWOOP
HUH? OH... YES. BE CARE-FUL.
WHAT SHOULD WE DO? WE CAN ASK AROUND IF ANYONE'S SEEN CHITOGE...
YES.
REMINDS ME OF WHEN MARIKA DISAPPEARED.
HEY, RAKU...YOU TWO WALKED HOME TOGETHER YESTERDAY, RIGHT?
YOU REALLY DIDN'T NOTICE ANYTHING DIFFERENT?
WELL... I DID GET THE SENSE THAT SOMETHING WAS BOTHERING HER...

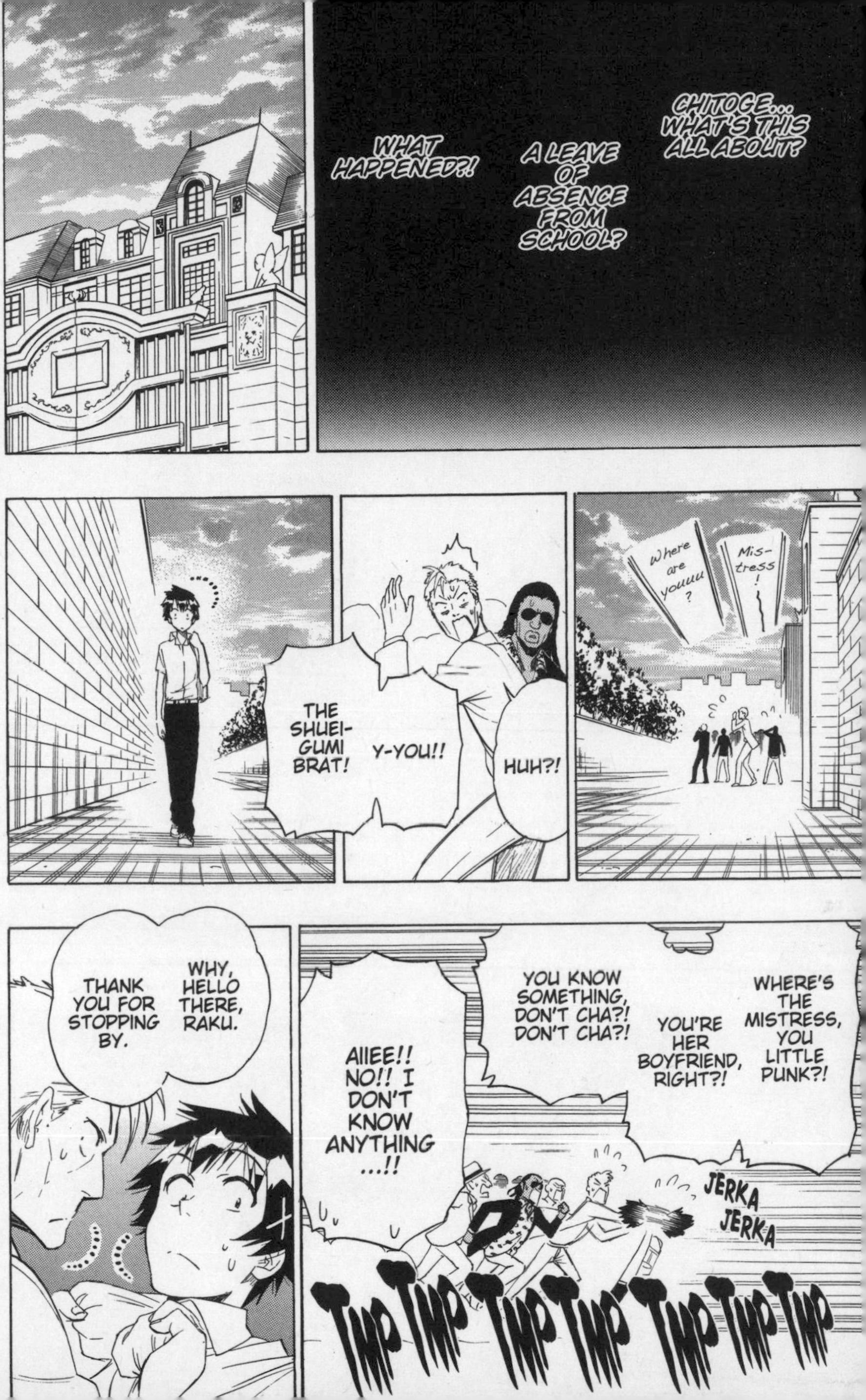
CHITOGE... WHAT'S THIS ALL ABOUT?
A LEAVE OF ABSENCE FROM SCHOOL?
WHAT HAPPENED?!
Mis-tress!
Where are youuu?
HUH?!
Y-YOU!!
THE SHUEI-GUMI BRAT!
WHERE'S THE MISTRESS, YOU LITTLE PUNK?!
YOU'RE HER BOYFRIEND, RIGHT?!
YOU KNOW SOMETHING, DON'T CHA?! DON'T CHA?!
AIIEE!! NO!! I DON'T KNOW ANYTHING...!!
JERKA JERKA
TMP TMP TMP TMP TMP TMP TMP
WHY, HELLO THERE, RAKU.
THANK YOU FOR STOPPING BY.

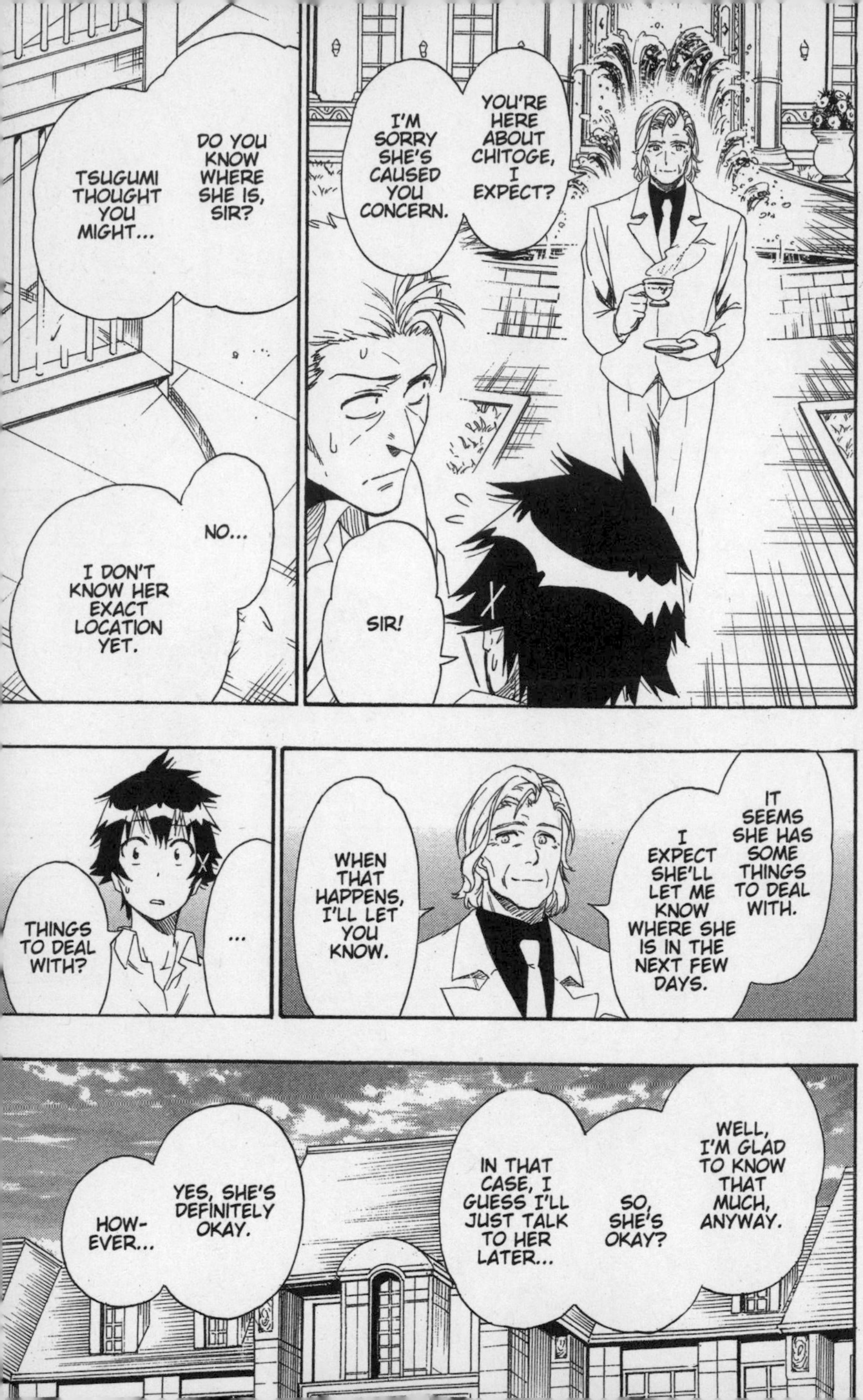
YOU'RE HERE ABOUT CHITOGE, I EXPECT?
I'M SORRY SHE'S CAUSED YOU CONCERN.
SIR!
DO YOU KNOW WHERE SHE IS, SIR?
TSUGUMI THOUGHT YOU MIGHT...
NO...
I DON'T KNOW HER EXACT LOCATION YET.
IT SEEMS SHE HAS SOME THINGS TO DEAL WITH.
I EXPECT SHE'LL LET ME KNOW WHERE SHE IS IN THE NEXT FEW DAYS.
WHEN THAT HAPPENS, I'LL LET YOU KNOW.
...
THINGS TO DEAL WITH?
WELL, I'M GLAD TO KNOW THAT MUCH, ANYWAY.
SO, SHE'S OKAY?
IN THAT CASE, I GUESS I'LL JUST TALK TO HER LATER...
YES, SHE'S DEFINITELY OKAY.
HOW-EVER...

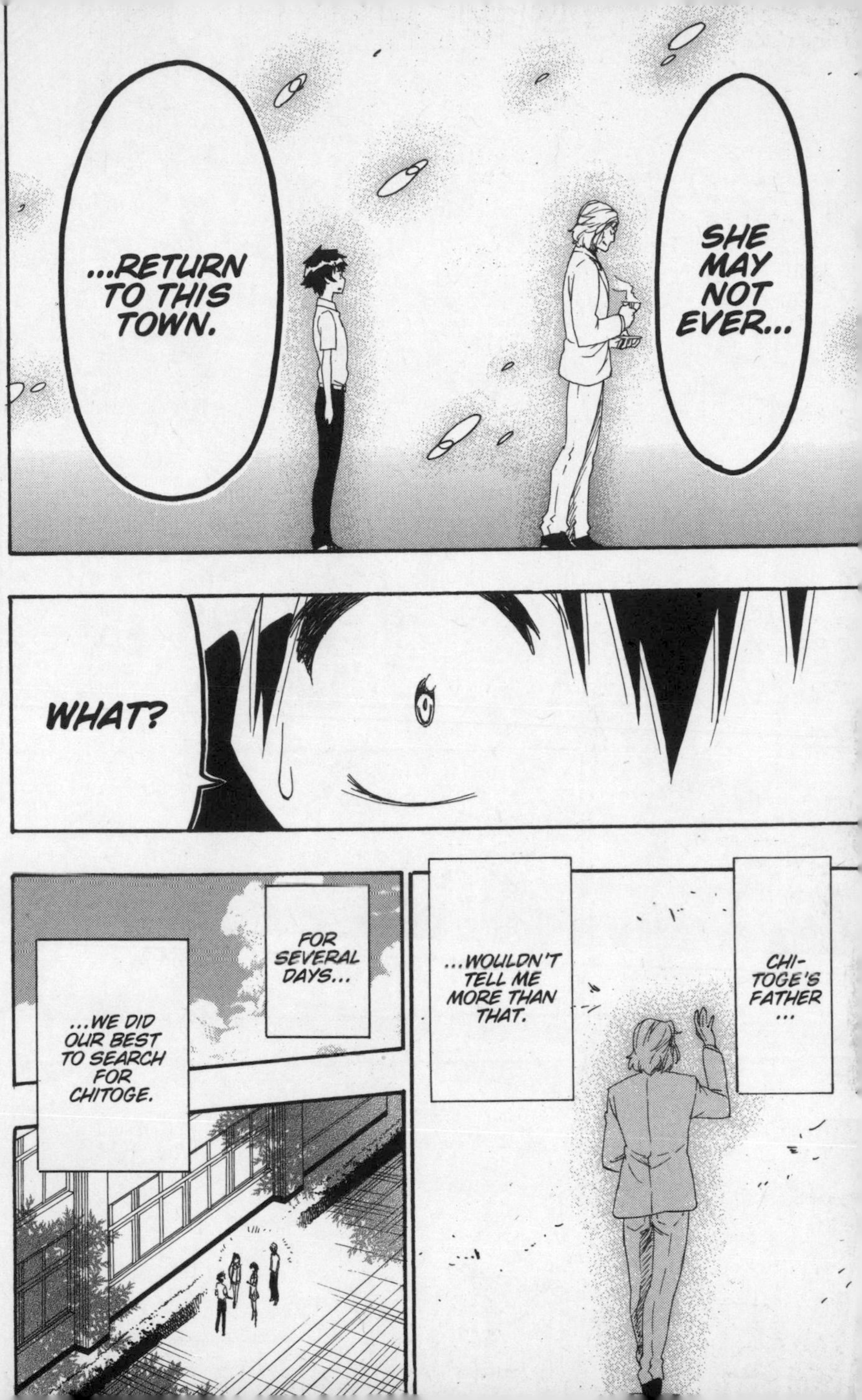
SHE MAY NOT EVER...
...RETURN TO THIS TOWN.
WHAT?
CHI-TOGE'S FATHER...
...WOULDN'T TELL ME MORE THAN THAT.
FOR SEVERAL DAYS...
...WE DID OUR BEST TO SEARCH FOR CHITOGE.

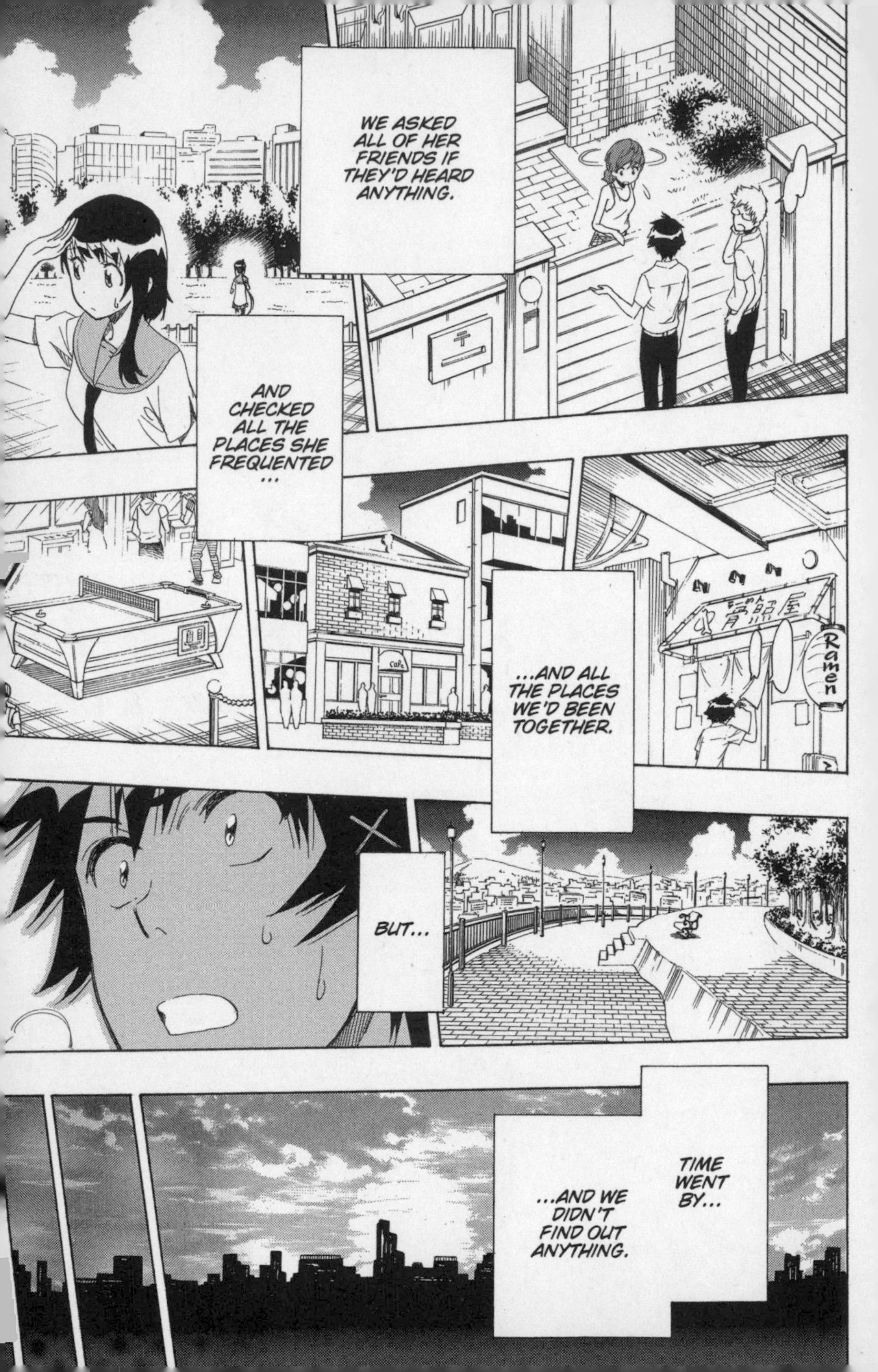
WE ASKED ALL OF HER FRIENDS IF THEY'D HEARD ANYTHING.
AND CHECKED ALL THE PLACES SHE FREQUENTED ...
Ramen
...AND ALL THE PLACES WE'D BEEN TOGETHER.
BUT...
TIME WENT BY...
...AND WE DIDN'T FIND OUT ANYTHING.

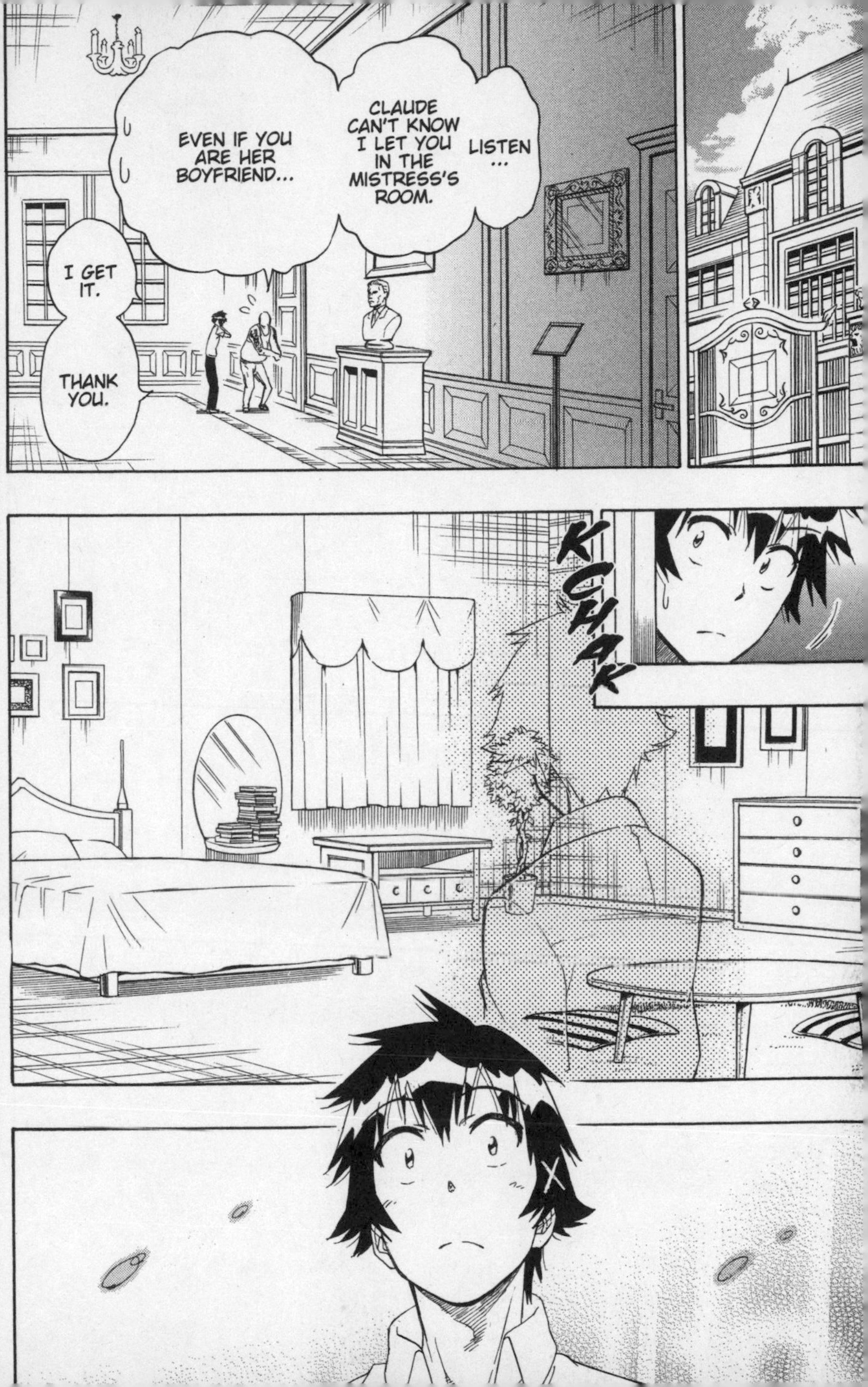
LISTEN ...
CLAUDE CAN'T KNOW I LET YOU IN THE MISTRESS'S ROOM.
EVEN IF YOU ARE HER BOYFRIEND...
I GET IT.
THANK YOU.
KCHAK

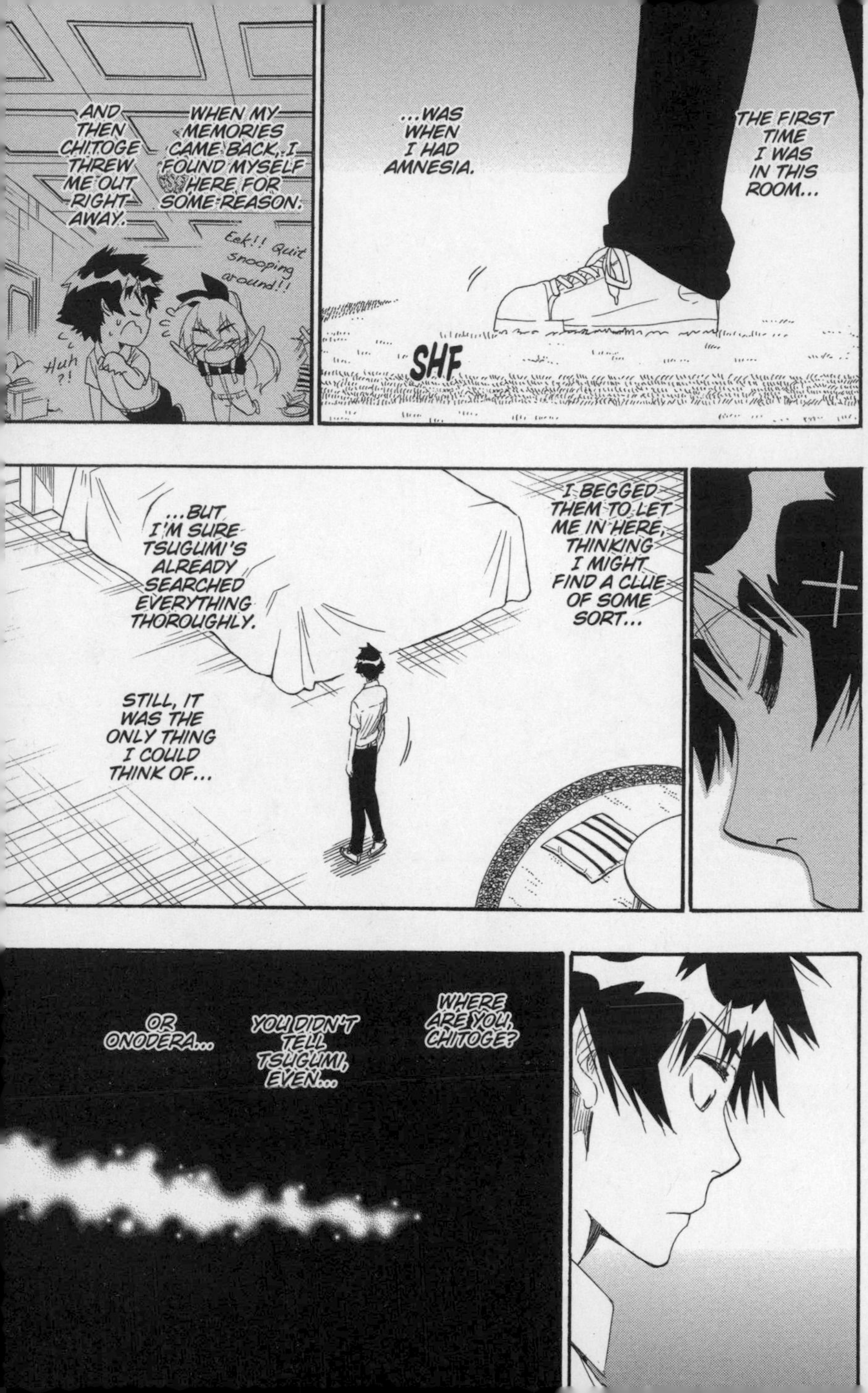
THE FIRST TIME I WAS IN THIS ROOM...
...WAS WHEN I HAD AMNESIA.
SHF
WHEN MY MEMORIES CAME BACK, I FOUND MYSELF HERE FOR SOME REASON.
AND THEN CHITOGE THREW ME OUT RIGHT AWAY.
Eek!! Quit snooping around!!
Huh?!
I BEGGED THEM TO LET ME IN HERE, THINKING I MIGHT FIND A CLUE OF SOME SORT...
...BUT I'M SURE TSUGUMI'S ALREADY SEARCHED EVERYTHING THOROUGHLY.
STILL, IT WAS THE ONLY THING I COULD THINK OF...
WHERE ARE YOU, CHITOGE?
YOU DIDN'T TELL TSUGUMI, EVEN...
OR ONODERA...

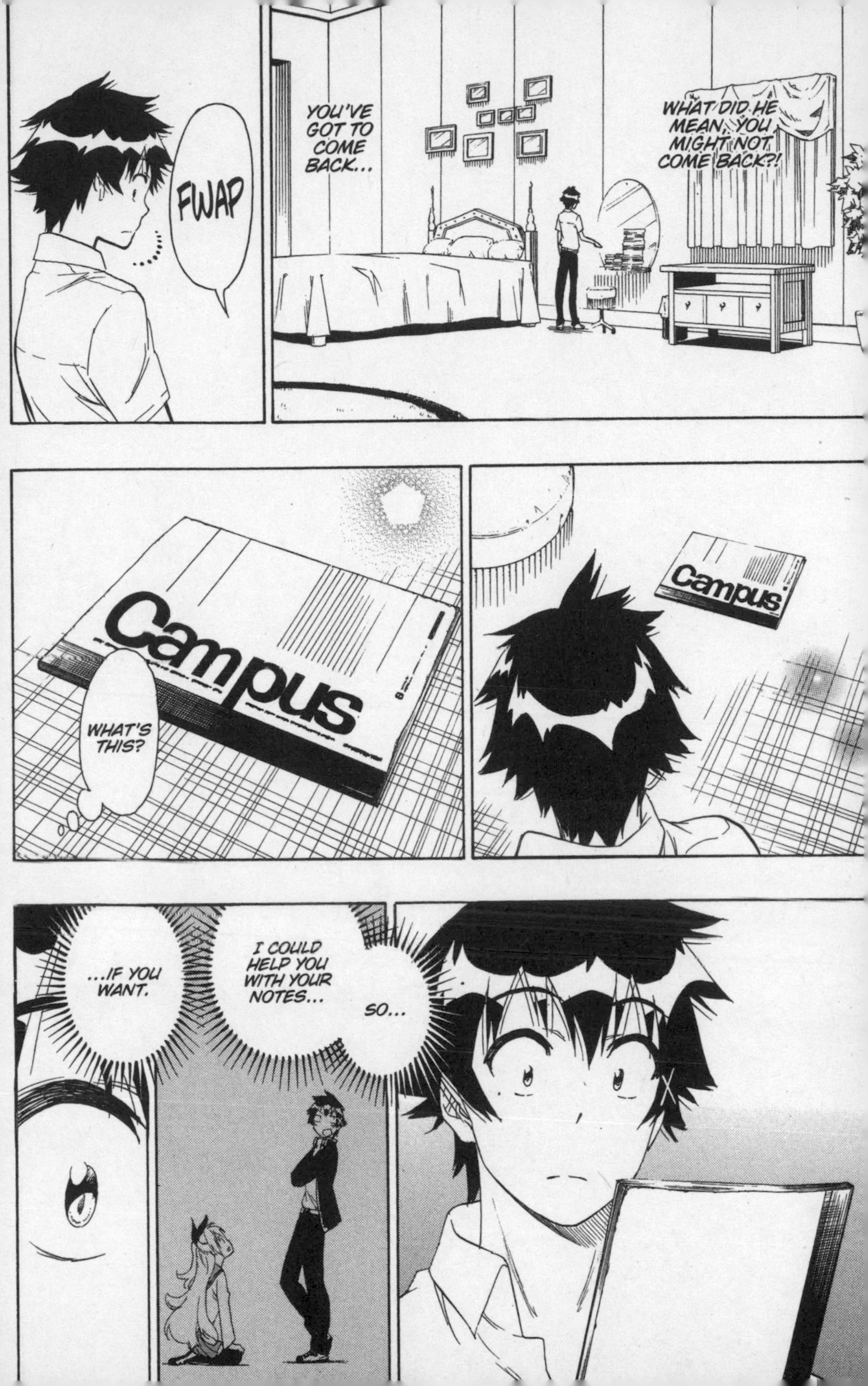
WHAT DID HE MEAN, YOU MIGHT NOT COME BACK?!
YOU'VE GOT TO COME BACK...
FWAP
...
WHAT'S THIS?
SO...
I COULD HELP YOU WITH YOUR NOTES...
...IF YOU WANT.

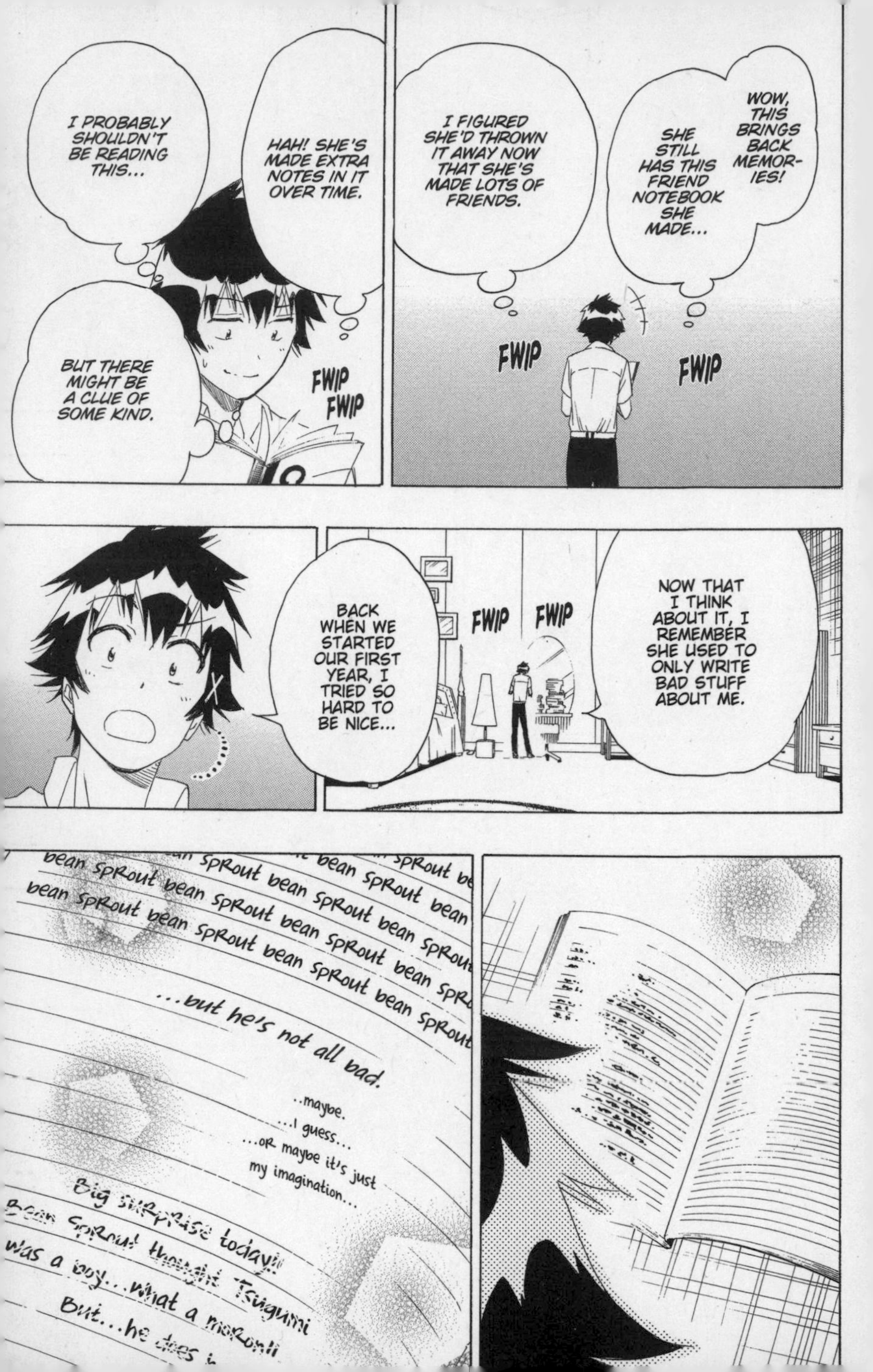
WOW, THIS BRINGS BACK MEMORIES!
SHE STILL HAS THIS FRIEND NOTEBOOK SHE MADE...
I FIGURED SHE'D THROWN IT AWAY NOW THAT SHE'S MADE LOTS OF FRIENDS.
FWIP
FWIP
HAH! SHE'S MADE EXTRA NOTES IN IT OVER TIME.
I PROBABLY SHOULDN'T BE READING THIS...
FWIP FWIP
BUT THERE MIGHT BE A CLUE OF SOME KIND.
NOW THAT I THINK ABOUT IT, I REMEMBER SHE USED TO ONLY WRITE BAD STUFF ABOUT ME.
FWIP
FWIP
BACK WHEN WE STARTED OUR FIRST YEAR, I TRIED SO HARD TO BE NICE...
bean sprout bean sprout bean
bean sprout bean sprout bean sprout
bean sprout bean sprout bean sprout bean sprout
...but he's not all bad.
..maybe.
...I guess...
...or maybe it's just my imagination...
Big surprise today!
Bean Sprout thought Tsugumi was a boy...what a moron!!
But...he does

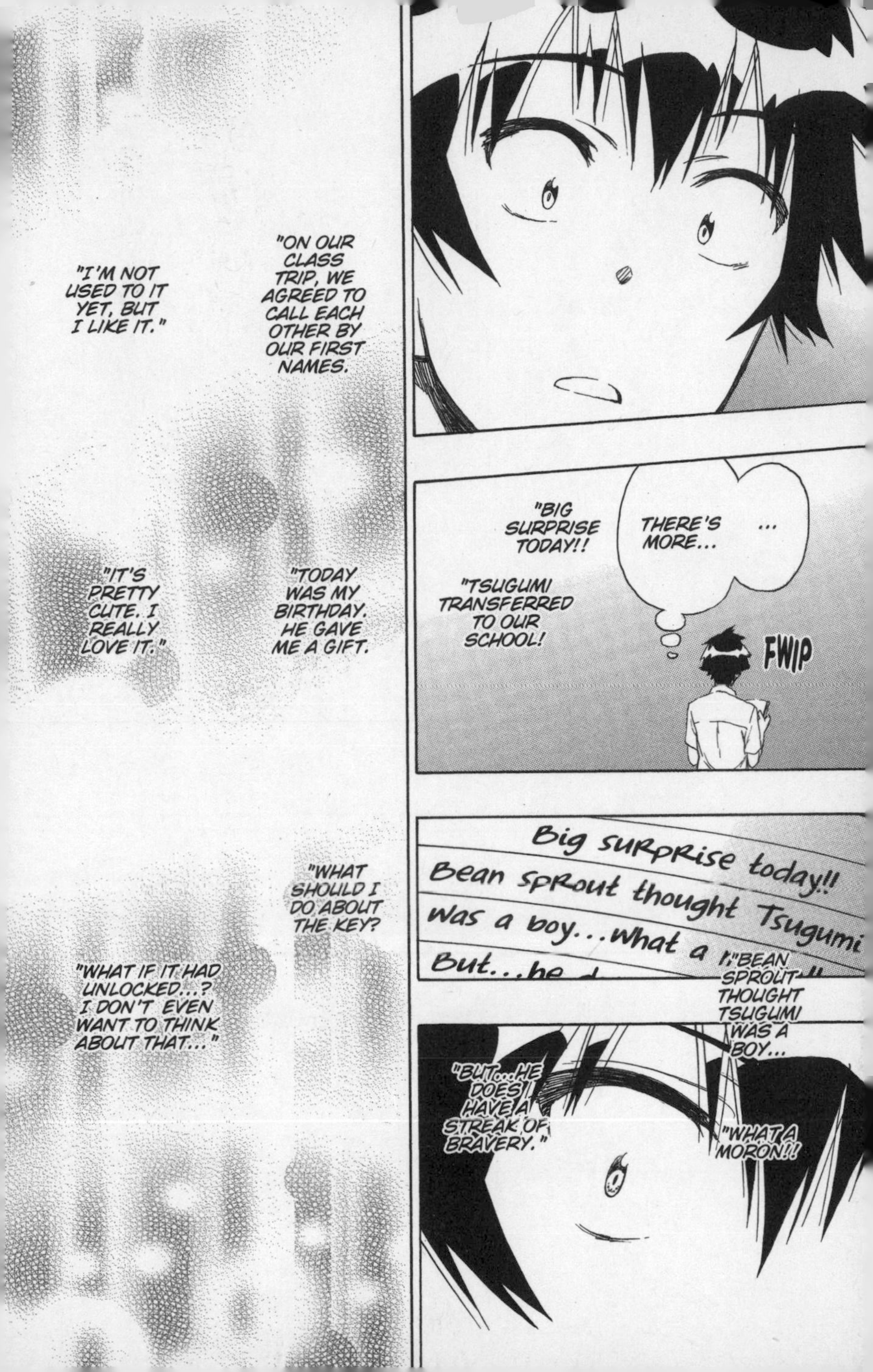
THERE'S MORE...
...
"BIG SURPRISE TODAY!!
"TSUGUMI TRANSFERRED TO OUR SCHOOL!
FWIP
Big surprise today!!
Bean sprout thought Tsugumi
was a boy...what a
But...he
"BEAN SPROUT THOUGHT TSUGUMI WAS A BOY...
"WHAT A MORON!!
"BUT...HE DOES HAVE A STREAK OF BRAVERY."
"ON OUR CLASS TRIP, WE AGREED TO CALL EACH OTHER BY OUR FIRST NAMES.
"I'M NOT USED TO IT YET, BUT I LIKE IT."
"TODAY WAS MY BIRTHDAY. HE GAVE ME A GIFT.
"IT'S PRETTY CUTE. I REALLY LOVE IT."
"WHAT SHOULD I DO ABOUT THE KEY?
"WHAT IF IT HAD UNLOCKED...? I DON'T EVEN WANT TO THINK ABOUT THAT..."

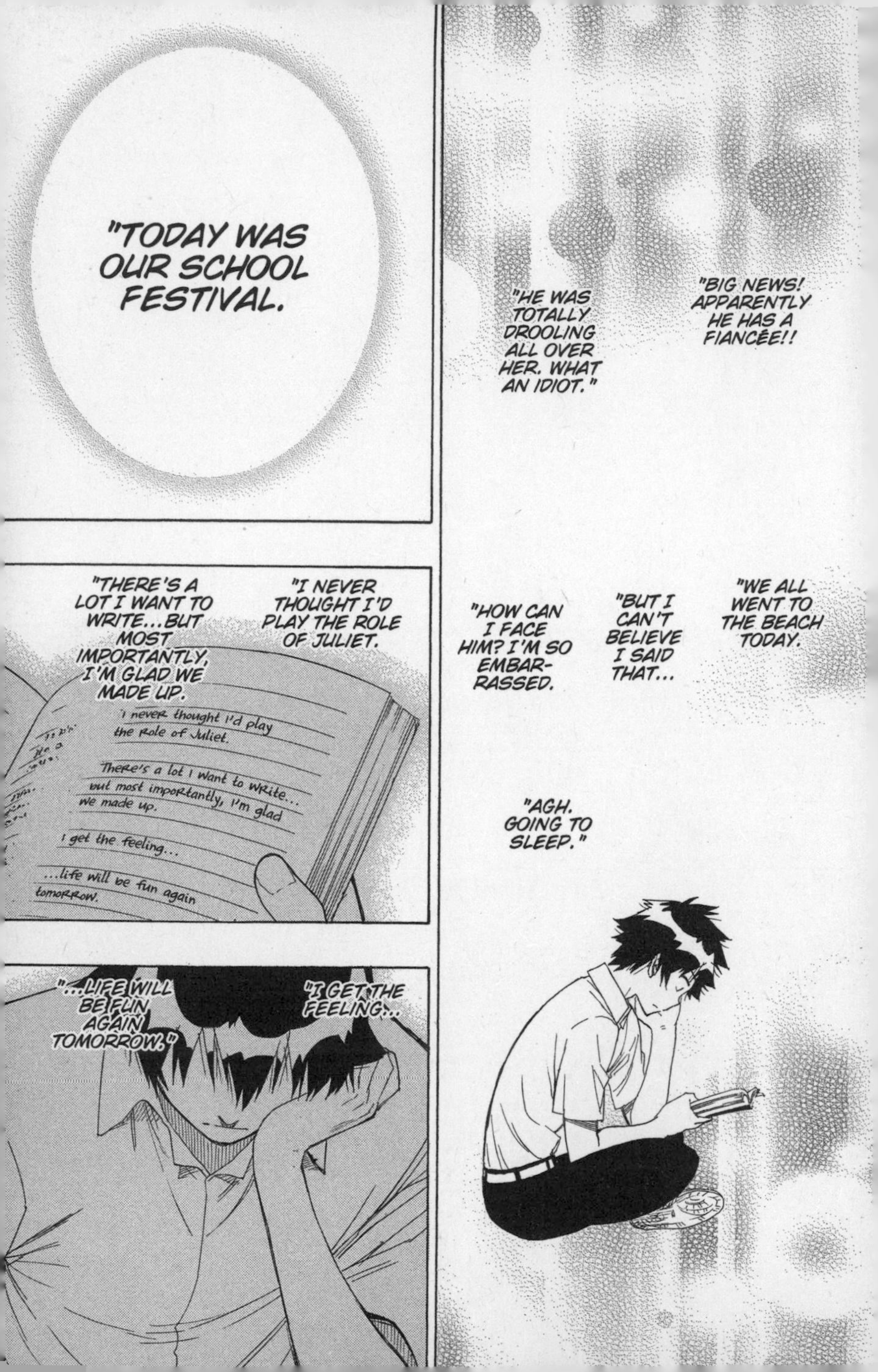
"BIG NEWS! APPARENTLY HE HAS A FIANCÉE!!
"HE WAS TOTALLY DROOLING ALL OVER HER. WHAT AN IDIOT."
"WE ALL WENT TO THE BEACH TODAY.
"BUT I CAN'T BELIEVE I SAID THAT...
"HOW CAN I FACE HIM? I'M SO EMBARRASSED.
"AGH. GOING TO SLEEP."
"TODAY WAS OUR SCHOOL FESTIVAL.
"I NEVER THOUGHT I'D PLAY THE ROLE OF JULIET.
"THERE'S A LOT I WANT TO WRITE...BUT MOST IMPORTANTLY, I'M GLAD WE MADE UP.
I never thought I'd play the Role of Juliet.
There's a lot I want to write... but most importantly, I'm glad we made up.
I get the feeling...
...life will be fun again tomorrow.
"I GET THE FEELING...
"...LIFE WILL BE FUN AGAIN TOMORROW."

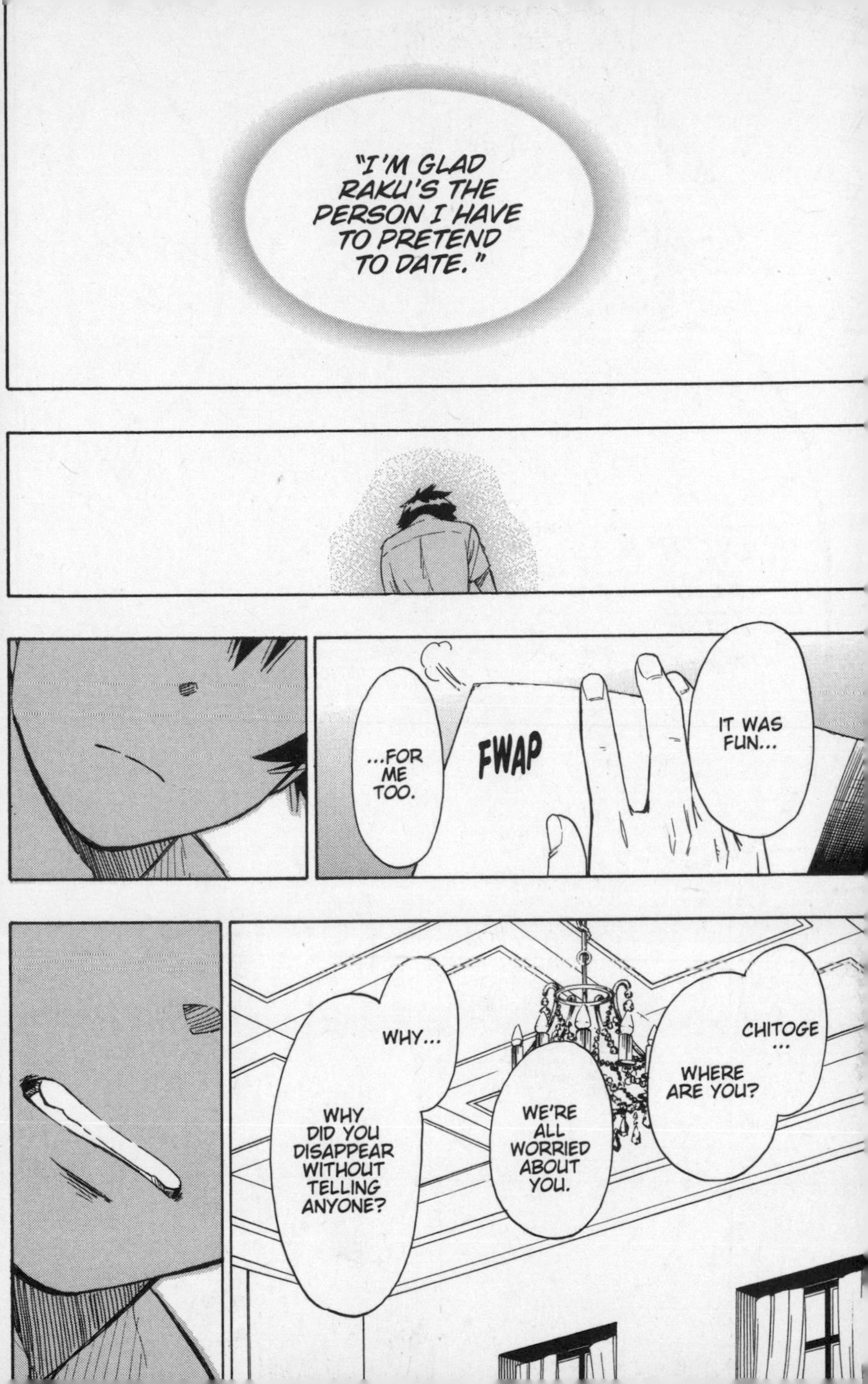
"I'M GLAD RAKU'S THE PERSON I HAVE TO PRETEND TO DATE."
IT WAS FUN...
FWAP
...FOR ME TOO.
CHITOGE... WHERE ARE YOU?
WE'RE ALL WORRIED ABOUT YOU.
WHY... WHY DID YOU DISAPPEAR WITHOUT TELLING ANYONE?

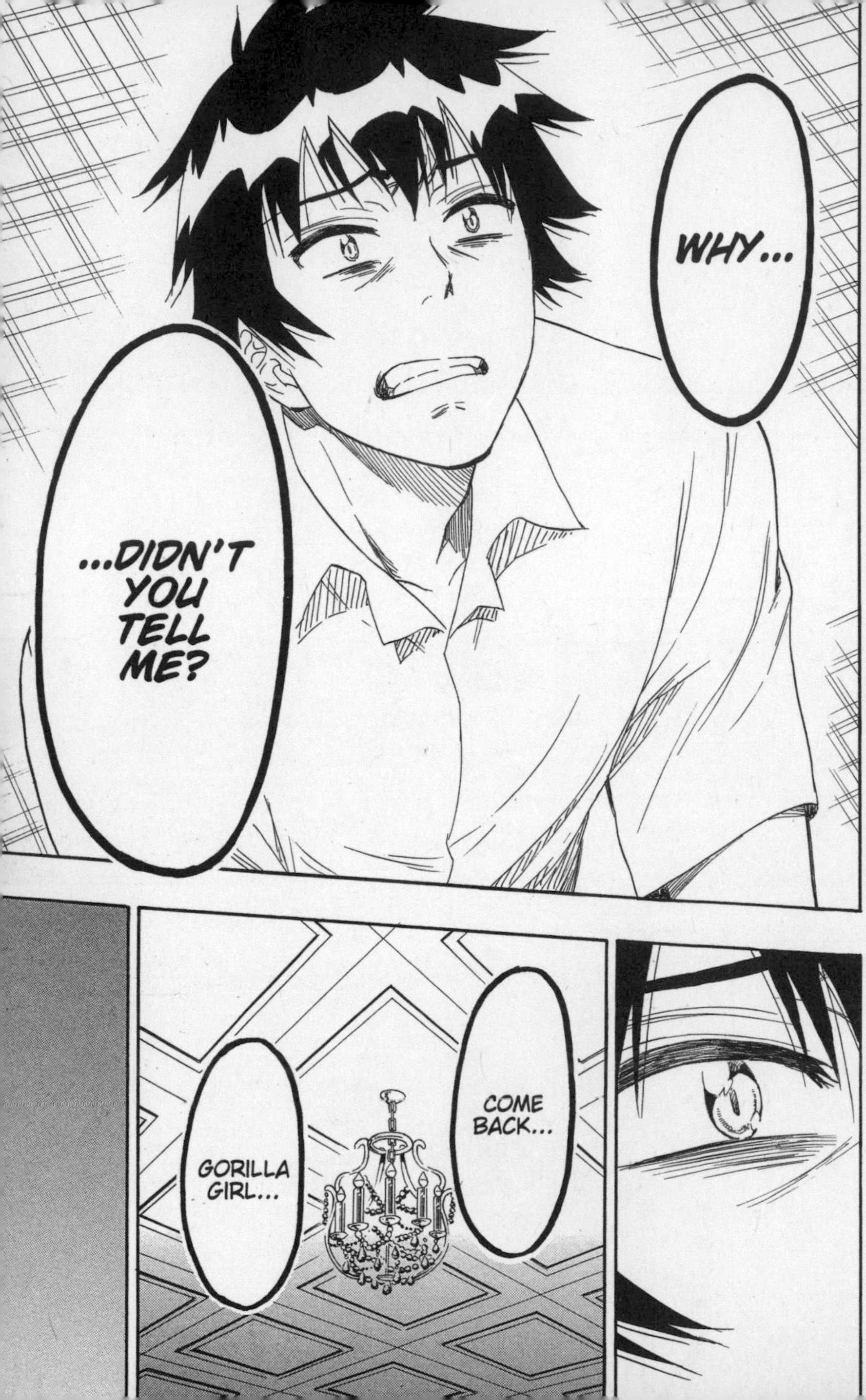
WHY...
...DIDN'T YOU TELL ME?
COME BACK...
GORILLA GIRL...

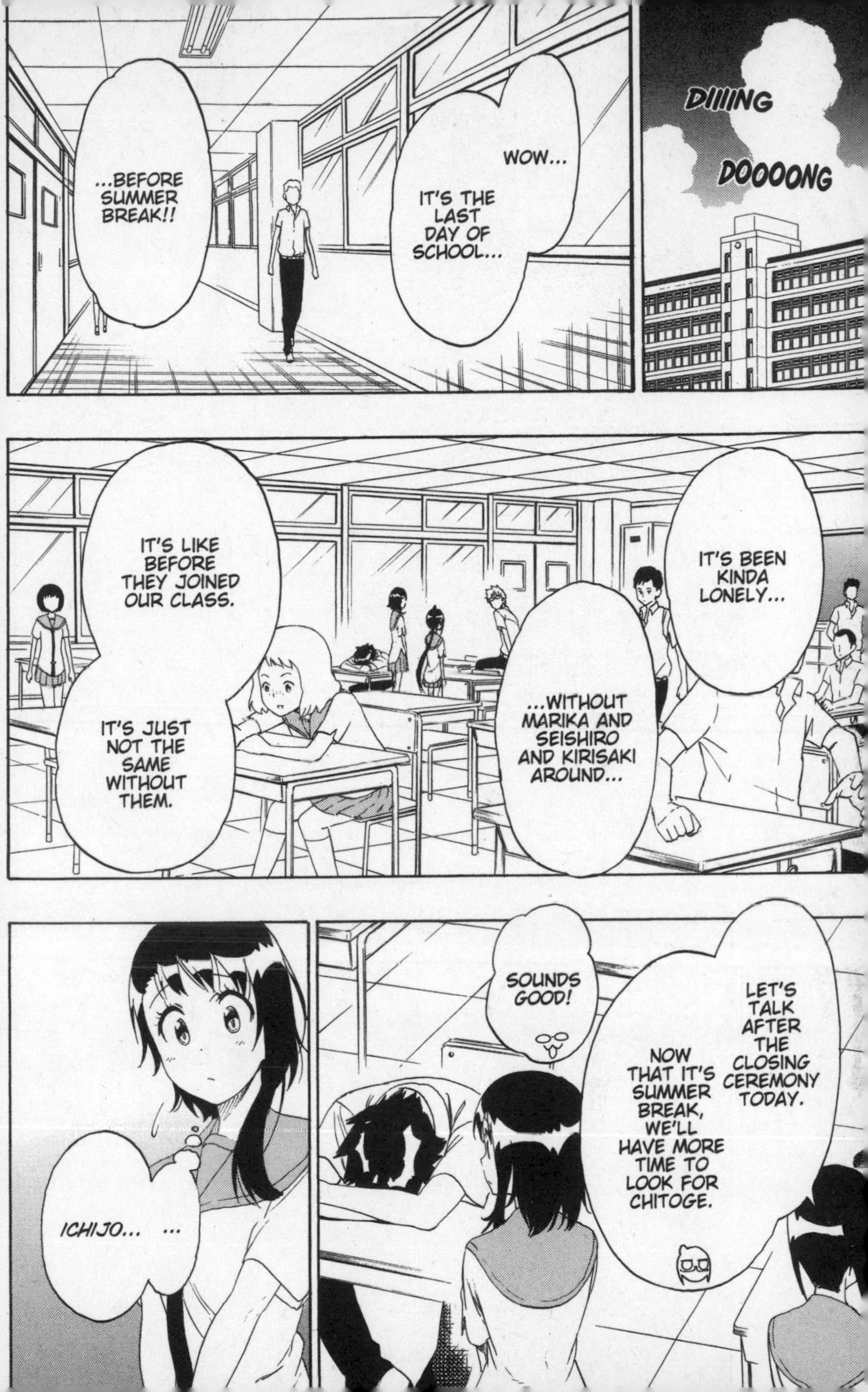
DIIING
DOOOONG
WOW... IT'S THE LAST DAY OF SCHOOL...
...BEFORE SUMMER BREAK!!
IT'S BEEN KINDA LONELY...
...WITHOUT MARIKA AND SEISHIRO AND KIRISAKI AROUND...
IT'S LIKE BEFORE THEY JOINED OUR CLASS.
IT'S JUST NOT THE SAME WITHOUT THEM.
LET'S TALK AFTER THE CLOSING CEREMONY TODAY.
NOW THAT IT'S SUMMER BREAK, WE'LL HAVE MORE TIME TO LOOK FOR CHITOGE.
SOUNDS GOOD!
ICHIJO... ...

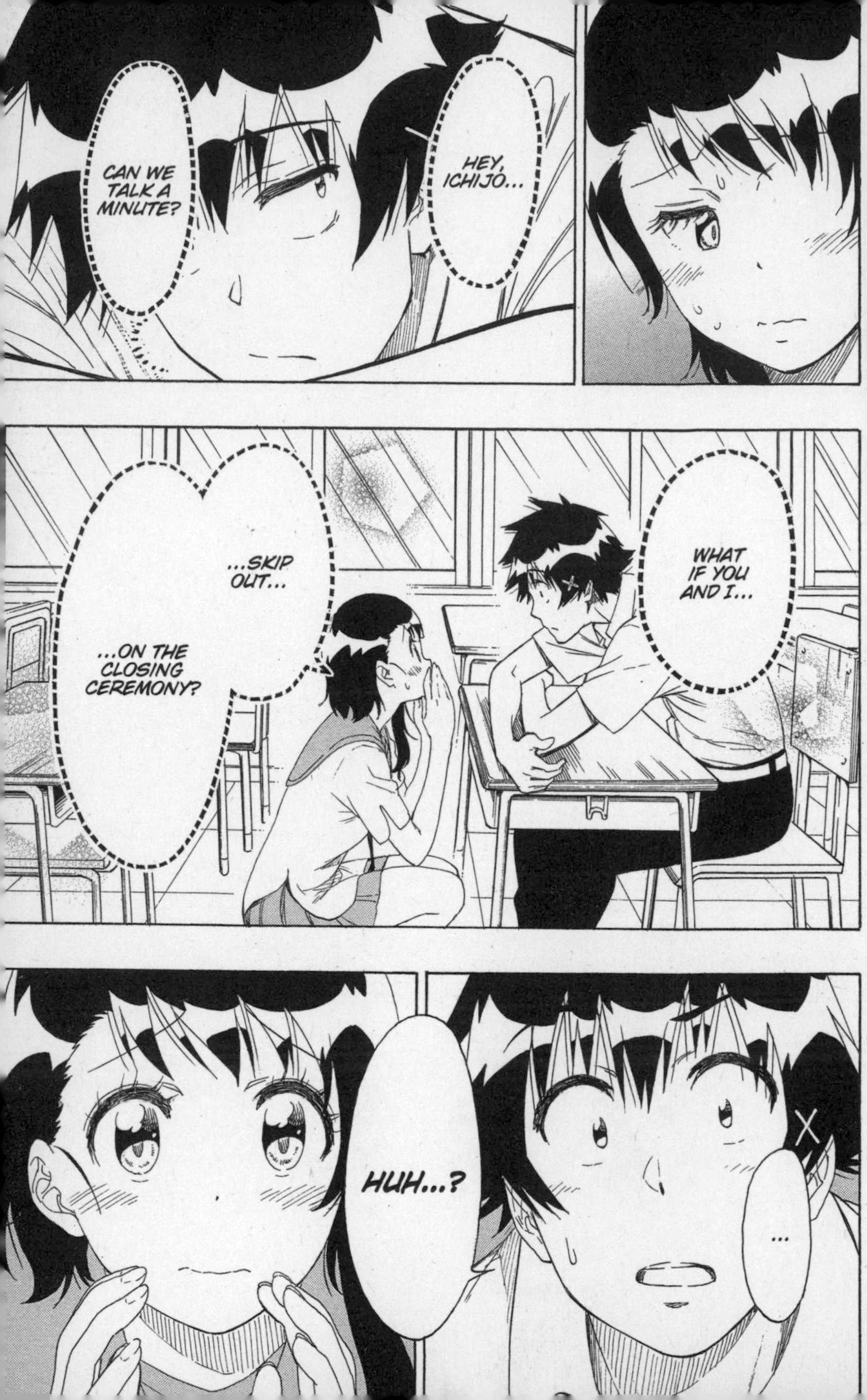
HEY, ICHIJO...
CAN WE TALK A MINUTE?
WHAT IF YOU AND I...
...SKIP OUT...
...ON THE CLOSING CEREMONY?
...
HUH...?

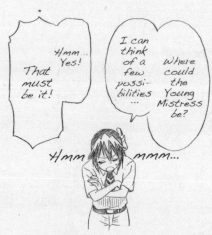

Where could the Young Mistress be?
I can think of a few possi-bilities...
Hmm... Yes!
That must be it!
Hmm mmm...

Where does Tsugumi think Chitoge is? Find out at the end of the next chapter!

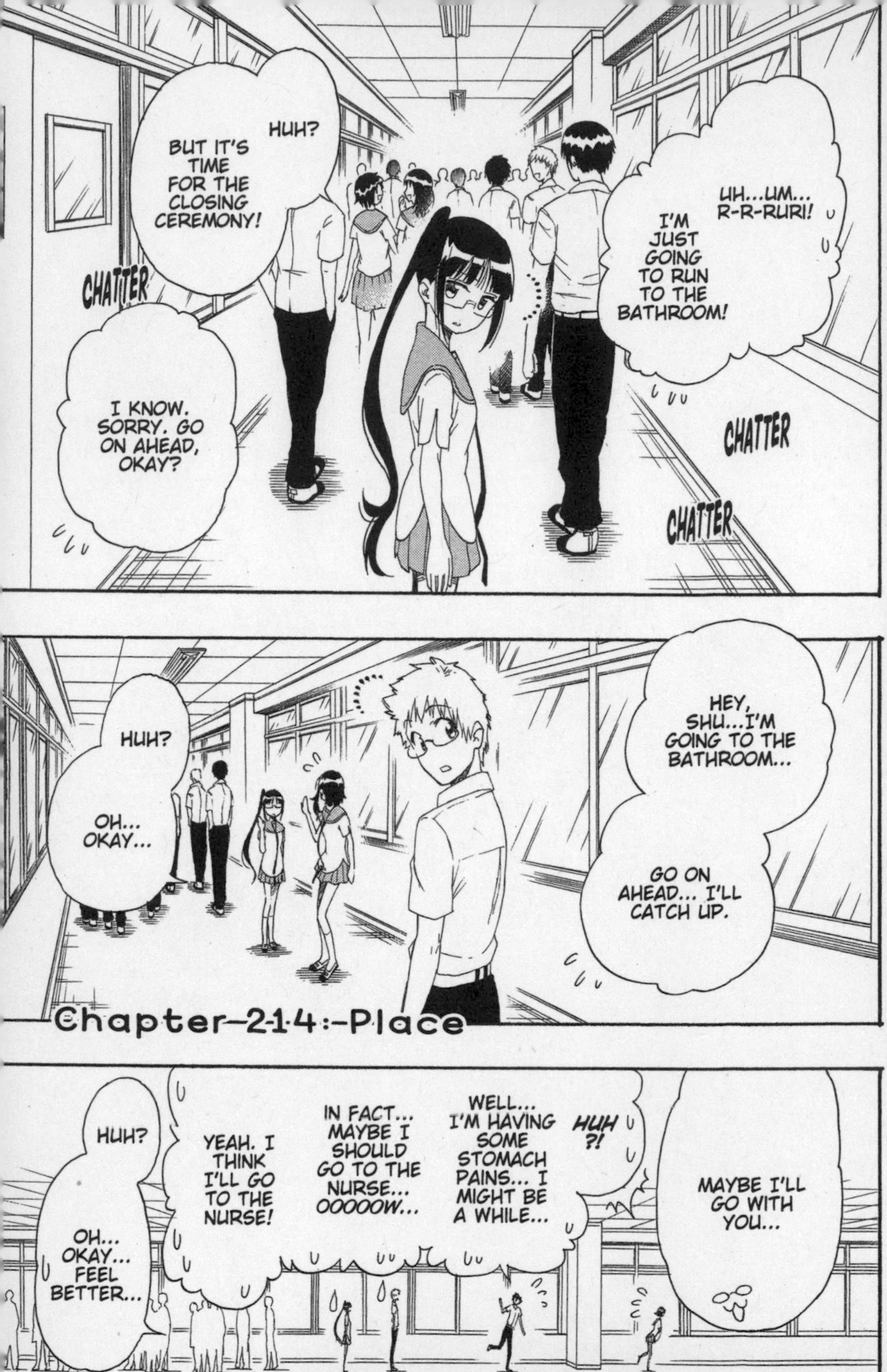
UH...UM... R-R-RURI!
I'M JUST GOING TO RUN TO THE BATHROOM!
CHATTER
CHATTER
HUH?
BUT IT'S TIME FOR THE CLOSING CEREMONY!
CHATTER
I KNOW. SORRY. GO ON AHEAD, OKAY?
HEY, SHU...I'M GOING TO THE BATHROOM...
GO ON AHEAD... I'LL CATCH UP.
HUH?
OH... OKAY...
Chapter 214: Place
MAYBE I'LL GO WITH YOU...
HUH ?!
WELL... I'M HAVING SOME STOMACH PAINS... I MIGHT BE A WHILE...
IN FACT... MAYBE I SHOULD GO TO THE NURSE... OOOOOW...
YEAH. I THINK I'LL GO TO THE NURSE!
HUH?
OH... OKAY... FEEL BETTER...

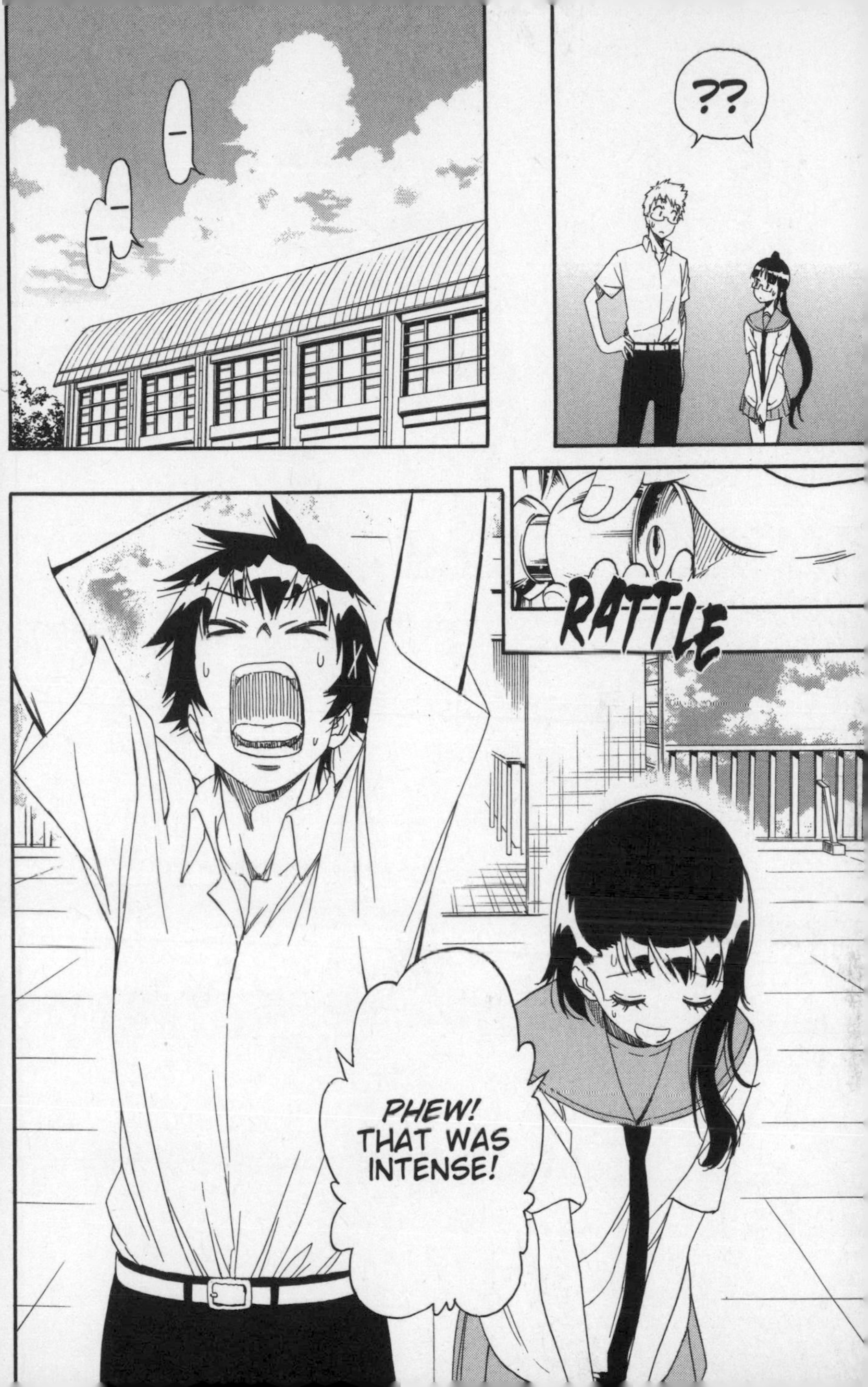
??
—
—
—
RATTLE
PHEW! THAT WAS INTENSE!

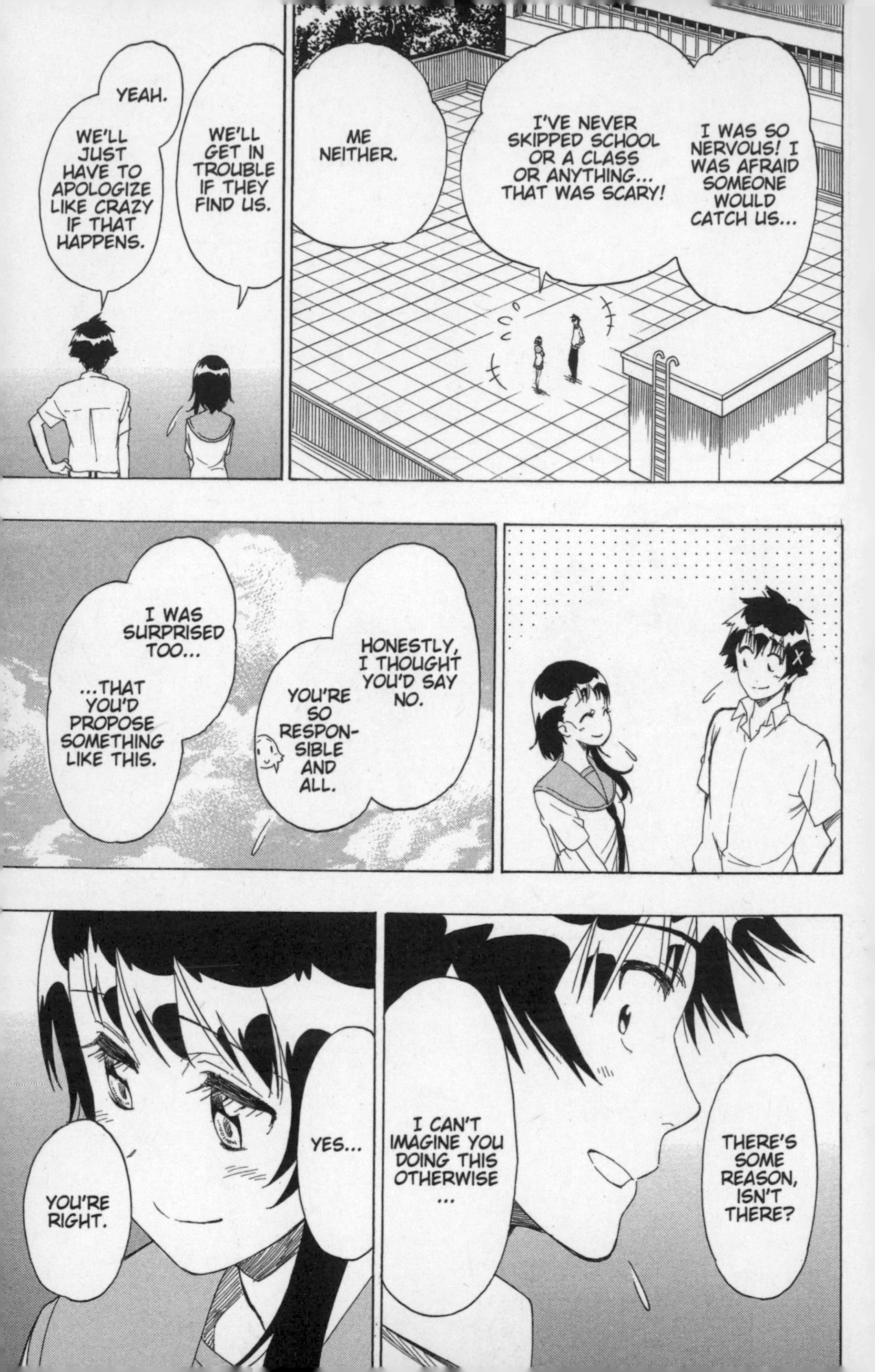
I WAS SO NERVOUS! I WAS AFRAID SOMEONE WOULD CATCH US...
I'VE NEVER SKIPPED SCHOOL OR A CLASS OR ANYTHING... THAT WAS SCARY!
ME NEITHER.
WE'LL GET IN TROUBLE IF THEY FIND US.
YEAH.
WE'LL JUST HAVE TO APOLOGIZE LIKE CRAZY IF THAT HAPPENS.
HONESTLY, I THOUGHT YOU'D SAY NO.
YOU'RE SO RESPON-SIBLE AND ALL.
I WAS SURPRISED TOO...
...THAT YOU'D PROPOSE SOMETHING LIKE THIS.
THERE'S SOME REASON, ISN'T THERE?
I CAN'T IMAGINE YOU DOING THIS OTHERWISE...
YES...
YOU'RE RIGHT.

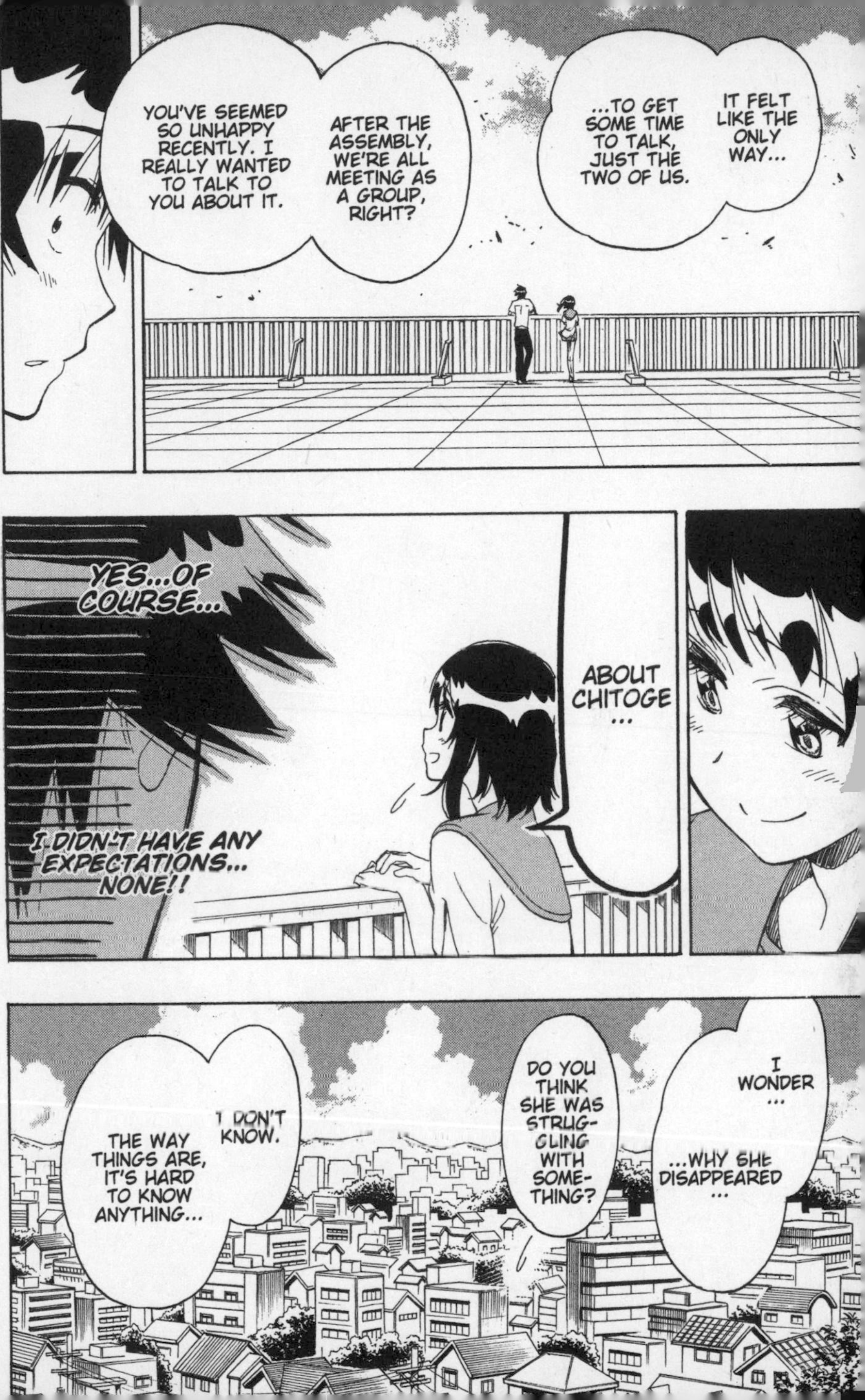
IT FELT LIKE THE ONLY WAY...
...TO GET SOME TIME TO TALK, JUST THE TWO OF US.
AFTER THE ASSEMBLY, WE'RE ALL MEETING AS A GROUP, RIGHT?
YOU'VE SEEMED SO UNHAPPY RECENTLY. I REALLY WANTED TO TALK TO YOU ABOUT IT.
ABOUT CHITOGE...
YES...OF COURSE...
I DIDN'T HAVE ANY EXPECTATIONS... NONE!!
I WONDER...
...WHY SHE DISAPPEARED...
DO YOU THINK SHE WAS STRUG-GLING WITH SOME-THING?
I DON'T KNOW.
THE WAY THINGS ARE, IT'S HARD TO KNOW ANYTHING...

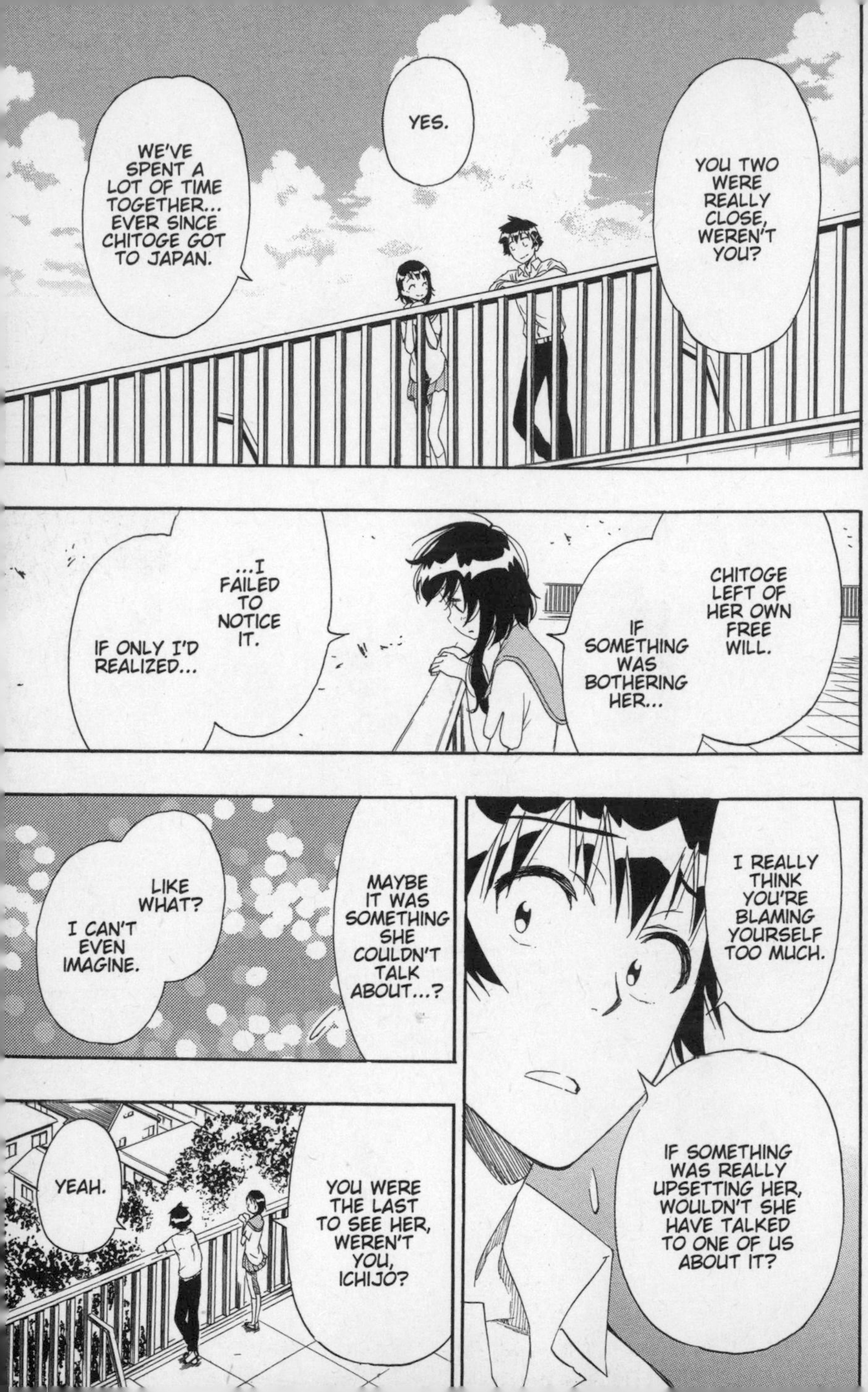
YOU TWO WERE REALLY CLOSE, WEREN'T YOU?
YES.
WE'VE SPENT A LOT OF TIME TOGETHER... EVER SINCE CHITOGE GOT TO JAPAN.
CHITOGE LEFT OF HER OWN FREE WILL.
IF SOMETHING WAS BOTHERING HER...
...I FAILED TO NOTICE IT.
IF ONLY I'D REALIZED...
I REALLY THINK YOU'RE BLAMING YOURSELF TOO MUCH.
IF SOMETHING WAS REALLY UPSETTING HER, WOULDN'T SHE HAVE TALKED TO ONE OF US ABOUT IT?
MAYBE IT WAS SOMETHING SHE COULDN'T TALK ABOUT...?
LIKE WHAT? I CAN'T EVEN IMAGINE.
YOU WERE THE LAST TO SEE HER, WEREN'T YOU, ICHIJO?
YEAH.

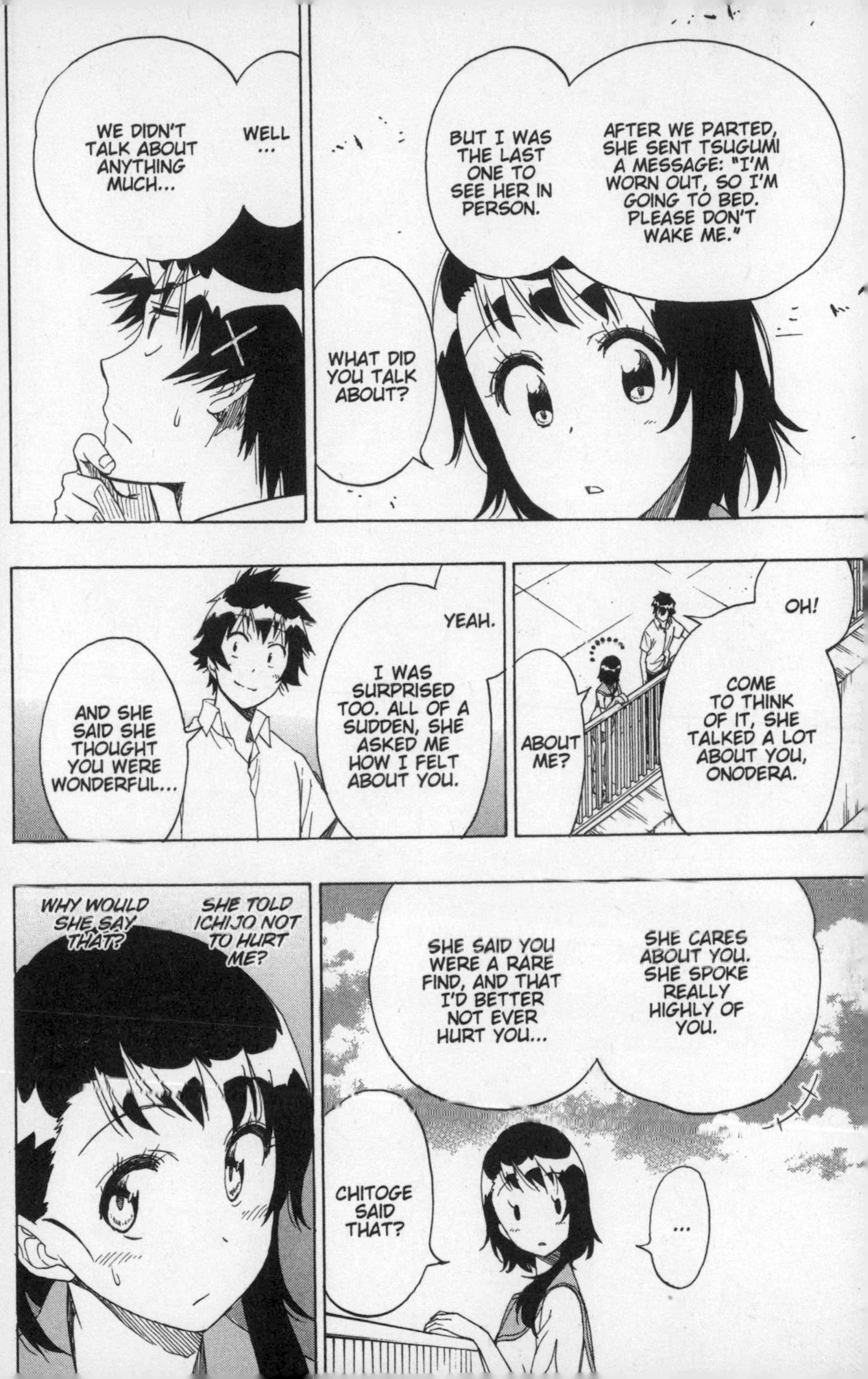
AFTER WE PARTED, SHE SENT TSUGUMI A MESSAGE: "I'M WORN OUT, SO I'M GOING TO BED. PLEASE DON'T WAKE ME."
BUT I WAS THE LAST ONE TO SEE HER IN PERSON.
WHAT DID YOU TALK ABOUT?
WELL...
WE DIDN'T TALK ABOUT ANYTHING MUCH...
OH!
COME TO THINK OF IT, SHE TALKED A LOT ABOUT YOU, ONODERA.
ABOUT ME?
YEAH.
I WAS SURPRISED TOO. ALL OF A SUDDEN, SHE ASKED ME HOW I FELT ABOUT YOU.
AND SHE SAID SHE THOUGHT YOU WERE WONDERFUL...
SHE CARES ABOUT YOU. SHE SPOKE REALLY HIGHLY OF YOU.
SHE SAID YOU WERE A RARE FIND, AND THAT I'D BETTER NOT EVER HURT YOU...
...
CHITOGE SAID THAT?
SHE TOLD ICHIJO NOT TO HURT ME?
WHY WOULD SHE SAY THAT?

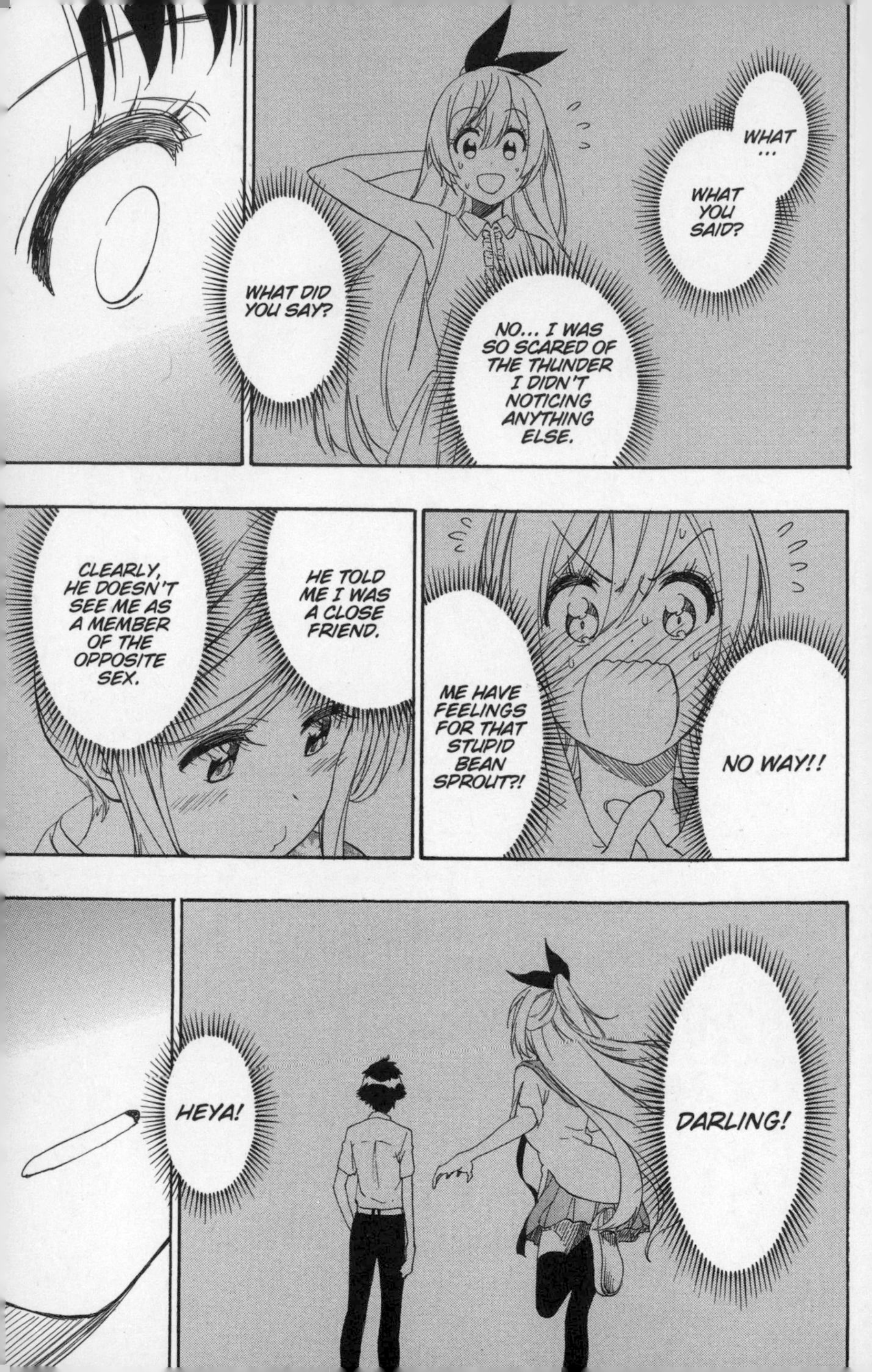
WHAT ... WHAT YOU SAID?
WHAT DID YOU SAY?
NO... I WAS SO SCARED OF THE THUNDER I DIDN'T NOTICING ANYTHING ELSE.
NO WAY!!
ME HAVE FEELINGS FOR THAT STUPID BEAN SPROUT?!
HE TOLD ME I WAS A CLOSE FRIEND.
CLEARLY, HE DOESN'T SEE ME AS A MEMBER OF THE OPPOSITE SEX.
DARLING!
HEYA!

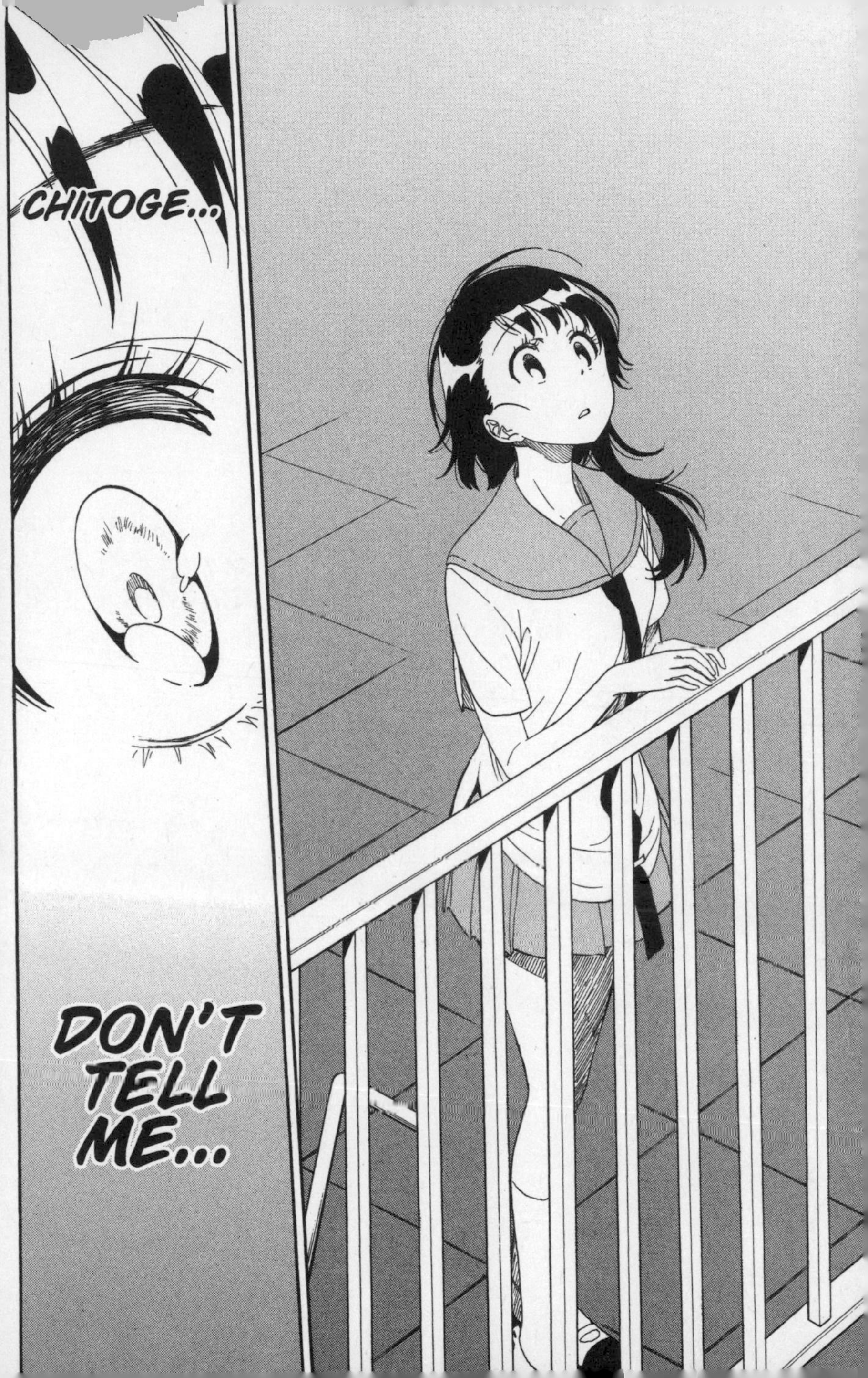
CHITOGE...
DON'T TELL ME...

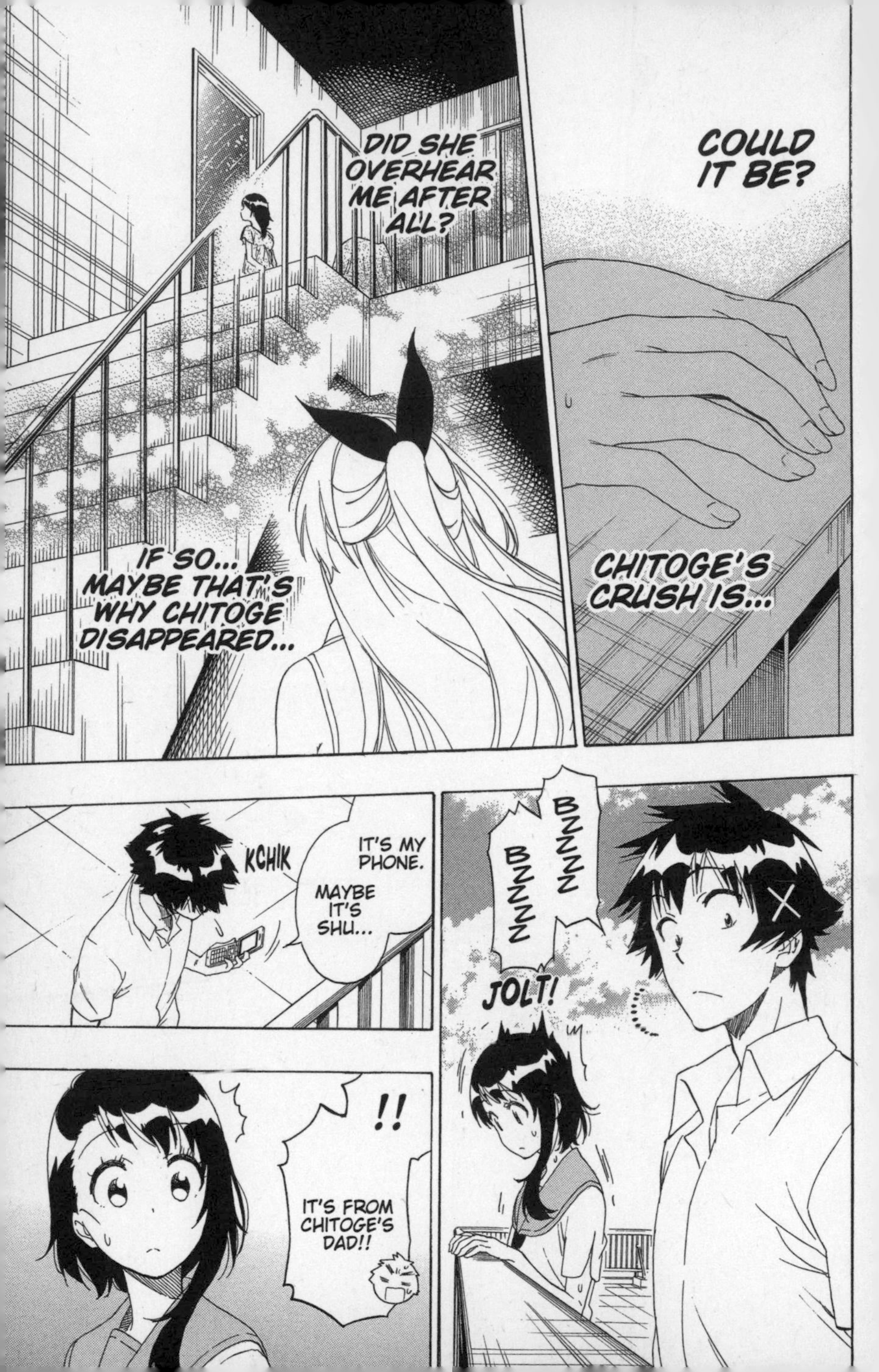
COULD IT BE?
CHITOGE'S CRUSH IS...
DID SHE OVERHEAR ME AFTER ALL?
IF SO... MAYBE THAT'S WHY CHITOGE DISAPPEARED...
BZZZZ
BZZZZ
JOLT!
KCHIK
IT'S MY PHONE.
MAYBE IT'S SHU...
!!
IT'S FROM CHITOGE'S DAD!!

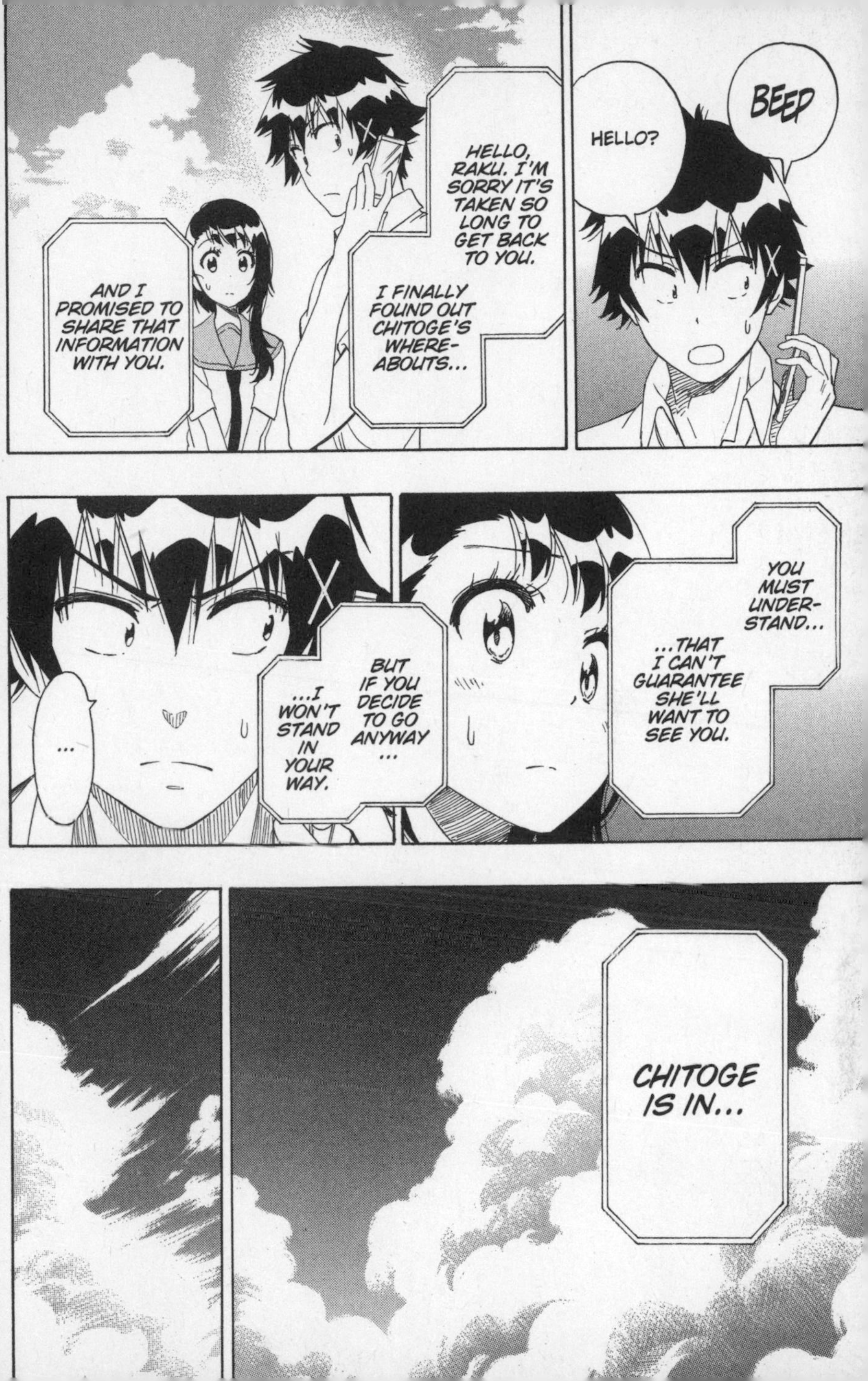
BEEP
HELLO?
HELLO, RAKU. I'M SORRY IT'S TAKEN SO LONG TO GET BACK TO YOU.
I FINALLY FOUND OUT CHITOGE'S WHEREABOUTS...
AND I PROMISED TO SHARE THAT INFORMATION WITH YOU.
YOU MUST UNDERSTAND...
...THAT I CAN'T GUARANTEE SHE'LL WANT TO SEE YOU.
BUT IF YOU DECIDE TO GO ANYWAY...
...I WON'T STAND IN YOUR WAY.
...
CHITOGE IS IN...

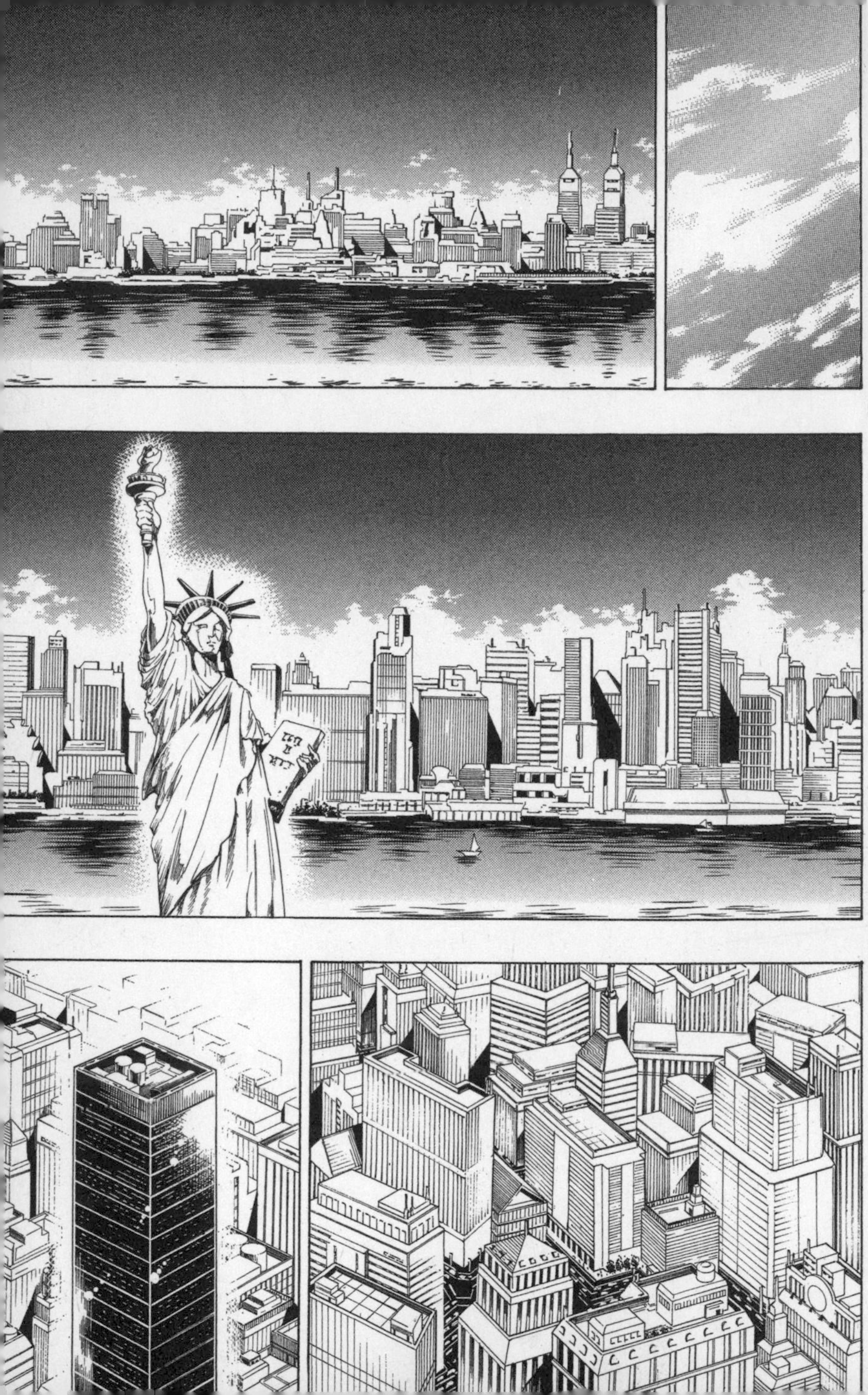

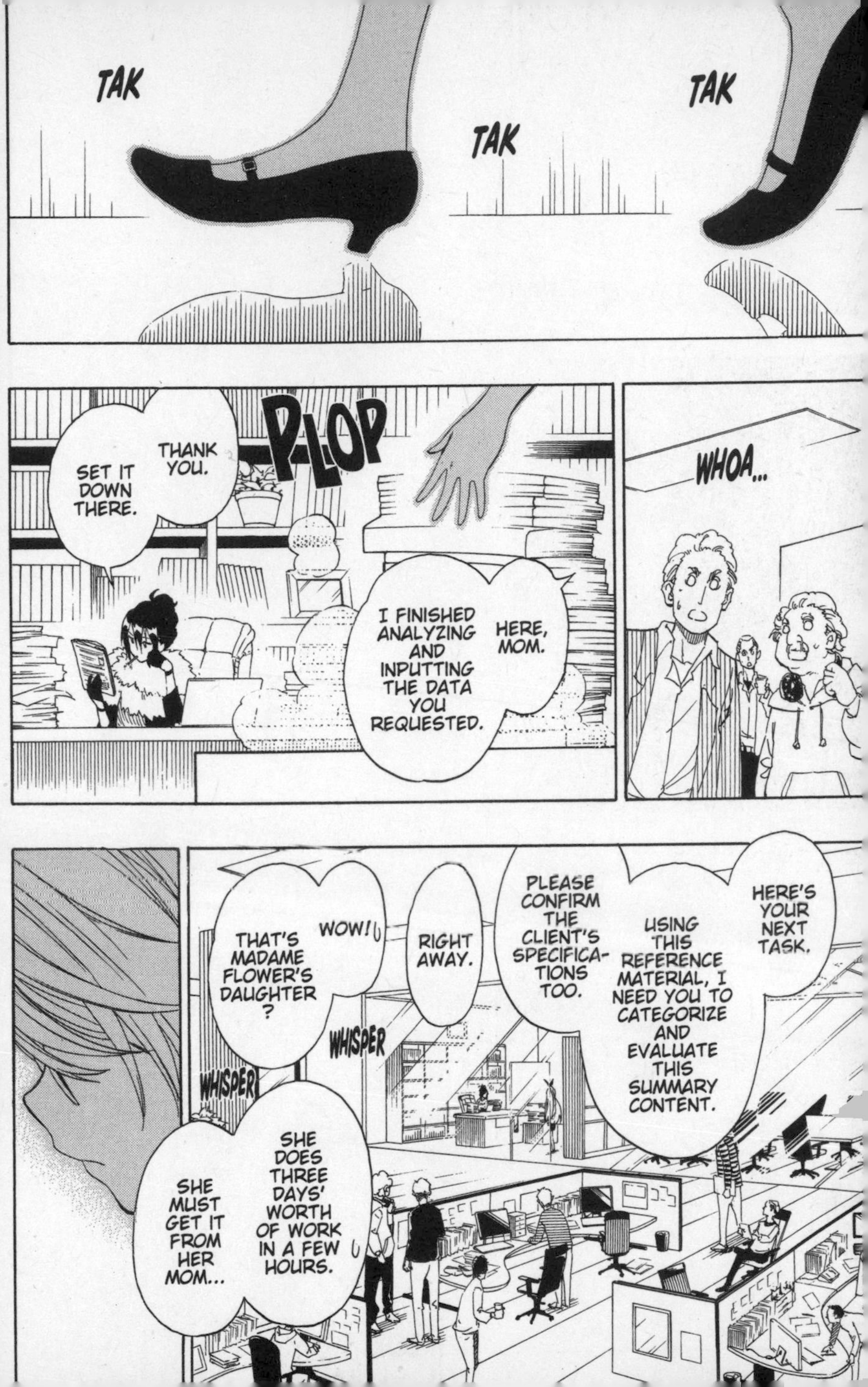

TAK
TAK
TAK
WHOA...
HERE, MOM.
I FINISHED ANALYZING AND INPUTTING THE DATA YOU REQUESTED.
THANK YOU.
SET IT DOWN THERE.
PLOP
HERE'S YOUR NEXT TASK.
USING THIS REFERENCE MATERIAL, I NEED YOU TO CATEGORIZE AND EVALUATE THIS SUMMARY CONTENT.
PLEASE CONFIRM THE CLIENT'S SPECIFICA-TIONS TOO.
RIGHT AWAY.
WOW!
THAT'S MADAME FLOWER'S DAUGHTER?
WHISPER
WHISPER
SHE DOES THREE DAYS' WORTH OF WORK IN A FEW HOURS.
SHE MUST GET IT FROM HER MOM...

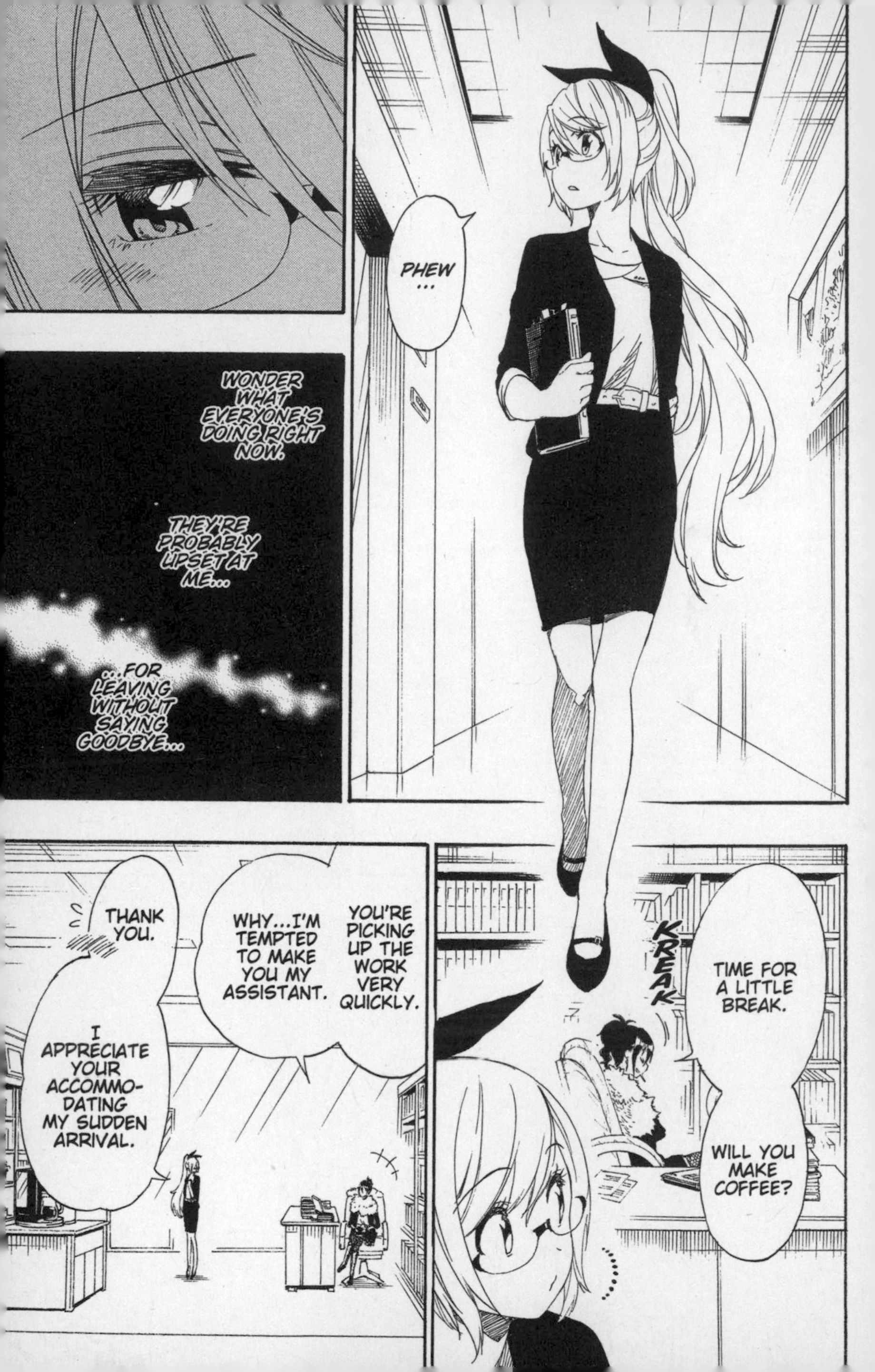
PHEW ...
WONDER WHAT EVERYONE'S DOING RIGHT NOW.
THEY'RE PROBABLY UPSET AT ME...
...FOR LEAVING WITHOUT SAYING GOODBYE...
KREAK
TIME FOR A LITTLE BREAK.
WILL YOU MAKE COFFEE?
YOU'RE PICKING UP THE WORK VERY QUICKLY.
WHY...I'M TEMPTED TO MAKE YOU MY ASSISTANT.
THANK YOU.
I APPRECIATE YOUR ACCOMMO-DATING MY SUDDEN ARRIVAL.

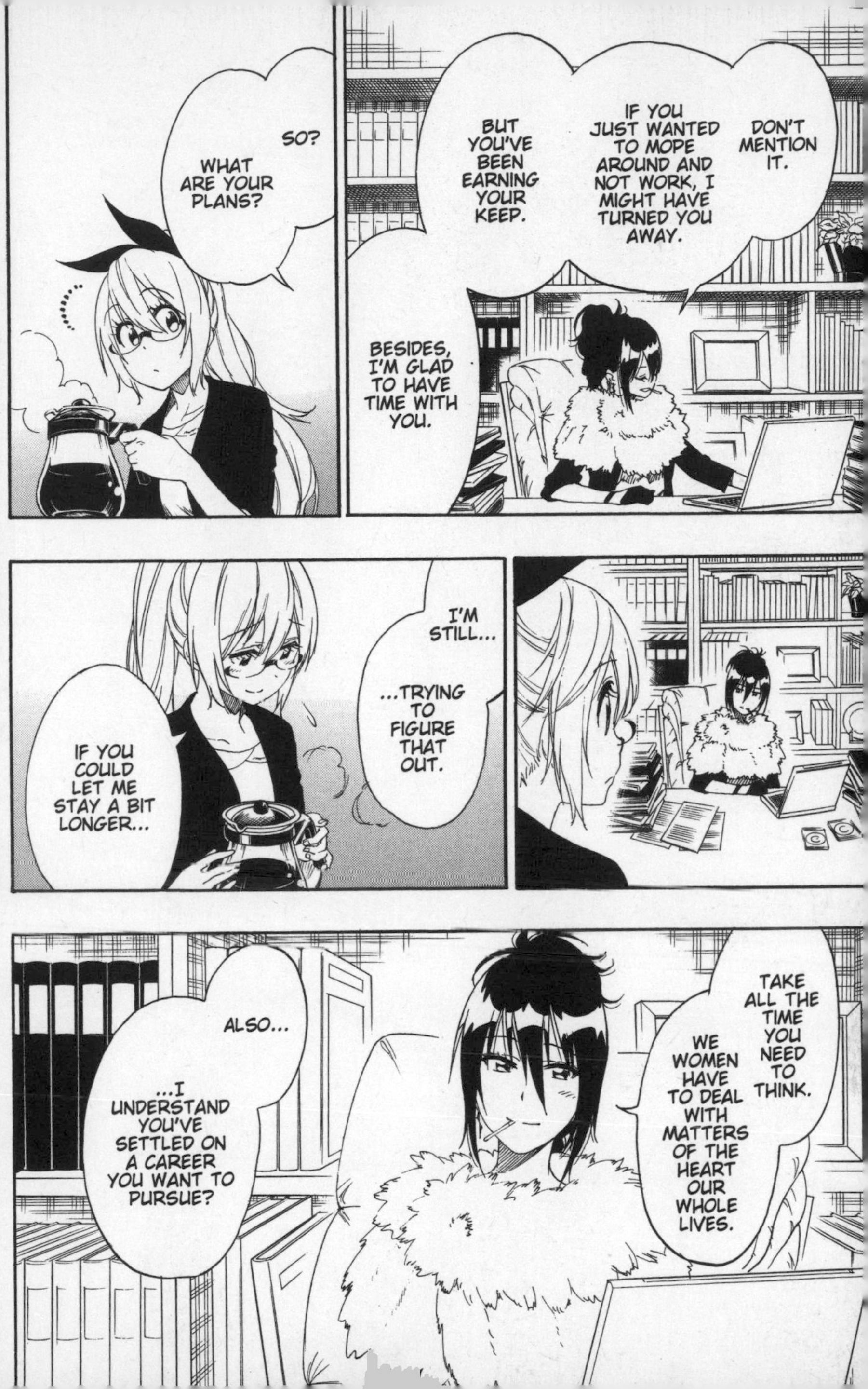
DON'T MENTION IT.
IF YOU JUST WANTED TO MOPE AROUND AND NOT WORK, I MIGHT HAVE TURNED YOU AWAY.
BUT YOU'VE BEEN EARNING YOUR KEEP.
BESIDES, I'M GLAD TO HAVE TIME WITH YOU.
SO?
WHAT ARE YOUR PLANS?
I'M STILL...
...TRYING TO FIGURE THAT OUT.
IF YOU COULD LET ME STAY A BIT LONGER...
TAKE ALL THE TIME YOU NEED TO THINK.
WE WOMEN HAVE TO DEAL WITH MATTERS OF THE HEART OUR WHOLE LIVES.
ALSO...
...I UNDERSTAND YOU'VE SETTLED ON A CAREER YOU WANT TO PURSUE?

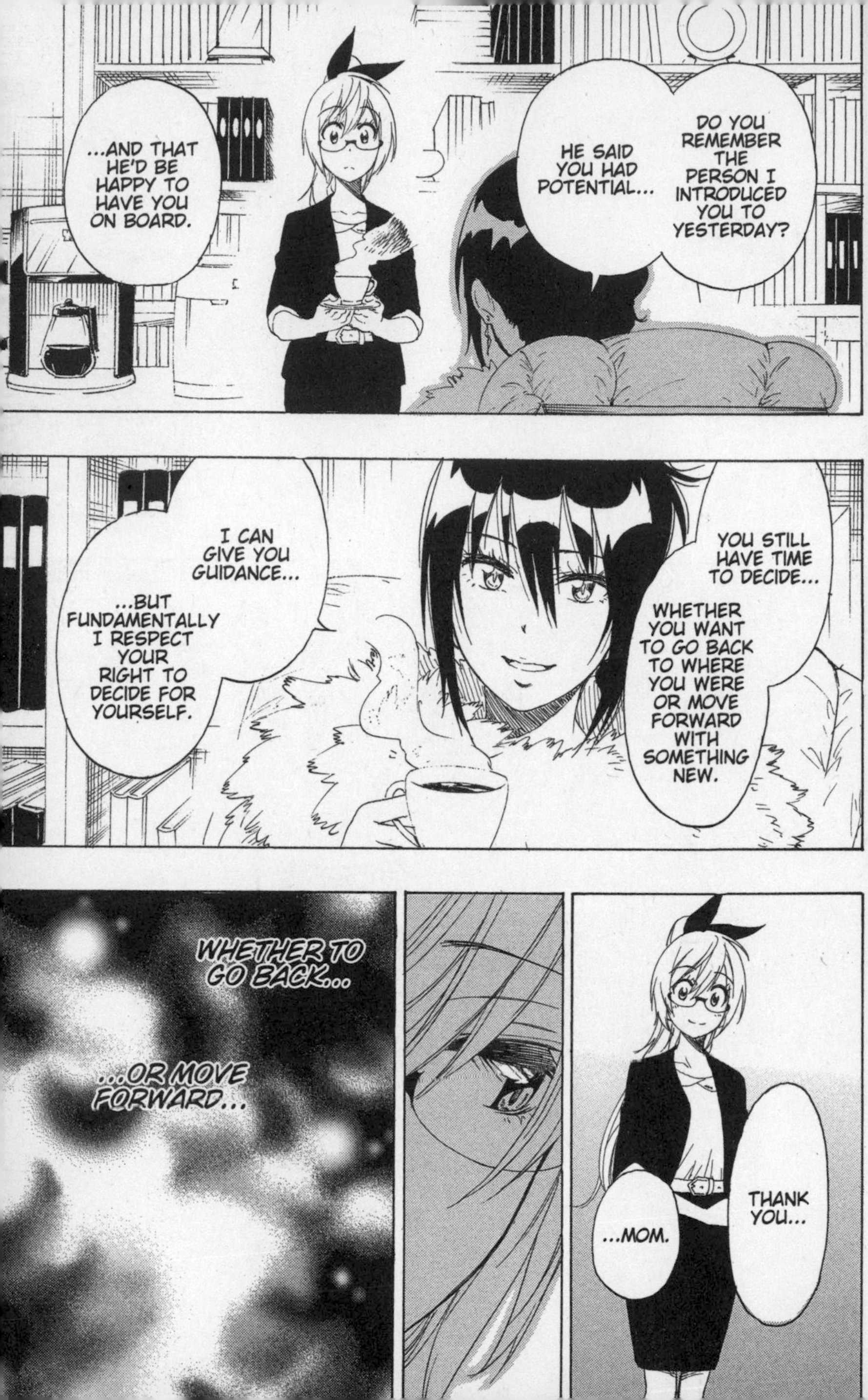
DO YOU REMEMBER THE PERSON I INTRODUCED YOU TO YESTERDAY?
HE SAID YOU HAD POTENTIAL...
...AND THAT HE'D BE HAPPY TO HAVE YOU ON BOARD.
YOU STILL HAVE TIME TO DECIDE...
WHETHER YOU WANT TO GO BACK TO WHERE YOU WERE OR MOVE FORWARD WITH SOMETHING NEW.
I CAN GIVE YOU GUIDANCE...
...BUT FUNDAMENTALLY I RESPECT YOUR RIGHT TO DECIDE FOR YOURSELF.
THANK YOU...
...MOM.
WHETHER TO GO BACK...
...OR MOVE FORWARD...

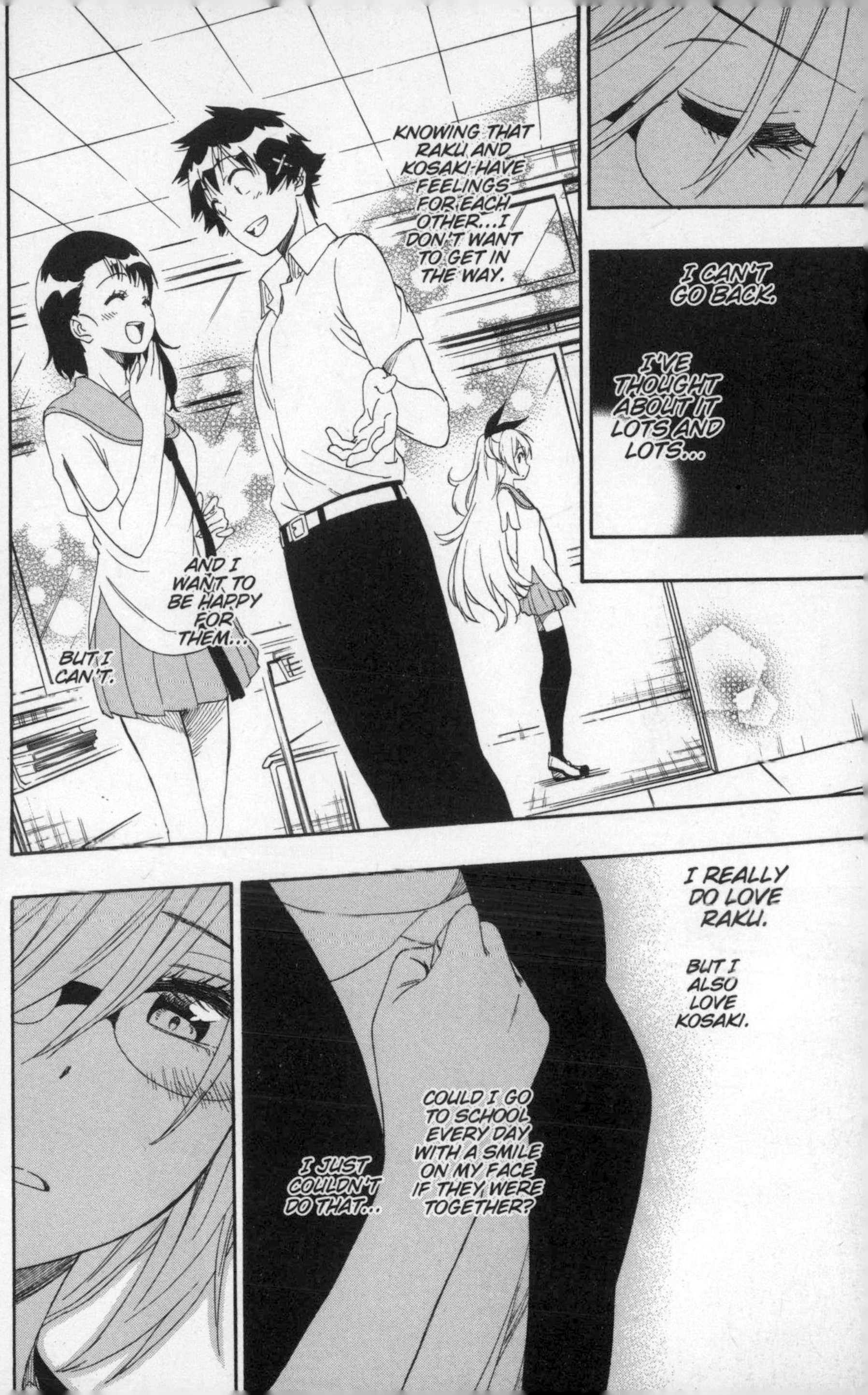
I CAN'T GO BACK.
I'VE THOUGHT ABOUT IT LOTS AND LOTS...
KNOWING THAT RAKU AND KOSAKI HAVE FEELINGS FOR EACH OTHER...I DON'T WANT TO GET IN THE WAY.
AND I WANT TO BE HAPPY FOR THEM...
BUT I CAN'T.
I REALLY DO LOVE RAKU.
BUT I ALSO LOVE KOSAKI.
COULD I GO TO SCHOOL EVERY DAY WITH A SMILE ON MY FACE IF THEY WERE TOGETHER?
I JUST COULDN'T DO THAT...

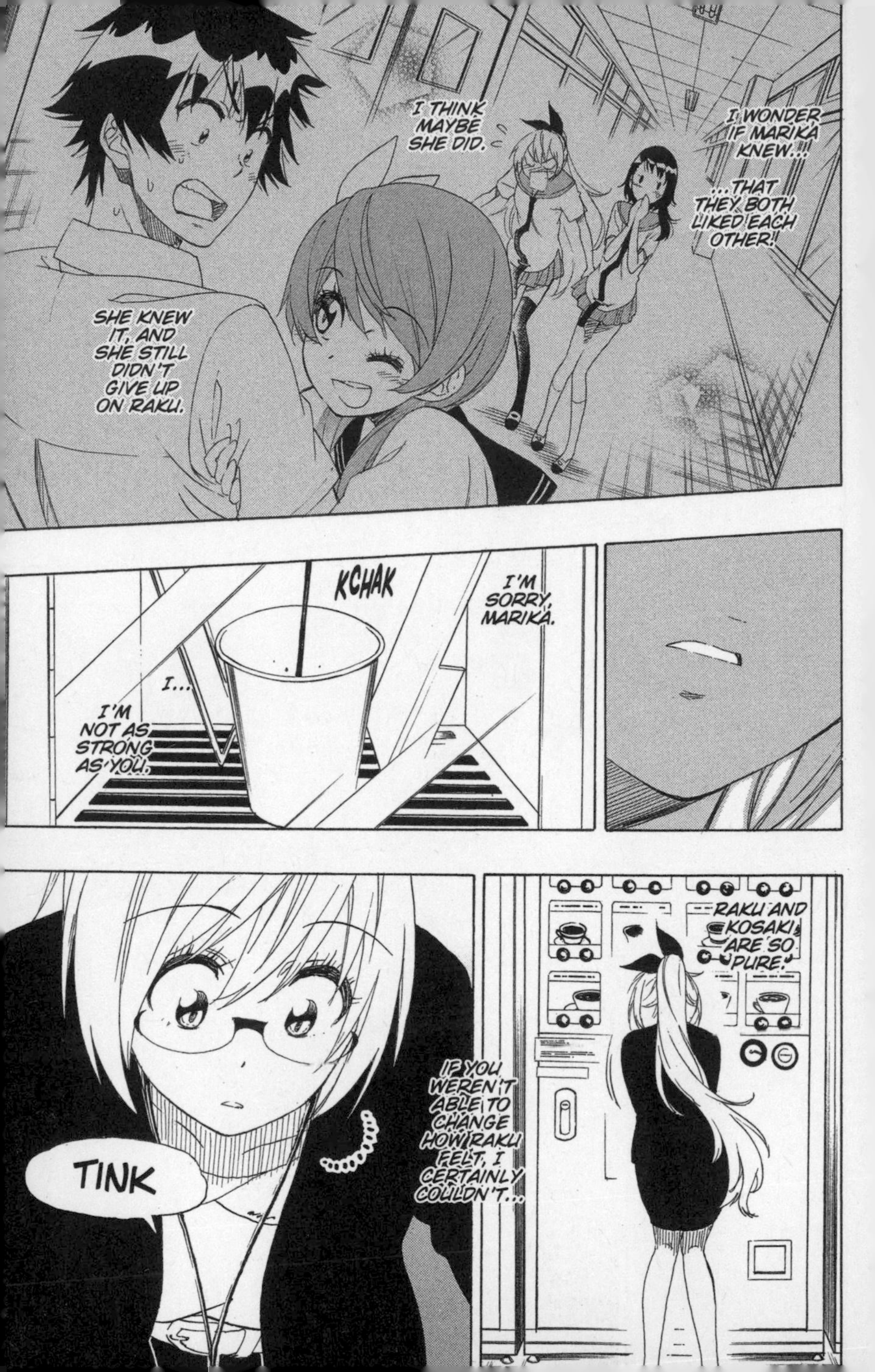
I WONDER IF MARIKA KNEW...
...THAT THEY BOTH LIKED EACH OTHER!
I THINK MAYBE SHE DID.
SHE KNEW IT, AND SHE STILL DIDN'T GIVE UP ON RAKU.
KCHAK
I'M SORRY, MARIKA.
I...
I'M NOT AS STRONG AS YOU.
RAKU AND KOSAKI ARE SO PURE.
IF YOU WEREN'T ABLE TO CHANGE HOW RAKU FELT, I CERTAINLY COULDN'T...
TINK

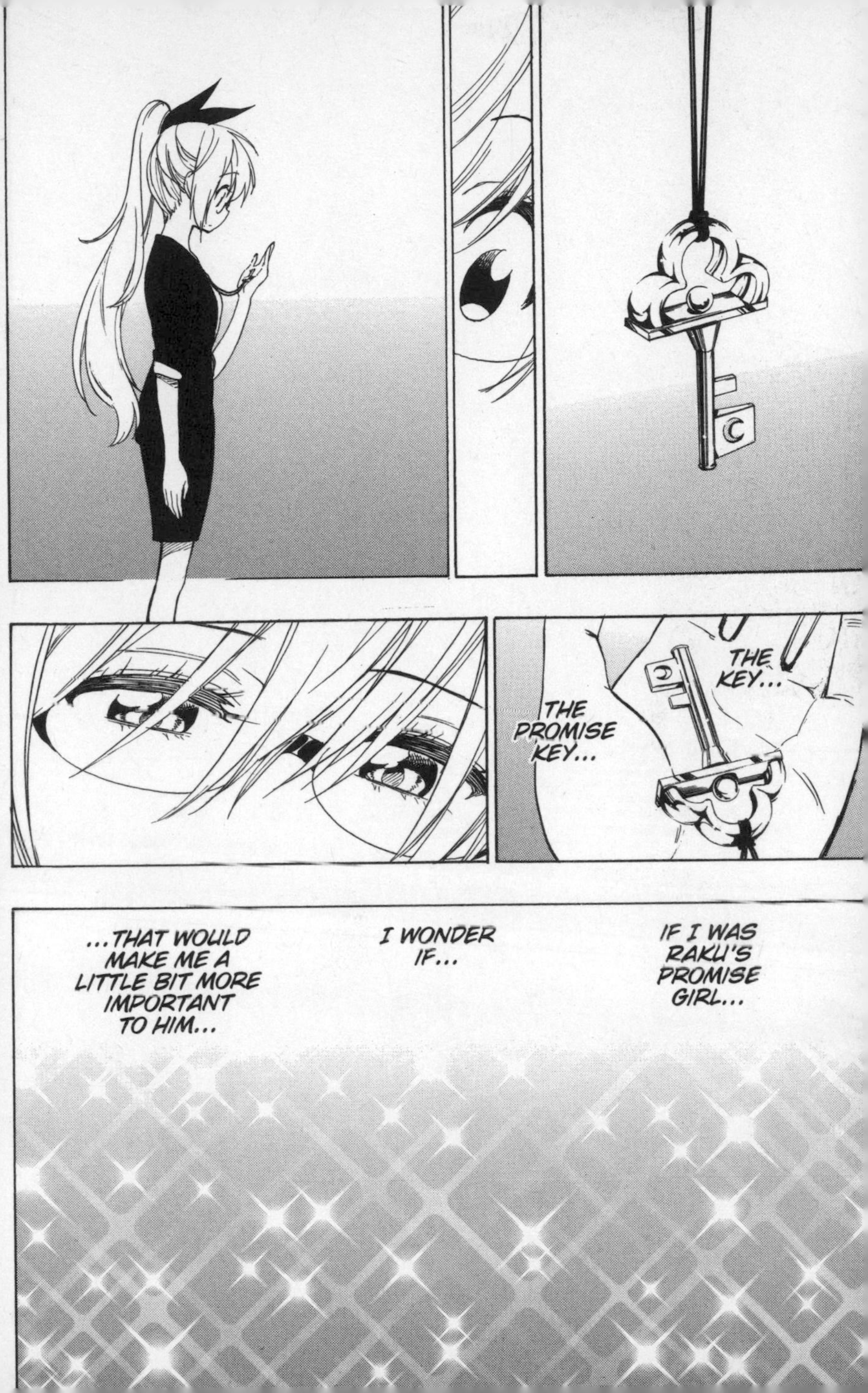
THE KEY...
THE PROMISE KEY...
IF I WAS RAKU'S PROMISE GIRL...
I WONDER IF...
...THAT WOULD MAKE ME A LITTLE BIT MORE IMPORTANT TO HIM...

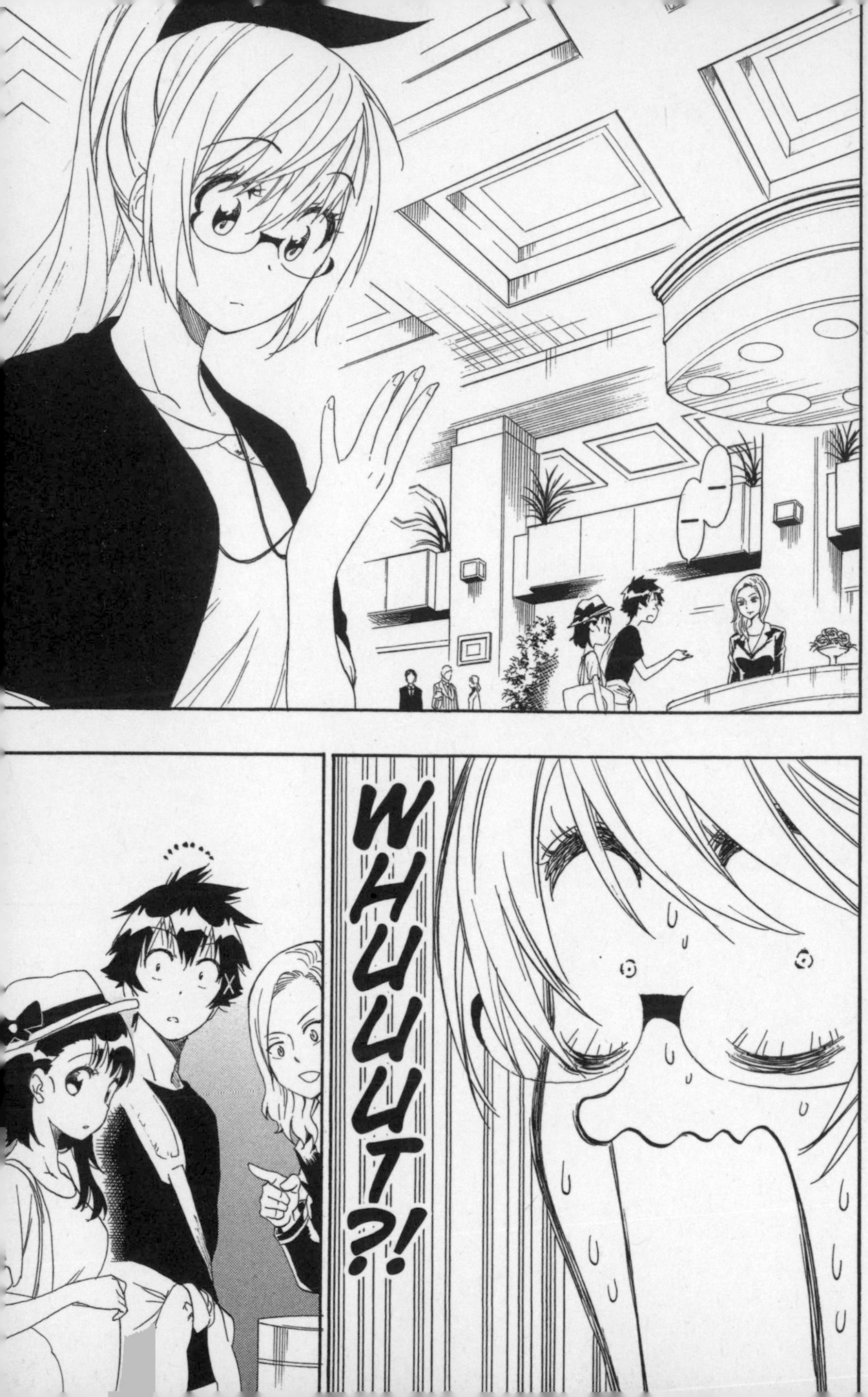
WHUUUT?!

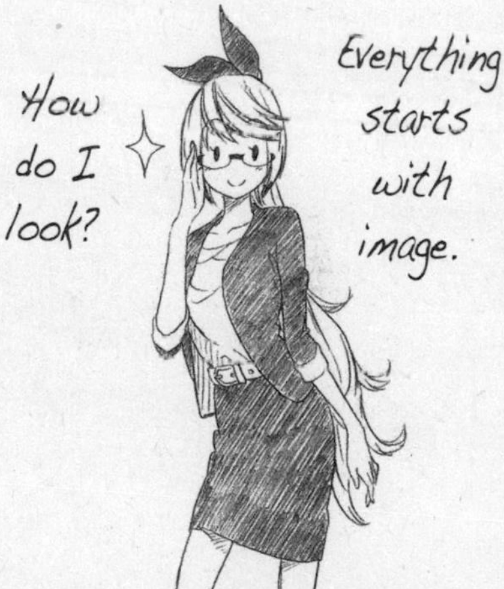
Everything starts with image.
How do I look?

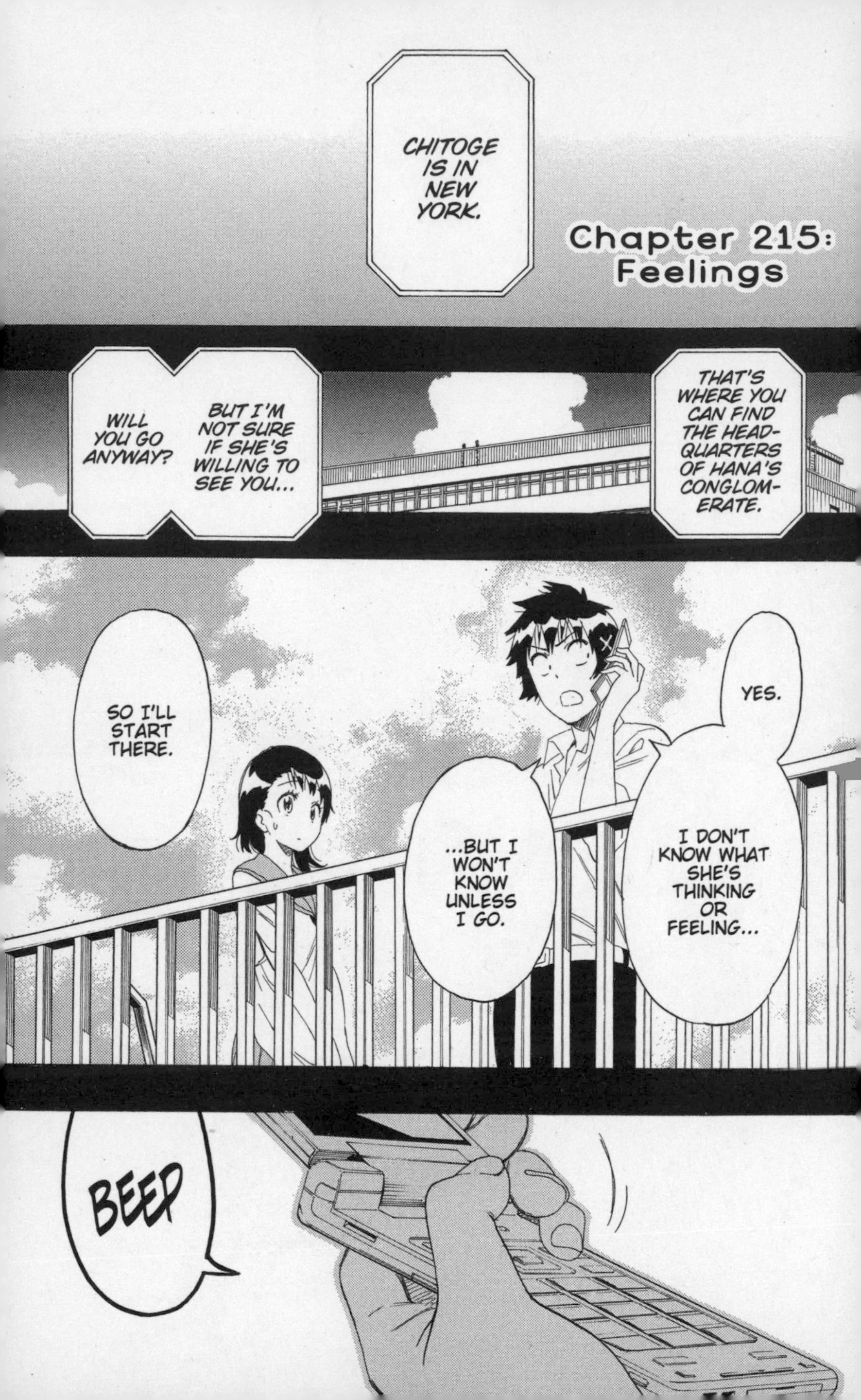
CHITOGE IS IN NEW YORK.
Chapter 215: Feelings
THAT'S WHERE YOU CAN FIND THE HEAD-QUARTERS OF HANA'S CONGLOM-ERATE.
BUT I'M NOT SURE IF SHE'S WILLING TO SEE YOU...
WILL YOU GO ANYWAY?
YES.
I DON'T KNOW WHAT SHE'S THINKING OR FEELING...
...BUT I WON'T KNOW UNLESS I GO.
SO I'LL START THERE.
BEEP

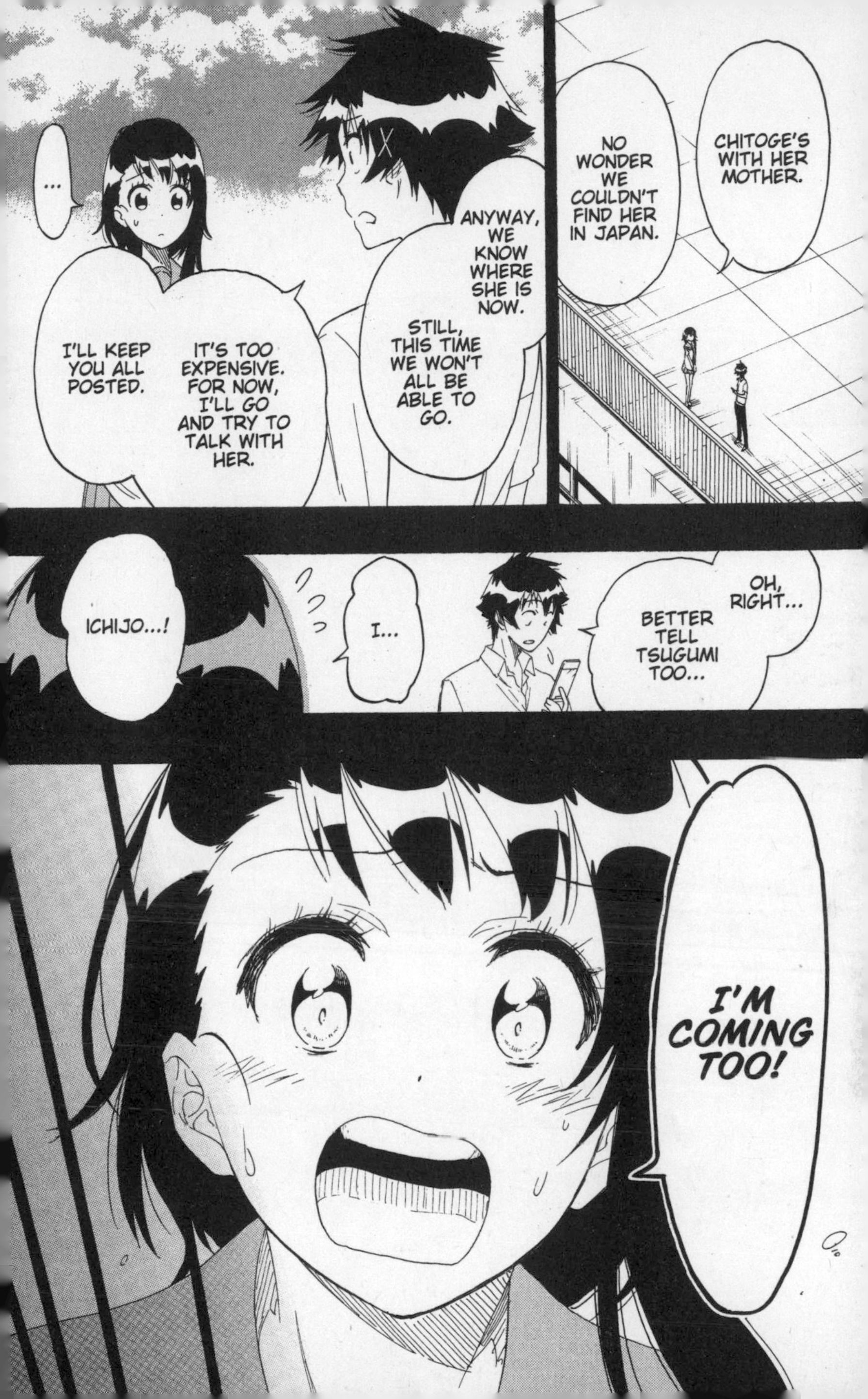

CHITOGE'S WITH HER MOTHER.
NO WONDER WE COULDN'T FIND HER IN JAPAN.
ANYWAY, WE KNOW WHERE SHE IS NOW.
STILL, THIS TIME WE WON'T ALL BE ABLE TO GO.
IT'S TOO EXPENSIVE. FOR NOW, I'LL GO AND TRY TO TALK WITH HER.
I'LL KEEP YOU ALL POSTED.
...
OH, RIGHT... BETTER TELL TSUGUMI TOO...
I...
ICHIJO...!
I'M COMING TOO!

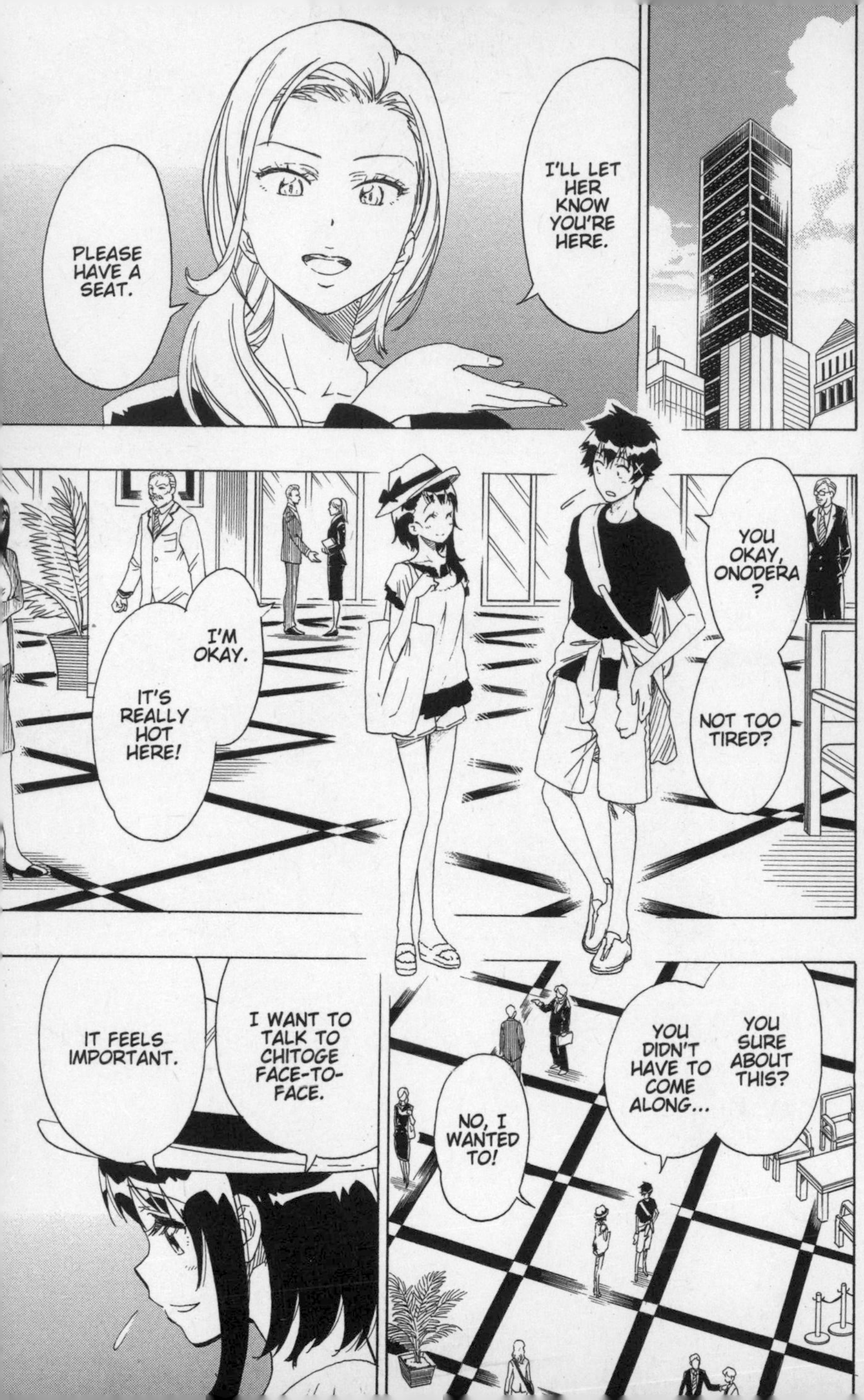
I'LL LET HER KNOW YOU'RE HERE.
PLEASE HAVE A SEAT.
YOU OKAY, ONODERA?
NOT TOO TIRED?
I'M OKAY.
IT'S REALLY HOT HERE!
YOU SURE ABOUT THIS?
YOU DIDN'T HAVE TO COME ALONG...
NO, I WANTED TO!
I WANT TO TALK TO CHITOGE FACE-TO-FACE.
IT FEELS IMPORTANT.

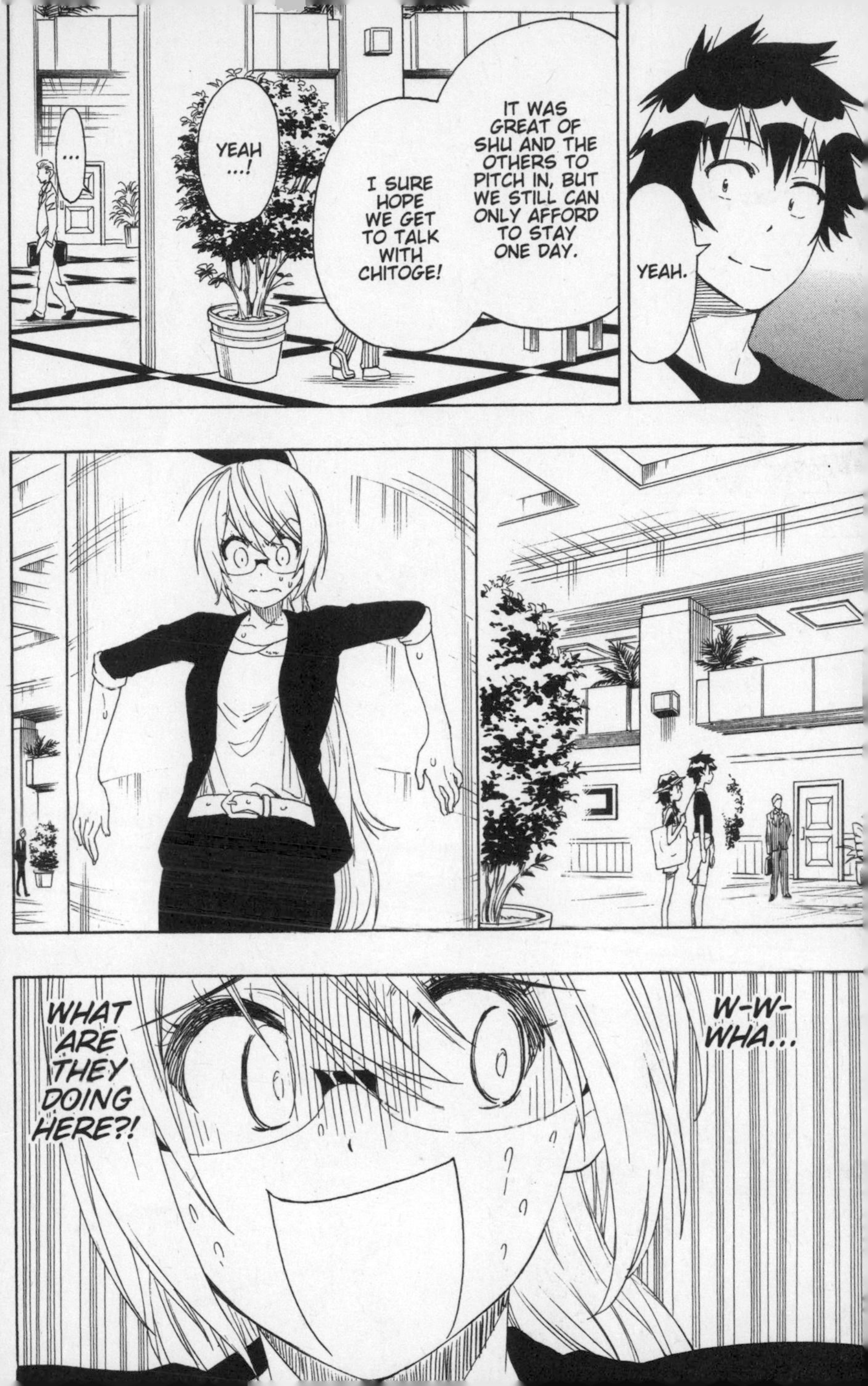
YEAH.
IT WAS GREAT OF SHU AND THE OTHERS TO PITCH IN, BUT WE STILL CAN ONLY AFFORD TO STAY ONE DAY.
I SURE HOPE WE GET TO TALK WITH CHITOGE!
YEAH ...!
...
W-W-WHA...
WHAT ARE THEY DOING HERE?!

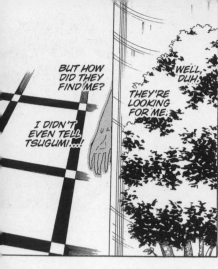

I'M NOT DREAMING, AM I?!
IT'S REALLY RAKU AND KOSAKI?!
WHY ON EARTH...
WELL, DUH.
THEY'RE LOOKING FOR ME.
BUT HOW DID THEY FIND ME?
I DIDN'T EVEN TELL TSUGUMI...!
I'M SO STUPID!
I KNOW IT'S WRONG...
BUT THERE'S A PART OF ME THAT'S HAPPY TO SEE THEM.
AAAUGH!! BUT I CAN'T SEE THEM!!
HOW CAN I POSSIBLY EXPLAIN WHY I LEFT?!
HOW CAN I EVEN FACE THEM?!
I'VE GOTTA GET OUT OF HERE...!
BEEP
BEEP
BEEP
BEEP
BEEP
BEEP

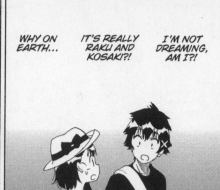

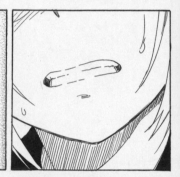

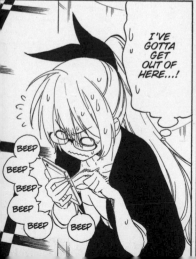

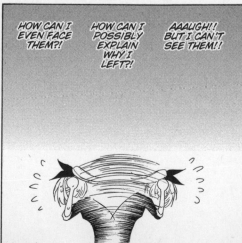

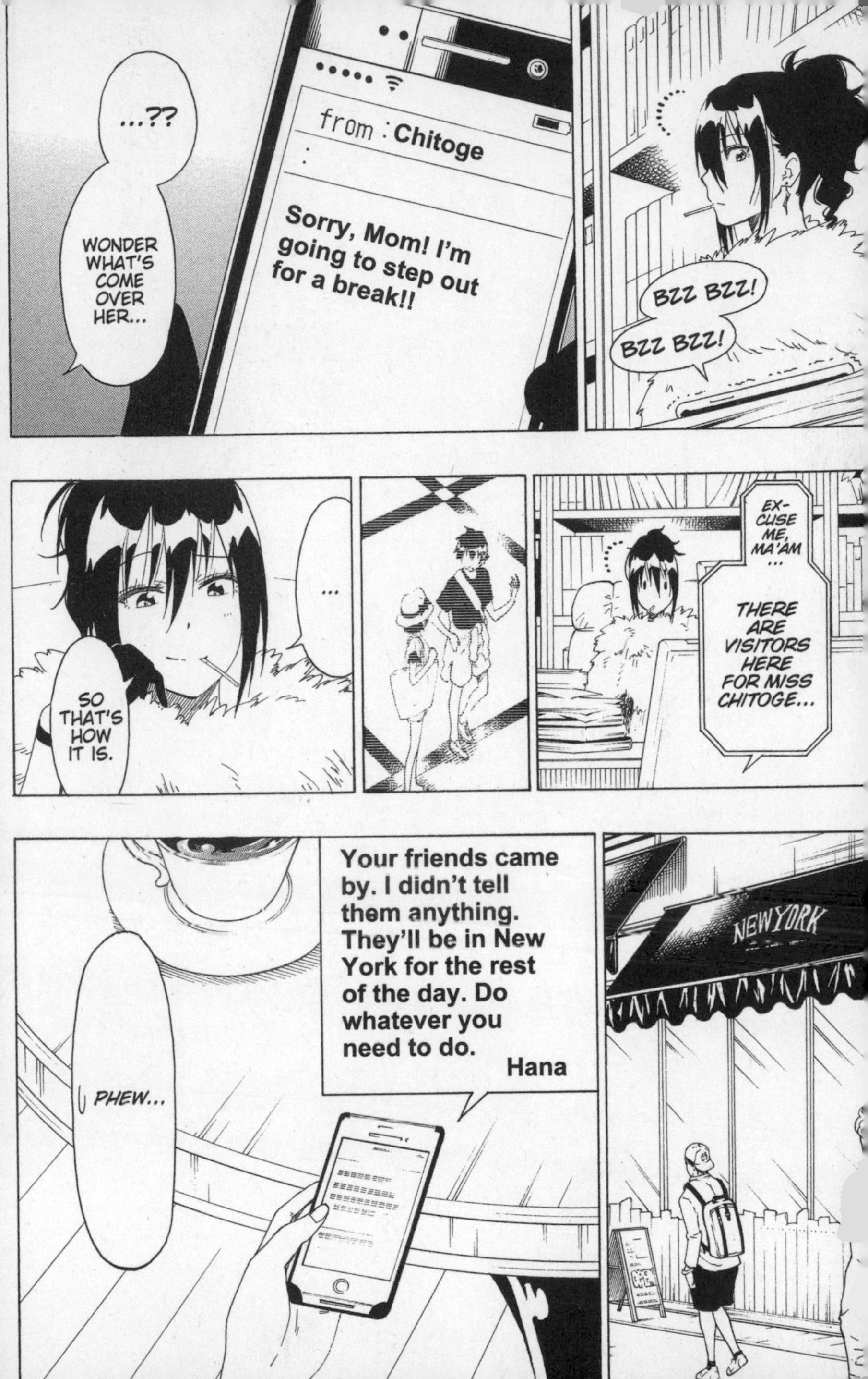
BZZ BZZ!
BZZ BZZ!
from : Chitoge
Sorry, Mom! I'm going to step out for a break!!
...??
WONDER WHAT'S COME OVER HER...
EXCUSE ME, MA'AM...
THERE ARE VISITORS HERE FOR MISS CHITOGE...
...
SO THAT'S HOW IT IS.
NEWYORK
Your friends came by. I didn't tell them anything. They'll be in New York for the rest of the day. Do whatever you need to do.
Hana
PHEW...

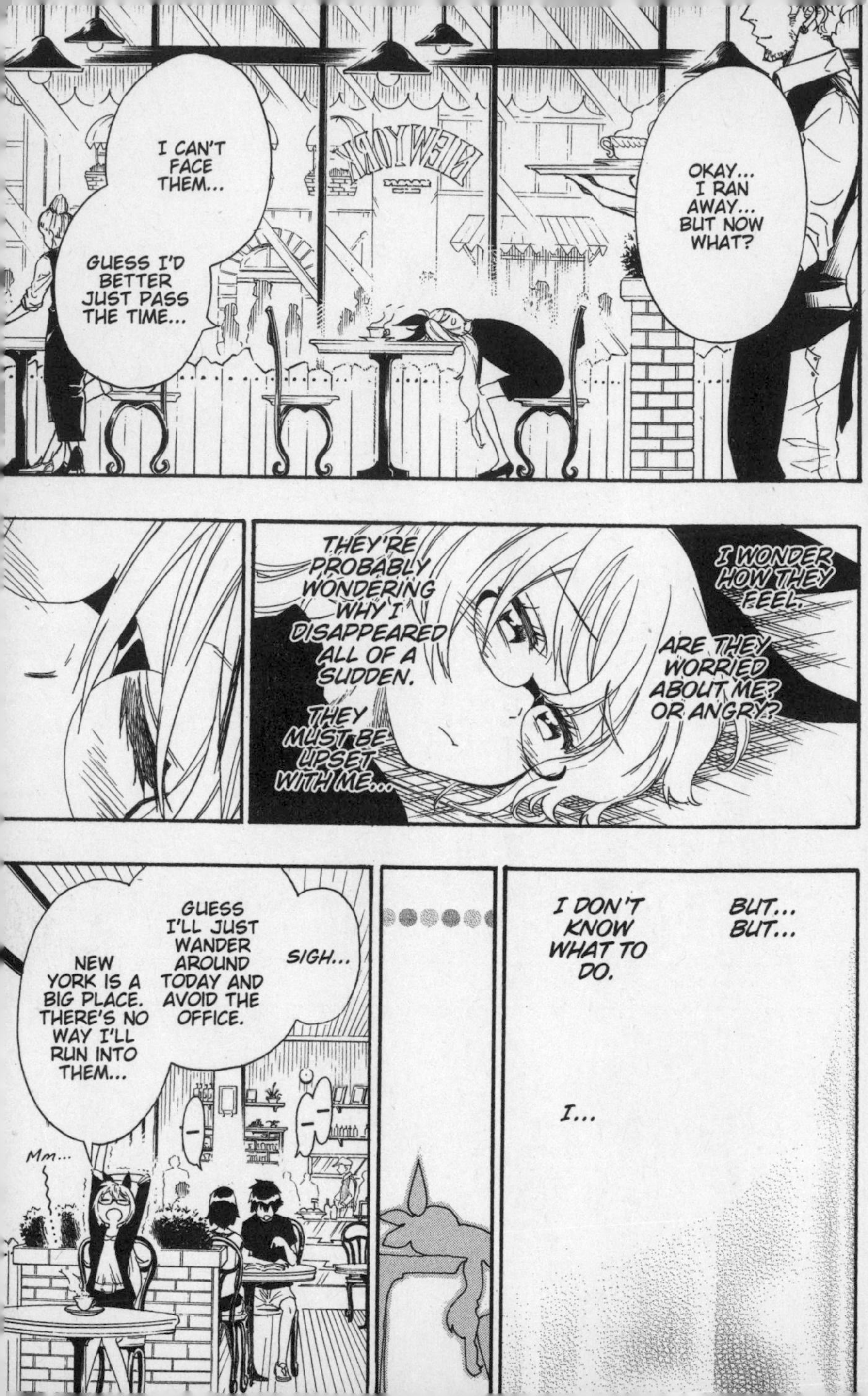
OKAY... I RAN AWAY... BUT NOW WHAT?
I CAN'T FACE THEM...
GUESS I'D BETTER JUST PASS THE TIME...
I WONDER HOW THEY FEEL.
ARE THEY WORRIED ABOUT ME? OR ANGRY?
THEY'RE PROBABLY WONDERING WHY I DISAPPEARED ALL OF A SUDDEN.
THEY MUST BE UPSET WITH ME...
BUT... BUT...
I DON'T KNOW WHAT TO DO.
I...
SIGH...
GUESS I'LL JUST WANDER AROUND TODAY AND AVOID THE OFFICE.
NEW YORK IS A BIG PLACE. THERE'S NO WAY I'LL RUN INTO THEM...
Mm...

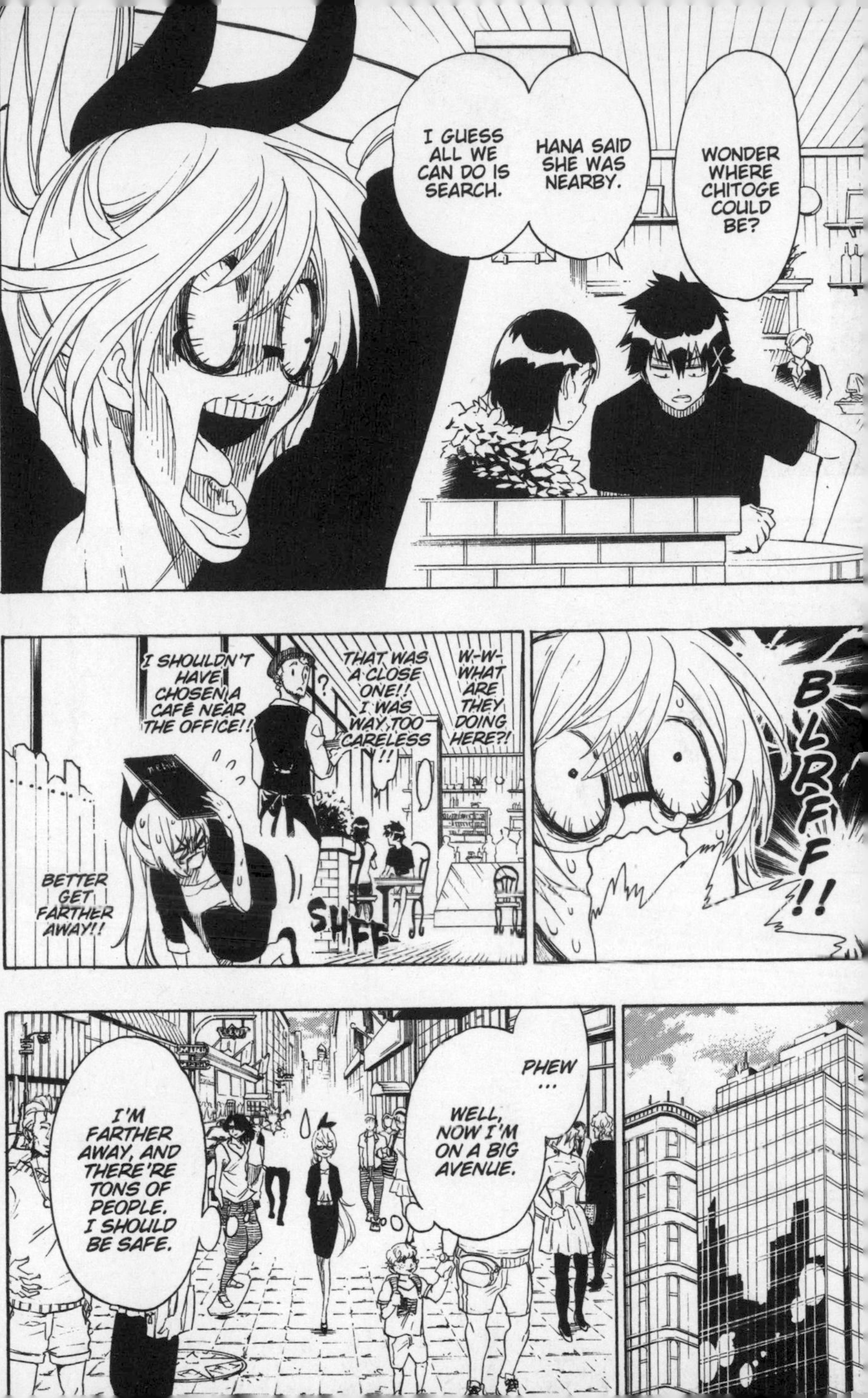
WONDER WHERE CHITOGE COULD BE?
HANA SAID SHE WAS NEARBY.
I GUESS ALL WE CAN DO IS SEARCH.
BLRFF!!
W-W-WHAT ARE THEY DOING HERE?!
THAT WAS A CLOSE ONE!! I WAS WAY TOO CARELESS!!
I SHOULDN'T HAVE CHOSEN A CAFÉ NEAR THE OFFICE!!
SHFF
BETTER GET FARTHER AWAY!!
PHEW ...
WELL, NOW I'M ON A BIG AVENUE.
I'M FARTHER AWAY, AND THERE'RE TONS OF PEOPLE. I SHOULD BE SAFE.

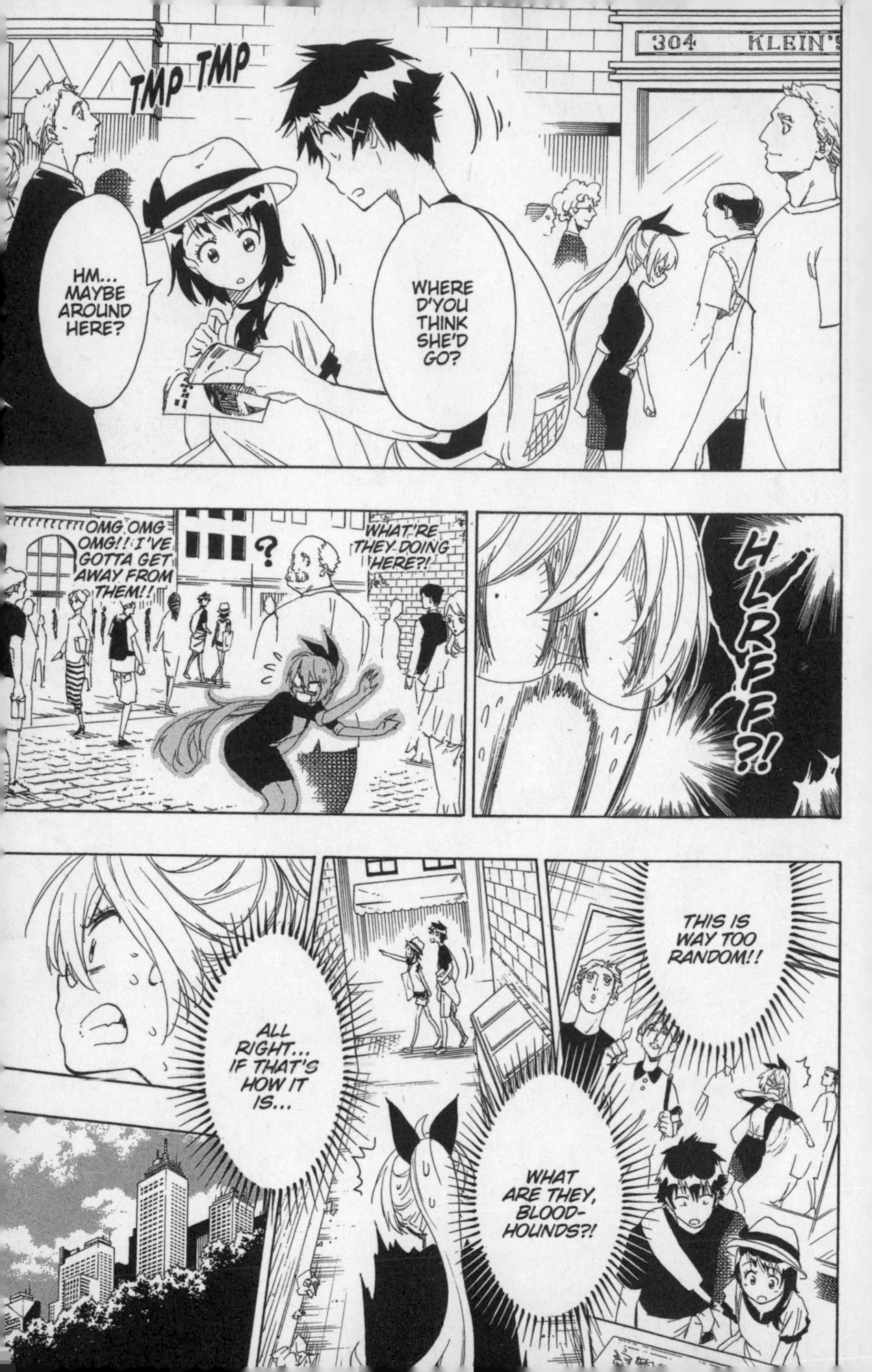
304 KLEIN'S
TMP TMP
WHERE D'YOU THINK SHE'D GO?
HM... MAYBE AROUND HERE?
HLRFF?!
WHAT'RE THEY DOING HERE?!
?
OMG OMG OMG!! I'VE GOTTA GET AWAY FROM THEM!!
THIS IS WAY TOO RANDOM!!
WHAT ARE THEY, BLOOD-HOUNDS?!
ALL RIGHT... IF THAT'S HOW IT IS...

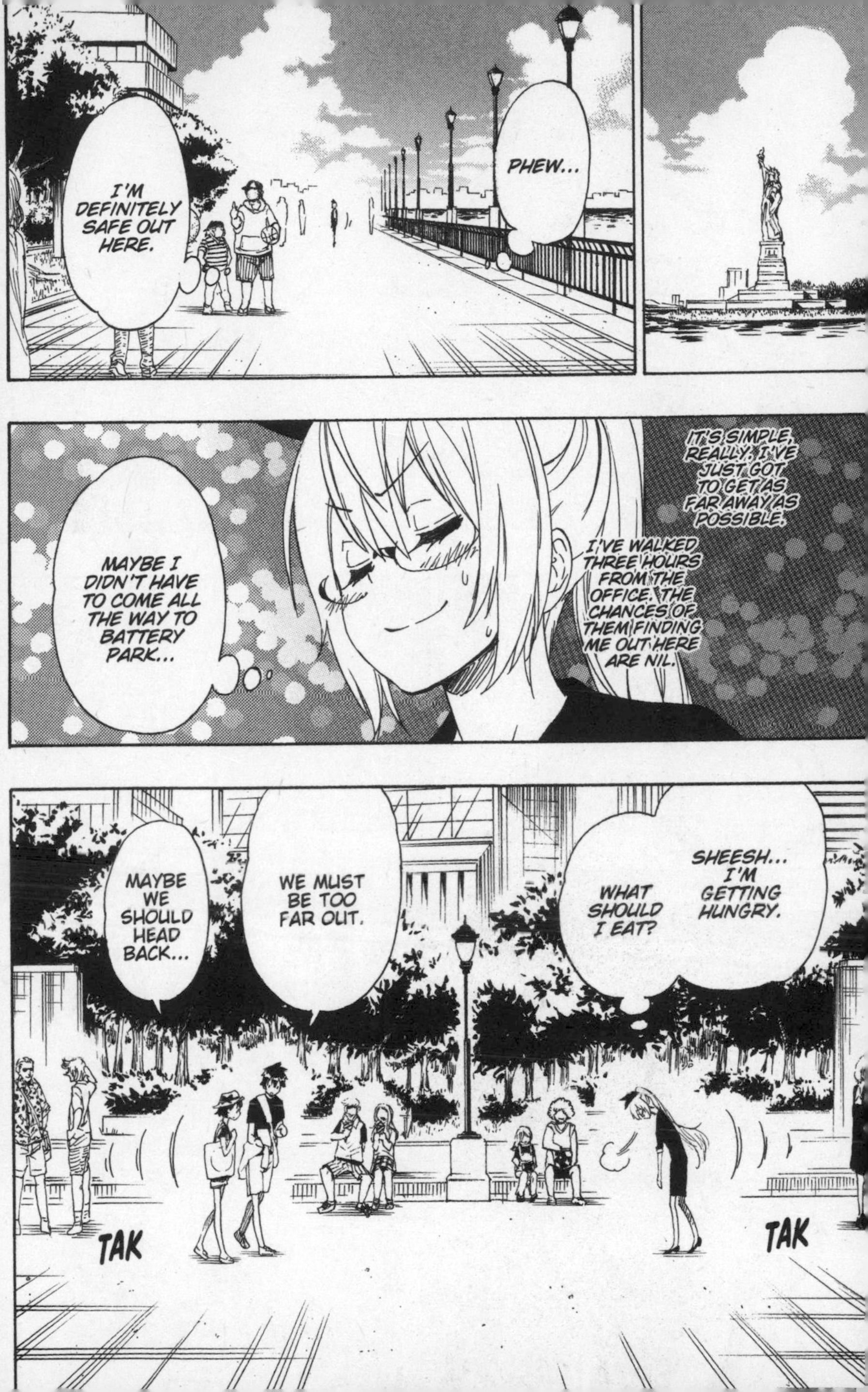
PHEW...
I'M DEFINITELY SAFE OUT HERE.
IT'S SIMPLE, REALLY. I'VE JUST GOT TO GET AS FAR AWAY AS POSSIBLE.
I'VE WALKED THREE HOURS FROM THE OFFICE. THE CHANCES OF THEM FINDING ME OUT HERE ARE NIL.
MAYBE I DIDN'T HAVE TO COME ALL THE WAY TO BATTERY PARK...
SHEESH... I'M GETTING HUNGRY.
WHAT SHOULD I EAT?
TAK
WE MUST BE TOO FAR OUT.
MAYBE WE SHOULD HEAD BACK...
TAK

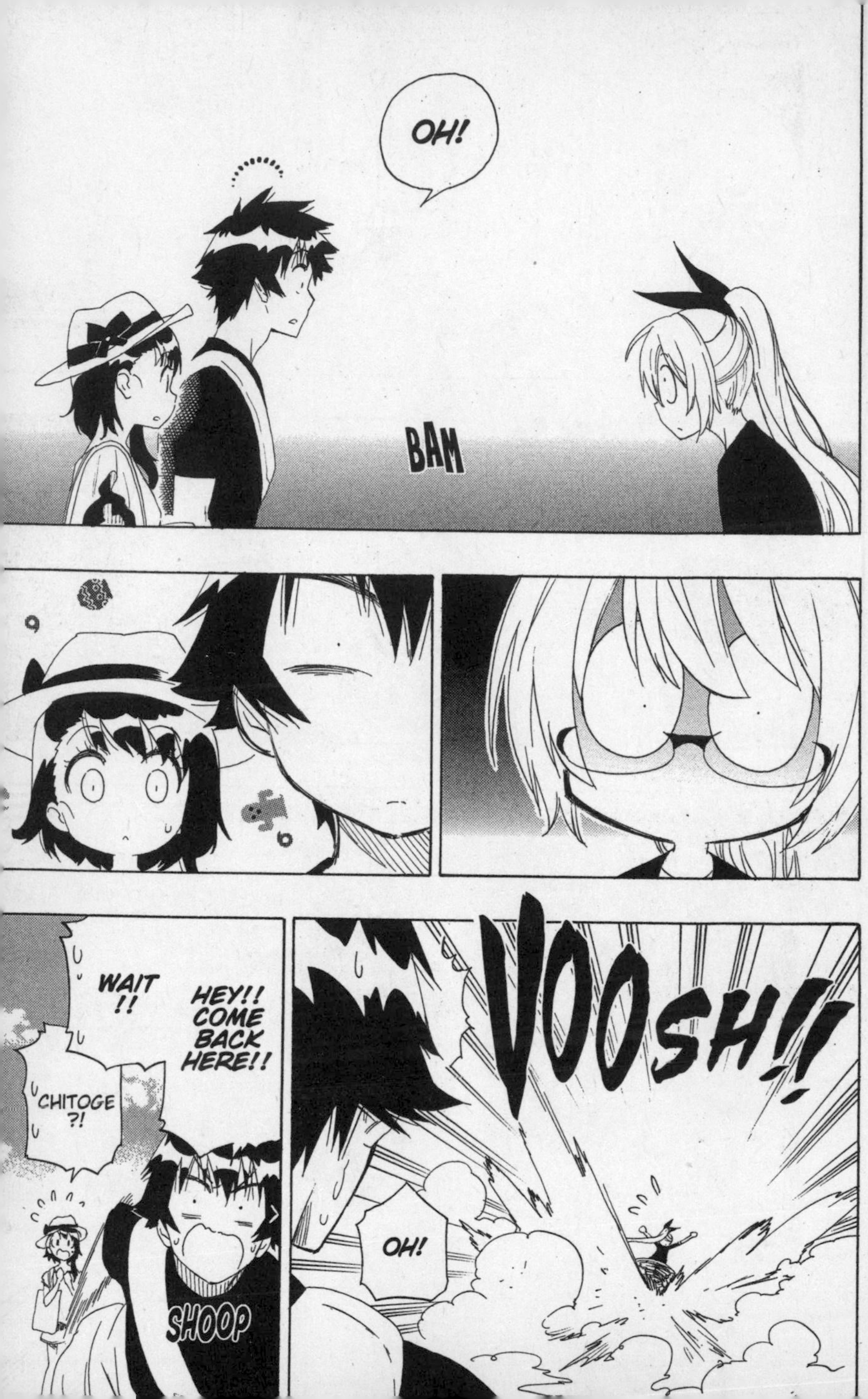
OH!
BAM
VOOSH!!
OH!
HEY!! COME BACK HERE!!
WAIT !!
CHITOGE ?!
SHOOP

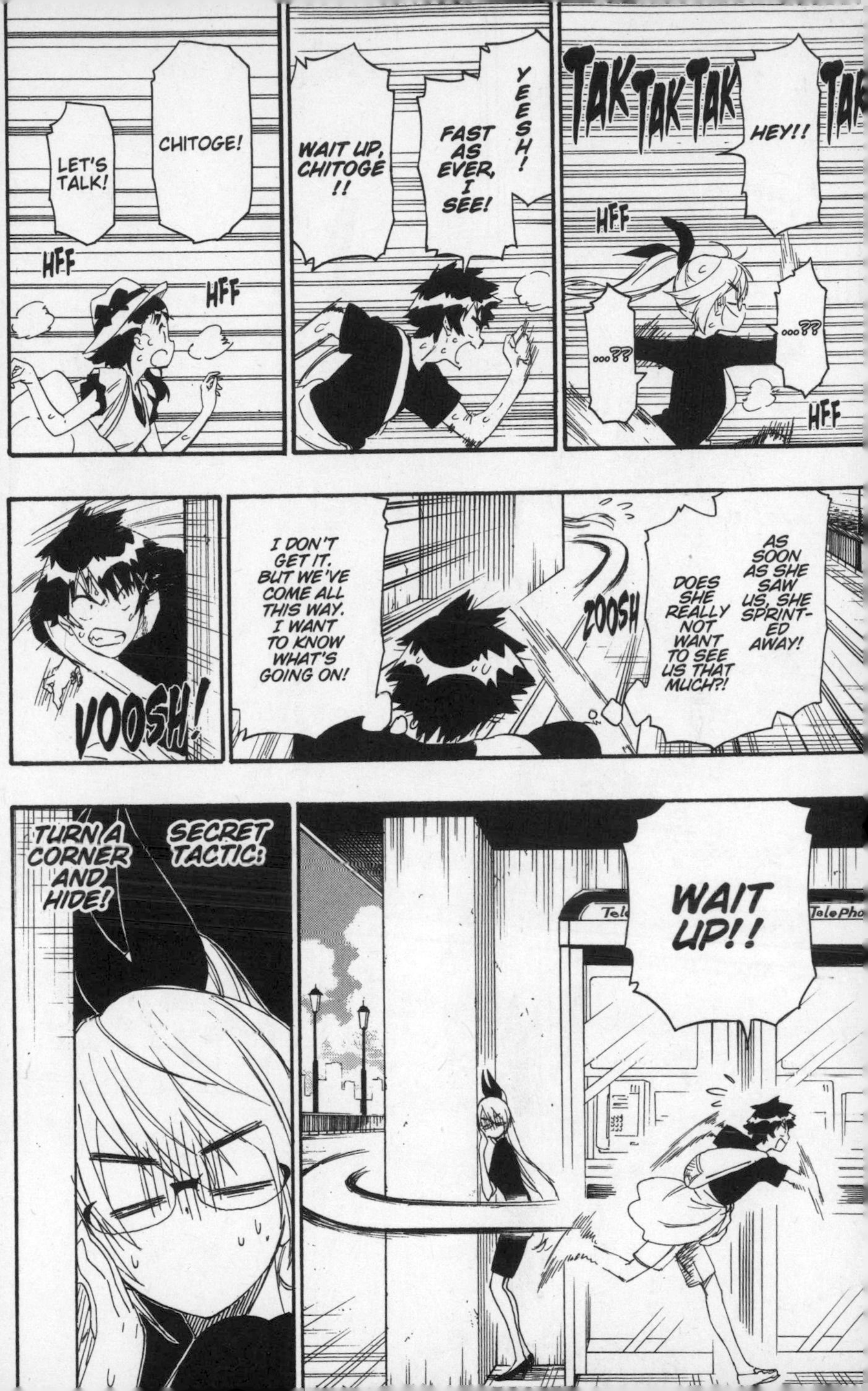
TAK TAK TAK
TAK
HEY!!
...??
...??
HFF
HFF
YEESH!
FAST AS EVER, I SEE!
WAIT UP, CHITOGE!!
CHITOGE!
LET'S TALK!
HFF
HFF
AS SOON AS SHE SAW US, SHE SPRINTED AWAY!
DOES SHE REALLY NOT WANT TO SEE US THAT MUCH?!
ZOOSH
I DON'T GET IT. BUT WE'VE COME ALL THIS WAY. I WANT TO KNOW WHAT'S GOING ON!
VOOSH!
WAIT UP!!
SECRET TACTIC:
TURN A CORNER AND HIDE!

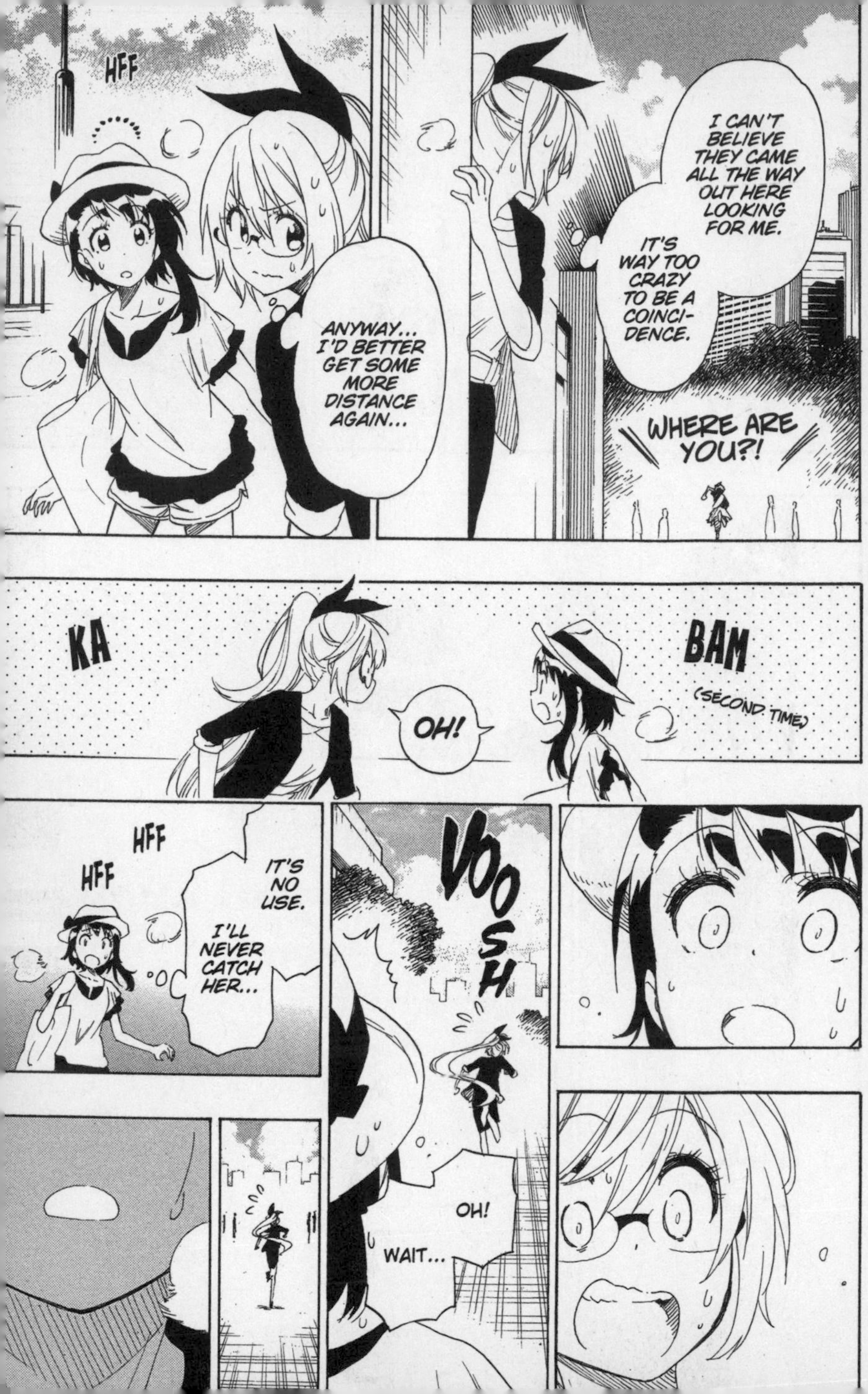
I CAN'T BELIEVE THEY CAME ALL THE WAY OUT HERE LOOKING FOR ME.
IT'S WAY TOO CRAZY TO BE A COINCIDENCE.
WHERE ARE YOU?!
HFF
ANYWAY... I'D BETTER GET SOME MORE DISTANCE AGAIN...
BAM
(SECOND TIME)
OH!
KA
VOOSH
HFF
HFF
IT'S NO USE.
I'LL NEVER CATCH HER...
OH!
WAIT...

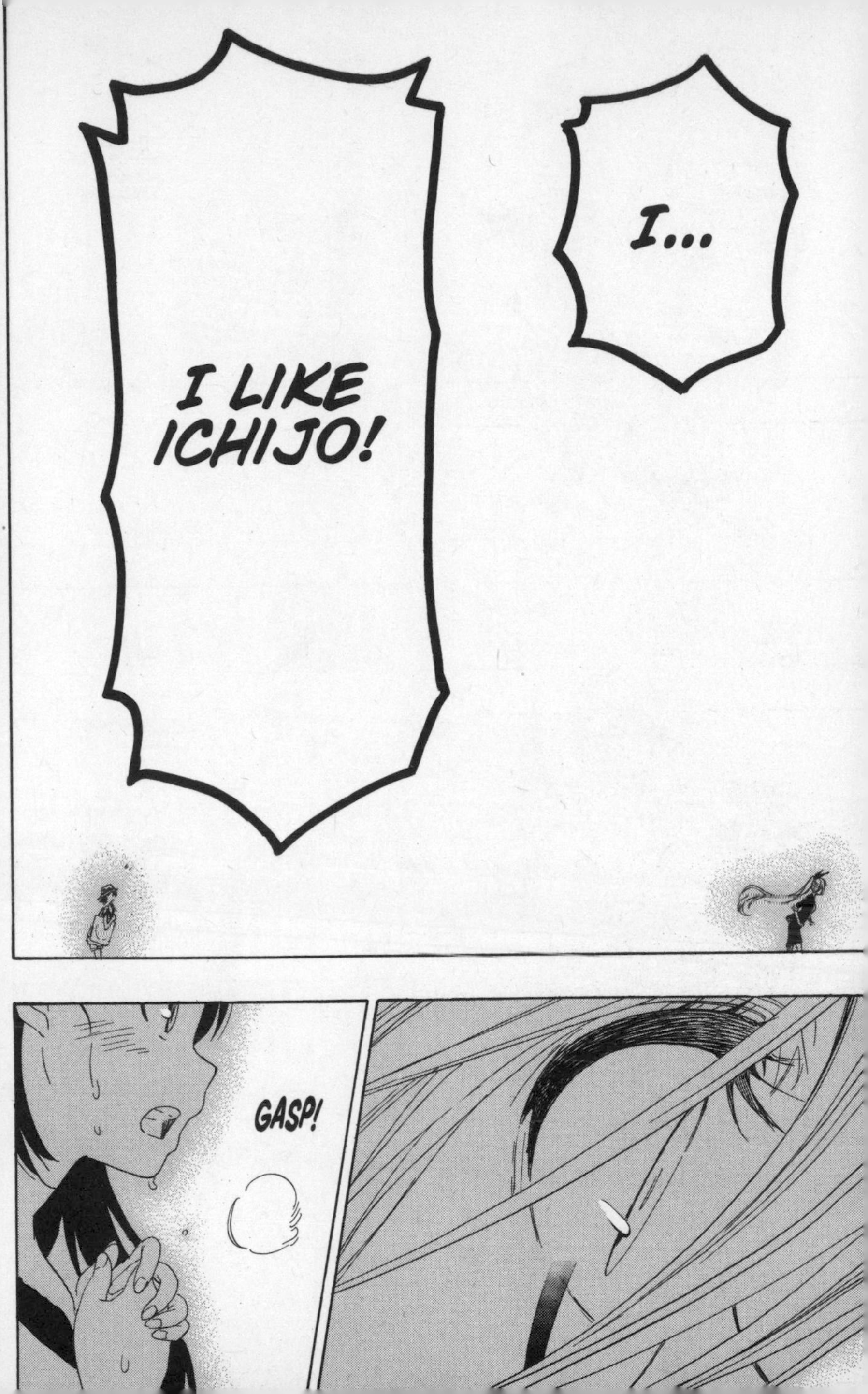
I...
I LIKE ICHIJO!
GASP!

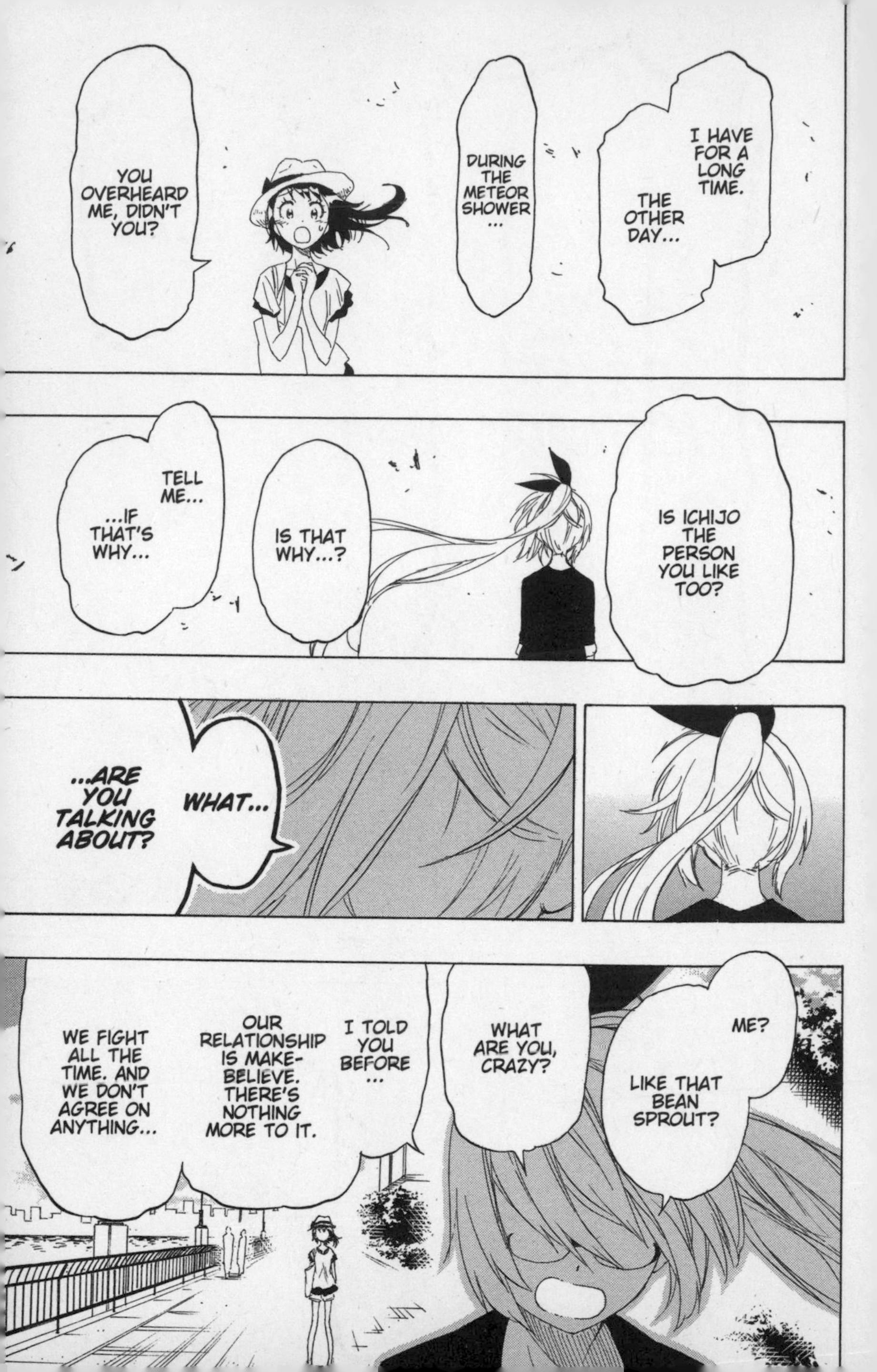
I HAVE FOR A LONG TIME.
THE OTHER DAY...
DURING THE METEOR SHOWER...
YOU OVERHEARD ME, DIDN'T YOU?
IS ICHIJO THE PERSON YOU LIKE TOO?
IS THAT WHY...?
TELL ME...
...IF THAT'S WHY...
WHAT...
...ARE YOU TALKING ABOUT?
ME?
LIKE THAT BEAN SPROUT?
WHAT ARE YOU, CRAZY?
I TOLD YOU BEFORE...
OUR RELATIONSHIP IS MAKE-BELIEVE. THERE'S NOTHING MORE TO IT.
WE FIGHT ALL THE TIME. AND WE DON'T AGREE ON ANYTHING...

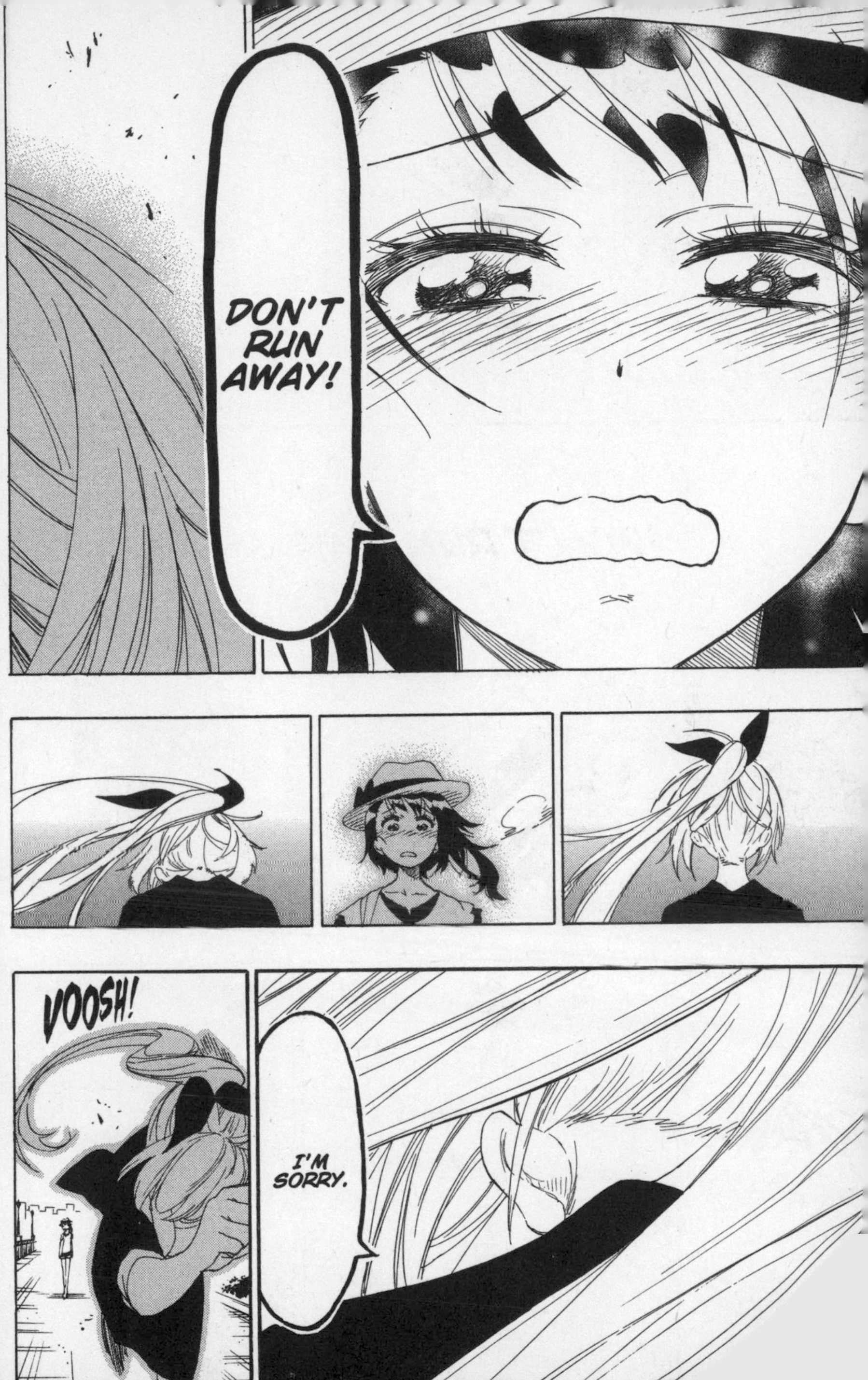
DON'T RUN AWAY!
I'M SORRY.
VOOSH!

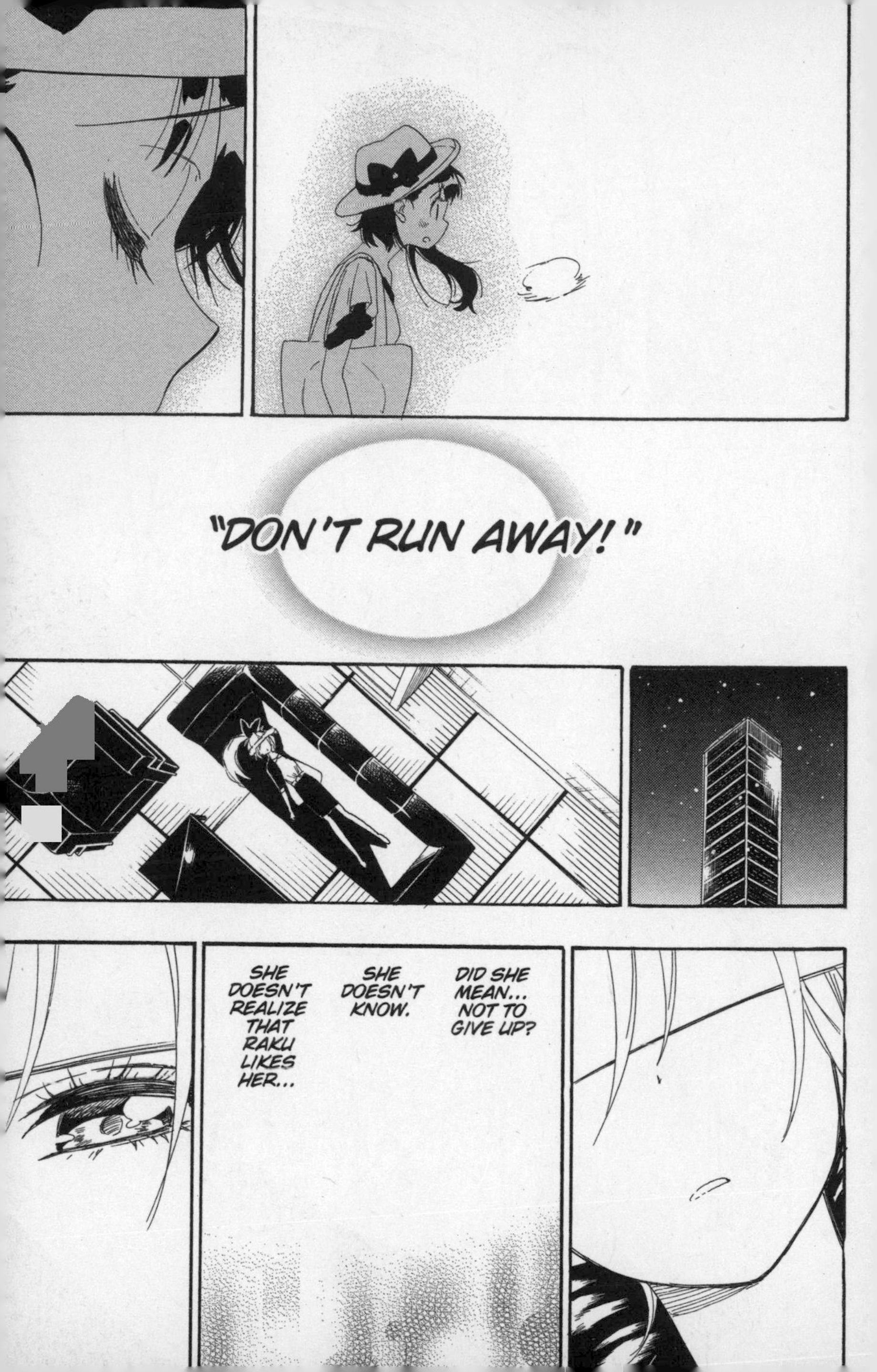
"DON'T RUN AWAY!"
DID SHE MEAN... NOT TO GIVE UP?
SHE DOESN'T KNOW.
SHE DOESN'T REALIZE THAT RAKU LIKES HER...

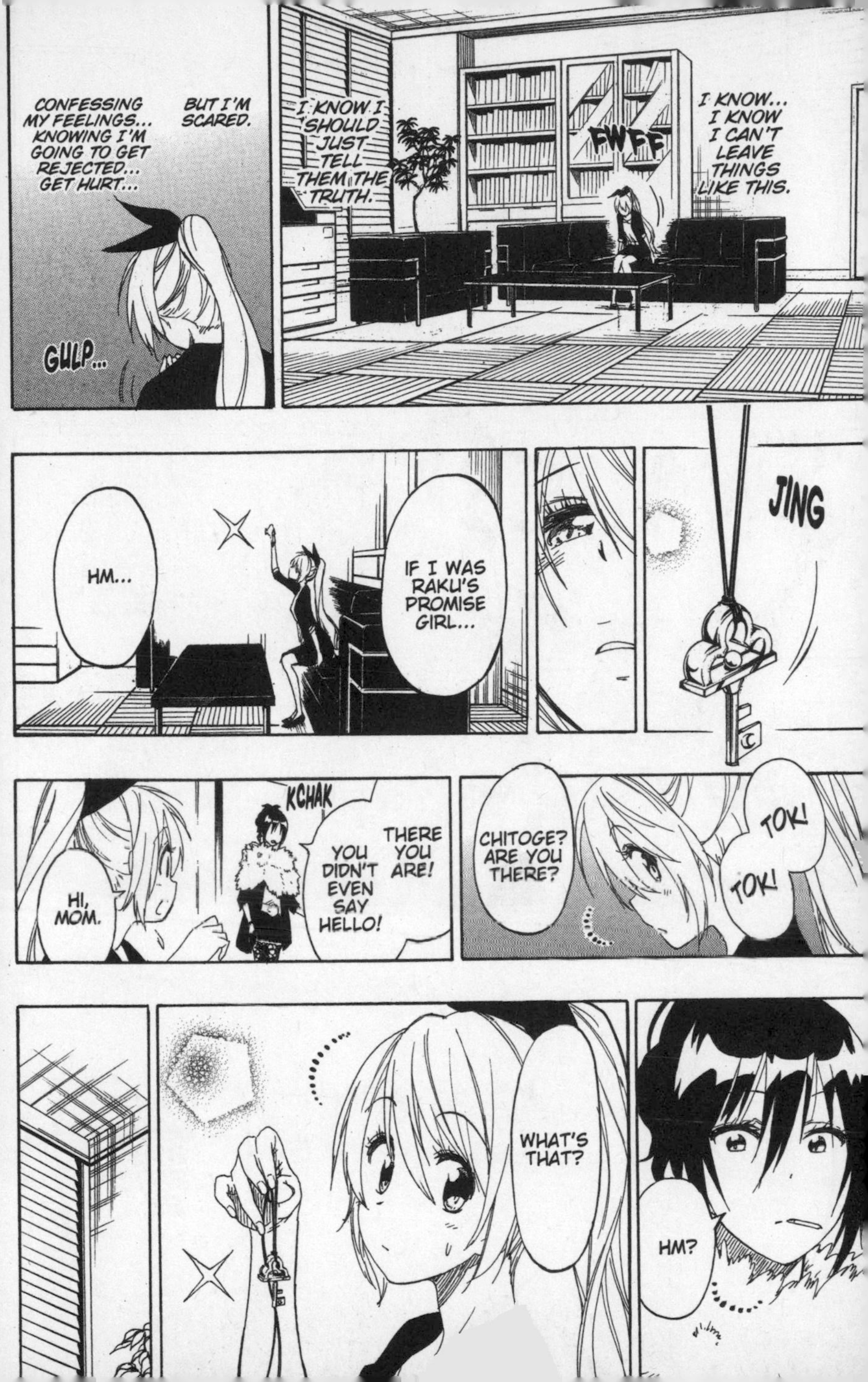
I KNOW... I KNOW I CAN'T LEAVE THINGS LIKE THIS.
FWFF
I KNOW I SHOULD JUST TELL THEM THE TRUTH.
BUT I'M SCARED.
CONFESSING MY FEELINGS... KNOWING I'M GOING TO GET REJECTED... GET HURT...
GULP...
JING
IF I WAS RAKU'S PROMISE GIRL...
HM...
TOK!
TOK!
CHITOGE? ARE YOU THERE?
KCHAK
THERE YOU ARE!
YOU DIDN'T EVEN SAY HELLO!
HI, MOM.
HM?
WHAT'S THAT?

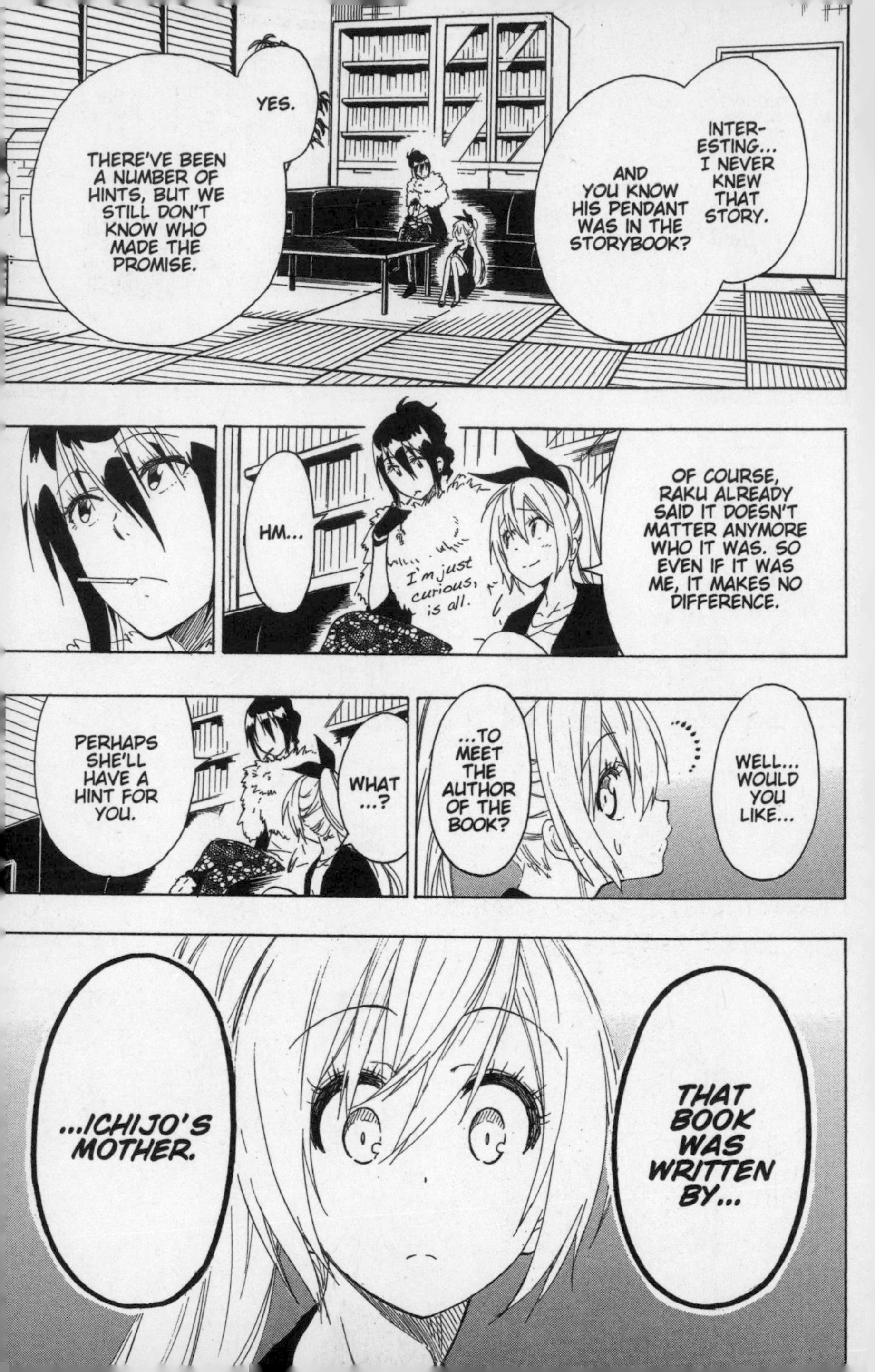
INTERESTING... I NEVER KNEW THAT STORY.
AND YOU KNOW HIS PENDANT WAS IN THE STORYBOOK?
YES.
THERE'VE BEEN A NUMBER OF HINTS, BUT WE STILL DON'T KNOW WHO MADE THE PROMISE.
OF COURSE, RAKU ALREADY SAID IT DOESN'T MATTER ANYMORE WHO IT WAS. SO EVEN IF IT WAS ME, IT MAKES NO DIFFERENCE.
I'm just curious, is all.
HM...
WELL... WOULD YOU LIKE...
...TO MEET THE AUTHOR OF THE BOOK?
WHAT...?
PERHAPS SHE'LL HAVE A HINT FOR YOU.
THAT BOOK WAS WRITTEN BY...
...ICHIJO'S MOTHER.

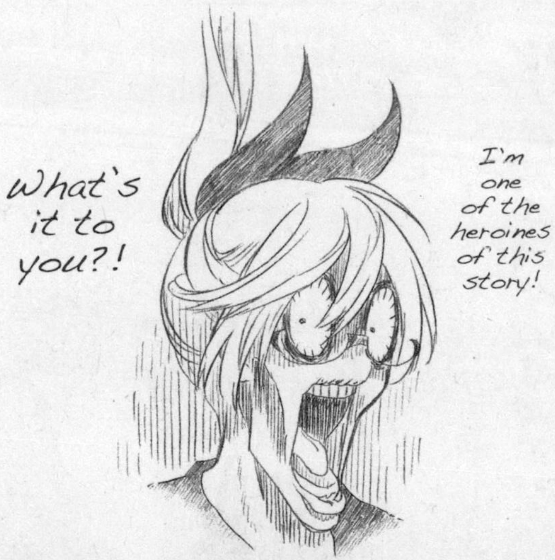
I'm one of the heroines of this story!
What's it to you?!

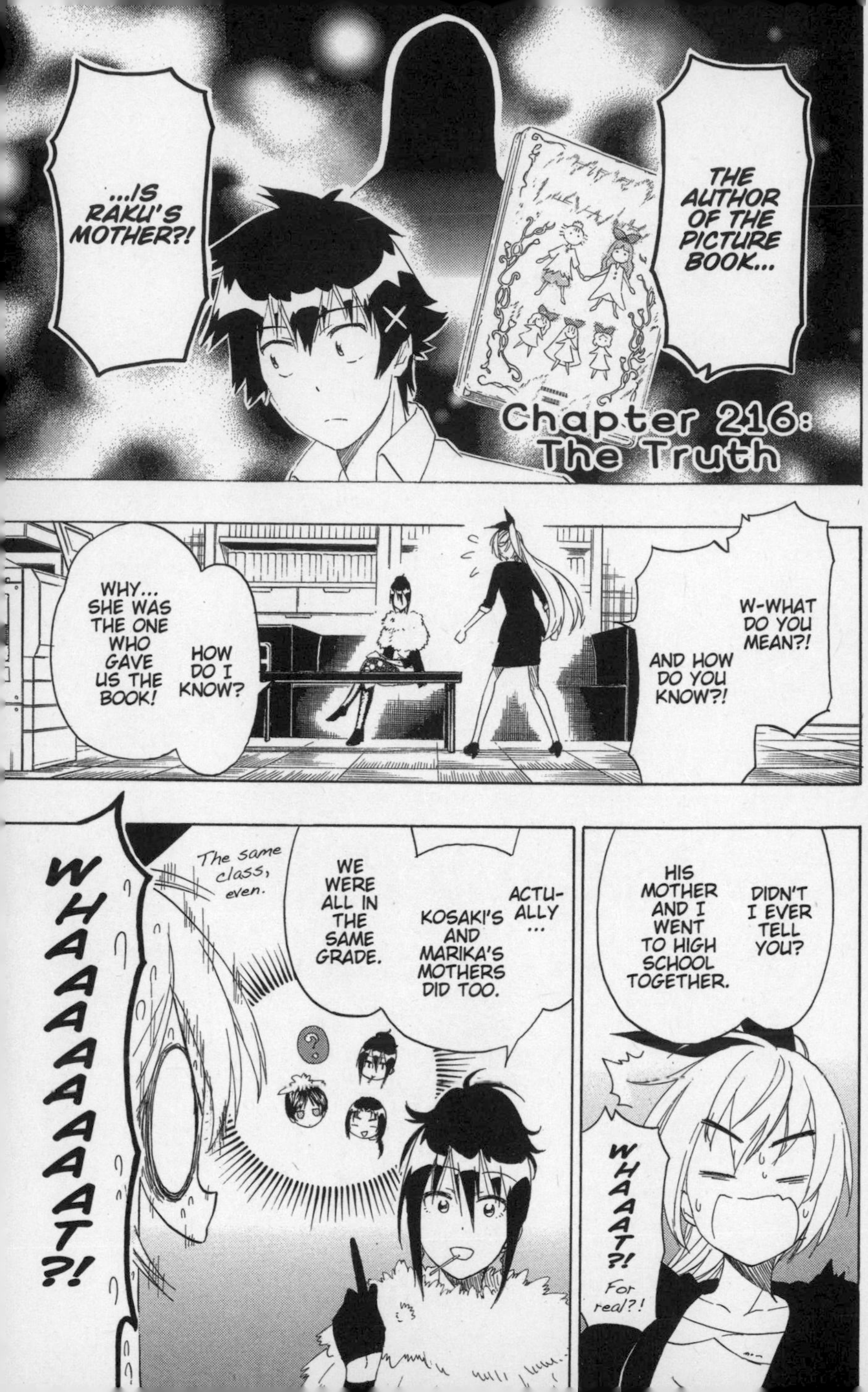
THE AUTHOR OF THE PICTURE BOOK...
...IS RAKU'S MOTHER?!
Chapter 216: The Truth
W-WHAT DO YOU MEAN?!
AND HOW DO YOU KNOW?!
HOW DO I KNOW?
WHY... SHE WAS THE ONE WHO GAVE US THE BOOK!
DIDN'T I EVER TELL YOU?
HIS MOTHER AND I WENT TO HIGH SCHOOL TOGETHER.
WHAAAT?!
For real?!
ACTU-ALLY...
KOSAKI'S AND MARIKA'S MOTHERS DID TOO.
WE WERE ALL IN THE SAME GRADE.
The same class, even.
WHAAAAAAAAT?!

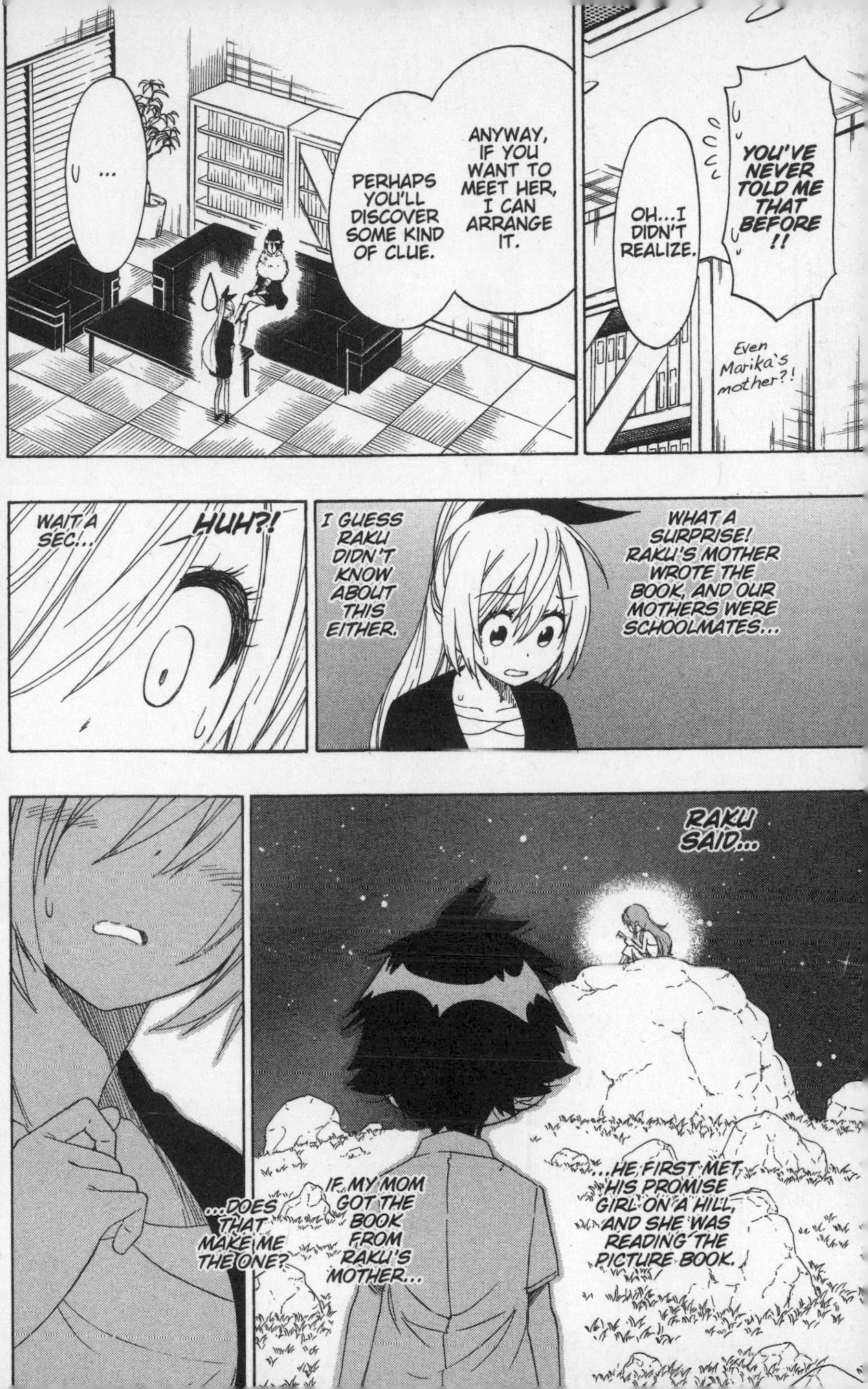
YOU'VE NEVER TOLD ME THAT BEFORE!!
OH...I DIDN'T REALIZE.
Even Marika's mother?!
ANYWAY, IF YOU WANT TO MEET HER, I CAN ARRANGE IT.
PERHAPS YOU'LL DISCOVER SOME KIND OF CLUE.
...
WHAT A SURPRISE! RAKU'S MOTHER WROTE THE BOOK, AND OUR MOTHERS WERE SCHOOLMATES...
I GUESS RAKU DIDN'T KNOW ABOUT THIS EITHER.
HUH?!
WAIT A SEC...
RAKU SAID...
...HE FIRST MET HIS PROMISE GIRL ON A HILL, AND SHE WAS READING THE PICTURE BOOK.
IF MY MOM GOT THE BOOK FROM RAKU'S MOTHER...
...DOES THAT MAKE ME THE ONE?

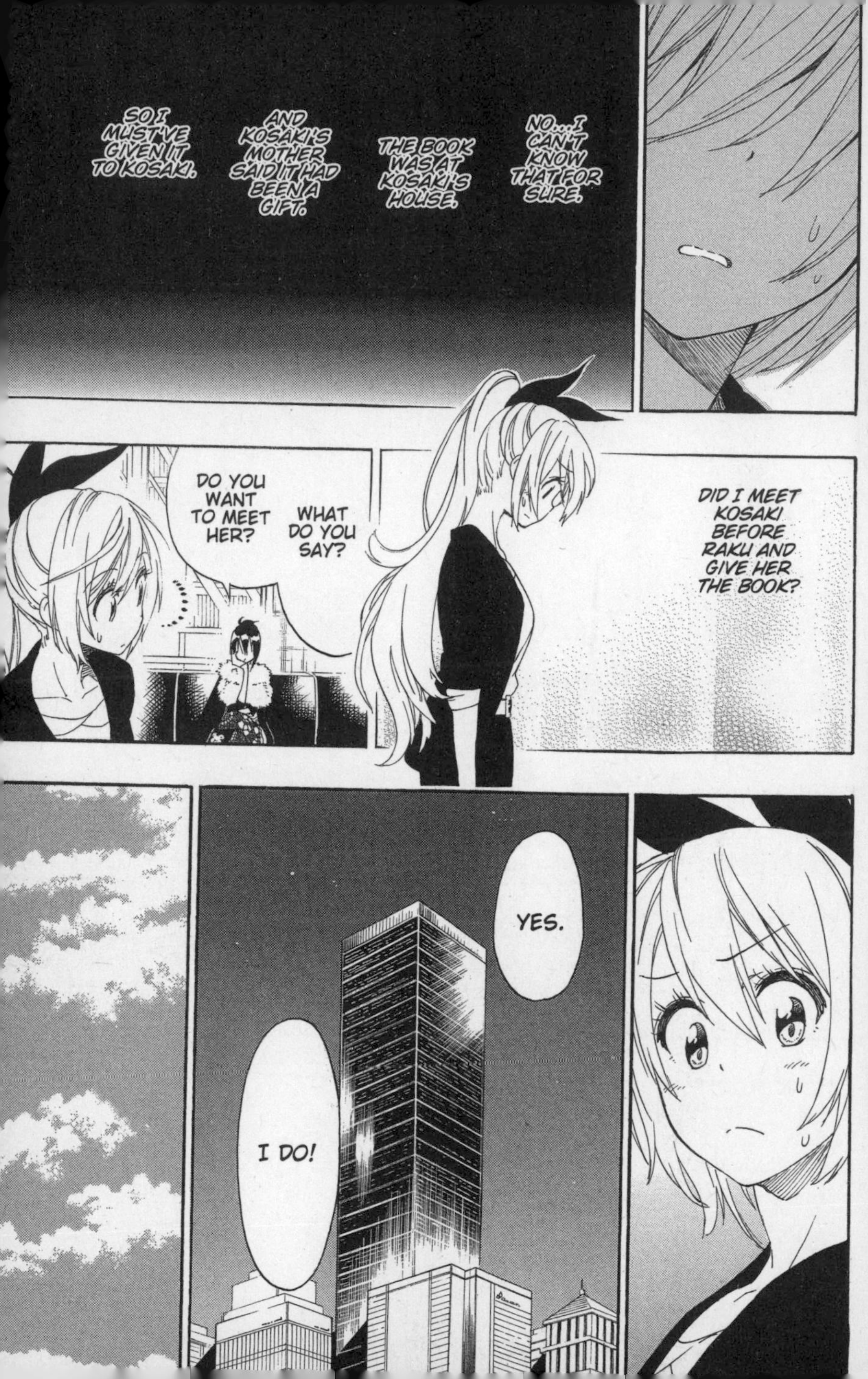
NO... I CAN'T KNOW THAT FOR SURE.
THE BOOK WAS AT KOSAKI'S HOUSE.
AND KOSAKI'S MOTHER SAID IT HAD BEEN A GIFT.
SO I MUST'VE GIVEN IT TO KOSAKI.
DID I MEET KOSAKI BEFORE RAKU AND GIVE HER THE BOOK?
DO YOU WANT TO MEET HER? WHAT DO YOU SAY?
YES.
I DO!

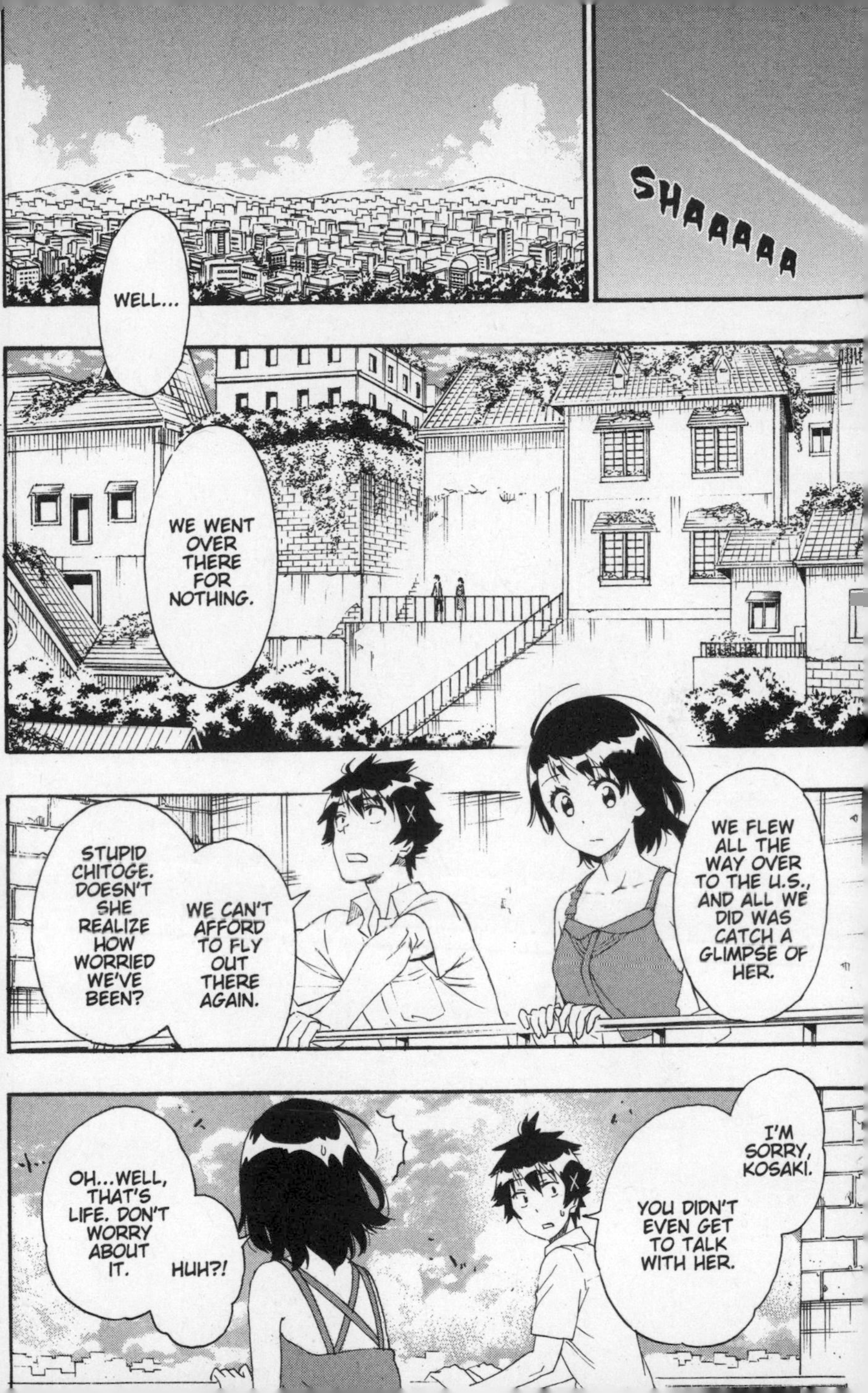
SHAAAAA
WELL...
WE WENT OVER THERE FOR NOTHING.
WE FLEW ALL THE WAY OVER TO THE U.S., AND ALL WE DID WAS CATCH A GLIMPSE OF HER.
WE CAN'T AFFORD TO FLY OUT THERE AGAIN.
STUPID CHITOGE. DOESN'T SHE REALIZE HOW WORRIED WE'VE BEEN?
I'M SORRY, KOSAKI.
YOU DIDN'T EVEN GET TO TALK WITH HER.
OH...WELL, THAT'S LIFE. DON'T WORRY ABOUT IT.
HUH?!

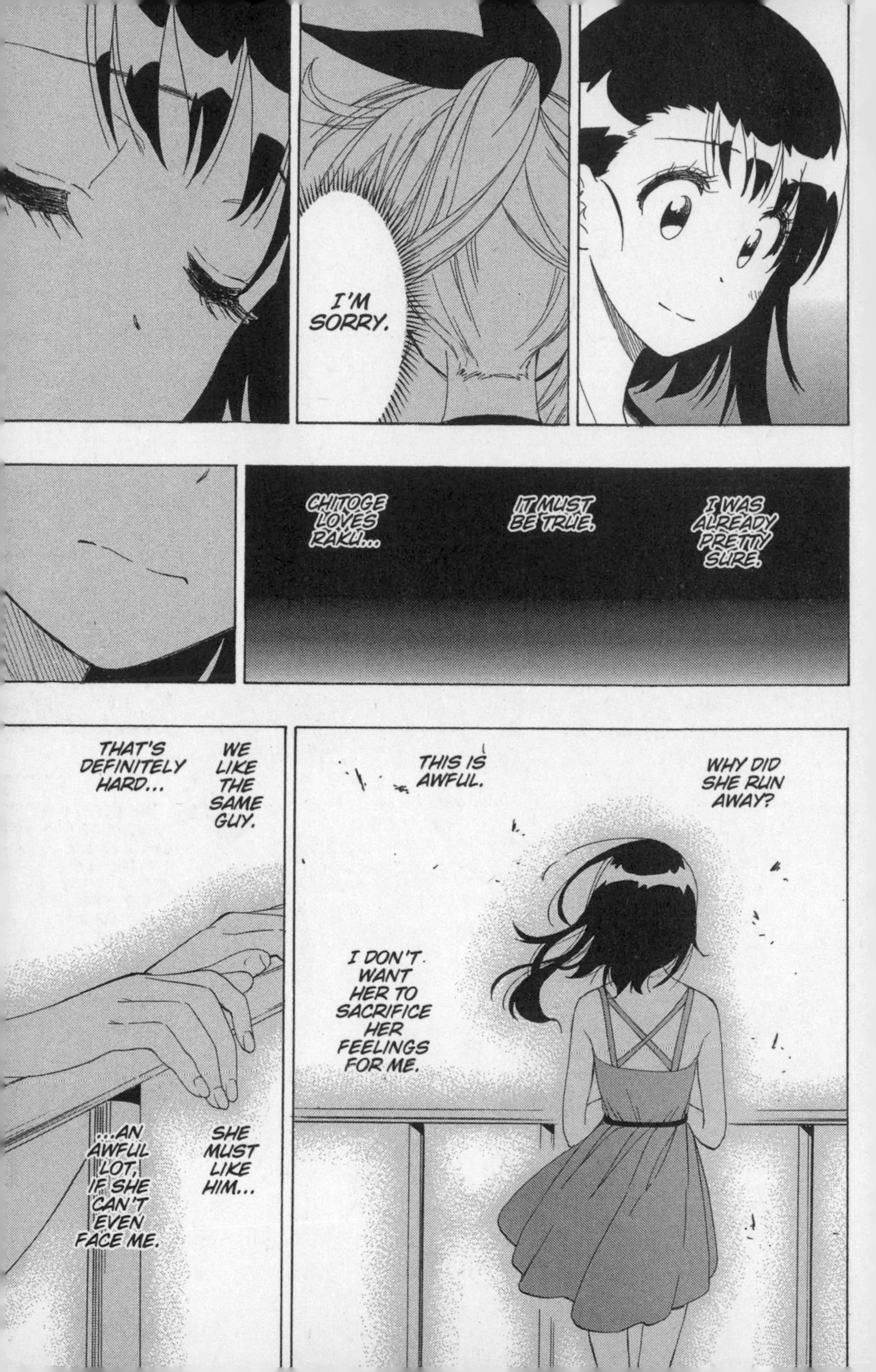
I'M SORRY.
I WAS ALREADY PRETTY SURE.
IT MUST BE TRUE.
CHITOGE LOVES RAKU...
WHY DID SHE RUN AWAY?
THIS IS AWFUL.
I DON'T WANT HER TO SACRIFICE HER FEELINGS FOR ME.
WE LIKE THE SAME GUY.
THAT'S DEFINITELY HARD...
SHE MUST LIKE HIM...
...AN AWFUL LOT, IF SHE CAN'T EVEN FACE ME.

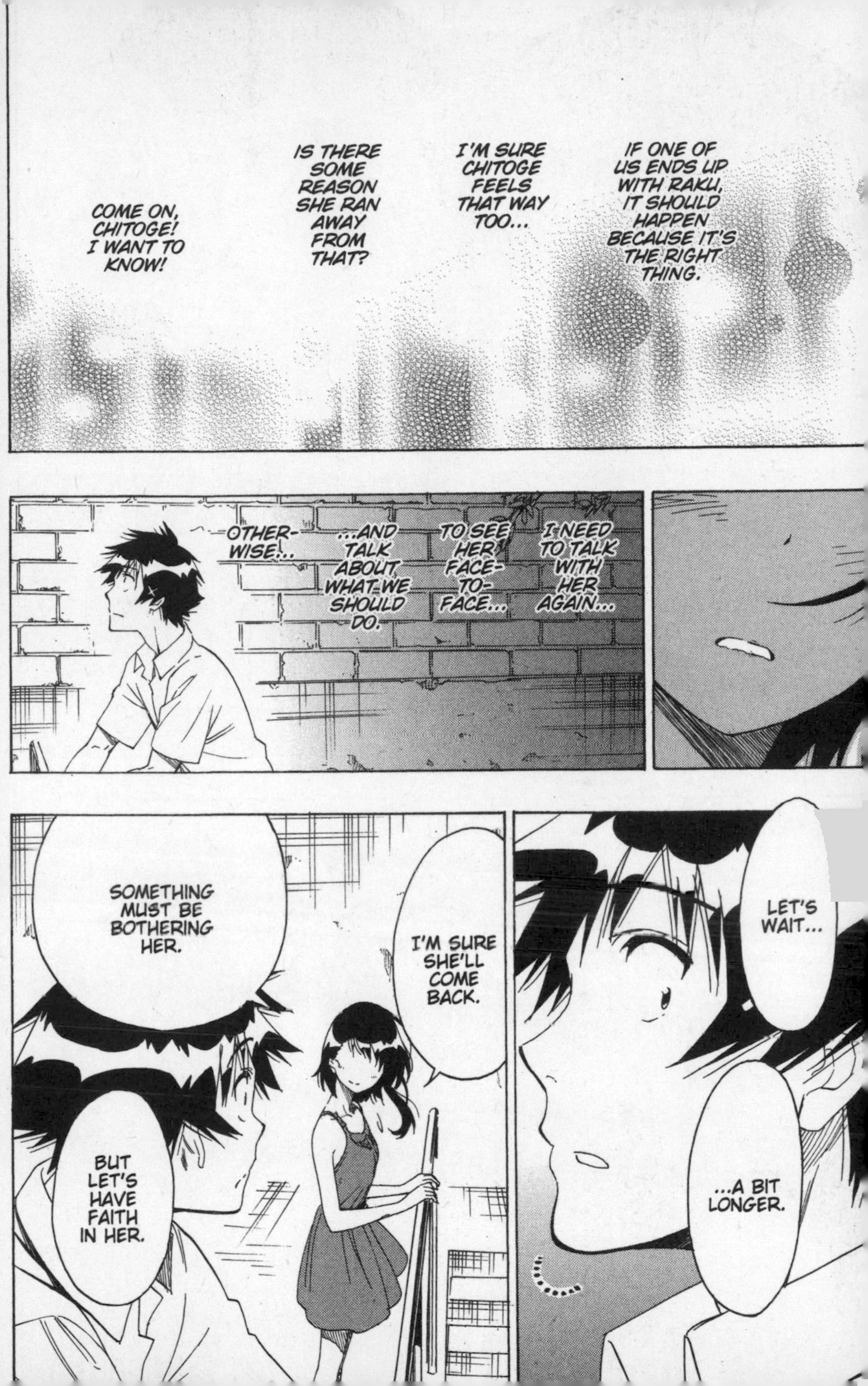
IF ONE OF US ENDS UP WITH RAKU, IT SHOULD HAPPEN BECAUSE IT'S THE RIGHT THING.
I'M SURE CHITOGE FEELS THAT WAY TOO...
IS THERE SOME REASON SHE RAN AWAY FROM THAT?
COME ON, CHITOGE! I WANT TO KNOW!
I NEED TO TALK WITH HER AGAIN...
TO SEE HER FACE-TO-FACE...
...AND TALK ABOUT WHAT WE SHOULD DO.
OTHER-WISE...
LET'S WAIT...
...A BIT LONGER.
I'M SURE SHE'LL COME BACK.
SOMETHING MUST BE BOTHERING HER.
BUT LET'S HAVE FAITH IN HER.

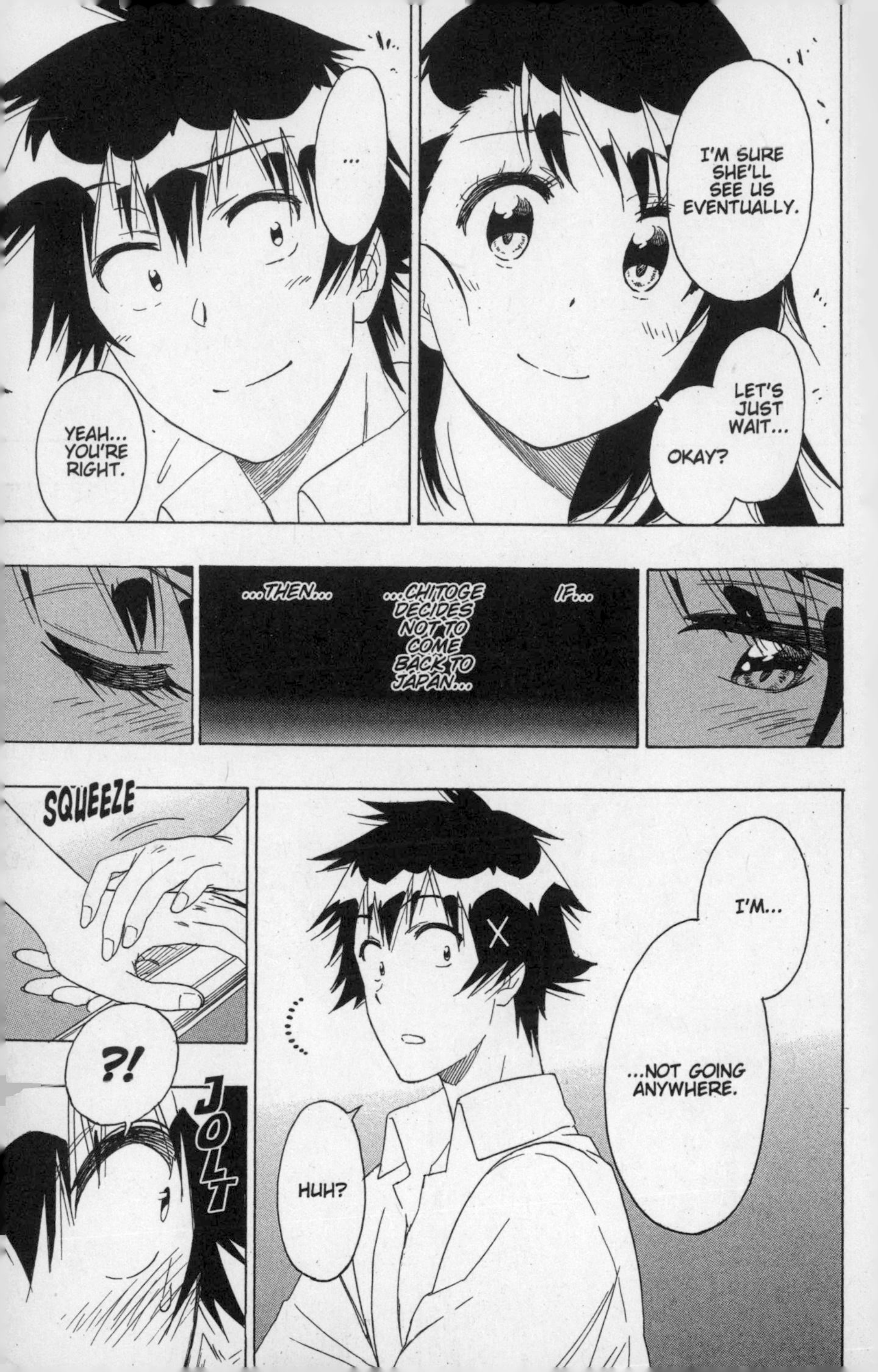
I'M SURE SHE'LL SEE US EVENTUALLY.
LET'S JUST WAIT...
OKAY?
...
YEAH... YOU'RE RIGHT.
IF...
...CHITOGE DECIDES NOT TO COME BACK TO JAPAN...
...THEN...
I'M...
...NOT GOING ANYWHERE.
HUH?
SQUEEZE
?!
JOLT

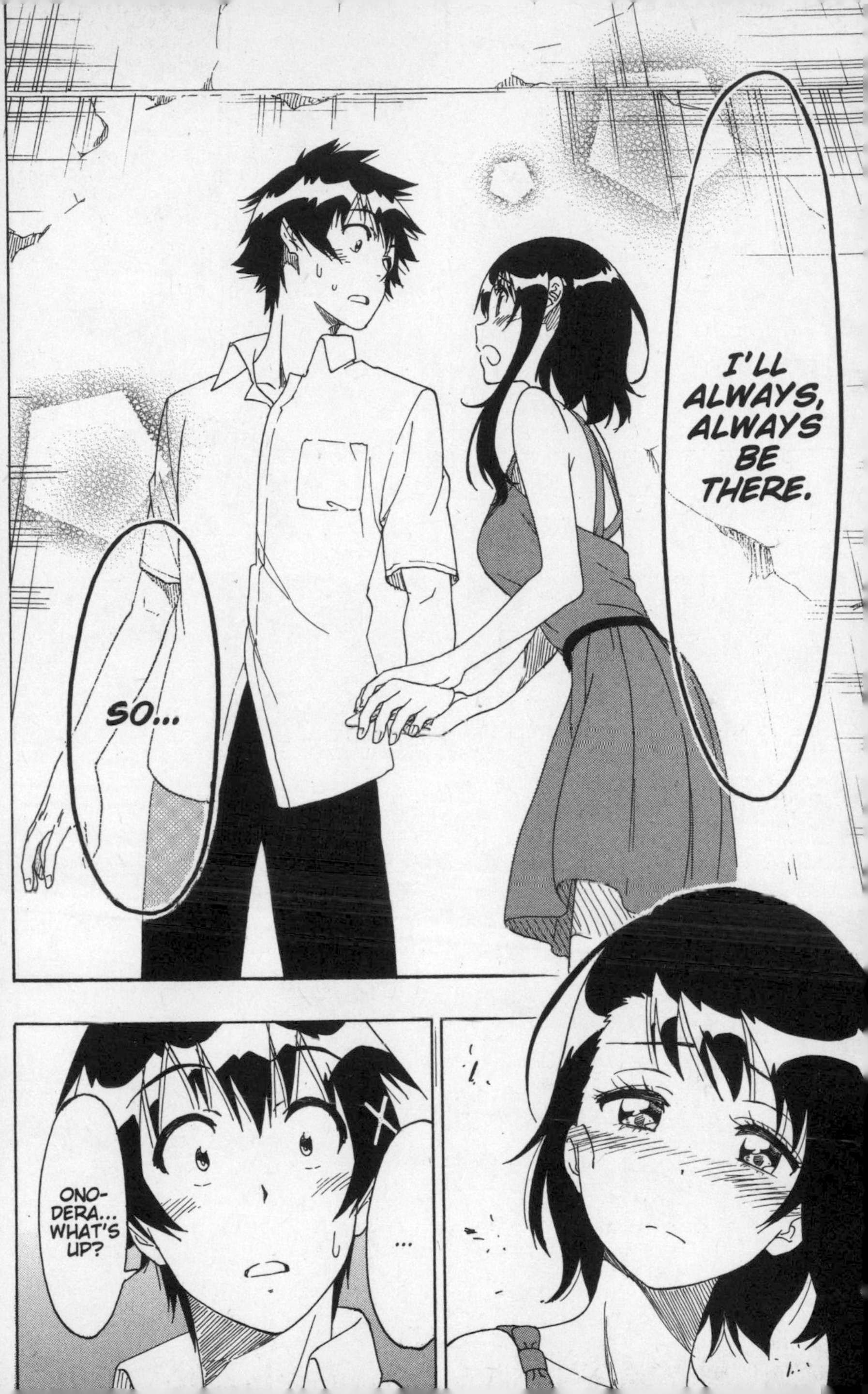
I'LL ALWAYS, ALWAYS BE THERE.
SO...
...
ONO-DERA... WHAT'S UP?

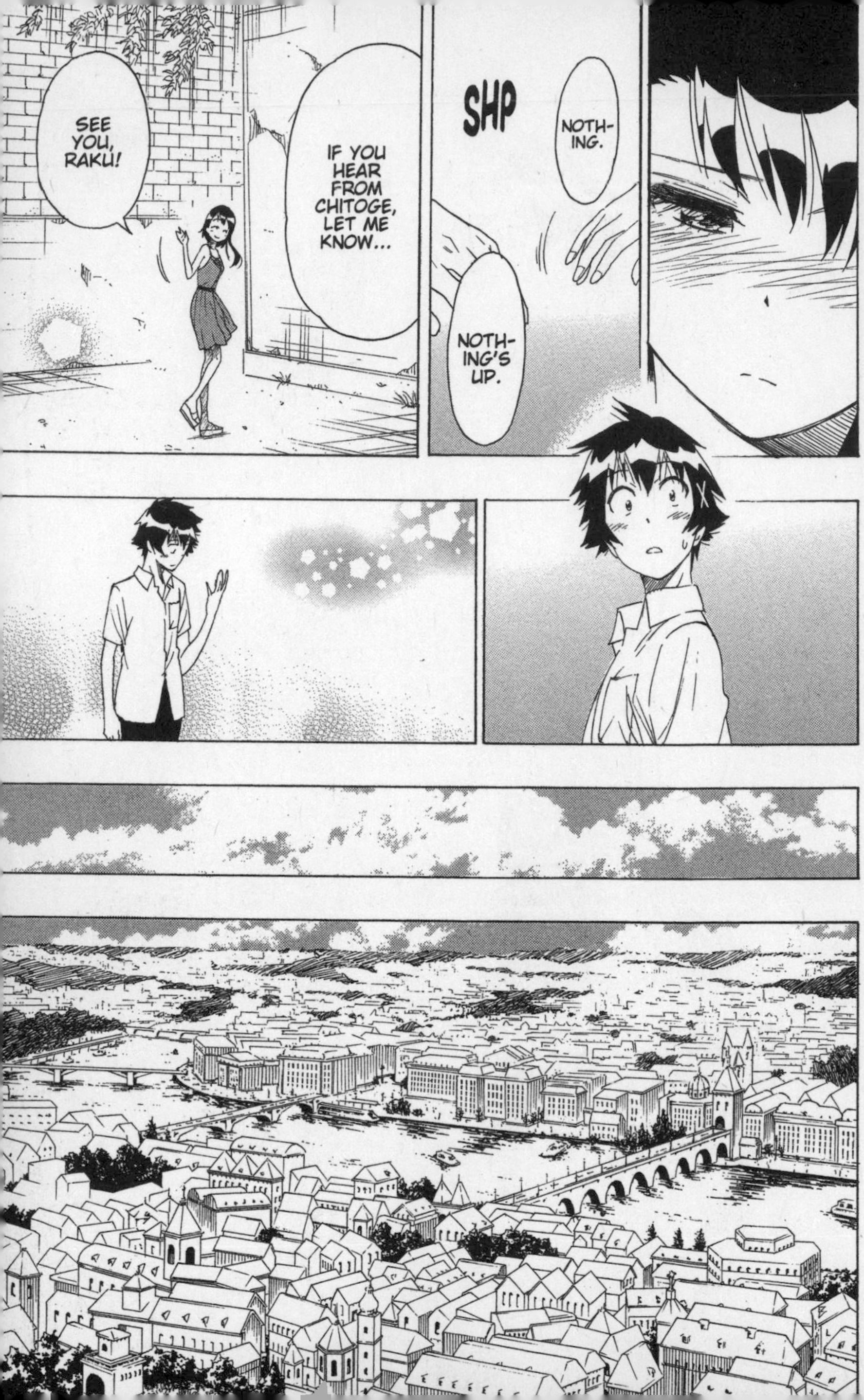
NOTHING.
SHP
NOTHING'S UP.
IF YOU HEAR FROM CHITOGE, LET ME KNOW...
SEE YOU, RAKU!

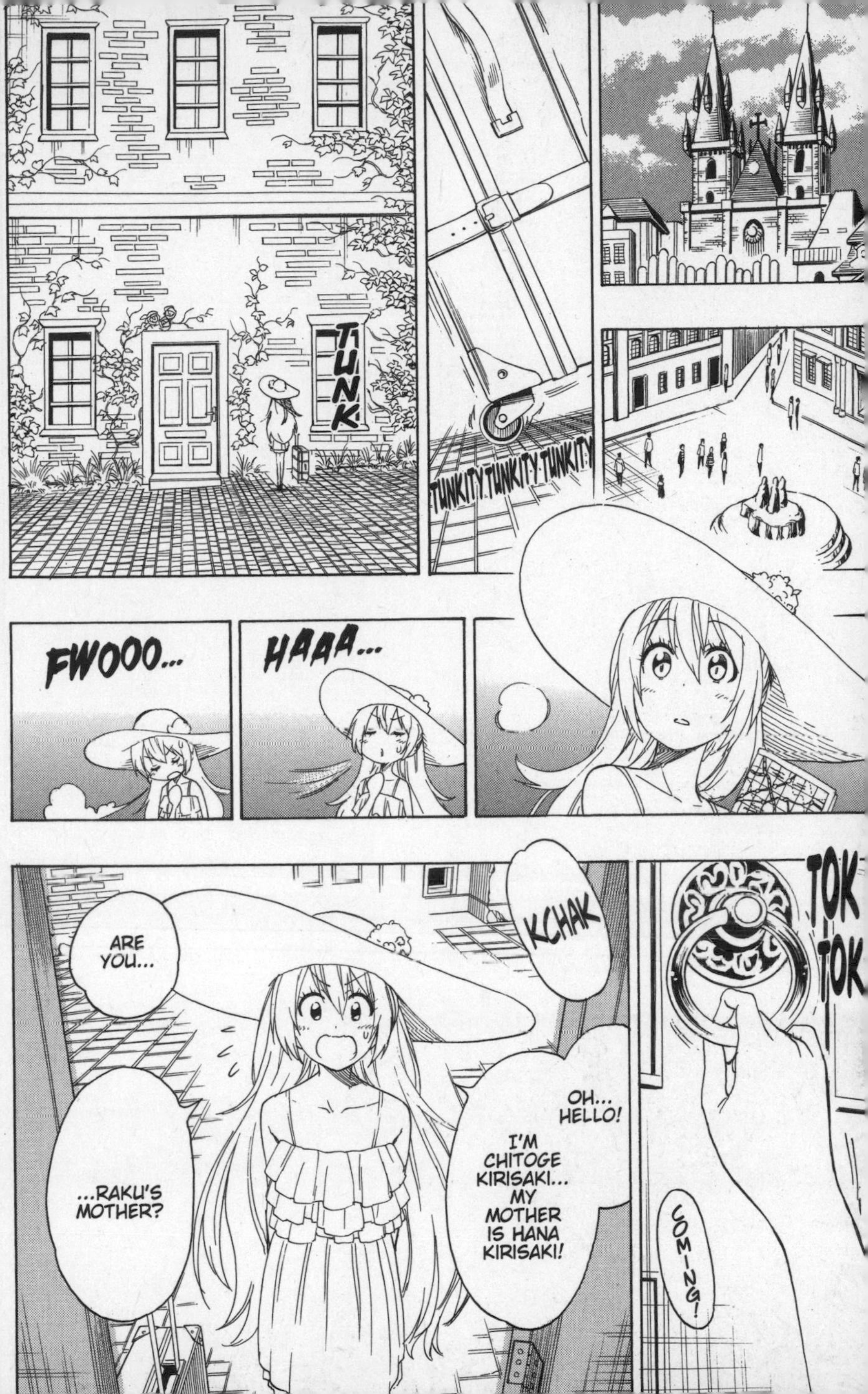
TUNKITY TUNKITY TUNKITY
TUNK
HAAA...
FWOOO...
TOK TOK
COMING!
KCHAK
OH... HELLO!
I'M CHITOGE KIRISAKI... MY MOTHER IS HANA KIRISAKI!
ARE YOU...
...RAKU'S MOTHER?

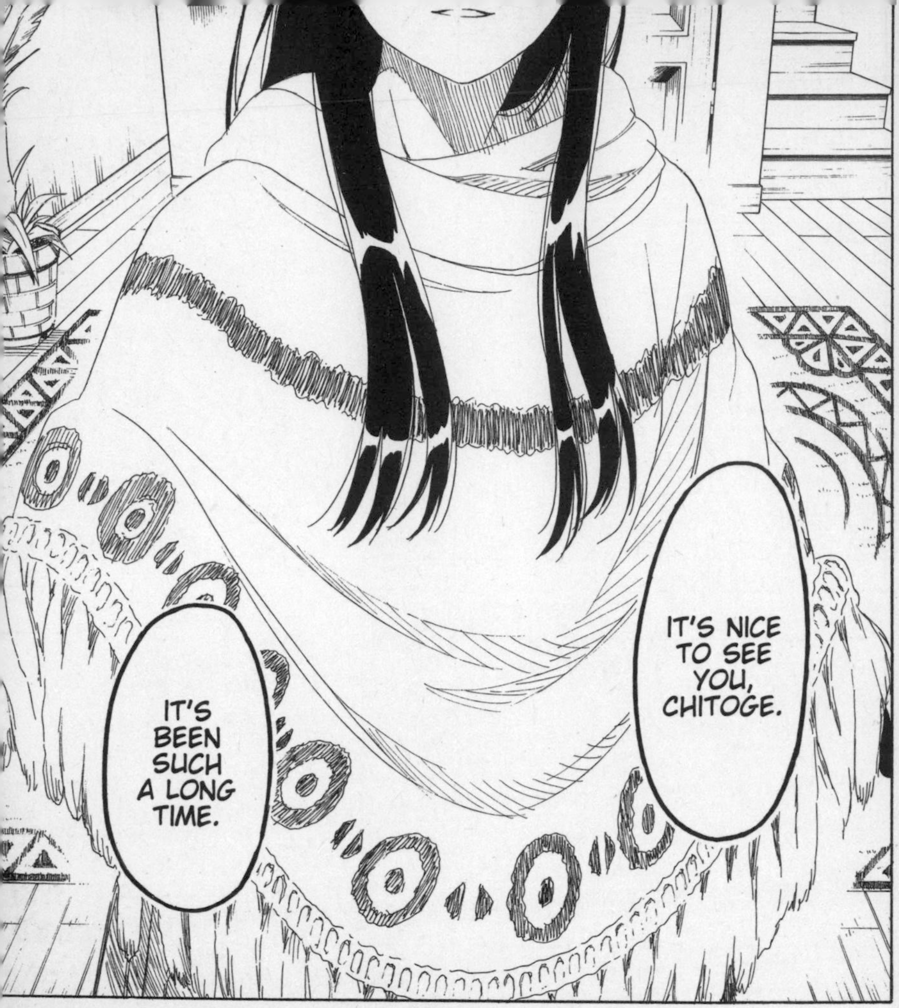
IT'S NICE TO SEE YOU, CHITOGE.
IT'S BEEN SUCH A LONG TIME.
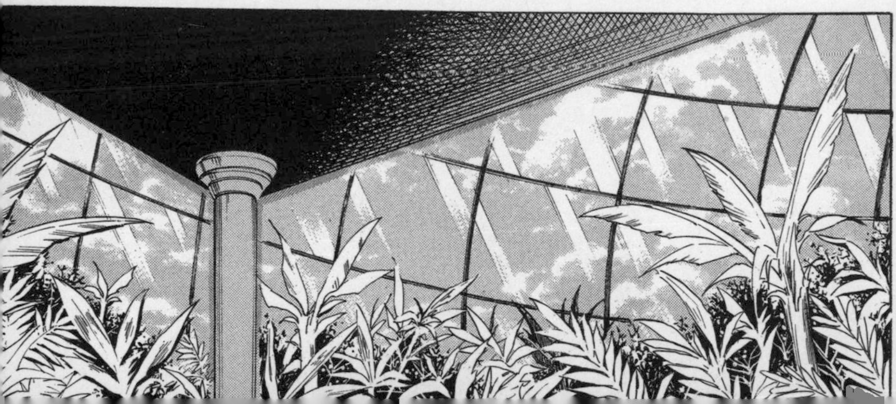

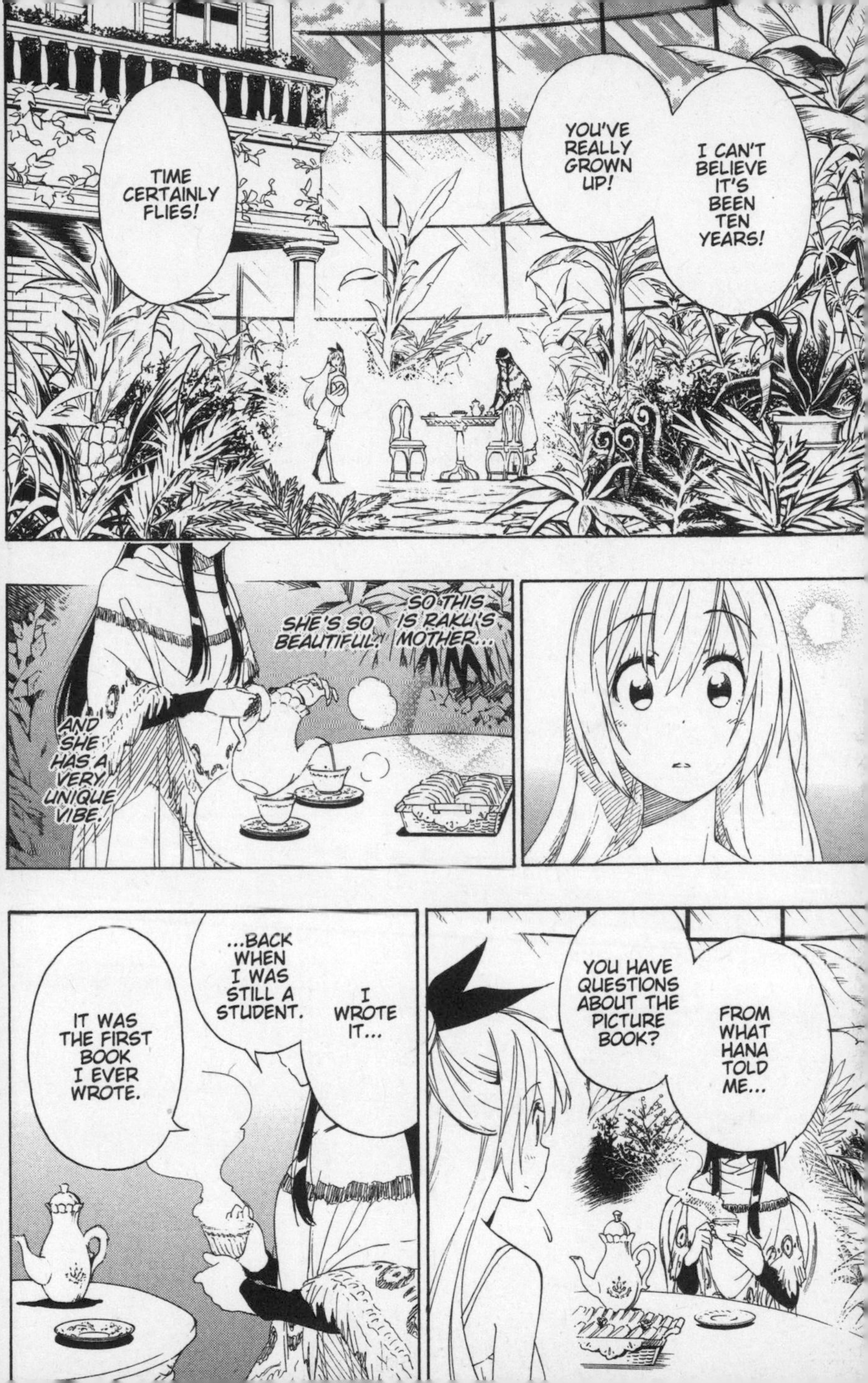
I CAN'T BELIEVE IT'S BEEN TEN YEARS!
YOU'VE REALLY GROWN UP!
TIME CERTAINLY FLIES!
SO THIS IS RAKU'S MOTHER...
SHE'S SO BEAUTIFUL.
AND SHE HAS A VERY UNIQUE VIBE.
FROM WHAT HANA TOLD ME...
YOU HAVE QUESTIONS ABOUT THE PICTURE BOOK?
I WROTE IT...
...BACK WHEN I WAS STILL A STUDENT.
IT WAS THE FIRST BOOK I EVER WROTE.

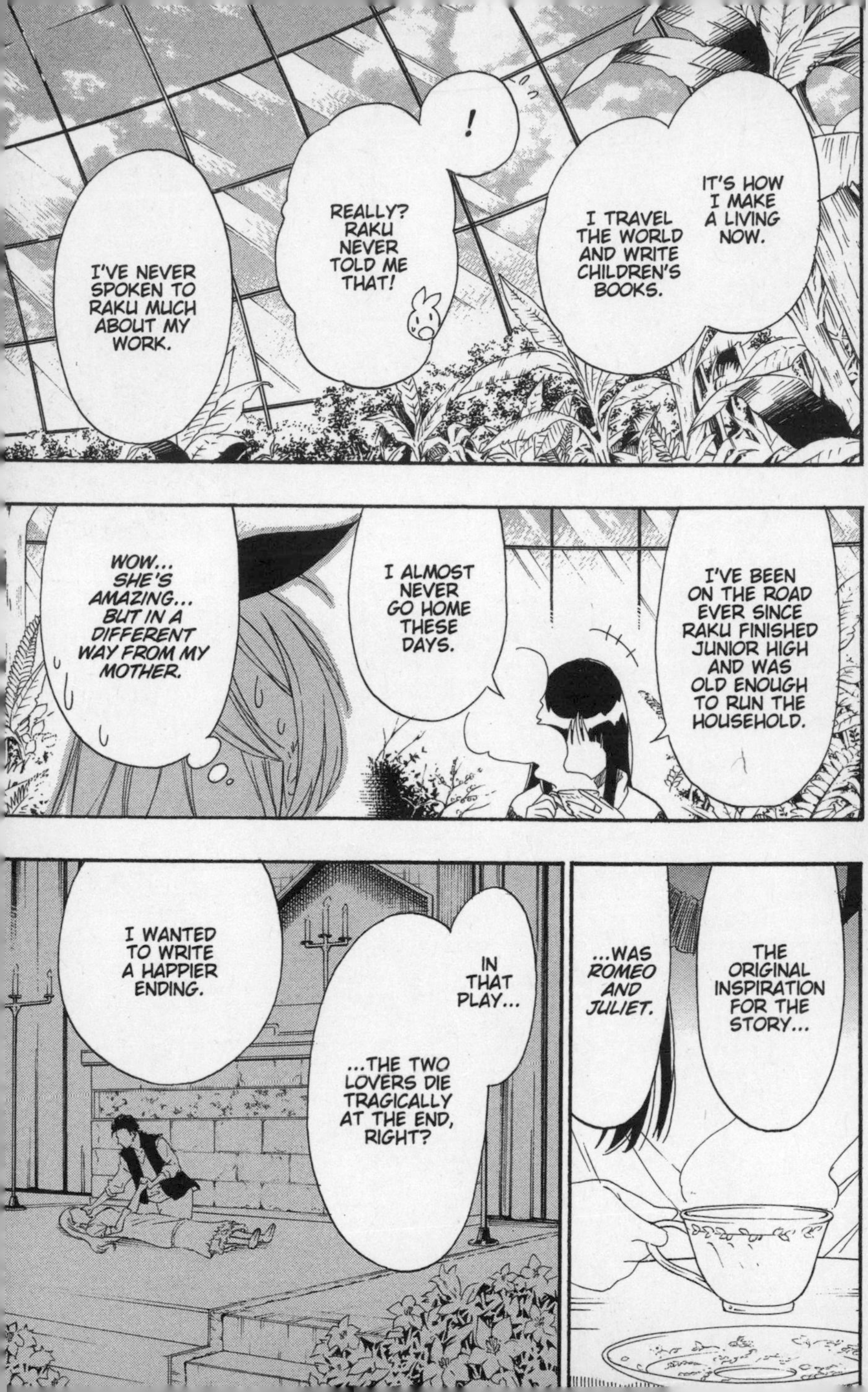
I TRAVEL THE WORLD AND WRITE CHILDREN'S BOOKS. IT'S HOW I MAKE A LIVING NOW.
!
REALLY? RAKU NEVER TOLD ME THAT!
I'VE NEVER SPOKEN TO RAKU MUCH ABOUT MY WORK.
I'VE BEEN ON THE ROAD EVER SINCE RAKU FINISHED JUNIOR HIGH AND WAS OLD ENOUGH TO RUN THE HOUSEHOLD.
I ALMOST NEVER GO HOME THESE DAYS.
WOW... SHE'S AMAZING... BUT IN A DIFFERENT WAY FROM MY MOTHER.
THE ORIGINAL INSPIRATION FOR THE STORY...
...WAS *ROMEO AND JULIET.*
IN THAT PLAY...
...THE TWO LOVERS DIE TRAGICALLY AT THE END, RIGHT?
I WANTED TO WRITE A HAPPIER ENDING.

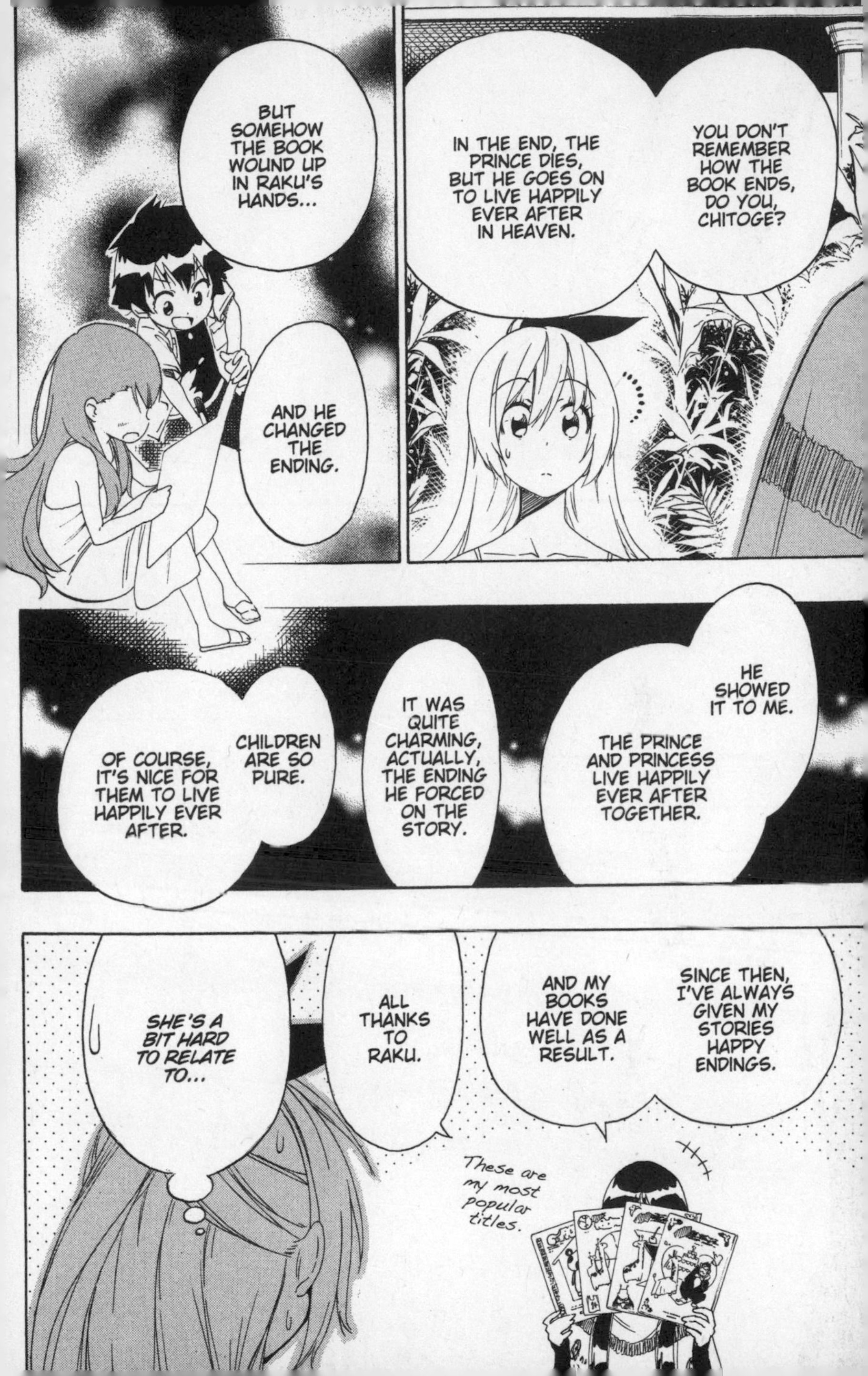
YOU DON'T REMEMBER HOW THE BOOK ENDS, DO YOU, CHITOGE?
IN THE END, THE PRINCE DIES, BUT HE GOES ON TO LIVE HAPPILY EVER AFTER IN HEAVEN.
BUT SOMEHOW THE BOOK WOUND UP IN RAKU'S HANDS...
AND HE CHANGED THE ENDING.
HE SHOWED IT TO ME.
THE PRINCE AND PRINCESS LIVE HAPPILY EVER AFTER TOGETHER.
IT WAS QUITE CHARMING, ACTUALLY, THE ENDING HE FORCED ON THE STORY.
CHILDREN ARE SO PURE.
OF COURSE, IT'S NICE FOR THEM TO LIVE HAPPILY EVER AFTER.
SINCE THEN, I'VE ALWAYS GIVEN MY STORIES HAPPY ENDINGS.
AND MY BOOKS HAVE DONE WELL AS A RESULT.
ALL THANKS TO RAKU.
These are my most popular titles.
SHE'S A BIT HARD TO RELATE TO...

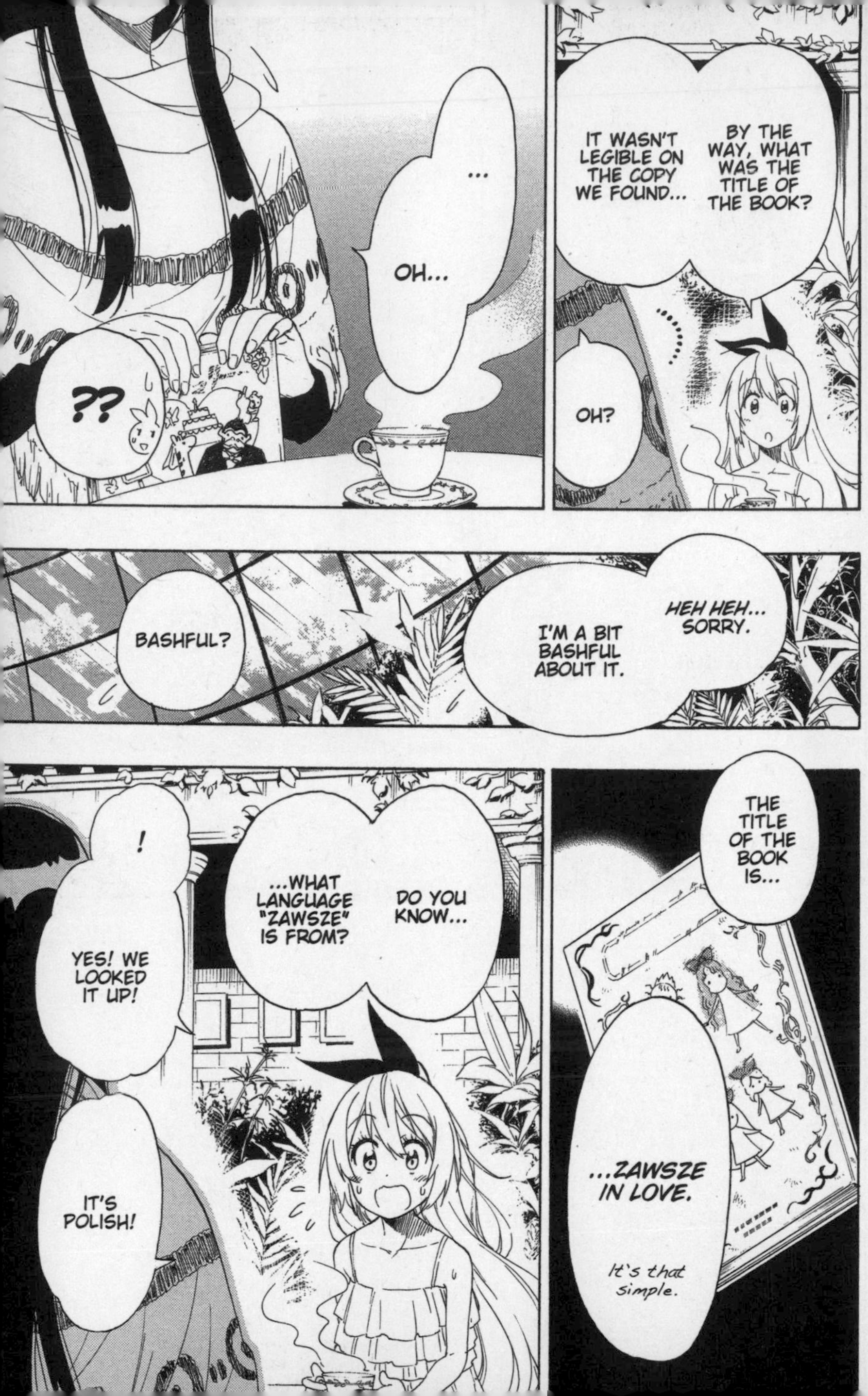
BY THE WAY, WHAT WAS THE TITLE OF THE BOOK?
IT WASN'T LEGIBLE ON THE COPY WE FOUND...
OH?
...
OH...
??
HEH HEH... SORRY.
I'M A BIT BASHFUL ABOUT IT.
BASHFUL?
THE TITLE OF THE BOOK IS...
...ZAWSZE IN LOVE.
It's that simple.
DO YOU KNOW...
...WHAT LANGUAGE "ZAWSZE" IS FROM?
!
YES! WE LOOKED IT UP!
IT'S POLISH!

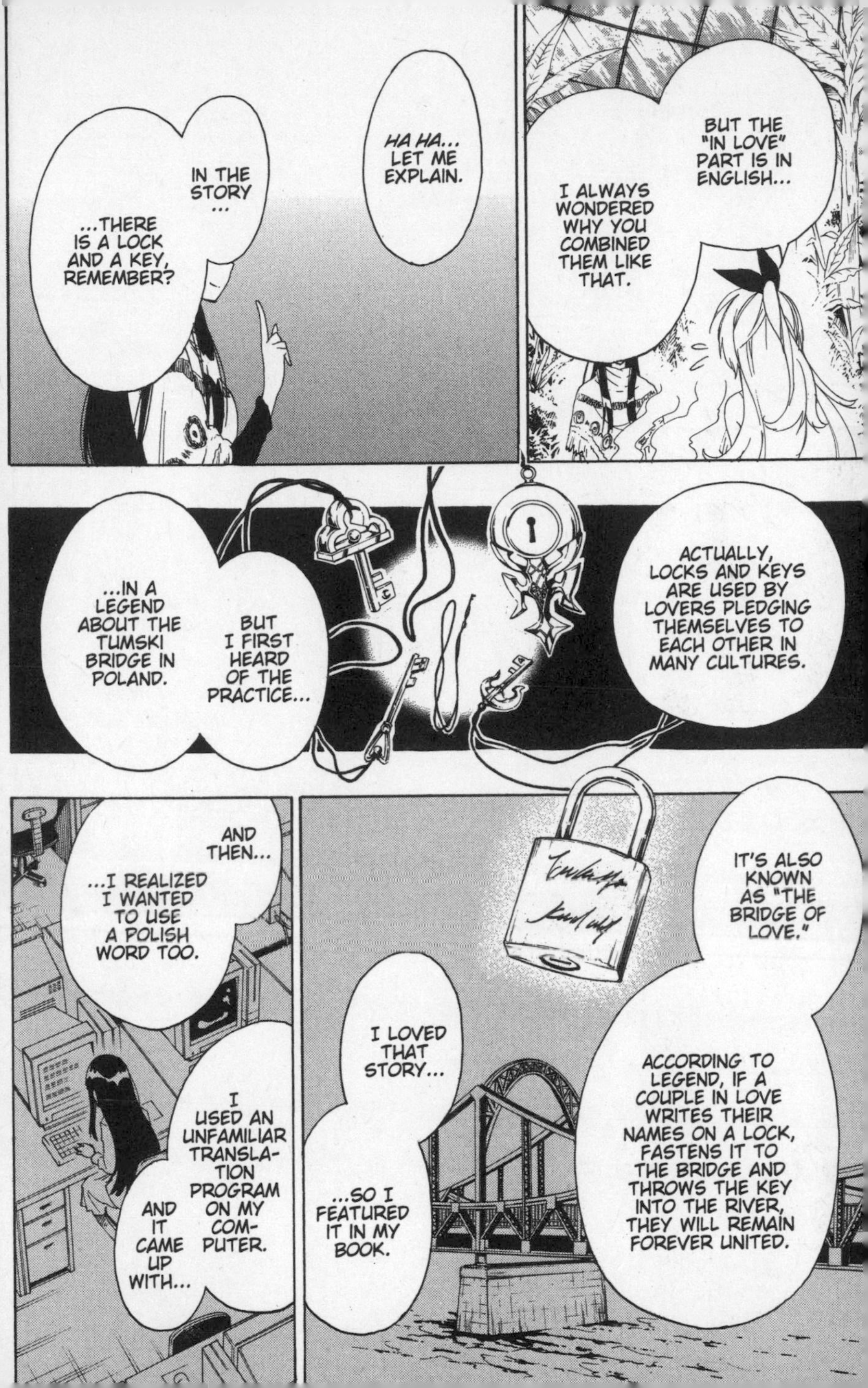
BUT THE "IN LOVE" PART IS IN ENGLISH...
I ALWAYS WONDERED WHY YOU COMBINED THEM LIKE THAT.
HA HA... LET ME EXPLAIN.
IN THE STORY...
...THERE IS A LOCK AND A KEY, REMEMBER?
ACTUALLY, LOCKS AND KEYS ARE USED BY LOVERS PLEDGING THEMSELVES TO EACH OTHER IN MANY CULTURES.
BUT I FIRST HEARD OF THE PRACTICE...
...IN A LEGEND ABOUT THE TUMSKI BRIDGE IN POLAND.
IT'S ALSO KNOWN AS "THE BRIDGE OF LOVE."
ACCORDING TO LEGEND, IF A COUPLE IN LOVE WRITES THEIR NAMES ON A LOCK, FASTENS IT TO THE BRIDGE AND THROWS THE KEY INTO THE RIVER, THEY WILL REMAIN FOREVER UNITED.
I LOVED THAT STORY...
...SO I FEATURED IT IN MY BOOK.
AND THEN...
...I REALIZED I WANTED TO USE A POLISH WORD TOO.
I USED AN UNFAMILIAR TRANSLATION PROGRAM ON MY COMPUTER.
AND IT CAME UP WITH...

Japanese		Polish
愛を永遠に	translate	Zawsze in Love

YES. IT WAS JUST A MISTRANSLATION.

TRANSLATION SOFTWARE WAS PRETTY PRIMITIVE IN THOSE DAYS.

SO...

I ONLY REALIZED THE MISTAKE AFTER THE BOOK WAS FINISHED.

WHEN HANA TOLD ME, I WAS SO EMBARRASSED I ERASED THE TITLE MYSELF.

BUT HANA WOULDN'T LET ME THROW IT AWAY. "IF YOU DON'T WANT IT, GIVE IT TO ME," SHE SAID.

Apparently it should be Zawsze w Miłości!

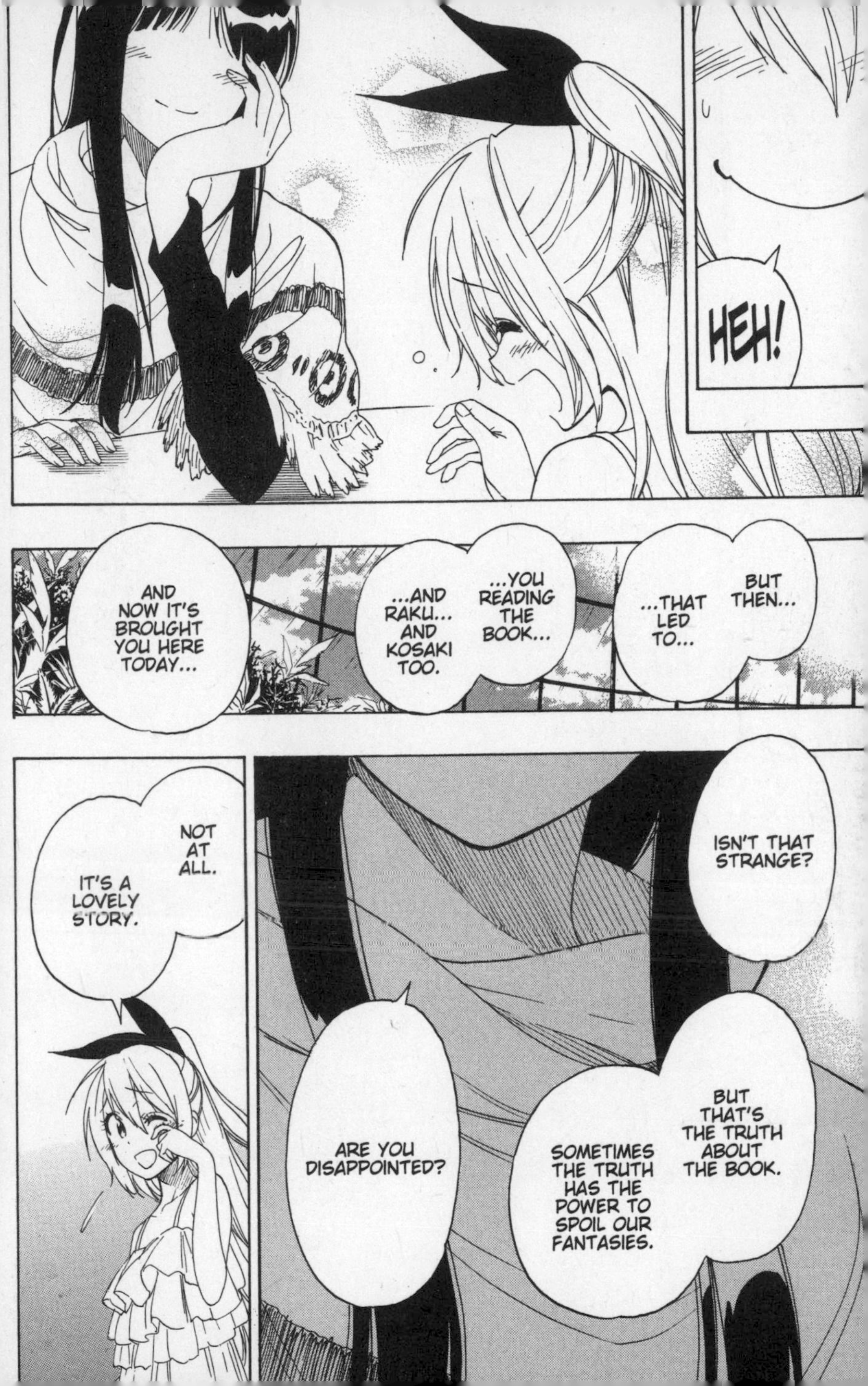
HEH!
BUT THEN... ...THAT LED TO...
...YOU READING THE BOOK... ...AND RAKU... AND KOSAKI TOO.
AND NOW IT'S BROUGHT YOU HERE TODAY...
ISN'T THAT STRANGE?
BUT THAT'S THE TRUTH ABOUT THE BOOK.
SOMETIMES THE TRUTH HAS THE POWER TO SPOIL OUR FANTASIES.
ARE YOU DISAPPOINTED?
NOT AT ALL.
IT'S A LOVELY STORY.

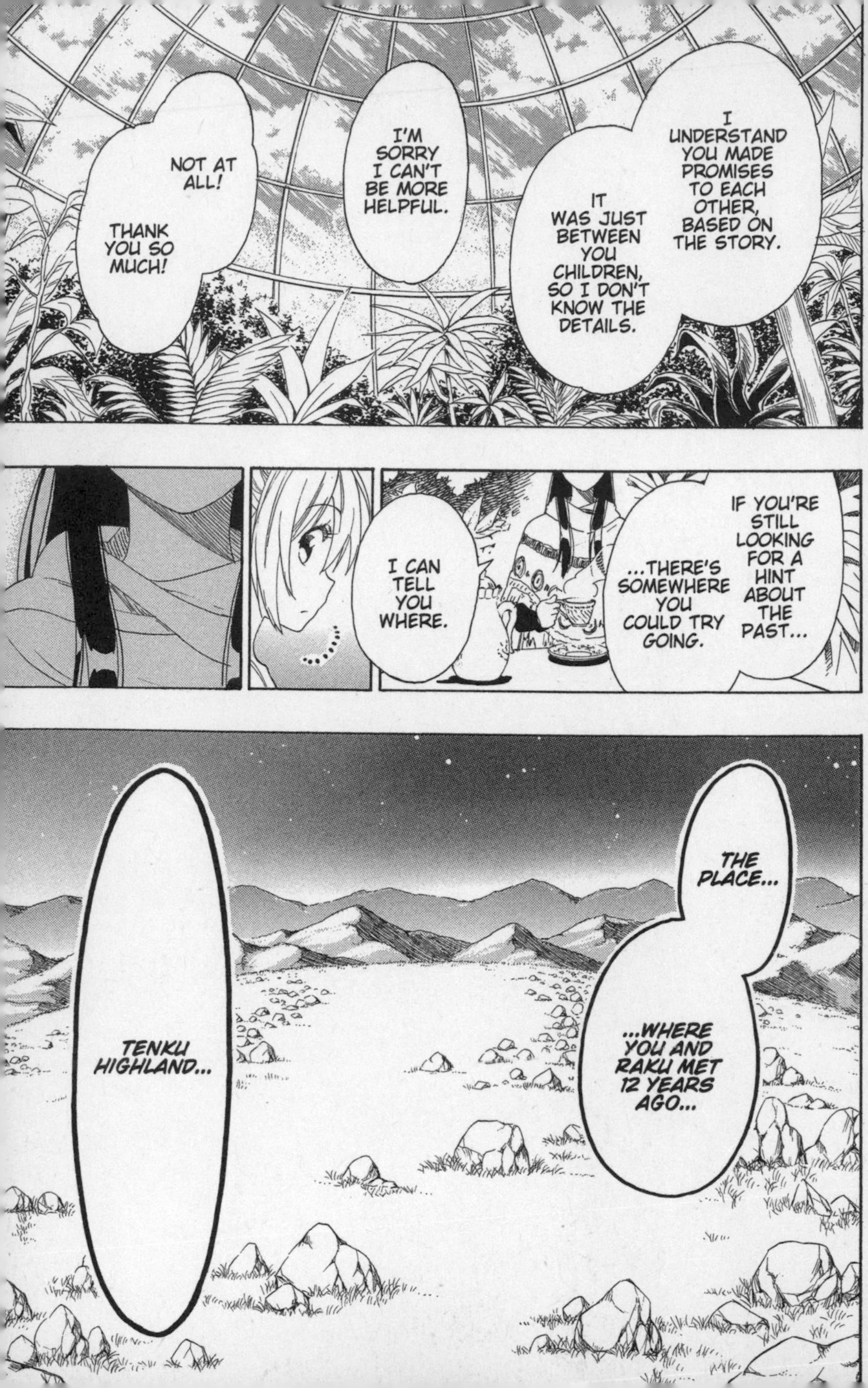
I UNDERSTAND YOU MADE PROMISES TO EACH OTHER, BASED ON THE STORY.
IT WAS JUST BETWEEN YOU CHILDREN, SO I DON'T KNOW THE DETAILS.
I'M SORRY I CAN'T BE MORE HELPFUL.
NOT AT ALL!
THANK YOU SO MUCH!
IF YOU'RE STILL LOOKING FOR A HINT ABOUT THE PAST...
...THERE'S SOMEWHERE YOU COULD TRY GOING.
I CAN TELL YOU WHERE.
THE PLACE...
...WHERE YOU AND RAKU MET 12 YEARS AGO...
TENKU HIGHLAND...

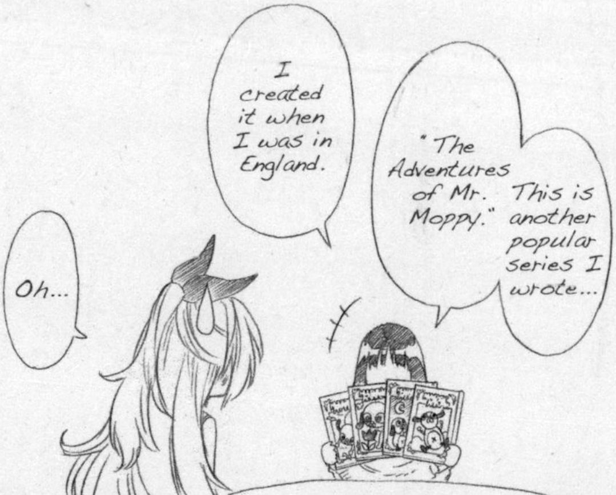
"The Adventures of Mr. Moppy." This is another popular series I wrote...
I created it when I was in England.
Oh...

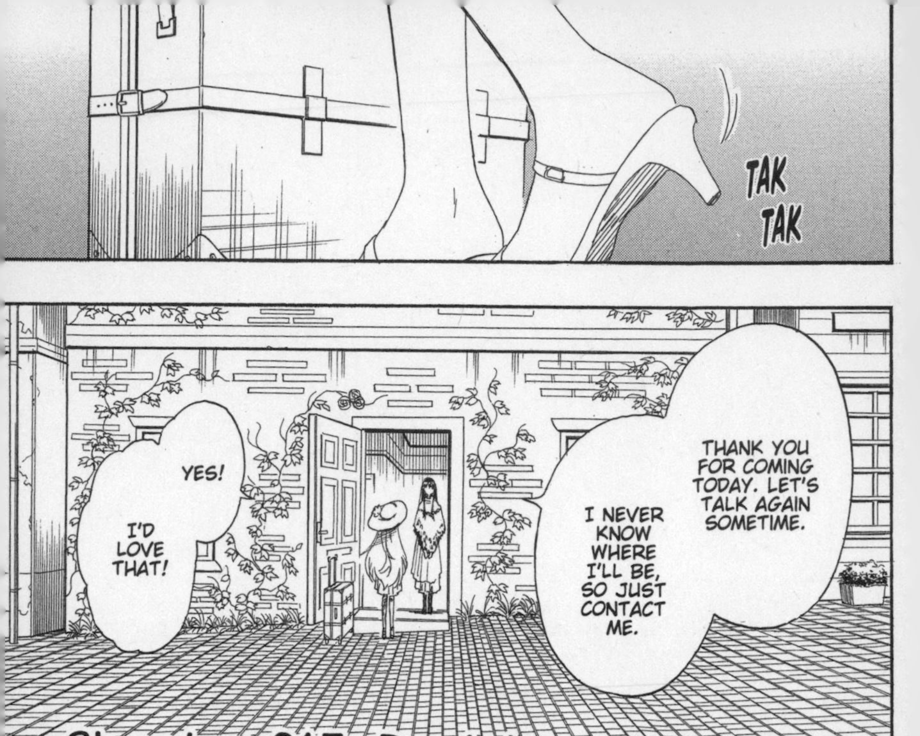
TAK
TAK
THANK YOU FOR COMING TODAY. LET'S TALK AGAIN SOMETIME.
I NEVER KNOW WHERE I'LL BE, SO JUST CONTACT ME.
YES!
I'D LOVE THAT!

Chapter 217: Decision

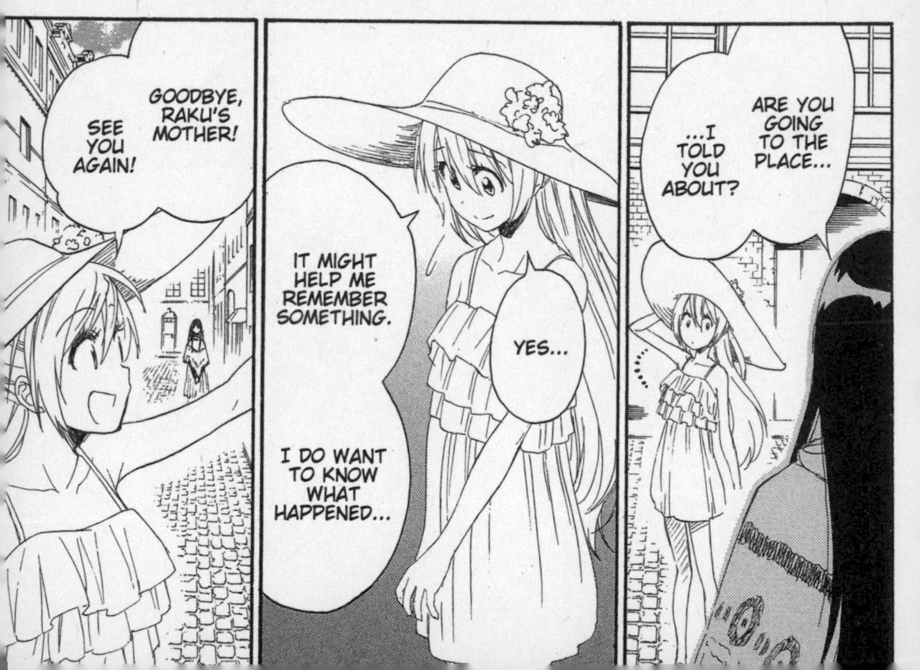
ARE YOU GOING TO THE PLACE...
...I TOLD YOU ABOUT?
YES...
IT MIGHT HELP ME REMEMBER SOMETHING.
I DO WANT TO KNOW WHAT HAPPENED...
GOODBYE, RAKU'S MOTHER!
SEE YOU AGAIN!

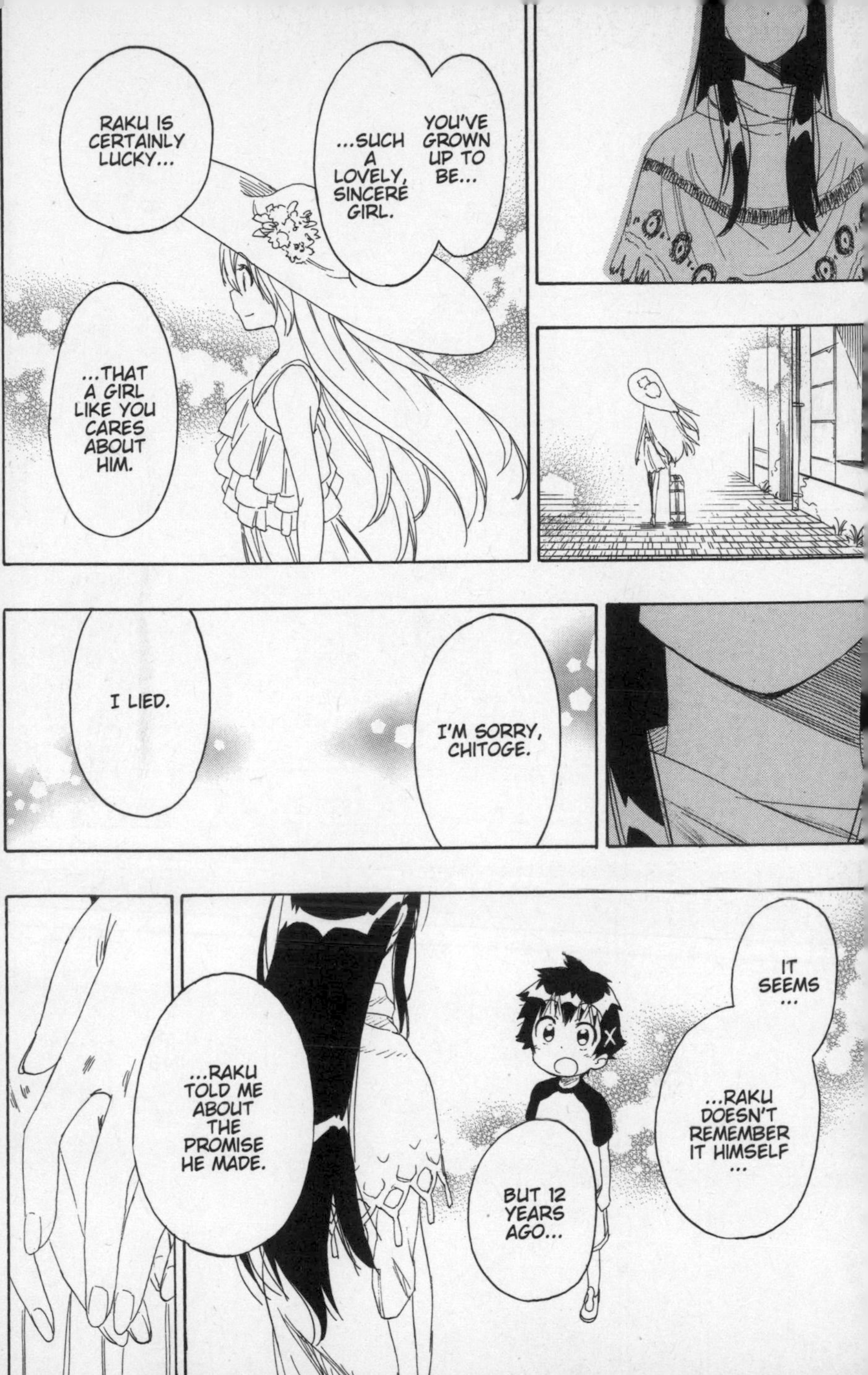
YOU'VE GROWN UP TO BE...
...SUCH A LOVELY, SINCERE GIRL.
RAKU IS CERTAINLY LUCKY...
...THAT A GIRL LIKE YOU CARES ABOUT HIM.
I'M SORRY, CHITOGE.
I LIED.
IT SEEMS...
...RAKU DOESN'T REMEMBER IT HIMSELF...
BUT 12 YEARS AGO...
...RAKU TOLD ME ABOUT THE PROMISE HE MADE.

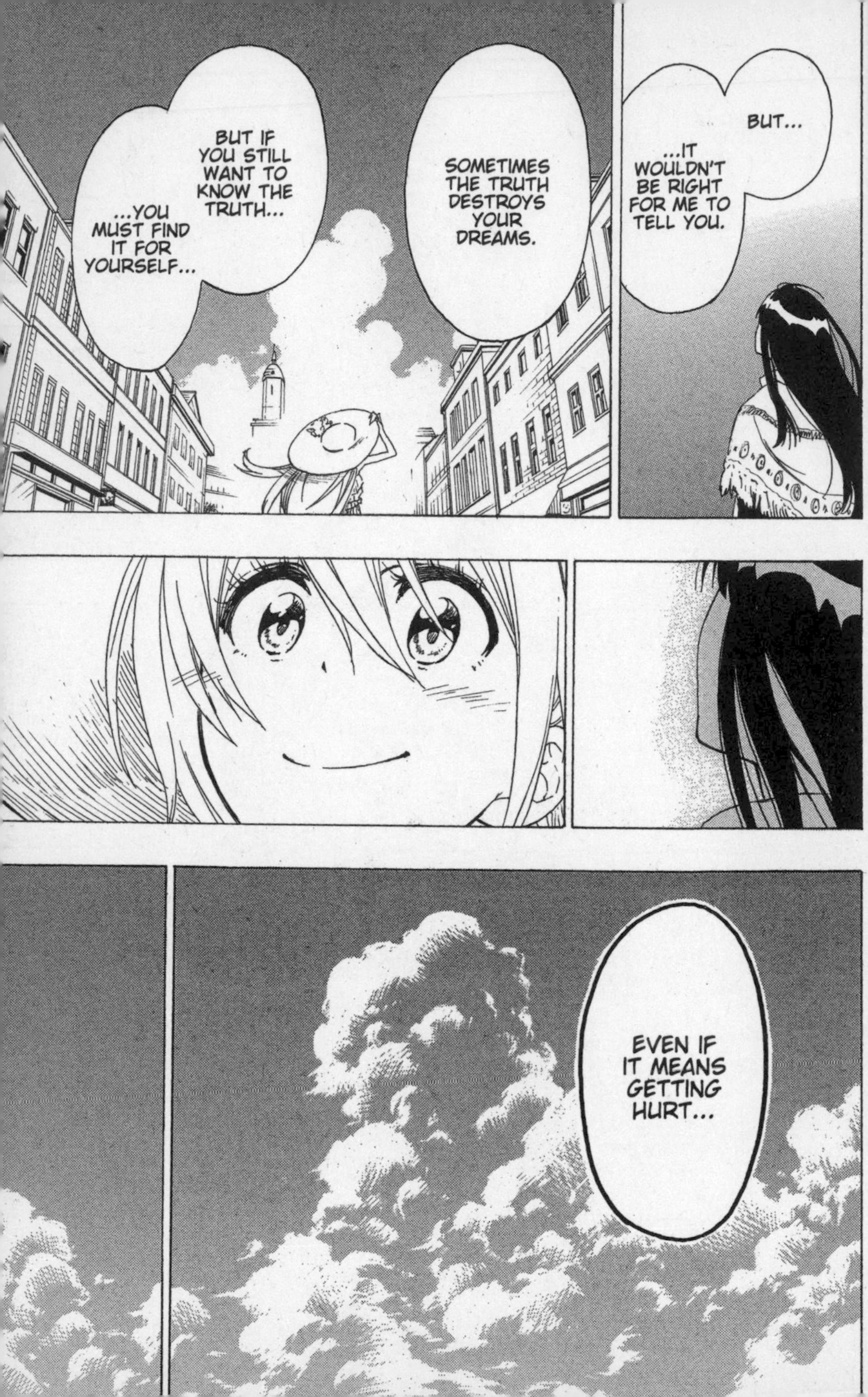
BUT...
...IT WOULDN'T BE RIGHT FOR ME TO TELL YOU.
SOMETIMES THE TRUTH DESTROYS YOUR DREAMS.
BUT IF YOU STILL WANT TO KNOW THE TRUTH...
...YOU MUST FIND IT FOR YOURSELF...
EVEN IF IT MEANS GETTING HURT...

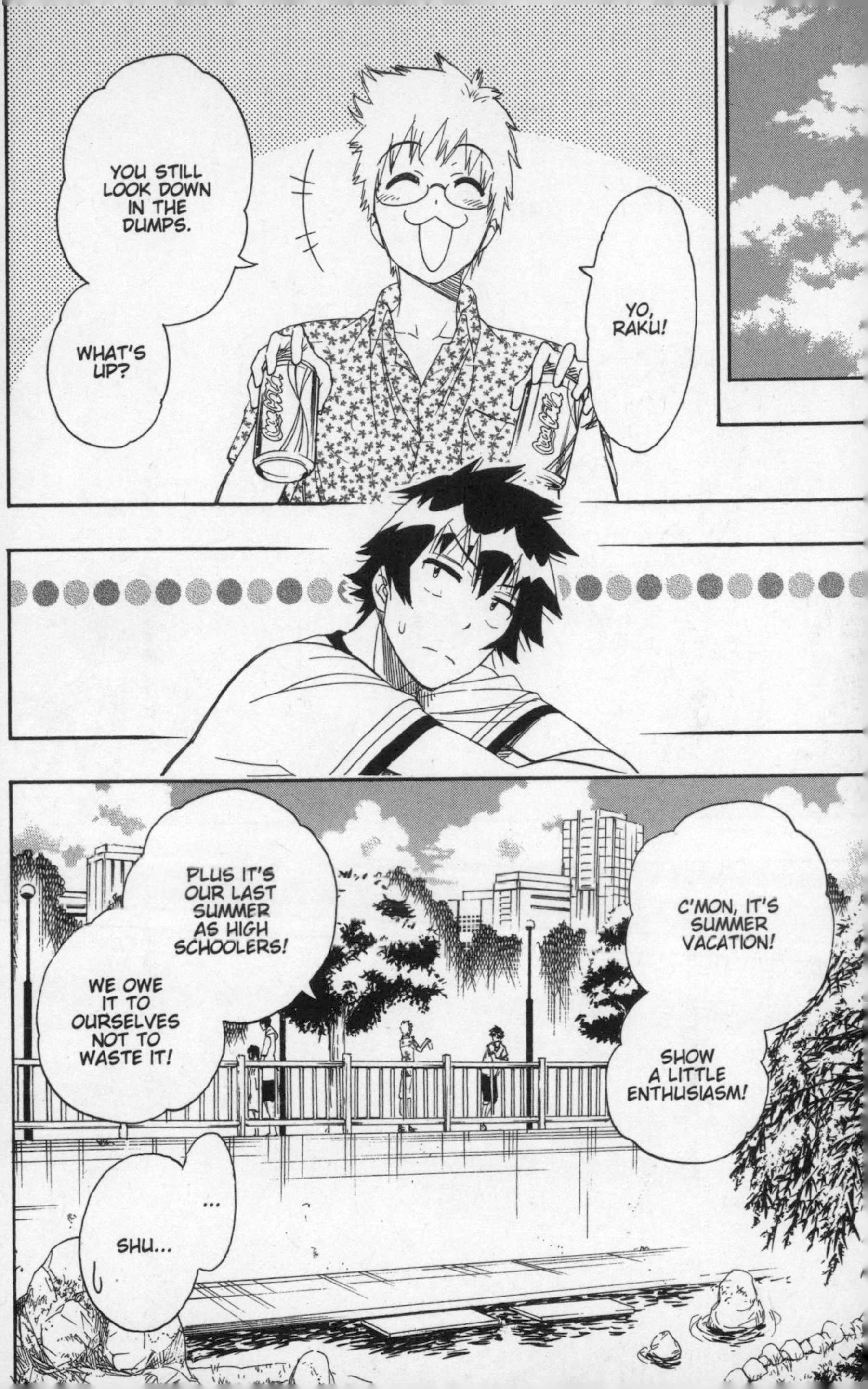
YO, RAKU!
YOU STILL LOOK DOWN IN THE DUMPS.
WHAT'S UP?
C'MON, IT'S SUMMER VACATION!
SHOW A LITTLE ENTHUSIASM!
PLUS IT'S OUR LAST SUMMER AS HIGH SCHOOLERS!
WE OWE IT TO OURSELVES NOT TO WASTE IT!
...
SHU...

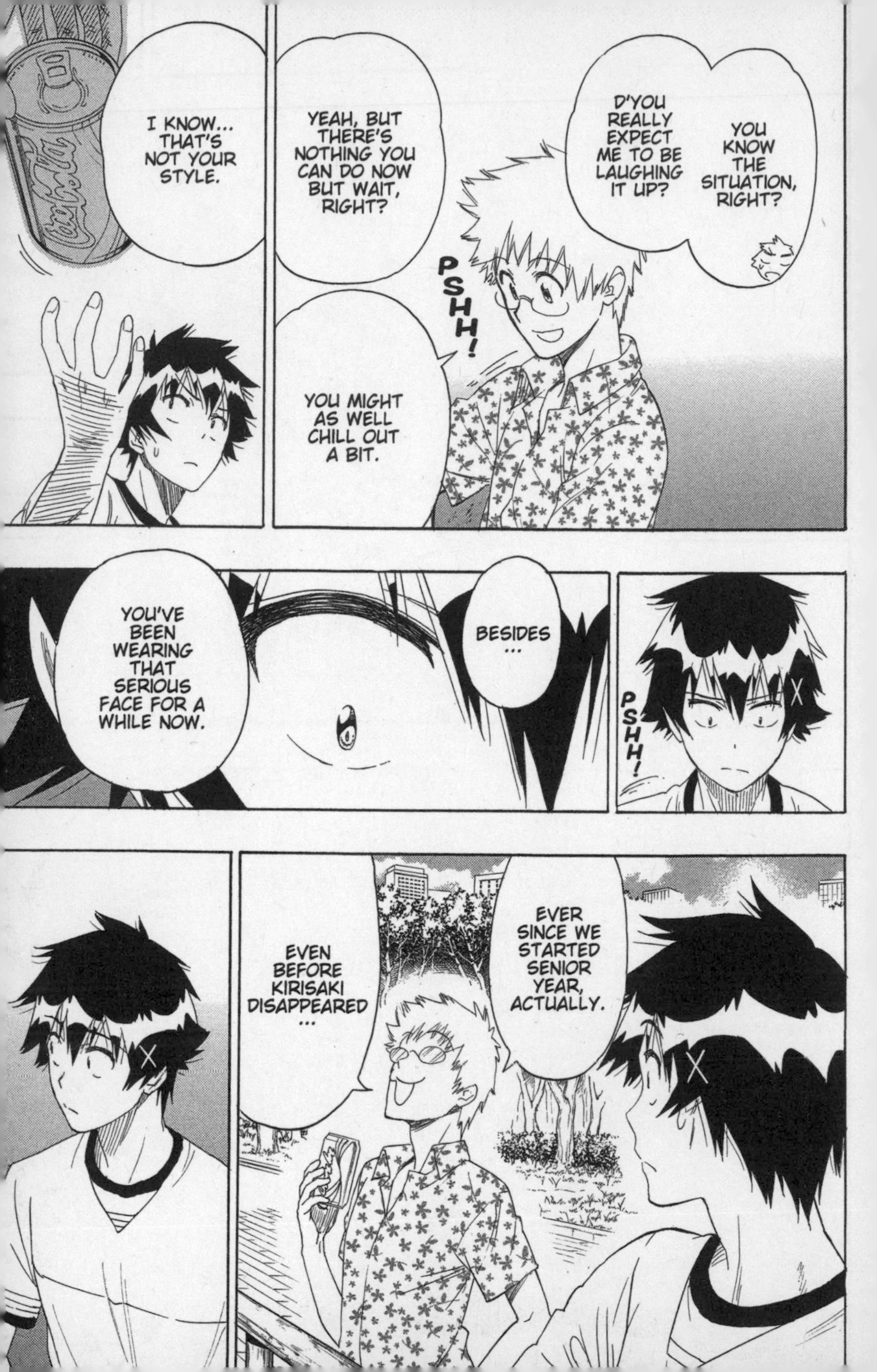
YOU KNOW THE SITUATION, RIGHT?
D'YOU REALLY EXPECT ME TO BE LAUGHING IT UP?
PSHH!
YEAH, BUT THERE'S NOTHING YOU CAN DO NOW BUT WAIT, RIGHT?
YOU MIGHT AS WELL CHILL OUT A BIT.
I KNOW... THAT'S NOT YOUR STYLE.
PSHH!
BESIDES...
YOU'VE BEEN WEARING THAT SERIOUS FACE FOR A WHILE NOW.
EVER SINCE WE STARTED SENIOR YEAR, ACTUALLY.
EVEN BEFORE KIRISAKI DISAPPEARED...

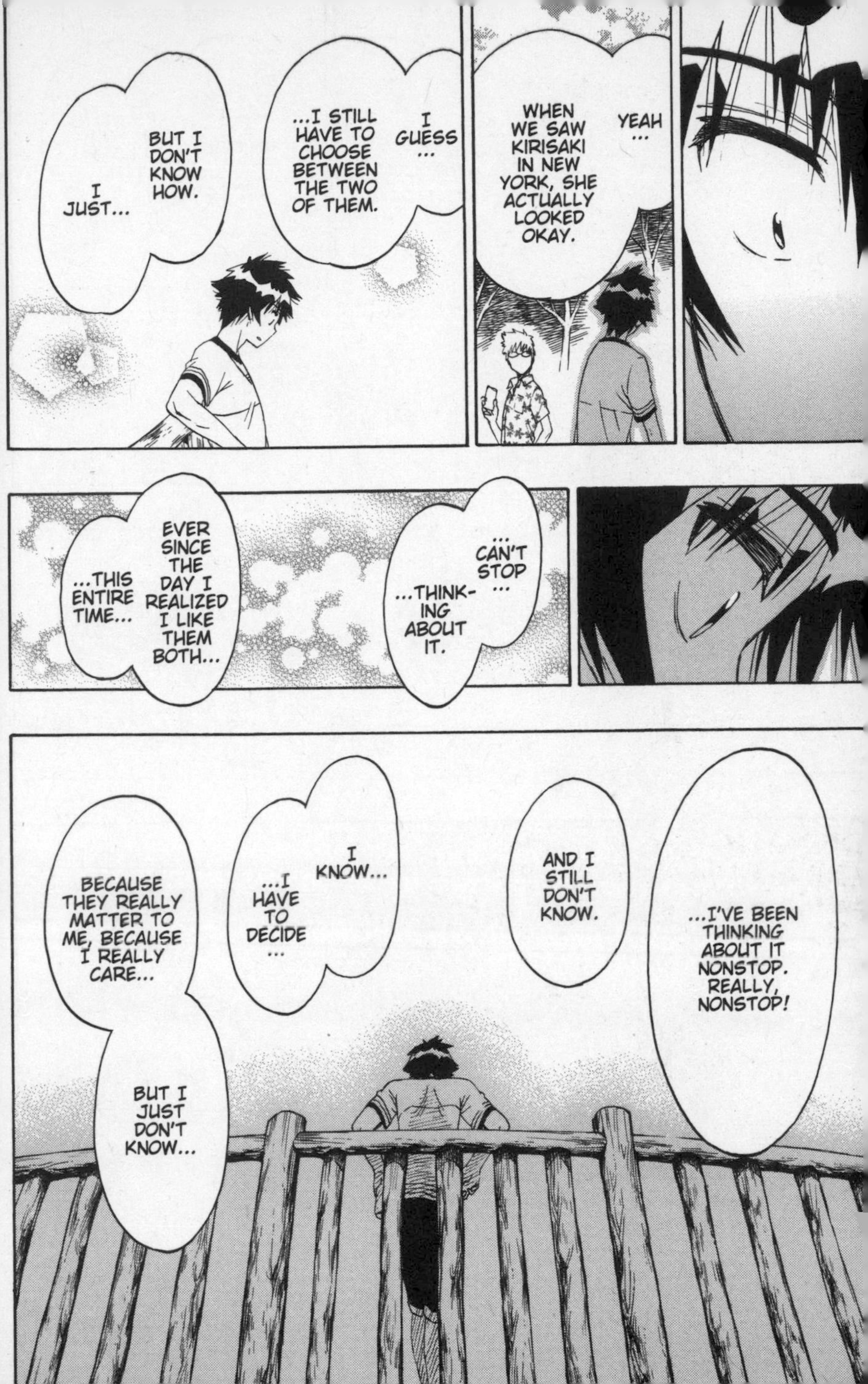
YEAH...
WHEN WE SAW KIRISAKI IN NEW YORK, SHE ACTUALLY LOOKED OKAY.
I GUESS...
...I STILL HAVE TO CHOOSE BETWEEN THE TWO OF THEM.
BUT I DON'T KNOW HOW.
I JUST...
...CAN'T STOP...
...THINKING ABOUT IT.
EVER SINCE THE DAY I REALIZED I LIKE THEM BOTH...
...THIS ENTIRE TIME...
...I'VE BEEN THINKING ABOUT IT NONSTOP. REALLY, NONSTOP!
AND I STILL DON'T KNOW.
I KNOW...
...I HAVE TO DECIDE...
BECAUSE THEY REALLY MATTER TO ME, BECAUSE I REALLY CARE...
BUT I JUST DON'T KNOW...

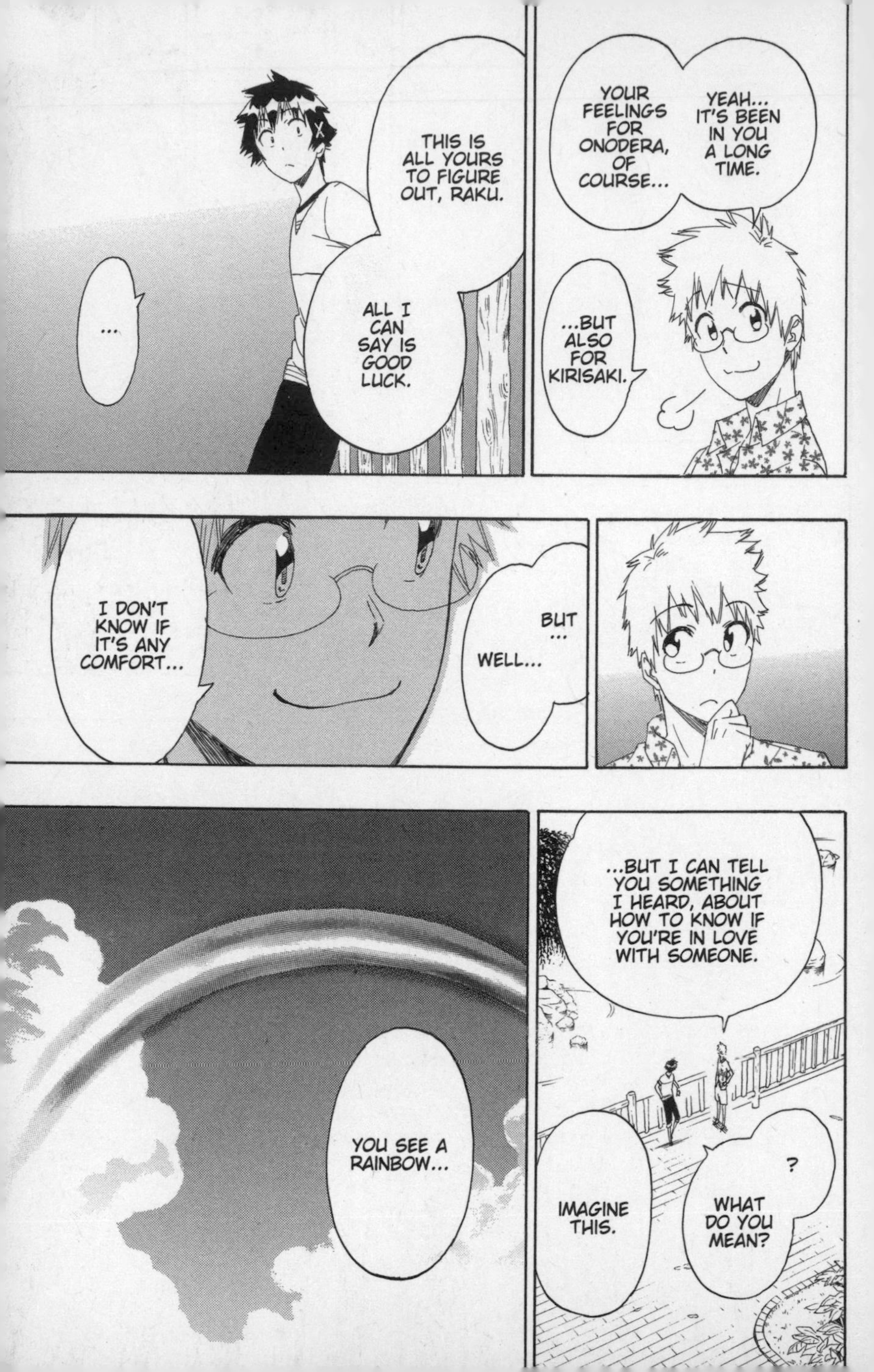
YEAH... IT'S BEEN IN YOU A LONG TIME.
YOUR FEELINGS FOR ONODERA, OF COURSE...
...BUT ALSO FOR KIRISAKI.
THIS IS ALL YOURS TO FIGURE OUT, RAKU.
ALL I CAN SAY IS GOOD LUCK.
...
BUT...
WELL...
I DON'T KNOW IF IT'S ANY COMFORT...
...BUT I CAN TELL YOU SOMETHING I HEARD, ABOUT HOW TO KNOW IF YOU'RE IN LOVE WITH SOMEONE.
?
WHAT DO YOU MEAN?
IMAGINE THIS.
YOU SEE A RAINBOW...

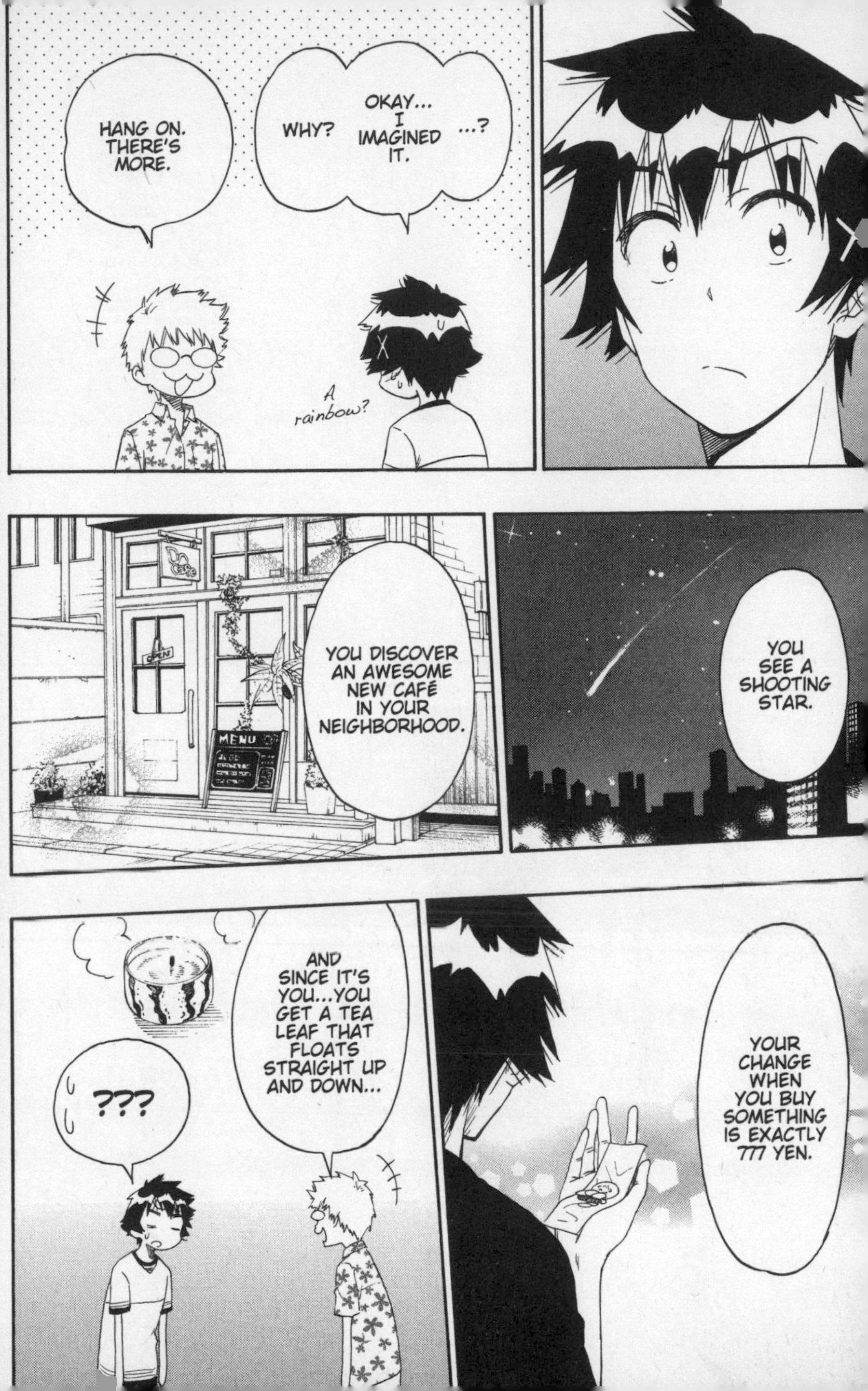
...?
OKAY... I IMAGINED IT.
WHY?
HANG ON. THERE'S MORE.
A rainbow?
YOU SEE A SHOOTING STAR.
YOU DISCOVER AN AWESOME NEW CAFÉ IN YOUR NEIGHBORHOOD.
MENU
YOUR CHANGE WHEN YOU BUY SOMETHING IS EXACTLY 777 YEN.
AND SINCE IT'S YOU...YOU GET A TEA LEAF THAT FLOATS STRAIGHT UP AND DOWN...
???

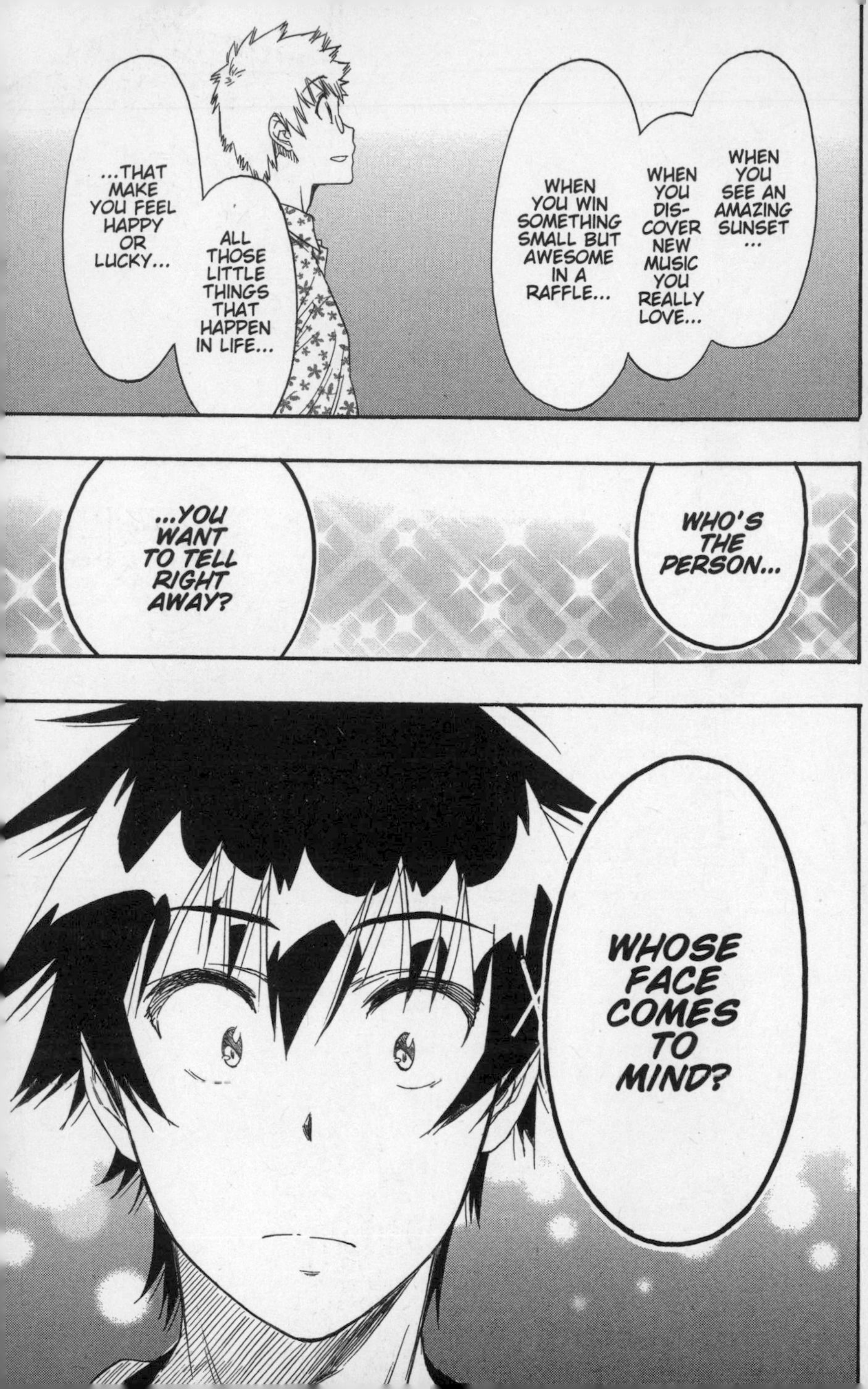
WHEN YOU SEE AN AMAZING SUNSET...
WHEN YOU DIS-COVER NEW MUSIC YOU REALLY LOVE...
WHEN YOU WIN SOMETHING SMALL BUT AWESOME IN A RAFFLE...
ALL THOSE LITTLE THINGS THAT HAPPEN IN LIFE...
...THAT MAKE YOU FEEL HAPPY OR LUCKY...
WHO'S THE PERSON...
...YOU WANT TO TELL RIGHT AWAY?
WHOSE FACE COMES TO MIND?

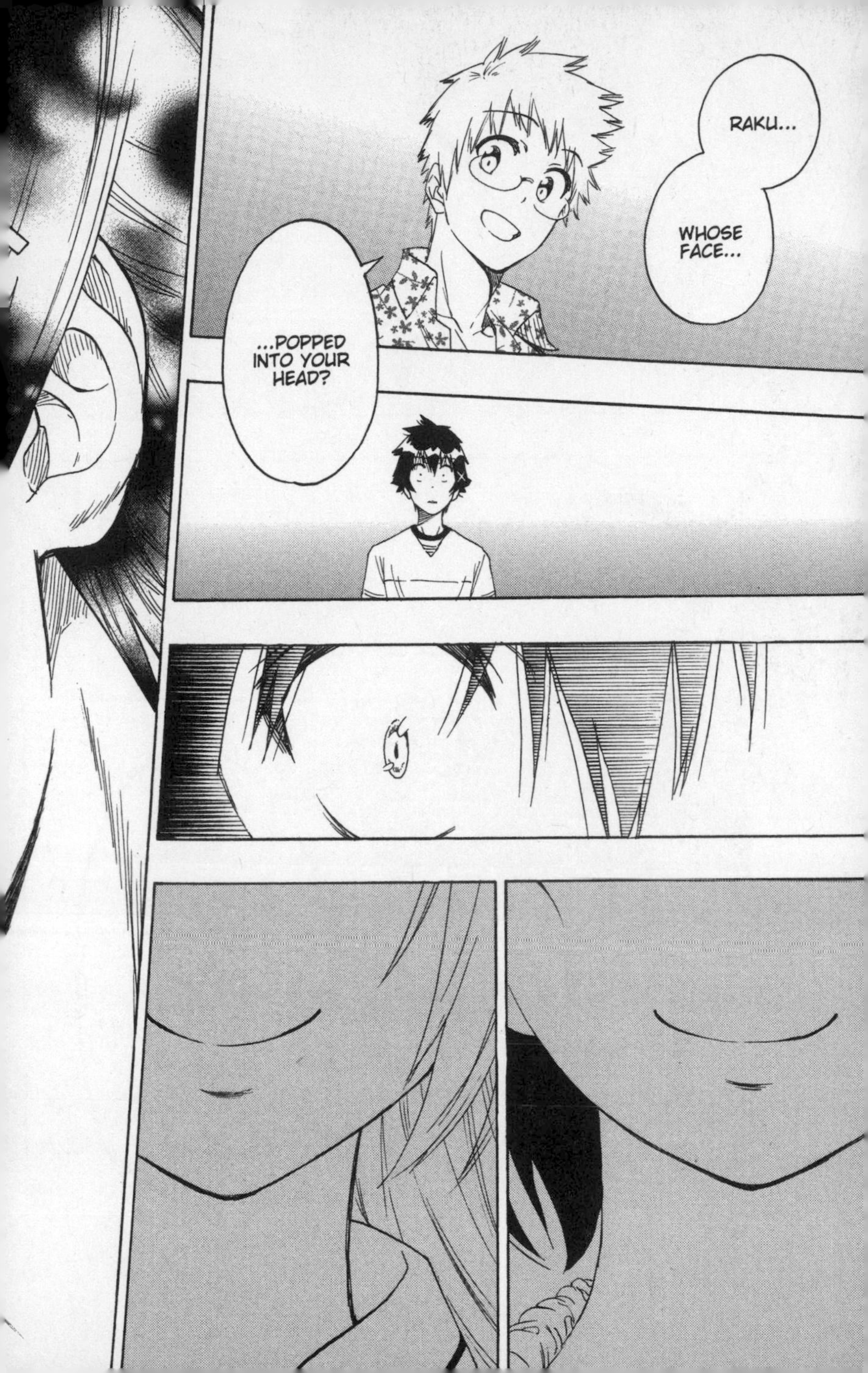
RAKU...
WHOSE FACE...
...POPPED INTO YOUR HEAD?

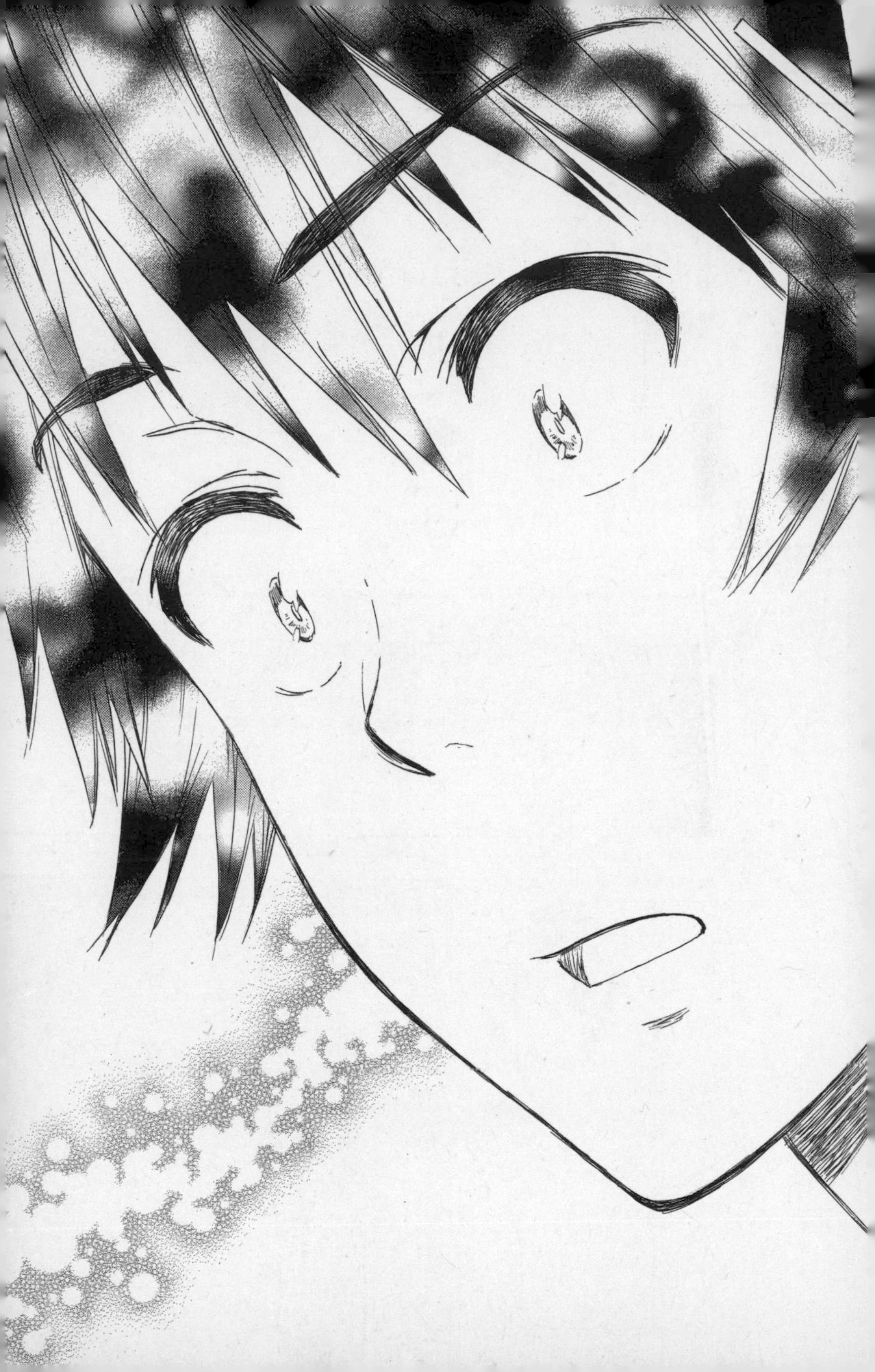

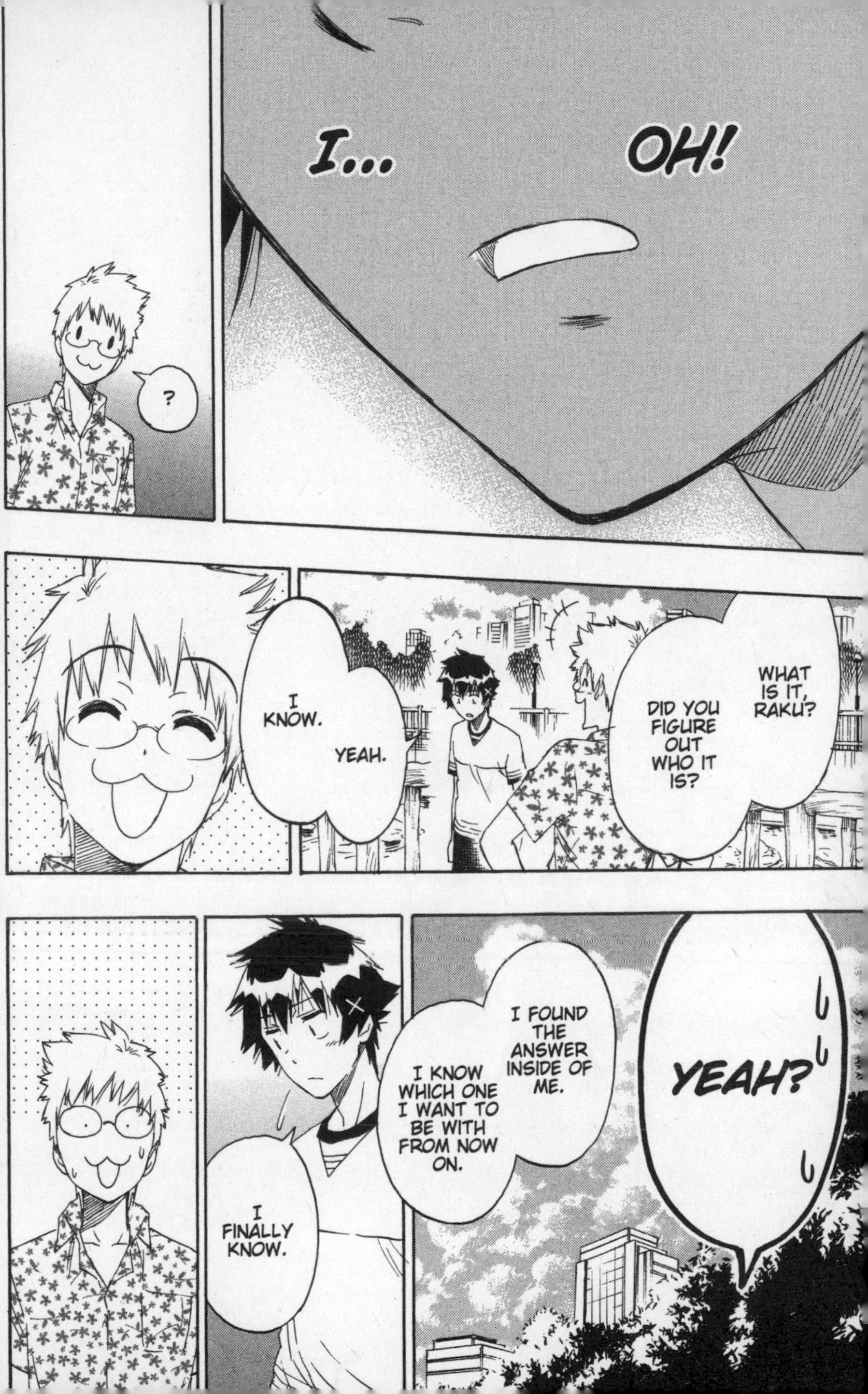
OH!
I...
?
WHAT IS IT, RAKU?
DID YOU FIGURE OUT WHO IT IS?
YEAH.
I KNOW.
YEAH?
I FOUND THE ANSWER INSIDE OF ME.
I KNOW WHICH ONE I WANT TO BE WITH FROM NOW ON.
I FINALLY KNOW.

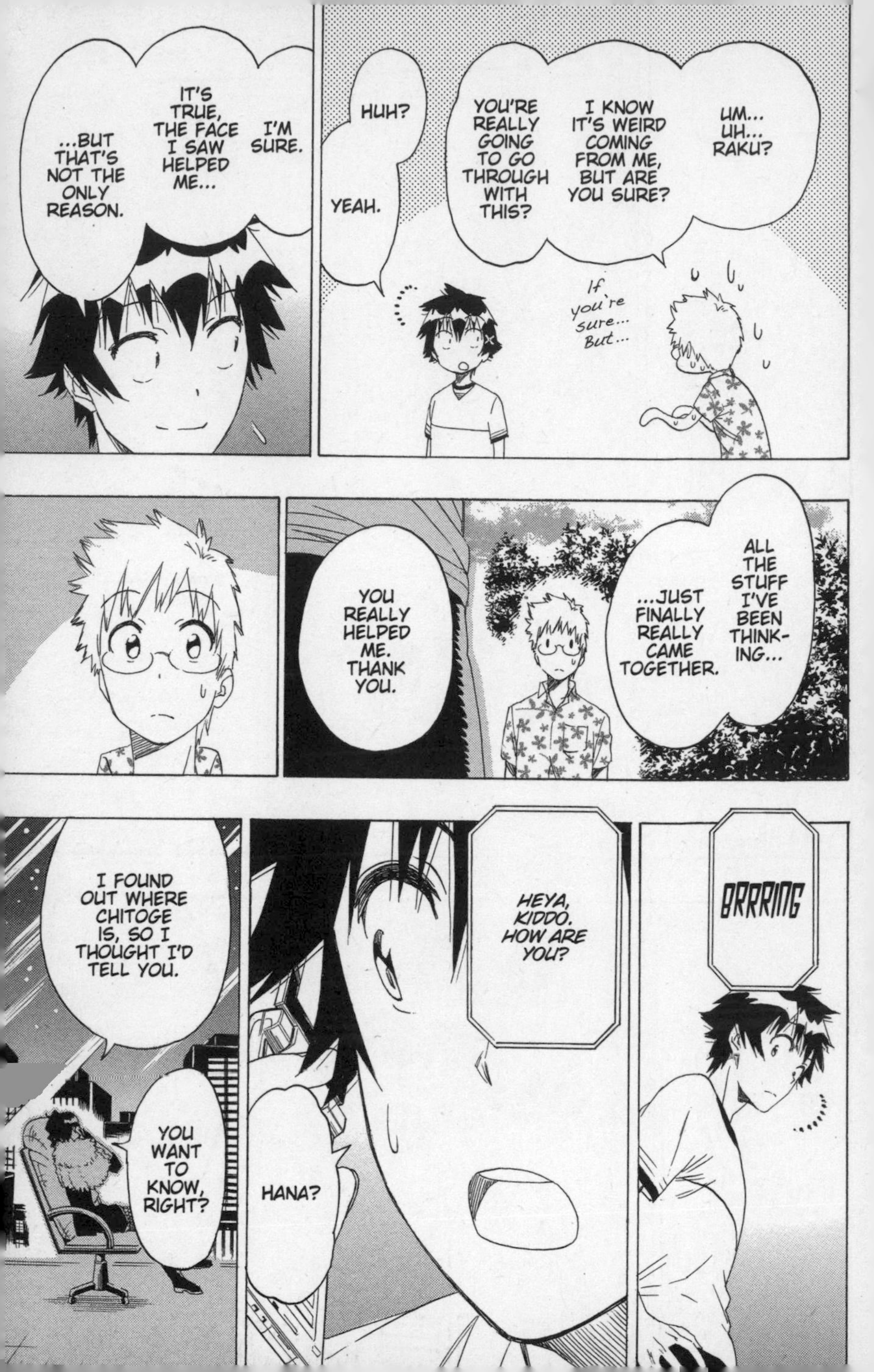
UM... UH... RAKU?
I KNOW IT'S WEIRD COMING FROM ME, BUT ARE YOU SURE?
YOU'RE REALLY GOING TO GO THROUGH WITH THIS?
If you're sure... But...
HUH?
YEAH.
I'M SURE.
IT'S TRUE, THE FACE I SAW HELPED ME...
...BUT THAT'S NOT THE ONLY REASON.
ALL THE STUFF I'VE BEEN THINKING...
...JUST FINALLY REALLY CAME TOGETHER.
YOU REALLY HELPED ME. THANK YOU.
BRRRING
HEYA, KIDDO. HOW ARE YOU?
HANA?
I FOUND OUT WHERE CHITOGE IS, SO I THOUGHT I'D TELL YOU.
YOU WANT TO KNOW, RIGHT?

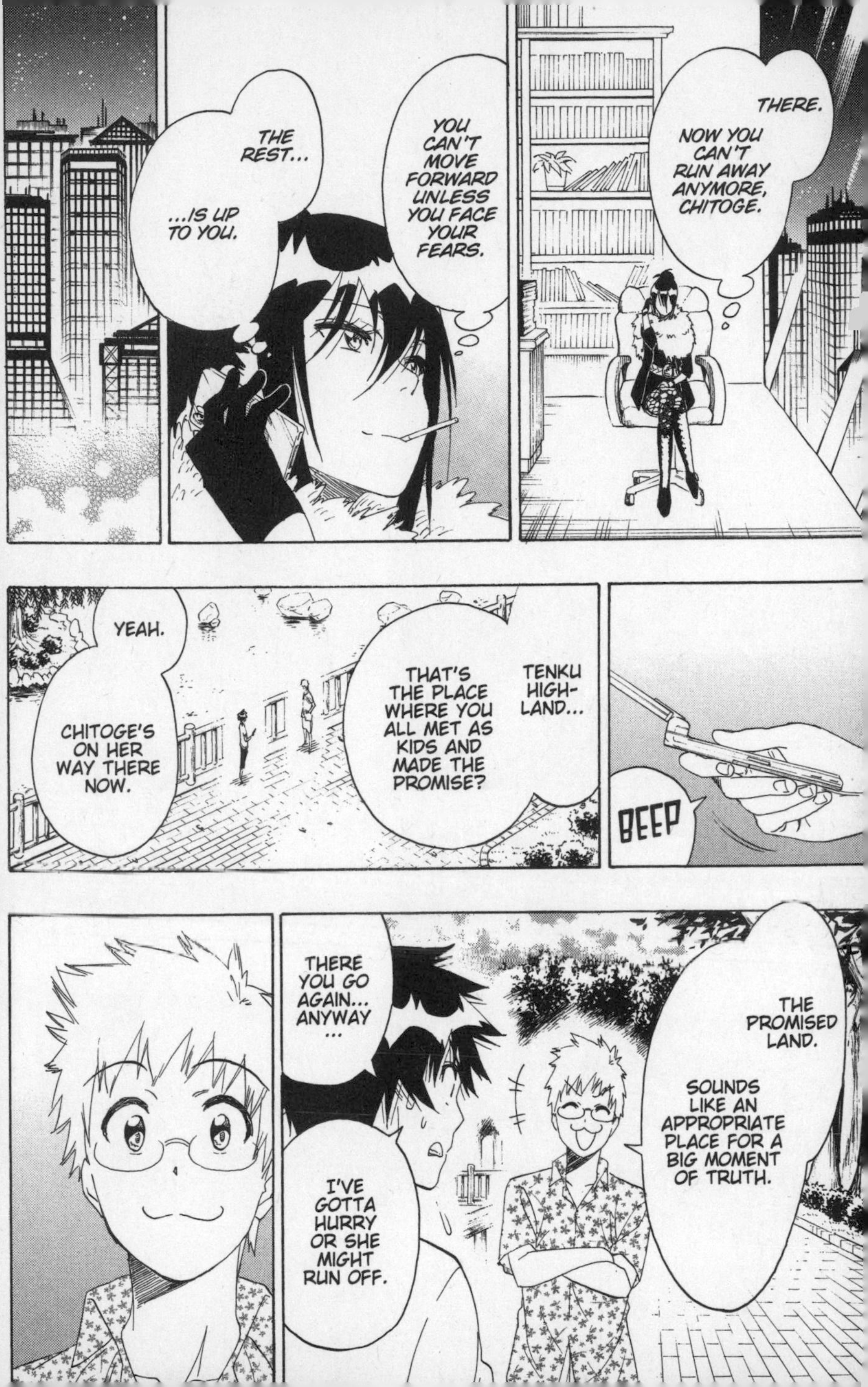
THERE.
NOW YOU CAN'T RUN AWAY ANYMORE, CHITOGE.
YOU CAN'T MOVE FORWARD UNLESS YOU FACE YOUR FEARS.
THE REST...
...IS UP TO YOU.
BEEP
TENKU HIGHLAND...
THAT'S THE PLACE WHERE YOU ALL MET AS KIDS AND MADE THE PROMISE?
YEAH.
CHITOGE'S ON HER WAY THERE NOW.
THE PROMISED LAND.
SOUNDS LIKE AN APPROPRIATE PLACE FOR A BIG MOMENT OF TRUTH.
THERE YOU GO AGAIN... ANYWAY...
I'VE GOTTA HURRY OR SHE MIGHT RUN OFF.

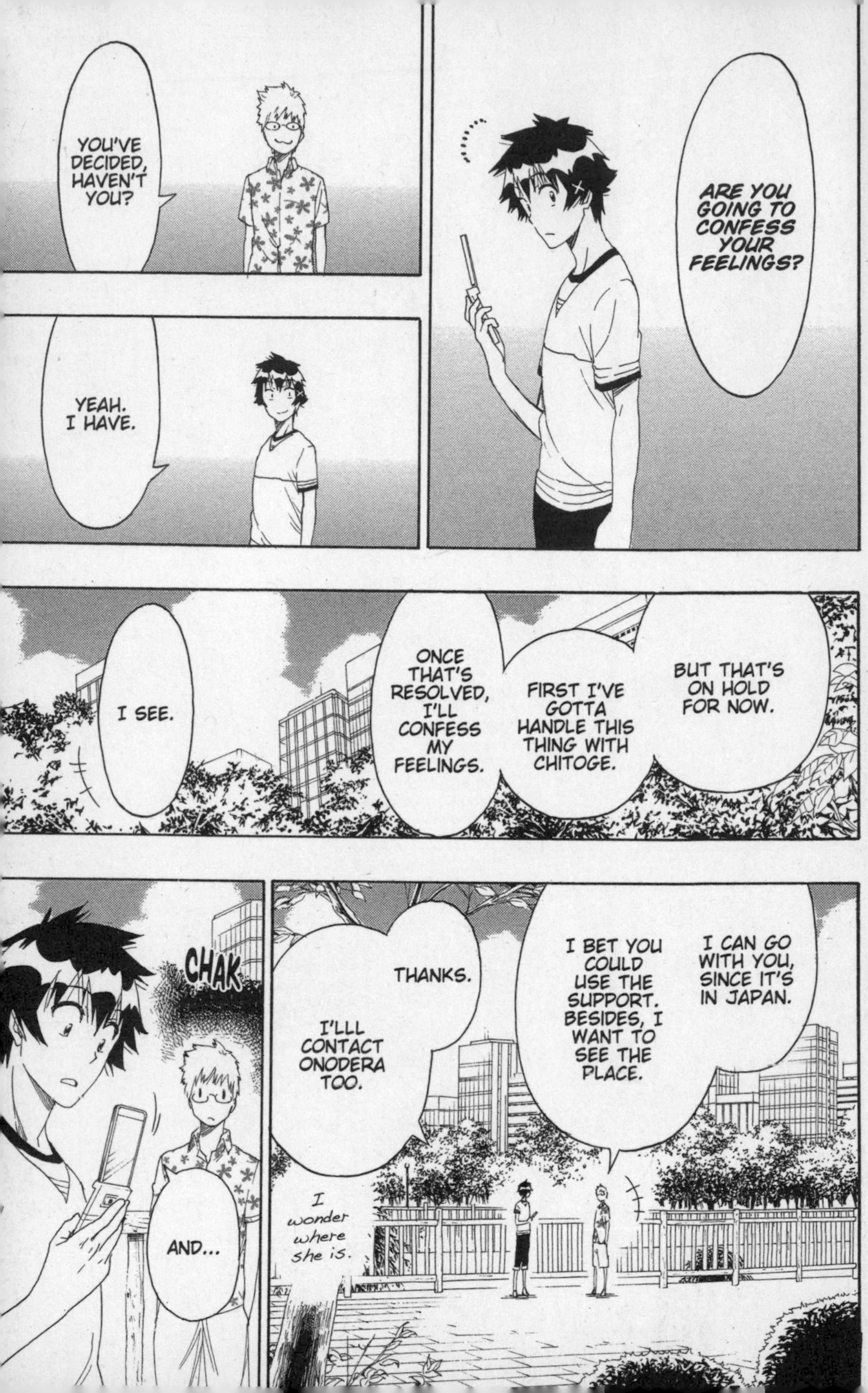
ARE YOU GOING TO CONFESS YOUR FEELINGS?
YOU'VE DECIDED, HAVEN'T YOU?
YEAH. I HAVE.
BUT THAT'S ON HOLD FOR NOW.
FIRST I'VE GOTTA HANDLE THIS THING WITH CHITOGE.
ONCE THAT'S RESOLVED, I'LL CONFESS MY FEELINGS.
I SEE.
I CAN GO WITH YOU, SINCE IT'S IN JAPAN.
I BET YOU COULD USE THE SUPPORT. BESIDES, I WANT TO SEE THE PLACE.
THANKS.
I'LLL CONTACT ONODERA TOO.
I wonder where she is.
CHAK
AND...

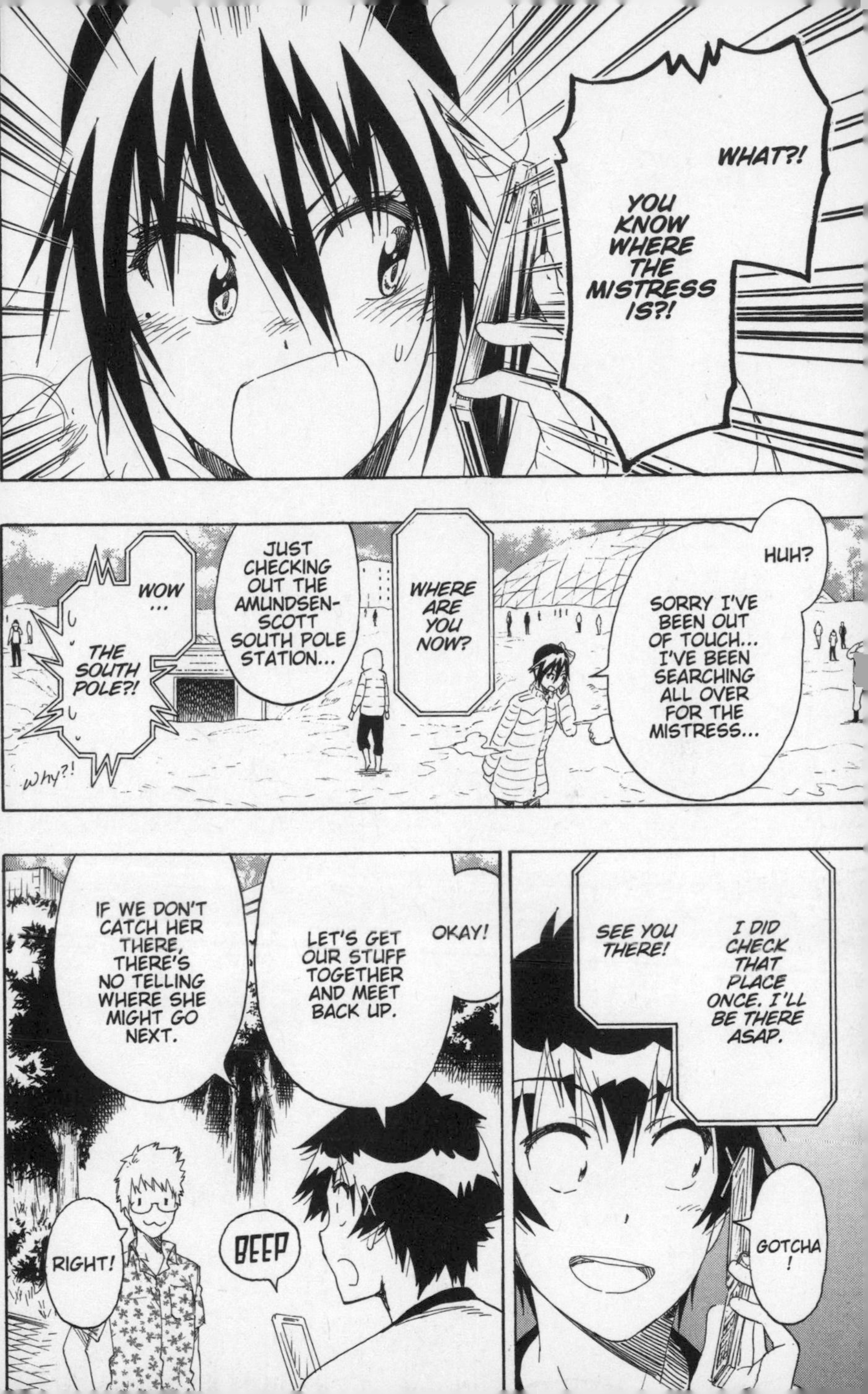
WHAT?!
YOU KNOW WHERE THE MISTRESS IS?!
HUH?
SORRY I'VE BEEN OUT OF TOUCH... I'VE BEEN SEARCHING ALL OVER FOR THE MISTRESS...
WHERE ARE YOU NOW?
JUST CHECKING OUT THE AMUNDSEN-SCOTT SOUTH POLE STATION...
WOW ...
THE SOUTH POLE?!
why?!
I DID CHECK THAT PLACE ONCE. I'LL BE THERE ASAP.
SEE YOU THERE!
GOTCHA!
OKAY!
LET'S GET OUR STUFF TOGETHER AND MEET BACK UP.
IF WE DON'T CATCH HER THERE, THERE'S NO TELLING WHERE SHE MIGHT GO NEXT.
BEEP
RIGHT!

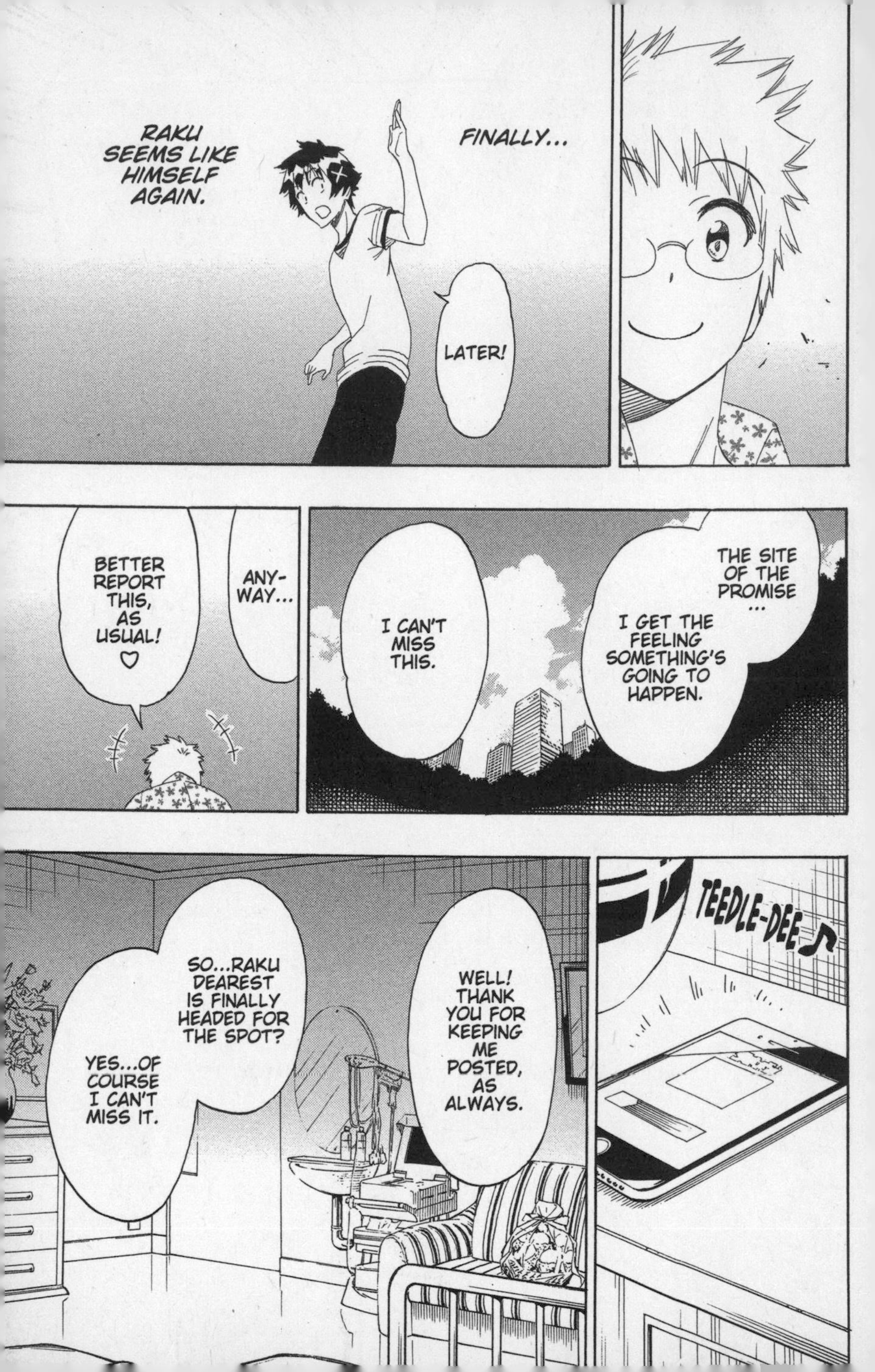
FINALLY...
RAKU SEEMS LIKE HIMSELF AGAIN.
LATER!
THE SITE OF THE PROMISE...
I GET THE FEELING SOMETHING'S GOING TO HAPPEN.
I CAN'T MISS THIS.
ANY-WAY...
BETTER REPORT THIS, AS USUAL! ♡
TEEDLE-DEE♪
WELL! THANK YOU FOR KEEPING ME POSTED, AS ALWAYS.
SO...RAKU DEAREST IS FINALLY HEADED FOR THE SPOT?
YES...OF COURSE I CAN'T MISS IT.

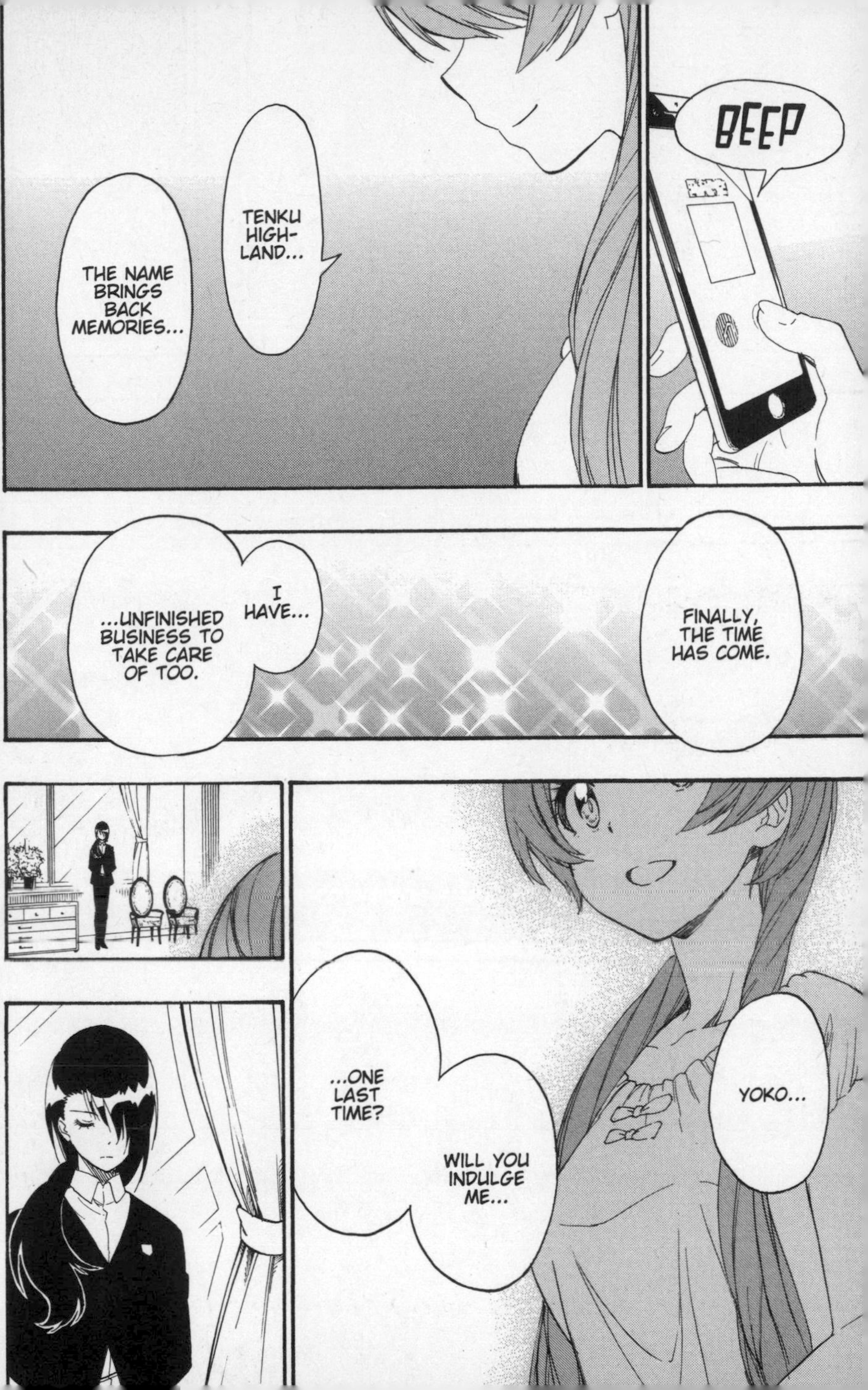
BEEP
TENKU HIGH-LAND...
THE NAME BRINGS BACK MEMORIES...
FINALLY, THE TIME HAS COME.
I HAVE...
...UNFINISHED BUSINESS TO TAKE CARE OF TOO.
YOKO...
WILL YOU INDULGE ME...
...ONE LAST TIME?

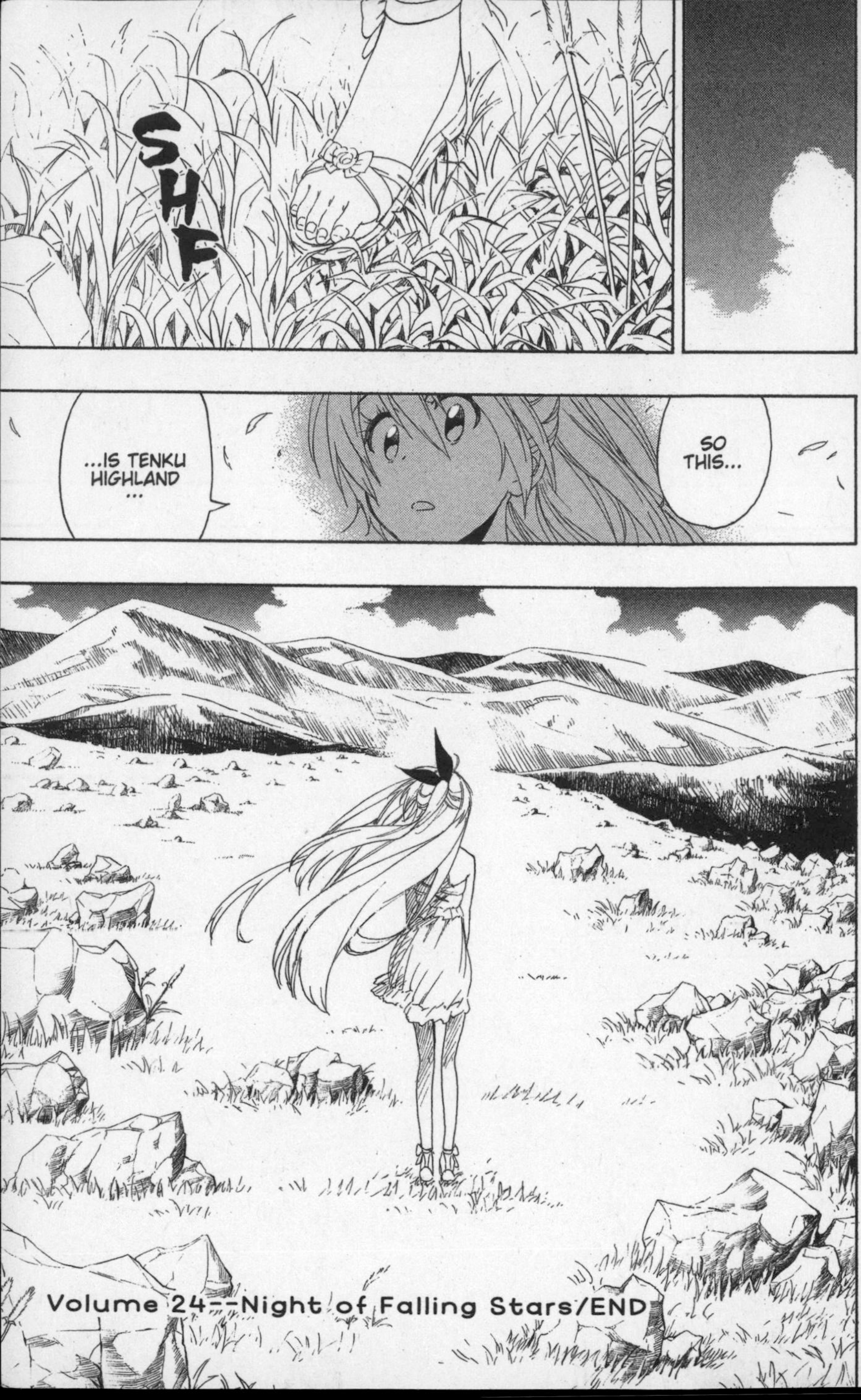
SHF
SO THIS...
...IS TENKU HIGHLAND ...
Volume 24--Night of Falling Stars/END

SEARCH

"TENGU HIGHLAND!!"

CLIK   **Tengu Highland**

Another shameless plug!

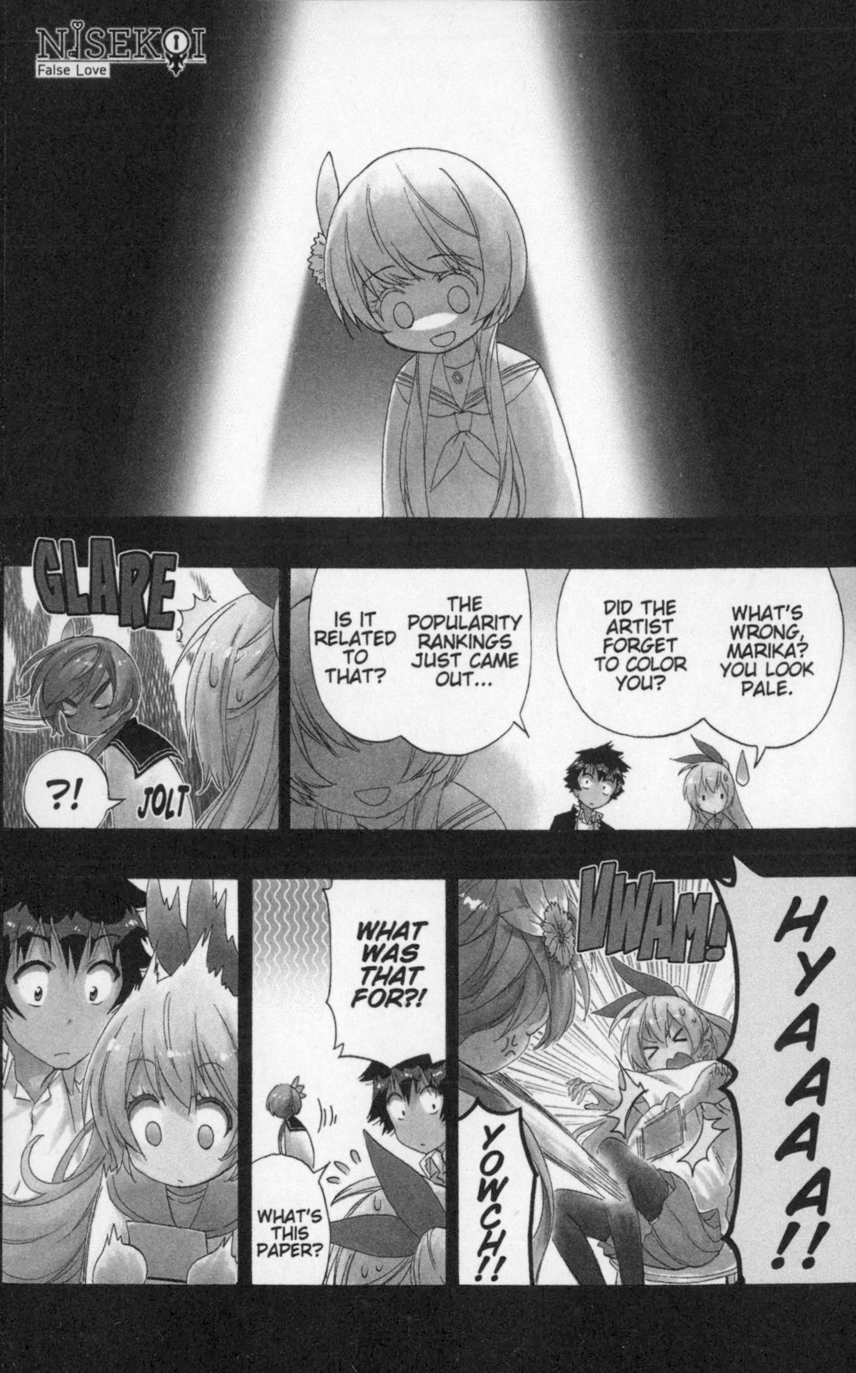
WHAT'S WRONG, MARIKA? YOU LOOK PALE.
DID THE ARTIST FORGET TO COLOR YOU?
THE POPULARITY RANKINGS JUST CAME OUT...
IS IT RELATED TO THAT?
GLARE
?!
JOLT
HYAAAAA!!
VWAM!
YOWCH!!
WHAT WAS THAT FOR?!
WHAT'S THIS PAPER?

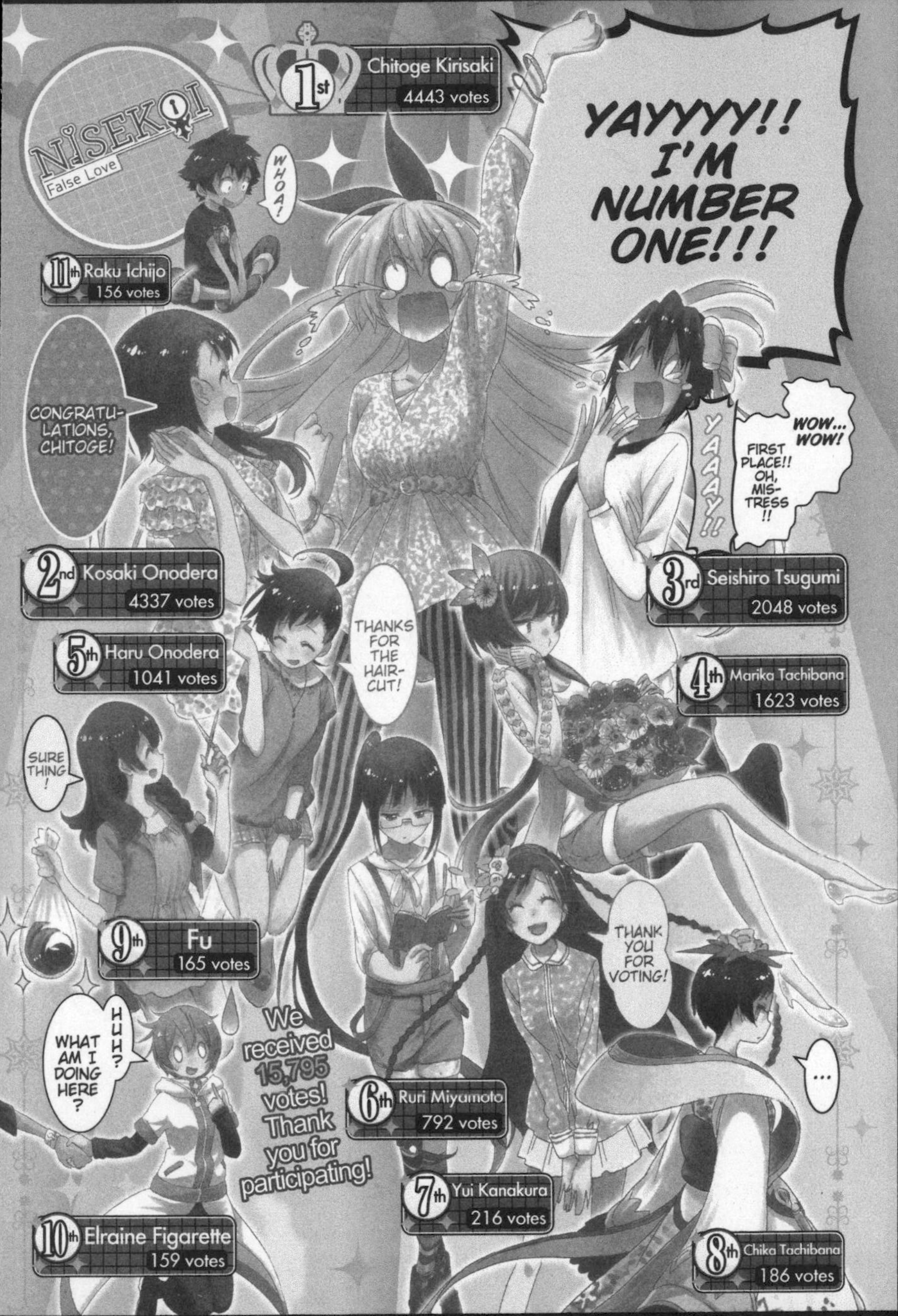

1st Chitoge Kirisaki
4443 votes
YAYYYY!! I'M NUMBER ONE!!!
NISEKOI
False Love
WHOA!
11th Raku Ichijo
156 votes
WOW... WOW!
FIRST PLACE!! OH, MISTRESS!!
YAAAAY!!
CONGRATULATIONS, CHITOGE!
2nd Kosaki Onodera
4337 votes
3rd Seishiro Tsugumi
2048 votes
THANKS FOR THE HAIRCUT!
5th Haru Onodera
1041 votes
4th Marika Tachibana
1623 votes
SURE THING!
9th Fu
165 votes
THANK YOU FOR VOTING!
...
HUH?
WHAT AM I DOING HERE?
We received 15,795 votes! Thank you for participating!
6th Ruri Miyamoto
792 votes
7th Yui Kanakura
216 votes
10th Elraine Figarette
159 votes
8th Chika Tachibana
186 votes

3rd NISEKOI False Love Character Popularity Ranking!!

12th Place and Beyond!

Here are the rankings for 12th place and beyond. Did your favorite character make the list?!

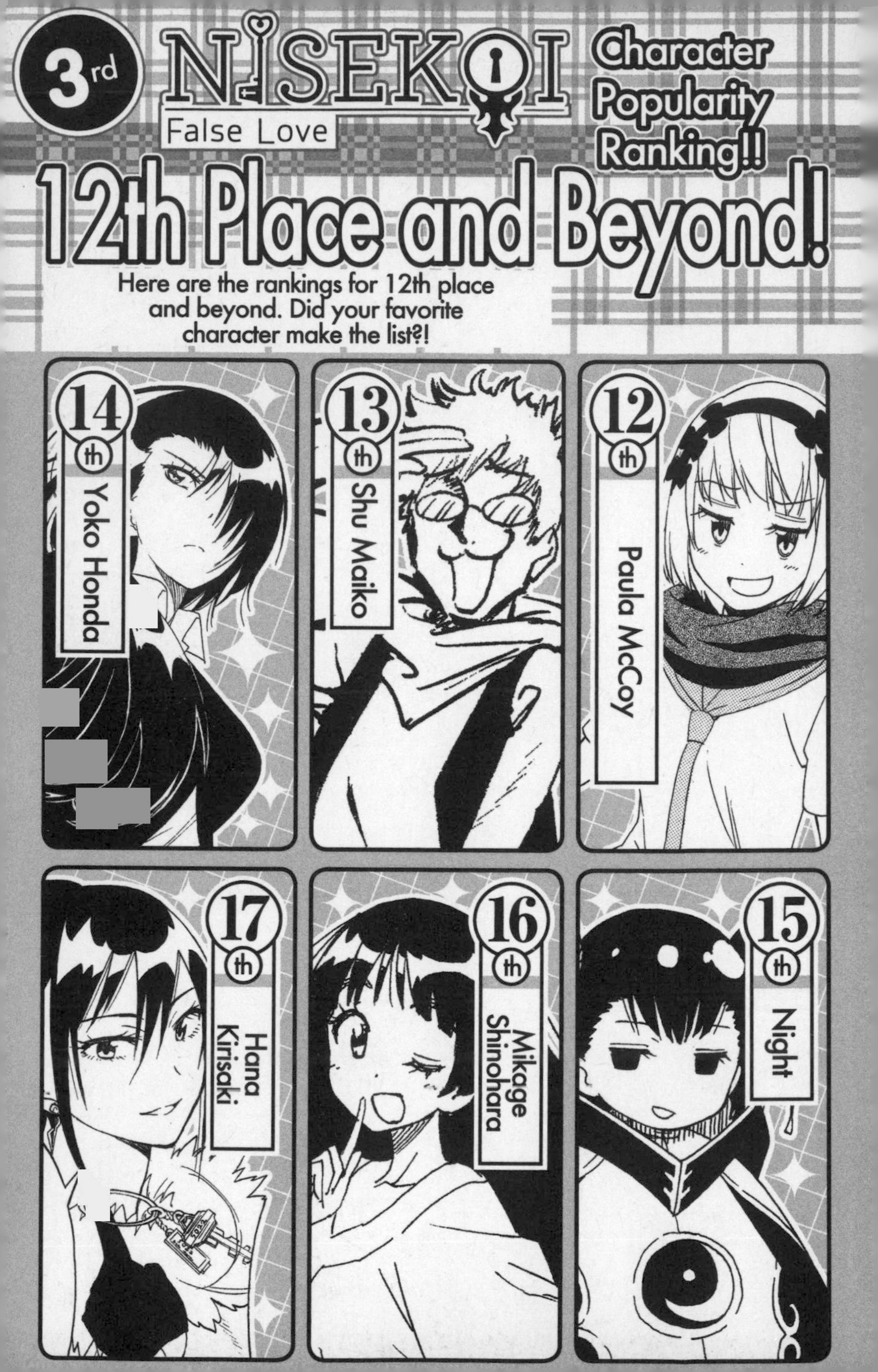
12th
Paula McCoy
13th
Shu Maiko
14th
Yoko Honda
15th
Night
16th
Mikage Shinohara
17th
Hana Kirisaki

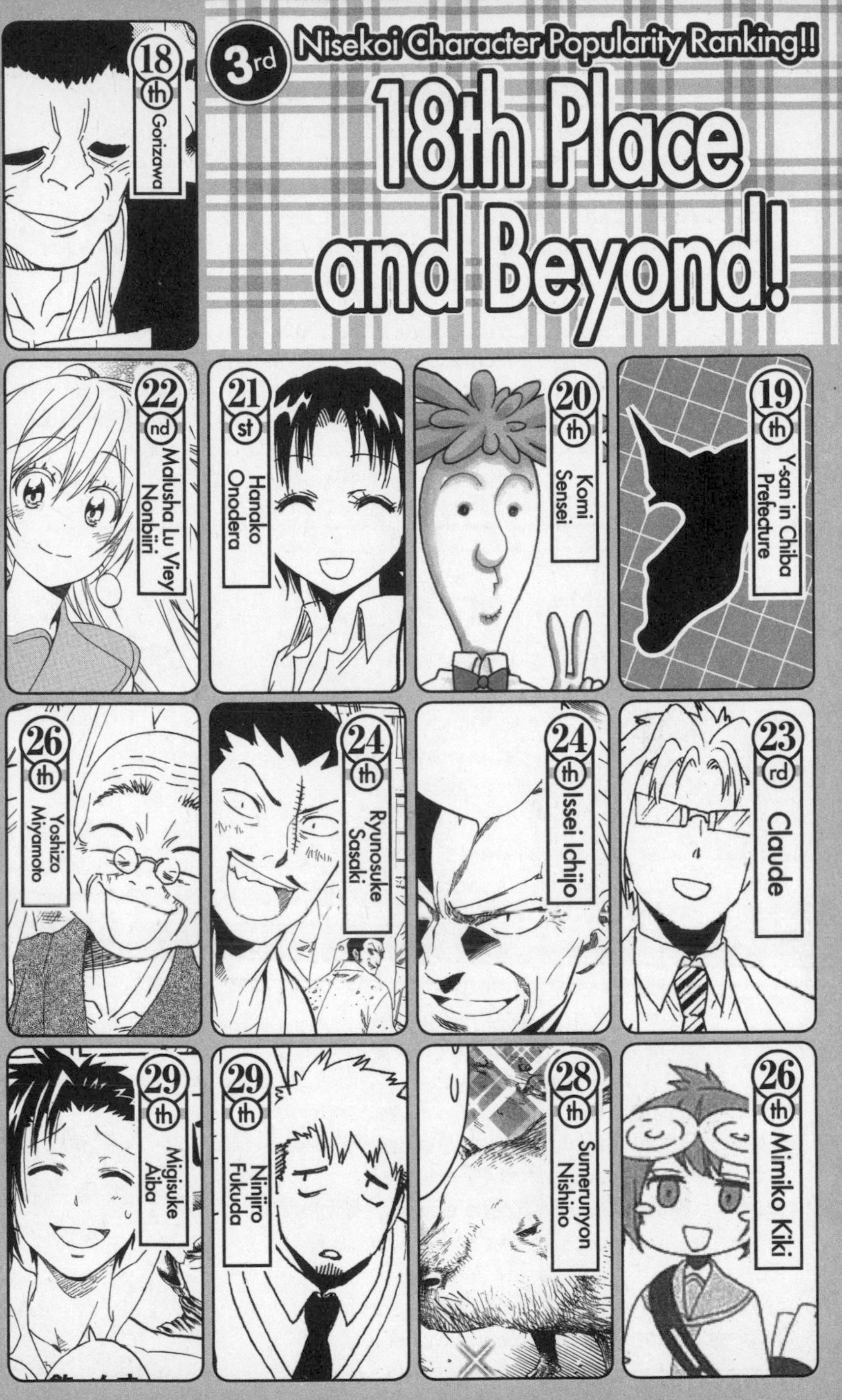
3rd Nisekoi Character Popularity Ranking!!
18th Place and Beyond!
18th Gorizawa
19th Y-san in Chiba Prefecture
20th Komi Sensei
21st Hanako Onodera
22nd Malusha Lu Viey Nonbiiri
23rd Claude
24th Issei Ichijo
24th Ryunosuke Sasaki
26th Yoshizo Miyamoto
26th Mimiko Kiki
28th Sumerunyon Nishino
29th Ninjiro Fukuda
29th Migisuke Aiba

• Surprise Entries! •

Yuka Minoshita, Chika Tachibana in high school, Ruri's younger friend, Shu's glasses, Taishi Tsutsui Sensei, Lord Hyumeron, Margarita de Sato, Beauty Edelweiss Sakurako, Takeo Goda, Koro Sensei, Onodera in middle school when she gets mad at Raku for stepping on her good-luck charm, Jessica Miralda, Kiri Luchile (of *Double Arts*), Magical Chocolatier Haru, Haru as a little girl reading a picture book, Itakeshi Sakurai Sensei of NISEKOI, Haru's teddy bear undies, Tsugumi's ribbon, KOSAKI, Mari's groom, Chitoge Kirsaki's boogers, Yu Saito, Jo Otsuki, Hikaru Nanakusa, Toru Susuya, the cat Raku rescues during the running race, Goriraku (Raku's weird face in chapter 199), Nao Toyama, Mari as a little girl, Mikakoshi, the MIKAKO dish held by Yamada in panel 3, page 2, chapter 155, the chicken on the wrapper of the piece of chocolate Tsugumi gave Raku, the shaggy-haired scientist guy of the Beehive R&D department from the Table of Contents illustration in volume 12

⦿ Reflections ⦿

It's been two years since our last character ranking. This is the first time Chitoge has been honored with the number one spot!! Kosaki came in a close second. There was quite a lot of reshuffling this time at the top of the chart. A cutting-edge special interest group backed Marika's mother, boosting her to eighth place. And a character from *Double Arts*, a different project by Komi Sensei, came in tenth! But the biggest shocker was Marika in fourth place. Fourth place is nothing to sneeze at, but for some reason Y-san in Chiba didn't support her this time with mass votes. I was feeling a bit sad about it one day when a bouquet of flowers and a pair of glass slippers were delivered for Marika. You can see her with them in the illustration. Our love for the characters takes many forms! That's the lesson I learned from this popularity ranking!

THANK YOU FOR VOTING, EVERY-ONE!

BONUS COMIC

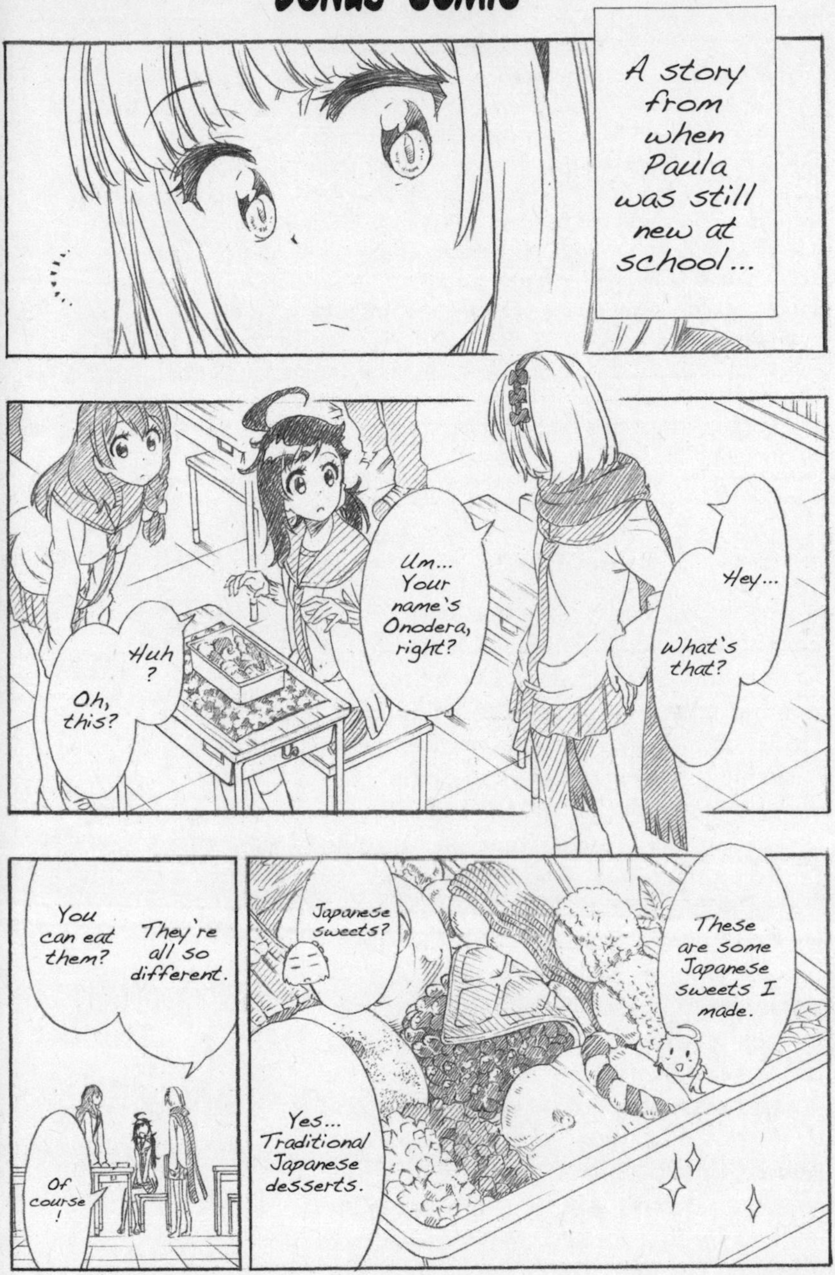

A story from when Paula was still new at school...
Hey...
What's that?
Um... Your name's Onodera, right?
Huh?
Oh, this?
These are some Japanese sweets I made.
Japanese sweets?
Yes... Traditional Japanese desserts.
They're all so different.
You can eat them?
Of course!

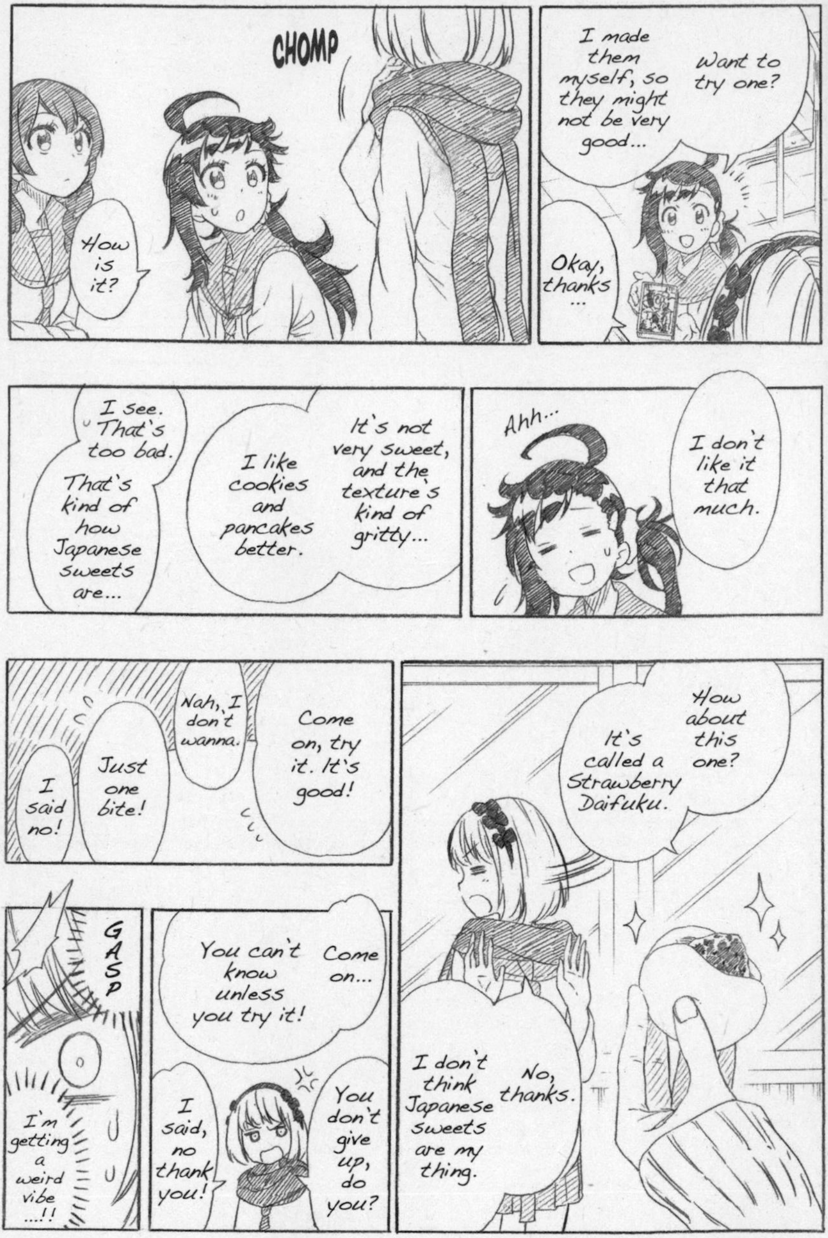
Want to try one?
I made them myself, so they might not be very good...
Okay, thanks ...
CHOMP
How is it?
I don't like it that much.
Ahh...
It's not very sweet, and the texture's kind of gritty...
I like cookies and pancakes better.
I see. That's too bad.
That's kind of how Japanese sweets are...
How about this one?
It's called a Strawberry Daifuku.
No, thanks.
I don't think Japanese sweets are my thing.
Come on, try it. It's good!
Nah, I don't wanna.
Just one bite!
I said no!
Come on...
You can't know unless you try it!
You don't give up, do you?
I said, no thank you!
GASP
I'm getting a weird vibe ....!!

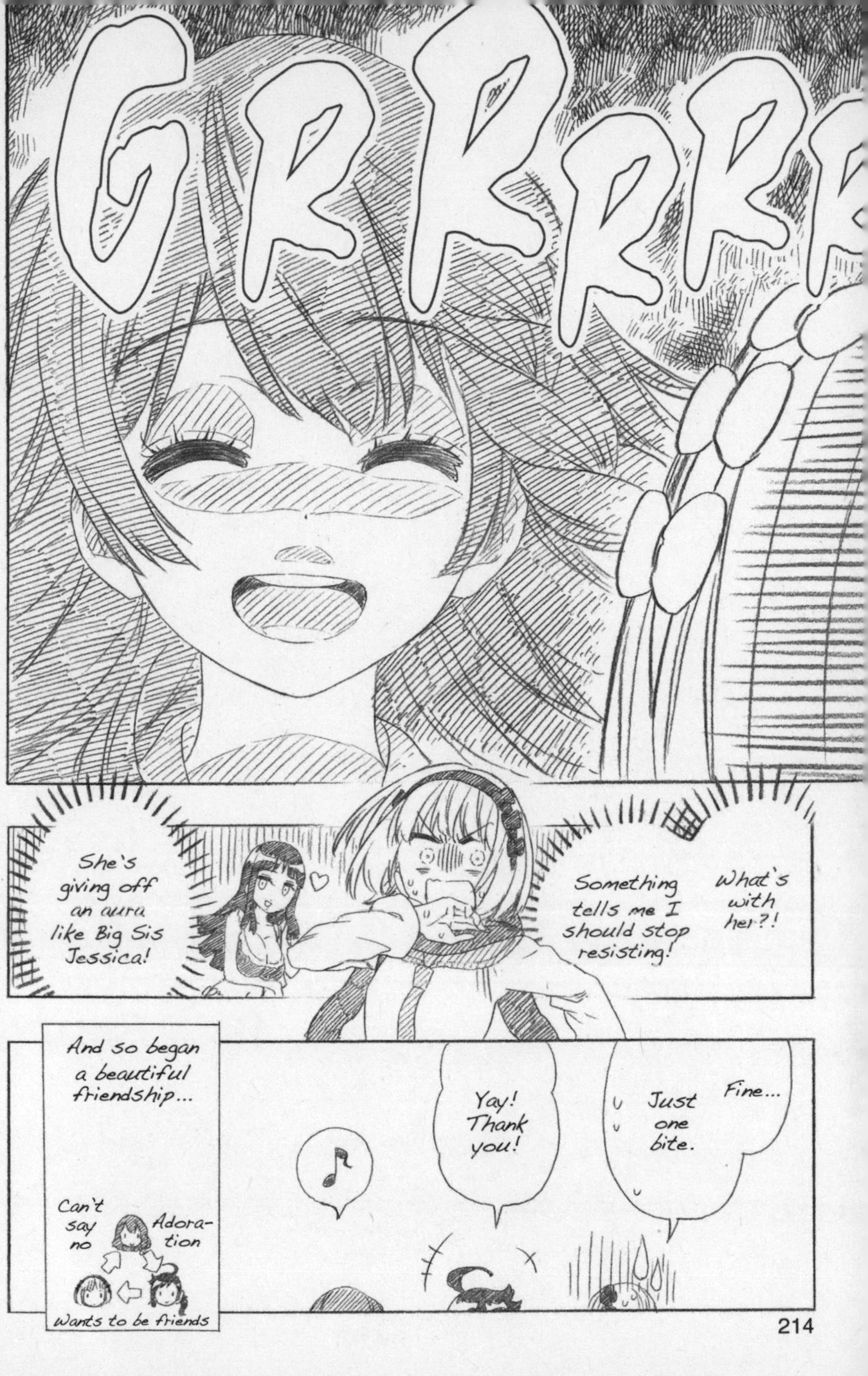
GRRRR
What's with her?!
Something tells me I should stop resisting!
She's giving off an aura like Big Sis Jessica!
Fine...
Just one bite.
Yay! Thank you!
♪
And so began a beautiful friendship...
Can't say no
Adoration
Wants to be friends

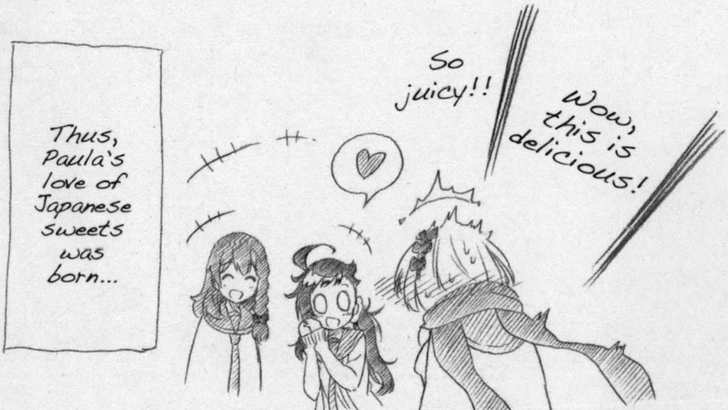
Wow, this is delicious!
So juicy!!
Thus, Paula's love of Japanese sweets was born...

You're
WRONG WAY!

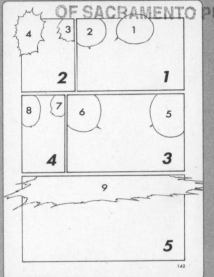

		4	3	2	1
2					1
8	7	6			5
4					3
		9			
					5

142

NISEKOI reads from right to left,
starting in the upper-right corner.
Japanese is read from right to left,
meaning that action, sound effects,
and word-balloon order are completely
reversed from English order.